Inventive Methods

Social and cultural research has changed dramatically in the last few years in response to changing conceptions of the empirical, an intensification of interest in interdisciplinary work, and the growing need to communicate with diverse users and audiences. Methods texts, however, have not kept pace with these changes.

This volume provides a set of new approaches for the investigation of the contemporary world. Building on the increasing importance of methodologies that cut across disciplines, more than twenty expert authors explain the utility of 'devices' for social and cultural research – their essays cover such diverse devices as the list, the pattern, the event, the photograph, the tape recorder and the anecdote.

This fascinating collection stresses the open-endedness of the social world, and explores the ways in which each device requires the user to reflect critically on the value and status of contemporary ways of making knowledge. With a range of genres and styles of writing, each chapter presents the device as a hinge between theory and practice, ontology and epistemology, and explores whether and how methods can be inventive. The book will be a valuable resource for students and scholars of sociology and cultural studies.

Celia Lury is Director of the Centre for Interdisciplinary Methodologies at University of Warwick. Her substantive research interests are focused on the sociology of culture and feminist theory. She explores contemporary developments in the culture industry with a special focus on changing cultural forms. Her recent publications include the jointly authored book *The Global Culture Industry: The Mediation of Things* (with Lash, Polity, 2007) and the Introduction to a Special Issue of the *European Journal of Social Theory* on 'What is the empirical?'. More recently, she has become interested in the relations between methods, space and representation in the context of an exploration of the value of topology for social science.

Nina Wakeford is Reader in Sociology at Goldsmiths College, University of London and a visual artist. Her interests include the ways in which collaborations can be forged between social science and design, and the way in which ethnography has been put to use in the design of new technologies. She is particularly concerned with the ways in which contemporary social and cultural theory can play a part in the design process, and how aspects of practice-led disciplines can be brought back into sociology, in particular though science and technology studies. Amongst her publications are papers on virtual methodologies, queer identities, and visual representations in design work.

Culture, Economy and the Social
A new series from CRESC – the ESRC Centre for Research on Socio-cultural Change

The *Culture, Economy and the Social* series is committed to innovative contemporary, comparative and historical work on the relations between social, cultural and economic change. It publishes empirically based research that is theoretically informed, that critically examines the ways in which social, cultural and economic change is framed and made visible, and that is attentive to perspectives that tend to be ignored or side-lined by grand theorizing or epochal accounts of social change. The series addresses the diverse manifestations of contemporary capitalism, and considers the various ways in which the 'social', 'the cultural' and 'the economic' are apprehended as tangible sites of value and practice. It is explicitly comparative, publishing books that work across disciplinary perspectives, cross-culturally, or across different historical periods.

The series is actively engaged in the analysis of the different theoretical traditions that have contributed to the development of the 'cultural turn' with a view to clarifying where these approaches converge and where they diverge on a particular issue. It is equally concerned to explore the new critical agendas emerging from current critiques of the cultural turn: those associated with the descriptive turn, for example. Our commitment to interdisciplinarity thus aims at enriching theoretical and methodological discussion, building awareness of the common ground that has emerged in the past decade, and thinking through what is at stake in those approaches that resist integration to a common analytical model.

E·S·R·C
ECONOMIC
& SOCIAL
RESEARCH
COUNCIL

Centre for Research on
Socio-Cultural Change

Inventive Methods

The happening of the social

**Edited by
Celia Lury and
Nina Wakeford**

Routledge
Taylor & Francis Group

LONDON AND NEW YORK

Hardback edition published 2012

Paperback edition published 2014
by Routledge
2 Park Square, Milton Park, Abingdon, Oxon OX14 4RN

Simultaneously published in the USA and Canada
by Routledge
711 Third Avenue, New York, NY 10017

Routledge is an imprint of the Taylor & Francis Group,
an informa business

British Library Cataloguing in Publication Data
A catalogue record for this book is available from the British Library

Library of Congress Cataloging-in-Publication Data
    Inventive methods: the happening of the social/edited by Celia
    Lury and Nina Wakeford.—1st ed.
    p. cm.—(Culture, economy, and the social)
    Includes bibliographical references and index.
    1. Social sciences—Research—Methodology. I. Lury, Celia.
    II. Wakeford, Nina.
    H62.I678 2012
    300.72—dc23
    2011048418

ISBN: 978-0-415-57481-5 (hbk)
ISBN: 978-0-415-72110-3 (pbk)
ISBN: 978-0-203-85492-1 (ebk)

Typeset in Times New Roman
by Florence Production Ltd, Stoodleigh, Devon, UK

Contents

Figures

Notes on contributors

Les Back is Professor of Sociology at Goldsmiths, University of London. His main fields of interest are the sociology of racism, popular culture and city life. His work attempts to create a sensuous or live sociology committed to searching for new modes of sociological writing and representation.

Vikki Bell is Professor of Sociology at Goldsmiths, University of London. Author of *Feminist Imagination* (Sage, 1999) and *Culture and Performance* (Berg, 2007), she has published numerous academic articles across the social sciences and theoretical humanities. She has written about cultural-aesthetic aspects of transition in Northern Ireland and Argentina, as well as about contemporary art.

Kirsten Boehner is a Visiting Fellow at the Interaction Research Studio at Goldsmiths, University of London. Her research focuses on intersections of divergent perspectives and practices in both design and evaluation. Kirsten holds a PhD from Cornell University in Communication with a focus on Human Computer Interaction.

Andy Boucher is Senior Research Fellow at the Interaction Research Studio at Goldsmiths, University of London. His research interests focus on practice-based design research with a particular emphasis on the design, fabrication and long-term *in situ* deployment of computational devices for varied user-groups. He holds a Masters in Industrial Design from the Royal College of Art.

Steven D. Brown is Professor of Social and Organisational Psychology at the University of Leicester. His research interests are around social memory. Recent books include *The Social Psychology of Experience* (Sage, 2005) and *Psychology without Foundations* (Sage, 2009).

Matthew Fuller's books include *Media Ecologies: Materialist Energies in Art and Technoculture, Behind the Blip: Essays on the Culture of Software* and *Elephant and Castle*. He works at the Centre for Cultural Studies, Goldsmiths, University of London (www.spc.org/fuller/).

William Gaver is Professor of Design and Leader of the Interaction Research Studio at Goldsmiths, University of London. His research focuses on design-led methodologies and thought-provoking technologies for everyday life.

Olga Goriunova is Senior Lecturer in Media Practice at London Metropolitan University. She is the author of *Art Platforms and Cultural Production on the Internet* (Routledge, 2011).

Cori Hayden is Associate Professor of Anthropology at the University of California, Berkeley. The author of *When Nature Goes Public* (Princeton, 2003), her research examines, among other things, the technics and politics of innovation and appropriation.

Janis Jefferies is Professor of Visual Arts at Goldsmiths, University of London. She is researching electronic communication in cloth and convenes highly successful MFA and PhD practice-based programmes in Arts and Computational Technology for the Department of Computing. Recent publications include 'The Artist as Researcher in a Computer Mediated Culture', in *Art Practices in a Digital Culture*, eds Gardiner and Gere (Ashgate Publishing), 'Loving Attention: An outburst of craft in contemporary art', in *Extra/ordinary: Craft Culture and Contemporary Art*, ed. Maria Buszek, Kansas City Art Institute, USA (Duke University Press), and 'Wires and Wearables', in *This Persuasive Day: The Potential and Perils of Pervasive Computing*, ed. Jeremy V. Pitt (Imperial College Press).

Adrian Mackenzie is Reader in the Centre for Social and Economic Aspects of Genomics, Lancaster University. He has published work on technology which includes *Transductions: Bodies and Machines at Speed* (2002/6), *Cutting Code: Software and Sociality* (2006), and *Wirelessness: Radical Empiricism in Network Cultures* (2010). He is currently working on the circulation of data-intensive methods across science, government, and business in network media.

Noortje Marres is Lecturer in Sociology and Co-Director of the Centre for the Study of Invention and Social Process (CSISP) at Goldsmiths, University of London.

Mike Michael is Professor of Sociology of Science and Technology at Goldsmiths, University of London. His interests include technoscience and everyday life, and biomedical innovation and culture.

Luciana Parisi is Senior Lecturer at the Centre for Cultural Studies, Goldsmiths, University of London, where she runs the Interactive Media MA programme. In 2004 she published *Abstract Sex: Philosophy, Biotechnology, and the Mutations of Desire* (Continuum). She has since published articles on the relation between cybernetics, evolution and digital culture, and on modalities of perception and control. She is currently completing a monograph entitled *Contagious Architecture* (MIT Press, forthcoming).

Andrea Phillips is Reader in Fine Art and Director of Research Progammes in the Art Department, Goldsmiths, University of London. She publishes internationally on the public politics of art objects.

Evelyn S. Ruppert is an Open University Senior Research Fellow with the Centre for Research on Socio-cultural Change (CRESC) and co-convenes the Social Life of Methods theme.

AbdouMaliq Simone is an urbanist focusing on African and Southeast Asian cities. He is Professor of Sociology at Goldsmiths, University of London and Visiting Professor at the African Centre for Cities, University of Cape Town.

Paul Stenner is Professor of Social Psychology at the Open University. In *Psychology without Foundations* (Sage, 2009, with S. D. Brown), he proposes a transdisciplinary relational process oriented social psychology.

Lucy Suchman is Professor of Anthropology of Science and Technology in the Department of Sociology at Lancaster University, and Co-Director of Lancaster's Centre for Science Studies. Her research includes ethnographic studies of everyday practices of technology design and use, critical engagement with projects in the design of human-like machines, and interdisciplinary and participatory interventions in new technology design.

Helen Verran is Reader in History and Philosophy of Science at the University of Melbourne, Australia. Her *Science and an African Logic* (University of Chicago Press, 2001), a study of Yoruba numbers and scientific numbers and how we can know them, won the 2003 Ludwick Fleck Prize. She is currently working on the manuscript of a book provisionally titled *Nature as Humanity's Infrastructure: The Challenges of Environmental Services*.

1 Introduction

A perpetual inventory

Celia Lury and Nina Wakeford

How to use this book

Before we begin this introduction, we think it might be helpful to say a little about the organization of the book, and its inclusion of some, but not other inventive methods.[1] In a broad sense, the collection is a response to the current renewal of interest in the politics of method in some social sciences (Burrows and Savage, 2007; Thrift, 2007; Adkins and Lury, 2009; Rabinow and Marcus, 2009), as evidenced by the recent discussion of research methods and dissemination activities that critically engage theory and practice, including participatory and action research methods; performative and non-representational investigations; the acknowledgement of non-human agencies; as well as interdisciplinary and collaborative and beyond-the-academy working practices. It responds and hopes to make a contribution to the 'new empiricism of sensation' (Clough and Halley, 2007), to help expand the repertoire of 'materially innovative methods' (Law, 2004) and address the limits of the phenomenal. More specifically, the book refers back to a workshop that the editors organized in 2009, and includes chapters based on presentations made there. In thinking about this collection, however, we have also drawn upon accounts of methods of conducting research that are not included here, but are relevant in relation to the patterns (see Chapters 9 and 10) we see emerging in this collection. These include Haraway (1985) on cyborg, Serres (2007) on parasite, Agamben (2009) on apparatus, Berlant (2007) on the case, Fraser (2010) on event, Kwinter (1998) on diagram, Rabinow and Marcus (2009) and Parker (2012, forthcoming) on contraption, Riles (2001) on network, and Stark (2009) on search, all of which are models, ideals or exemplars that we believe deserve imitation.

The collection makes use of an alphabetical listing, an ordering that is explicitly presented in the form of an 'index'. Although, like numbers, letters may be used not only to list, but also to rank (as in a school report), their use here is purely alphabetical, and is intended to encourage – perhaps even incite – you, the reader, not to read from A through to Z, but rather to make a selective entry into the collection, to use your own principles of inclusion and exclusion, of ordering and valuing. Our hope is thus that the alphabetical list – familiar from other uses – will nonetheless act as an experimental and alternative ordering to an academic book (see also Pile and Thrift, 2000). We invite you to make your own associations – draw a line – across and between the chapters in ways that we may anticipate but do not want to predetermine. You might want to: establish relations of equivalence between methods; make groups or sets; draw distinctions; compare and contrast; or see how one method is included or configured in relation to others. What always becomes clear, however – if you read more than one entry, no matter what order you read them in – is that inventiveness is not intrinsic to methods; it is rather something that emerges in relation to the purposes to which they are put. The listing of methods is thus also intended to act as a provocation to you, the reader, to consider (more) methods in relation to your own purposes, to begin devising yourself.

You will, in any case, soon find out how each chapter refuses to be ordered by this introduction: they have been left – more or less – to their own devices. Each is written with a different voice, to different effect. The entries deliberately and systematically employ a range of styles of writing. From an editorial point of view, the retention of this diversity of modes of address is a way of acknowledging the significance of the semiotic materiality of the methods they describe and the radical heterogeneity of the worlds that they enact. Disciplinary differences are not erased or minimized, but acknowledged. Nor is there any attempt to present the collection as complete; we do not aspire to either unity or completeness; a fact to which attention is drawn – paradoxically – by the way in which some methods are represented by one entry, while others are represented by more than one. This variability testifies that there is no way to complete a list of inventive methods, not even by doubling or multiplying an entry, no way to fill all the gaps. Yet, although the collection is incomplete, we also believe that, if, as readers, you bring together the chapters together variously, there are many possible books here. The collection is designed as a perpetual inventory (Krauss, 2010): testimony to the irreducibly unstable relations between elements and parts, inclusion and belonging, sensing, knowing and doing.

Beginning, or refrain

The guiding aim in putting together this collection is to provide a resource, an inventory of methods or devices that may be used to conduct research that is explicitly oriented towards an investigation of the open-endedness of the social world. Our hope is that the methods collected here will variously enable *the happening* of the social world – its ongoingness, relationality, contingency and sensuousness – to be investigated. Our belief is that, to address these dimensions of social life, the full actuality of the world, its indeterminateness, what AbdouMaliq Simone describes as 'the unregulated thickening of relationships among things of all kinds', it is not possible to apply a method as if it were indifferent or external to the problem it seeks to address, but that method must rather be made specific and relevant to the problem.[2] In short, inventive methods are ways to introduce answerability into a problem.[3] Further, if methods are to be inventive, they should not leave that problem untouched.

The methods or devices included here are various. They are: anecdote (Mike Michael), category (Evelyn Ruppert), configuration (Lucy Suchman), experiment (Steve Brown; Noortje Marres), list (Andrea Phillips), number (Helen Verran), pattern (Janis Jefferies; Paul Stenner), photo-image (Vikki Bell), phrase (Matthew Fuller and Olga Goriunova), population (Cori Hayden), probe (Kirsten Boehner, William Gaver and Andy Boucher), screen (AbdouMaliq Simone), set (Adrian Mackenzie), speculation (Luciana Parisi) and tape recorder (Les Back). As such, they appear a somewhat heterogeneous collection of research 'methods', with some, such as tape recorder, appearing closer to a device or instrument than a method or knowledge practice, while others, such as anecdote, not seeming at first glance to belong to an academic repertoire of methods at all. Many are more easily seen as a method once they are introduced as a verb: to probe, to categorize, to list, to pattern, to record, but still they are heterogeneous. Some are in between a thing and a practice; some are more or less the monopoly of social researchers; others are an everyday activity of 'lay' people; some have acquired legitimacy in their use by governments or by business; while others are more frequently deployed by those without authority. Each, however, is discussed here in relation to their use to conduct (popular and professional, lay and academic) research, whether this is in cities in the urban south (screen), computer programming and software packages (phrase, set), the carrying out of a census in Canada (category), socio-technical projects in the UK (anecdote), USA and southern India (configuration), a pharmaceutical chain in Mexico (population), the making of the art world (list, pattern), swarms of swallows and textiles (pattern), soundscapes (tape recorder), the home (probe), the valuation of natural resources (number), reality television, social and developmental psychology and blogs about green living (experiment), thought experiments and AI (speculation).

One of the principal claims the book makes is that there is a need to (re)consider the relevance of method (Fraser, 2008, 2009) to the empirical investigation of the here and now, the contemporary (Rabinow and Marcus, 2009). The methods the book includes make this possible because of the ways in which, as they are discussed here, they require their user to reflect critically upon the value, status and significance of knowledge today. So, for example, the methods of anecdote, category, configuration, phrase and population do not presume that the subjects and objects of the research imagination are discrete, or stand in external relation to each other, although they allow such distinctions to be drawn. There is no presumption that time and space operate in a standardized relation to each other; rather the methods of list, pattern and screen open up the issues of scale, calibration and measurement. They do not rely upon external measures but are rather revealed to be 'things that scale' (Tsing, 2004; Holbraad and Pedersen, 2009). Nor do the methods necessarily privilege either the quantitative or the qualitative: number is set alongside photo-image and anecdote, while others – such as set, population, pattern – draw on mathematical thinking in ways that do not adhere to a quantitative-qualitative divide. In addition, methods such as the photo-image and the probe do not presume the senses by which the social world is known, the medium in which data should be collected or argument is best communicated. They do not take the human as the only measure of the significance of the world, or as the only source of agency, as the discussion of cats and dogs in the case of the anecdote, swallows and ants in pattern, the chemical in relation to population, and batteries in the discussion of the tape recorder reveal. Instead, speculation and the other methods included here enable research to follow forked directions, to trace processes that are in disequilibrium or uncertain, to acknowledge and refract complex combinations of human and non-human agencies, supporting an investigation of what matters and how in ways that are open, without assuming a single fixed relation between epistemology and ontology.

While the methods collected here are focused on the *social* world, the book is not narrowly disciplinary. Rather, there is an exploration of interdisciplinarity through the juxtaposition of different disciplinary uses of methods and, in some cases – such as the list, the probe and the pattern – through explicit reflection on the possibilities and limits of interdisciplinary or cross-disciplinary approaches. Many of the methods discussed have, in any case, been developed in movements across and between disciplines in the social sciences, the humanities and the natural sciences. So, for example, the device of phrase has a linguistic and literary critical history but is taken up here in relation to computing and software studies, while the methods of experiment and pattern have multiple histories and may be situated in relation to both art and science. The refusal of the methods collected here to assume the operation of disciplinary distinctions is not meant to imply that disciplines do not matter, however. Rather it is intended to invite recognition of how methods participate – variously – in the making of disciplinary distinctions as well as interdisciplinary space.

There is, we would suggest, much to be gained from putting histories of social scientific method in relation to those of other traditions, including, for example, art movements. Jenny Shaw, for example, observes, 'If Surrealism and sociology appear to be light years apart from one another . . . they are not, and Mass Observation is the link'. For Mass Observation, she says, art and sociology were indivisible. Its adherents foregrounded the importance of irrational and subconscious processes; disruption and shock, rupture and breaks in routine, were used as methods of perception. In contrast, Ben Highmore has suggested that Mass Observation practiced a kind of 'radical positivism' that built on surrealism and yet differed from it: Mass Observation, in his view, insisted on attending to the everyday as a mass project of collecting 'facts', not so much commenting on the everyday as becoming coterminous with it (Highmore, 2000: 16). Such contested histories are necessary to understand the potential inventiveness of methods; that of Mass Observation, for example, provides a valuable context for the dream recorders that are one example of probes discussed by Boehner, Gaver and Boucher.

Methods that have the capacity to be inventive are also, as Noortje Marres puts it, 'multifarious instruments' in the sense that they have a variety and variability of purpose. The book speaks to the way in which methods such as the list, the tape recorder and the set may be encoded in everyday and specialized technologies and assemblages, and addresses the challenge currently posed to researchers thinking about the distinctiveness of academic and disciplinary knowledge when it is set alongside commercial and everyday knowledge-making practices. Indeed, this challenge is the explicit topic of some of the chapters. So, for example, Marres herself describes experiments in living as an example of 'collective practices of researching social and cultural change, as engaged in by actors who do not necessarily identify themselves as "social researchers"', and Simone focuses on the everyday uses of screening as a method in urban space, pointing out that, since people in cities 'step in and out of various "shells" of operation', they are necessarily involved in carrying out 'popular research', while Andrea Phillips' discussion of web-based art listings highlights the relationship of lists and ranking to commercial values and the market. She writes, pointedly:

> The conditions of production of such devices in art do so at the behest of an economy of alienation that is rarely acknowledged, even when artists turn to dispositifs that enable a relation, broadly, to the realm of the social (for this is what the list does).

The methods described here are thus not the monopoly of academics alone. Indeed, we would emphasize – as a way of resisting the fears raised by the notion of a crisis in empirical research in academic social science (Burrows and Savage, 2007) induced by the recognition that academic sociology is becoming less of an obligatory point of passage for the powerful agents of knowing capitalism – that methods of social research never have been so restricted in their use. They have always been distributed. Nevertheless, we recognize with Phillips that relationality and participation are dominant tropes of knowing capitalism,[4] and with Marres that the 'resources and techniques of social research are being redistributed among a variety of agencies inside and outside the university'. Indeed, Marres observes that the proliferation of social methods involves not just a displacement or 'democratization' of social methods – as in the slogan 'we are all social researchers now' – but is rather a question of the (re-)organization of processes of knowledge-making'.

Inventive methods – like any other methods – are, for good and ill, caught up in what Helga Nowotny (2002) describes as the expansion of the present, in which there is an ongoing maximization of the agencies involved in social life. As Adrian Mackenzie puts it in his discussion of the method of set-making, there are more and more techniques to determine the excess of the actual, 'to present it, to manage it, to undo it or to politicize it'. But if, as Marres says, 'the active participation of social actors in the conduct of research is today increasingly recognized across social life', *and* we cannot – and should not – foreclose the 'multiplicity of purposes' of social research, *and* there is no necessary relation between problems, solutions, invention and critique, should we not be a little more precise about how the inventiveness of the methods collected here are to be understood?

Inventiveness does not, for us, equate to new. Many methods, such as experiment, pattern or population, have a long history, although others, such as the anecdote, screen or speculation, are marginal to the established histories of natural and social sciences. Some – such as probe or phrase – are self-evidently methods in the making.[5] What unites them, however, is that they are methods or means by which the social world is not only investigated, but may also be engaged. Indeed, the book as a whole seeks to open up the question of how methods contribute to the framing of change; it aims to enable change to be understood not only as complex, contradictory and uncertain, but also as everyday, routine and ongoing: as something in which methods of social research are necessarily engaged. To describe them as inventive is to seek to realize the potential of this engagement, whether this is as intervention, interference or refraction (Haraway, 1992; Barad, 2007). Our proposal is that this potential can be realized through an exploration of how the knowledge of change they permit need not be limited to ascertaining what is going on now or predicting what will go on soon, but may rather be a matter of configuring what comes next. And here we are understanding 'next' not simply as a simple spatial equivalent of 'new', but rather as a way of exploring the potential of method to gain a purchase on the notion of adjacency outlined by Paul Rabinow in his discussion of the contemporary:

> "Adjacent: in close proximity . . ." Neither the overdrive of the universal intellectual nor the authoritative precision of the specific. Rather: a space of problems. Of questions. Of being behind or ahead. Belated or anticipatory. Out of synch. Too fast or too slow. Reluctant. Audacious. Annoying.
>
> (Rabinow, 2007: 40–1)

Let us try to expand on the annoyingness of inventive methods a little more – their capacity to be an irritant, as Michael says of anecdotalization – by way of a discussion of some of the ideas of the historian of science, Hans-Jörg Rheinberger. In his study of the development of an experimental system for synthesizing proteins in a test tube, Rheinberger (1997) uses the Derridean term 'differance' to characterize the specific, displacing dynamics that distinguish the research process he describes. The experimental system, he says, is involved in a process of differential reproduction. More exactly, he proposes that an experimental system that is organized in a way such that the production of differences becomes the orienting principle of its own reproduction is governed by, and at the same time creates a kind of subversive movement. Inventive methods, as we understand them, have the capacity to display a kind of self-displacing movement; that is, they comprise processes of imitation and repetition in which a surplus is created that allows an event – what happens, the happening of social life – to become inventive. Matthew Fuller and Olga Goriunova ask, for example, 'How does a phrase assemble itself together to become a real unity of an order and ensemble that is not predetermined?' and reply that this process is achieved in the differential reproduction of a system of which the phrase is a part, or rather: 'The permutational movement of such algorithms, the data they come into composition with, the multiple systems they are embedded in is itself expressive, that is, exudes phrases'. Evelyn Ruppert says of the category that it is 'a device that travels'; Lucy Suchman says of the artefact that it is produced through a method of configuration that it is both fixed and fluid: 'fixity is an effect of reiterative enactments' and 'fluidity articulates the inherent multiplicity of objects in ways that facilitate their travel'.

Our proposal, then, is that the inventiveness of methods is to be found in the relation between two moments: the addressing of a method – an anecdote, a probe, a category – to a specific problem, and the capacity of what emerges in the use of that method to change the problem. It is this combination, we suggest, that makes a method answerable to its problem, and provides the basis of its self-displacing movement, its inventiveness, although the likelihood of that inventiveness can never be known in advance of a specific use. Indeed, in Parisi's discussion of speculation, invention is necessarily a matter of retroduction.

Even within the tightly regulated experimental systems that Rheinberger describes, 'one never knows precisely how the set-up differentiates' (Rheinberger, 1997: 79–80). Thus, he emphasizes what he calls the 'Blind tactics of empirical wandering', and says that 'Event-riddenness . . . is at the heart of research experiments'. As Simone says of the use of screens in urban space: 'Research is then not a matter of identifying locations but explicitly inventing them in a context where residents endeavour to act as if the undecidability of their location in a larger world either doesn't exist or doesn't matter'. Along similar lines, Fuller and Goriunova advise that a phrase 'is a lucky device; it can occur, become fashionable or firm, can dilapidate. It may last only a moment', while in his discussion of the set as method Mackenzie draws on Badiou to emphasize the importance of 'an always aleatory decision which is only given through its effects'. All this is a way of saying that inventiveness is a matter of use, of collaboration, of situatedness, and does not imply the ineffectiveness of methods, only that their inventiveness – their capacity to address a problem and change that problem as it performs itself – cannot be secured in advance. Thus, while we might suggest that reflexivity in the pursuit of relevance is one of the principal requirements for anyone wishing to make inventive their own use of methods, inventiveness cannot be given in advance. Indeed, it is this characteristic that necessarily makes the book far more open-ended than a conventional set of 'how-to' recipes for research, or so we hope.

Devising methods

In trying to elucidate further how or what it might be about methods that afford the possibility of inventiveness, we were drawn to the term 'device', a word that has multiple everyday meanings, including an object, a method and a bomb. To adopt an anecdote, a screen or a list as a device is to make explicit how a method and its object are linked to each other and with what potentially explosive – or inventive – effects. Indeed, as Parisi observes in her discussion of the method of speculation, the notion of the device not only admits that object and methods are mutually constitutive, but also acknowledges that it is their relation that forces us to confront the new. As Katie King describes them, devices are 'jumpy materializations of practices, transforming and dissimilar agencies rather than elegantly inert guarantors of epistemological simplicity' (King, 2010).

In social and cultural analyses the notion of device has a lineage that may be traced back to Foucault's notion of *dispositif* or apparatus, which he defines as:

> a thoroughly heterogeneous ensemble consisting of discourses, institutions, architectural forms, regulatory decisions, laws, administrative measures, scientific statements, philosophical, moral and philanthropic propositions – in short, the said as much as the unsaid. Such are the elements of the apparatus. The apparatus itself is the system of relations that can be established between these elements.
>
> (Foucault, 1980: 194)

He continues this definition by suggesting that there is always an interplay of shifts of position and modifications of function among the elements of the apparatus, and that an apparatus has a strategic function, that is, it is organized in response to urgent needs. Giorgio Agamben draws on and extends this understanding:

> Further expanding the already large class of Foucauldian apparatuses, I shall call an apparatus literally anything that has in some way the capacity to capture, orient, determine, intercept, model, control, or secure the gestures, behaviors, opinions, or discourses of living beings.
>
> (Agamben, 2009: 14)

Importantly, then, locating the notion of device in relation to that of apparatus helps make clear that a device or method is never able to operate in isolation, since it is always in relations that are themselves always being reconfigured.

In this collection, for example, the device of the probe described by Kirsten Boehner, William Gaver and Andy Boucher is, typically, a carefully crafted artefact that 'bears the fingerprints of a designer', while the device in Les Back's chapter is quite evidently also a thing, a tape recorder. But both chapters situate their device or method in relation to a complex ensemble of practices that destabilize any sense that a device – even when it is a thing – is merely a tool, able to be used always and everywhere in the same way. So, while tape recorder is the title under which Back's chapter enters this collection, it might also – with a different emphasis – have been entered under 'interview', 'sound' or 'voice'. As Back reflects, the foregrounding of the tape recorder as device recognizes the centrality of instruments to social research – and here he draws an analogy with the doctor's stethoscope, but importantly also invites consideration of the part such instruments play in a complex, and constantly changing constellations of things, procedures, abstractions, mediations, sensitivities and sociabilities in the apparatuses, configurations or assemblages of social research. Focusing on the tape recorder as device enables Back to show how neither a 'thing' such as a recording machine nor a 'practice' such as the method of interviewing are static techniques that may be carried out in the same way, always and everywhere, but rather, brought together in a specific way, produce a very particular 'turning up of the background' of sound. And, importantly, the method of bringing together of things, techniques and practices is itself included here as configuration (Suchman), while it has been elaborated by others, elsewhere, as assemblage (Deleuze and Guattari, 1987; Law, 2004; Ong and Collier, 2005; DeLanda, 2006) and contraption (Rabinow and Marcus, 2009; Parker, 2012, forthcoming), as well as, of course, apparatus.[6]

This emphasis on the capacity of the device to capture that is associated with its links to the notion of dispositif also feeds into recent understandings of the performativity of methods in the enactment of the social (Haraway, 1992; Barad, 2003; Law, 2004; Law and Urry, 2004; Mol, 2005; Callon *et al.*, 2007). In this way of thinking, devices act as a hinge between concepts and practice, epistemology and ontology, the virtual and the actual, opening a door – or perhaps better acting as an automobile clutch (whose operation is necessary for the shifting of 'analytic gears' in the words of Cori Hayden) on to the practical investigation of the social world. Devices are 'terms for thinking about processes' (Wardrip-Fruin, 2009). Perhaps most importantly, they 'articulate actions, they act or make others act' (Callon *et al.*, 2007: 2). As Mike Michael says of the anecdote, the device 'not only reports events, but acts on them'; as Fuller and Goriunova assert in relation to phrases, 'they are something that happens that makes something happen'; and as Lucy Suchman says in relation to configuration, it 'comprises both a method through which things are made, and a resource for their analysis and un-/re-making'.

The term 'device' is also appealing to us, then, because it helps us to recognize that knowledge practices, technical artefacts and epistemic things (Rheinberger, 1997) are encoded in everyday and specialized technologies and assemblages in which agency is no longer the sole privilege of human actors. It restores an often-overlooked objecticity, materiality or thingness to methods; devices body-forth and grasp the problem they are designed to study (Karpik, 2010). A guiding image for the collection in this respect is that of the short film made by the artist Richard Serra: *Hand Catching Lead* (1968), discussed here by Andrea Phillips. A forearm and hand are framed by the film, the hand repeatedly opening and closing, and as it closes, sometimes catching a scrap of metal, pieces of which are repeatedly dropped from the top of the frame. The film speaks to the understanding of devices we are proposing, as some-thing' such as a hand, caught in the act of catching, catching itself – as well as, perhaps, something else – in an act, somewhere between a sensing, a doing and a knowing. The notion of device is thus also helpful to us because it draws attention to the existence of methods as variously constituted, distributed material-semiotic entities and to their complicatedly (re)presentational and temporal character.

However, although the notion of device is welcome insofar as it draws attention to the semiotic-material relational-doing-thingness of methods, the term can sometimes seem to imply a collapsing of action and effect, as Suchman makes explicit in her discussion of configuration. In this regard, it can obscure what *Hand Catching Lead* makes evident: the hand – or device – does not always catch what it seeks to grasp. So it is to draw attention to the uncertain but not unorganized relation between the action of a method and its effects that the term 'inventive methods' is (slightly) preferred here to that of 'devices', although in fact we and our contributors will use both terms more or less equally. In identifying this preference, we want to emphasize that the grasp of a device is not a fix, and that this lack of fixity is not necessarily a problem: so, for example, Boehner, Gaver and Boucher write in relation to the probe, 'Uncertainty is valued as a productive state for exploration rather than a condition to be resolved'; while Suchman suggests that contingency should be planned for in making configurations through a systematic process of under-specification. As John Law says elsewhere, using devices such as allegory can make space for ambivalence and ambiguity (Law, 2004).

In what follows, then, we will focus on three further aspects of devices or inventive methods. The first explores the specific and situated relations that are established by inventive methods to their problems or contexts of use. The second considers the generalizability of the knowledge that is created in their use. The third concerns what we believe to be a changing relation between the sensible and the knowable in the contemporary social world, and the affordance or grasp on this world offered by inventive methods.

The problem at hand

First, then, let us turn to the relation to a problem that is afforded by inventive methods; that is, where and how and to what effect can they be used? On the one hand, as noted above, inventive methods or devices are tools, instruments, techniques or distinct (material-semiotic) entities that are, in part, alienable from specific problems or situations, able to be used in multiple contexts and continually introduced into new ones (Fuller and Goriunova). On the other, they are also always part of an ensemble, assemblage, configuration or apparatus, modified in specific uses, undergoing transformation – being brought to life, body-ing forth, grasping – in relation to particular situations, particular problems. For example: 'The probes are not customized for a particular individual, yet they are customized for a project, and their situated nature is evident in their content and appearance'. Devices are thus not simply reproducible in multiple sites but are, rather, modifiable and modified in use. In the case described by Cori Hayden, for example, the method of making a population emerges differently when its operations are thought through the problems of chemistry rather than, as more usually, those of biology. In relation to the problems of the chemical, the method of population-making develops its capacity as a reproductive multiplicity by describing and producing – grasping – non-genealogical forms of reproduction, such as imitation, repetition and replication.

A further characteristic of an inventive method, however, is that its (repeated) use is always oriented towards making a difference. So, for example, Boehner, Gaver and Boucher assert of probes that, 'Developed in a design context, their purpose is not to capture what is so much as to inspire what might be', while phrases are methods that are 'a means of entering, triggering and sensing into the grammars and diagrams through which . . . techno-social dynamics can be built, felt, understood and changed' (Fuller and Goriunova). Let us explore this orientation towards making a difference further, by exploring one method in a little more detail, the method of the anecdote as described by Mike Michael. As he describes it, it is the way in which the telling of an anecdote sets up a relation to a specific context that enables anecdotilization to make a difference, and making this difference is what gives the anecdote both relevance and efficacy; it is what enables the anecdote to circulate. In the telling of an anecdote as a device or method, it is not that the researcher is made to accommodate the anecdote to the problem researched, or that the problem to be researched is cut down in size or complexity by the anecdote, but that they are defined anew in relation to each other, *and* in the process the relation of researcher to researched is transformed. If the (new) line it draws between itself and its context is successful, Michael suggests, the anecdote will add 'something new (or at least new-ish) to the conduct of research'; it will produce 'uninvited topics, unexpected insights, and untoward issues should emerge'.

To summarize: an inventive method addresses a specific problem, and is adapted in use in relation to that specificity; its use may be repeated, but the method is always oriented to making a difference. This orientation is linked, we suggest, to its double force (see Suchman for further discussion of this notion, taken from Castañeda, 2002): that is, to both its 'constitutive effects' and its capacity to contribute to its own 'generative circulation'. This double force is what enables a method to act as what Marres calls a 'multiplying genre': to continue the example of the anecdote, as method it both performs itself and is 'performative of researcher and researched'. To take another example: the method of population-making – when its substance and operation are thought through the chemical – multiplies in non-reproductive ways, most notably in the example of the Mexican pharmacy chain Farmacias Similares discussed by Cori Hayden, by processes of copying, imitation, repetition and replication. In short, that an inventive method can make a difference is linked to the way in which it makes itself, and in this making produces relations beyond itself. And this, we want to suggest, is a consequence of the particular ways in which such methods are able to articulate a problem – to make a problem answerable – through the operation of their boundaries.

To explore this further, let us move to another example: that of the Getting Things Done software discussed by Adrian Mackenzie in his discussion of the inventive method of the set. Mackenzie's focus is the operation of an algorithm that is used to sort what to include in a set (things to be done in the future) and what to exclude (things to be done immediately or not to be done at all). As he describes it, the algorithm organizes 'the problem' of the need for such a list to be both open and closed through its temporal organization of the method of the clopen set. The inventiveness of this method is to solve the problem of making a finite list of the never-ending things there are to do by telling the user what should be done next, repeatedly. The problem is not solved once and for all but, by re-presenting it, by giving it new (in this case temporal) limits – through the recursive organization of the set's own boundaries in relation to 'the same-but-ever-changing' context of things (still) to be done. Sadly, while the software may thus help you deal with anxiety that you have too much to do, it does not change the situation in which there are always more things to be done.

Inventive methods thus recognize specificity by addressing and including 'heres' and 'nows', but only as they are constituted in relation to 'theres' and 'thens' that are brought into being by the methods' own constitutive, self-organizing effects in relation to the context of a problem. In short, inventive methods grasp the excess of specificity that is always present in the actual by making a relation to elsewhere as they make themselves. Janis Jefferies says, 'pattern can always exceed itself and acts as an open-ended exchange between viewer and audience, text and reader'; Fuller and Goriunova show how phrases are 'one of a series of micro-to-macro objects, entities in their own terms at a certain scale, but also . . . mediations of part-whole relations'; Simone shows how screens take 'what intrudes from both the inside and outside, that comes from within and elsewhere – the strange that is familiar, and the familiar that is strange, and sutures a working connection'; Back says that sound flows 'invite an appreciation of how the "here and now" connects to a global elsewhere as well as the past'; Suchman says that the method assemblage of configuration can be understood as 'a device for articulating the relation between the "insides" of a socio-technical system and its constitutive "outsides", including all of those things that disappear in the system's figuration as an object'; while Michael claims, 'the anecdote is . . . useful for explicitly incorporating the performativity of the research – i.e. the way that research is not a mere reflection of something (e.g. one's experiences in relation to social or cultural process) out there, but is instrumental in, and a feature of, 'making out theres'.

More generally, we might say that the inventiveness of a method is to do with its ability to generate its own boundary conditions (Rheinberger, 1997: 20): to organize itself – to self-organize – in a (changing) relation to a (changing) context. Put very simply, this is a matter of exclusion and inclusion, closedness and openness to context, to act as what Simone describes as a semi-permeable boundary, to operate 'unspeakable frontiers'. Or rather, since inventive methods are neither totally inclusive nor exclusive, neither completely open nor completely closed, but instead are linguistic, perceptual and material manoeuvres that are able to give themselves over to the problem at hand without turning themselves in (Fuller and Goriunova), able to 'turn up' the background (Back), while 'tuning in' to the scale, texture or experience of a problem (Fuller and Goriunova), they can be seen as techniques for differential reproduction (Rheinberger, 1997; Mol, 2005). They are able to grasp the here and now in terms of somewhere else, and in doing so – *if* they can also change the problem to which they are addressed – they expand the actual, inventively (Nowotny, 2002).

The specific, the general and the universal

Our second point concerns the generalizability of the knowledge produced in inventive methods, an issue that is closely linked to their double force. To consider how this is so,[7] let us take the example of number. In her contribution to this collection, Helen Verran proposes that the remarkable capacities of numbers are two-fold: they participate in processes of ordering and in representing that order as value. The process of ordering involves the use of numbers as ordinals, while the valuing of order is primarily a function of number as cardinals. This dual role of number – ordering and valuing – is conflated in many routine everyday and scientific uses of number, in which their generalizations of whole-to-part and one-to-many are held together in the indexical use of number as a fixed (external) measure, a metric, or unit of quantity. In such uses, numbers act as coordinates of signification in a particular kind of way – they operate as apparently neutral, external markers of order and value in one; as Badiou says, 'What counts – in the sense of what is valued – is that which is counted' (Badiou, 2008: 2).

The indexical use of number in relation to an external metric that holds together the one-to-many and part-whole relations in one has been central to the ways in which methods used in the 'here and now' have been translated 'always and everywhere'. The work required to make this and other translations successful – that is, to secure the knowledge number produces in specific practices as universal – has been described by Bruno Latour (2000) as the work of extension in time. Latour proposes that recognizing this work should compel us to accept that the history of epistemic things (problems, measures, standards, facts, hypotheses) is an always relative existence: their capacity to endure, he says, is relative to the circumscribed and well-defined spatio-temporal envelope of their network of production. What is interesting to us, however, is that in many contemporary numbering practices there is no aspiration to the making of the spatio-temporal universalisms of always and everywhere. Rather, the relative existence of epistemic things between never-nowhere and always-everywhere is not simply acknowledged, but reflexively operated in. In these operations, a wider range of generalizations than universalization alone is given legitimacy. Problems and solutions are made in (many, multiple) general (not one, universal) space-times.

So, for example, in numerated entities such as models that simulate movements in city environments (Harvey, 2009), in the many mappings now being produced that are locative not territorial (Thrift, 2004), in measuring or judgement tools such as brand valuation techniques (Lury and Moor, 2010), the indexical capacities of numbers to order and value are brought together in relations in which the performative capacities of number are extended and intensified. In these uses, numbers open up new kinds of relations between the specific and the general as their inventive potential is enhanced by their use as indices of the (super-)positionality of multiple, coexisting relational coordinates. They produce what Nigel Thrift (2004) calls generalized spaces of 'awhereness', that is, they are constituted in and engender spaces of (post- or more-than-)representation that are not best understood in terms of external spatio-temporal coordinates of signification, but in which the coordinates participate in surfaces that are spaces in themselves, as operators in surfaces of coordinatization (Adkins and Lury, 2009). To put this in the terms of the material semiotics adopted by Verran (2001), the usefulness of one of the most important capacities of indices – to point to the actual, to indicate 'here', 'now' – a usefulness that has historically been limited by the positional situatedness of the relations it enacts is now being expanded as a resource for inventiveness by not only number, but also other methods or devices in which situatedness is understood not as a position but as a relation. These are, potentially at least, the relations of multiplicity.

In generalized spaces of 'awhereness', it is possible to explore the multiple possible states that a system may have, since entities are without extrinsic coordinatization, and are not limited by extrinsically defined measures or the assumption of a single unity. As Fuller and Goriunova say, these are spaces 'where we do not know how to exist, where we are not, and where, nevertheless, we are'. It is in such spaces, indeed, that methods are increasingly required to be inventive, for what is of interest in such spaces is that tendency is more and more 'part of the actual ... potential gains potency, and the possible is more and more part of the existent'. As Steven Connor notes, 'The strictness of the dichotomy between the actual and the possible is in large part a function of the kinds of relation we have to the latter' and 'It is possible to project and stage a much wider range of contingencies and possible relations to them than ever before, and those contingencies become more and more part of the tractable actual' (Connor, 2009: 9 of 12). Inventive methods are devices that are able to expand and explore the possibilities of this latency and laterality, to support the emergence of difference – or differentiation – by making relations in processes of generalization.

Inventive methods are thus devices of auto-spatialization, whose movement as Michael says of the anecdote, is both topological and nomadic: topological in that they bring together what might have seemed distant, and disconnected and nomadic in that they are processual, iterative, emergent and changeable. This is evident, for example, in Mackenzie's description of the introduction of movement into social life by way of the operation of clopen sets, Back's embrace of the sweep of sound, Ruppert's account of the iterative use of categories to make subject-citizens anew in the census, and Simone's discussion of the role of screening in the making of 'cognitive phase spaces'. Topological and nomadic, fixed and fluid, inventive methods have a multiple capacity for generalization that is precisely not monotheistic universalism.

But this capacity of inventive methods for generalization – to proliferate, to show up anywhere as Simone puts it – raises a number of concerns for academic and other researchers, including the problems of how to defend the value of the always relative existence of epistemic things, and the special legitimacy ('rigour') and distinctiveness or not of disciplinary knowledge. It is perhaps for these reasons that Verran, for example, seeks to make explicit the generative capacities of number, to develop our 'feeling' for number – so that we know how to judge the methods by which we make knowledge. Such concerns are also an explicit focus of discussion in some of the other chapters, including Ruppert on the category, Phillips on the list, Michael on the anecdote, Simone on the screen, Brown on the experiment, Mackenzie on the set, Parisi on speculation, Bell on the photo-image and Marres on the experiment in living.[8]

Let us focus on the last three. In her philosophical discussion of speculation, Parisi explicitly cautions us to be careful in our use of generalization. She draws on the philosopher Whitehead and others to make it clear that the process of generalization is not to be confused either with an appeal to a ('bigger', 'more inclusive') category, as with deductive method, or with a proved fact that can be universalized to others, as with an inductive method. But she also suggests that generalization – or at least the generalization of speculative reason – cannot make use of the concept of set as a basic concept – in contradistinction to the approach developed by Badiou and outlined by Mackenzie. This is because to generalize in her view means to describe the non-separability from particular rules of an object not as a one-to-many relation as she says is characteristic of set thinking, but as a constructivist endeavour 'in the nature of finite, actual, terminal entities'.

In her discussion of the contrast between the photo-image and the sociological text, Bell also draws out the problems of generalization: as she says, 'in the movement from image to text (as from text to image), there yawns a crucial panoply of possibilities, of tensions, of affirmations and contradictions'. Using the case of the book *Now Let Us Praise Famous Men* (2001; first published in 1941), with images by the photographer Walker Evans and text by James Agee, Bell highlights these tensions, focusing on what she sees as the possibility that the 'viewer's response will be one that contents itself with the sense of singularities, or otherwise of a "shared humanity", that routinely accompanies systematically reproduced inequities rather too easily'. This too-easy generalization is linked in her analysis to the specific mode of circulation associated with the image, that implicit in the photographic contract, in which 'the agreement to allow an image to be made is also an understanding that it may circulate and be witnessed'. For Bell, the sociologist's task 'cannot be content to leave it as undifferentiated as that; ours is a more critical, and a more political task'. The way in which an image can 'open up' is, she says, a process that 'cannot be captured as a positivity for social science, not least because it is not something that is in our control'.[9]

In Marres' discussion, the focus is also on the way in which methods are currently proliferating, enacting the social, making spaces: she describes in particular how experiments in living are multiplying across social life, circulating as a genre of publicity,[10] and asks whether and how the circulation of social research devices can be productive for social science. (Michael too observes of the anecdote that it is 'for the telling'; they 'seem to demand to be told, to be put into circulation'.) Marres observes how these processes of circulation are linked not only to the epistemology of the method in question but also to ontological politics, a distribution of agencies, techniques and bodies. She notes how living experiments are conducted by a range of government, scientific and for-profit organizations as well as individuals; and that they are used to serve a variety of objectives, which may not always be clearly distinguished, but range from 'technological innovation to marketing to awareness raising'. The conclusion Marres draws from this multiplicity of purpose, however, is 'that to the extent that some of these purposes are in tension with those of social research, sustainable living experiments must be defined as a critical site of research'. Inventive methods are critical for Marres not only because they are a way that (academic) social research may be contested, but also because they allow that social research can be renewed by being put in relation to – being put into alignment with – researching arrangements that are 'configuring in/as social practice'. As she says of sustainable living experiments conducted by, among others, journalists, mothers, engineers, policy-makers and artists:

> They invite us to focus not necessarily on what are the distinguishing features of social science that set it apart, or allow it to be demarcated, from research conducted elsewhere in society. But rather to explore how the circulation of social research techniques across social life can be rendered productive for social science.

This is an argument that has parallels with that developed in anthropology by George Marcus in his advocacy of para-ethnography – a 'collaborative' mode of research with expert subjects who are neither natives nor colleagues, but counterparts (Holmes and Marcus 2005; Marcus, 2005), and also, rather differently, by Michel Serres in his provocative discussion of the para-site (Serres, 2007). For Marcus, the need to consider new kinds of collaboration is not simply a response to the identification of new 'expert' research subjects (for example, elite knowledge workers), but instead is a response to a situation in which 'spontaneously generated para-ethnographies are built into the structure of the contemporary and give form and content to a continuously unfolding skein of experience' (Marcus, 2005). Indeed, Ruppert's discussion of the ways in which the putting into circulation of census categories contributes to a process of double identification of both state and subjects can be seen as an example of this. It is a kind of 'articulation work'. Ruppert writes:

> The question then is not how to improve techniques such as censuses to better 'capture' or describe the social world 'out there' but to examine how these very techniques are involved in both making up and legitimizing particular versions of the social world. From this perspective debates about whether categories of people are 'real' or 'constructed' are redundant for if we attend to the inventive capacities of categories in the ordering of our lives and that of others we see that categories have a formative and transformative potential. Indeed, it is a potential that has and can be activated by subjects.

In a similar spirit, Suchman cites Helen Verran's proposal to develop '"working knowledges together", that is, negotiating the creation of new, partially shared imaginaries without – and this is crucial – relying on one homogenizing translation into a dominant party's terms', while Simone asks of people living in cities: 'How do residents then perform this research; and if such research is a critical dimension of urban life, how is the research itself "researched"?'. Inventive methods as we understand them are one response to this question, ways of 'configuring possibilities for residents of a district to be in a larger world together – in ways that do not assume a past solidity of affiliations, a specific destination nor an ultimate collective formation to come'.

The sensible and the knowable

The visibility and speed of expansion of the multiple generalized spaces of 'awhereness' in the continuously unfolding contemporary is undoubtedly partly because 'the sheer amount of calculation going on in the world has undergone a major shift of late, as a result of the widespread application of computing power' (Thrift, 2004: 586). But the existence and generalization of such spaces is not new or a consequence of either computing or numbering practices alone, as the methods described here attest. As Simone writes:

> in contexts where once relied upon mediations grow weak, where clear interpretations of what is taking place are difficult to make with confidence, and where individuals feel they have few opportunities to make recourse to higher authorities or arbitration, individuals 'set screens' all of the time.

And once the capacities of the methods described here to create generalizing spaces of 'awhereness' is acknowledged, there follows a recognition of the importance of the properties of the medium – or media – of methods for whatever inventiveness happens. For example, that a probe is a handcrafted item, that it is 'tactile and situated', designed for a specific project, means that the researcher is not only able to register possibility in thought or calculation alone, but also to experience the haptic (as also described by Jefferies in relation to pattern), to 'hold the possible in our hand' (Connor, 2009: 9 of 12). Different methods support the methodological coordinates of signification – icons, indices and symbols, material graphemes, and various kinds of combinations between them, in different ways, and as a consequence have different material-semiotic capacities to introduce answerability into problems.

The inventive methods collected here variously make it possible to address the complex relations between the sensible and the knowable by deploying what Serra calls 'the logic of materials', and thus have different affordances for generalization. As Boehner, Gaver and Boucher put it, that a probe is specially designed for a project 'does not mean that the knowledge that emerges in its use is not generalizable, but that the generalization it makes possible necessarily takes place through the mediation of the matter of design'. Marres quotes Gay Hawkins, who proposes that what is distinctive about living experiments is that they 'involve intensities of the body' and as such may enable more intimate ways of 'understanding how new habits and sensibilities emerge'; and Simone proposes that the surface of social life 'no longer "screens" anything, but registers the body as immersed in the immediacy of experience'. What is being pointed to here is the way in which the materials and media of research are also agents – they have agency – in the research process, and this agency should not be seen as delegation, but as translation.

In his chapter, Back identifies the importance of the tape recorder as a device that stabilized the interview as a method of social research because of its capacity to 'give voice' to human subjects. He quotes early adopters of the tape recorder observing that, in contrast to what emerged in interview note-taking, 'you do get something which is heightened and more vivid and less hesitant, and smoothed out, by using those little tape recorders' (Marsden, 2010: 14). But he also suggests that, over time, the technological capacity to record voices accurately meant that researchers became 'less observant, less involved and this minimized their attentiveness to the social world'; a particular way of listening was stabilized in the use of the tape recorder to assist in conducting interviews, closing down the interviewer's other senses, helping to fix the subject of the interview as an authorial phenomenological conscious-ness. As he mourns the death of his tape recorder, Back welcomes the possibilities afforded by other devices to access 'auditory life', to extend what might count as data beyond 'recording human voices that are expected to tell the truth about society', and engage the 'surface of sonic vitality'. The traditional interview can – in relation with a variety of recording devices – enter the sociological imagination with an expanded set of affordances, beyond voice, including the material properties of sound. Such properties can themselves be explored and experimented with as indices of the relationality of subjects, objects and spaces: interviews can afford not only subjective depth, but also environmental acoustics and objectival volume.

What we want to emphasize here is the sensory plenitude afforded for knowledge and action by inventive methods. Such methods enable us to acknowledge that we are in *medias res*, in the middle of things, in 'mid-stream, always already embedded in a situation, one both settled and unsettled' as Rabinow puts it (Rabinow, 2007: 8). Simone, for example, describes the screen as 'a neurasthenic surface of the interplay of various sensations – visual, auditory, olfactory, gestural, and haptic – applicable to all cities'. And while the probes discussed by Boehner, Gaver and Boucher are created by a designer, the activity of screening used in research by city residents is, Simone says, less stable; it is 'a kind of probe involving various instances and forms of activation of which the individual is either an explicit or implicit target'. In these uses, the screen is a membrane, a mediation of interchange, a tissue 'that relays, switches, speeds up and slows down "the traffic of semiosis"'. Such a device, with its capacities for reflection and projection, 'a switchboard of connections', makes it possible to navigate in a space where 'on the one hand, everything remains to be figured out and, on the other hand, there is no longer a need for interpretation'.

The emphasis on the media of methods draws attention to the processes of giving form, figuring out, that are central to social inquiry. As Rabinow says, 'it is only through discovering and giving form to elements that are already present that the inquiry can proceed' (Rabinow, 2007: 9). Even the humble anecdote is 'an openly ambiguous textual form: combining the real and the constructed, holding them in tension' (Michael). In discussions of the ability of devices to format social action, the per-form-ativity of methods, and con-figure-ation, there is already an acknowledgement of the importance of form and figure, but many of the methods discussed here explicitly draw attention to what 'working with' methods might mean more explicitly in terms of form-giving, craft or imagination. So, for example, Steve Brown draws an explicit parallel between developments in the history of social psychology experimental methods and the German expressionist movement in the early twentieth century, which in part made use of ' "experiments with disruptive and inter-polative techniques" and include "montage and other devices of discontinuity" ' to focus on the ways in which psychological experimentation aims for 'a certain kind of purity of expression'. '[The experiment] attempts', he says, 'to make visible social phenomena in a form in which they could never possibly be lived, never otherwise made manifest'.

One further point follows from recognizing the medium-specificity of the methods described here, namely exploring and exploiting the possibilities of multiple temporalities that may accompany methods, including the 'automatism', self-regulating character or recursivity that is variously developed in media (Cavell, 1979; Kwinter, 2009).[11] The potential of exploiting such recursivity is perhaps most explicitly exemplified in Mackenzie's discussion of the set, where he notes the importance of the definition of a relation R as 'a set of sets' for the uses of the set in list-making and relational databases. As he observes, in allowing set-making to become recursive, this relation made it possible for mathematical operations coded in software to implement the method of the set (setting) in such a way as to allow relations between different sets to be organized sequentially (A as the set of 'things to be done' can be put in a recursive loop with a sub-set such as the set of 'things to be done before A, that is, 'things to be done'; and so on). Recursivity is thus fundamental to the power of sets in computing.

Recursivity is also evident in the title of another of Richard Serra's works discussed by Andrea Phillips: *Verb List Compilation: Actions to Relate to Oneself.* Peter Osborne, who Phillips quotes, suggests that, while this artwork has a speculative potential, it is dependent on its title to establish 'relations to acts of . . . production within the frozen objecthood of . . . results'. In contrast, patterning, as discussed by both Jefferies and Stenner, is organized in terms of repetition or recursivity; one chapter – that by Jefferies – emphasizes patterning as repetition in space, a 'textured medium', while the other – the chapter by Stenner – stresses repetition in time. Stenner says, 'we are dealing with something maximally temporal that, like a piece of live music, endures in only a minimally spatial manner'; a 'pulse of alternating pattern; playing the difference between gathering and dispersal; adding a little order to chaos and chaos to order'. Experiment, too, is also always a matter of reiterated and controlled adjustment; similarly, the categories of the census iteratively identify and close gaps, mediating the relationship between individuals and states; while configuration alerts us:

> to attend to the histories and encounters through which things are figured into meaningful existence, fixing them through reiteration but also always engaged in 'the perpetuity of coming to be' that characterizes the biographies of objects as well as subjects.

To be inventive, methods may need to be slow (as both Law and Marcus – 'the unbearable slowness of ethnography' – suggest), fast, or both, but always require attention to the mobile cluster of temporalities in which they are nested.

In different ways, all the methods we describe here can be seen in terms of the organization of a recursive relation to the excess of specificity that is the actual. This can be described in mathematical terms as the excess that comes from the internal non-cohesion of the set with itself, from the irreducibly unstable relations between the parts that belong and the elements that are included. It is the organization of the excess of representation over presentation (Badiou, 2008); sometimes this is a quantitative excess, the excess of data generated in transaction data sets, but it can also be the excess of sensory plenitude, of the non-representational and the more-and-less-than-rational. Grasping this excess, configuring it, is one of the principal sources of a method's capacity to be inventive, a capacity that can only be enhanced by the use of the material-semiotic properties of materials and media to expand relations between the sensible and the knowable. As Mariam Fraser (2009) has put it, a method can be inventive if it can be deployed to 'lure' materials into *posing their own problems*.

Conclusion, or refrain

To begin, again.

Notes

1 We would like to thank the editors of the book series, and in particular, Penny Harvey for not only pushing us to explicate our aims in adopting the method of the alphabetically ordered list to order the chapters in this volume, but also for their ideas about the role of the list, many of which we draw on here.

2 Of course, this is not a new proposal. One of the most influential advocates of such an approach is C. Wright Mills (1959). But it is a proposal that may usefully be refreshed by repetition.

3 And, some might say, questionability into methods.

4 In a related argument, Buscher, Urry and Witchger observe that the use of social research methods in 'forms and forces of surveillance and monitoring' is being extended in the development of 'powerful mobile computer-based methods' (Buscher *et al.*, 2011: 2).

5 Indeed, as Lucy Suchman says, 'Methods . . . like their research objects, are both well established and always in the making'.

6 The instability of such an assemblage (specifically the interview assemblage) is the subject of the method of anecdote described by Michael.

7 Which might also have been framed in terms of specificity – of under- or over-specificity, even un- or non-specificity.

8 They are also discussed in some detail by Verran (forthcoming).

9 Related concerns are the subject of Atkinson and Silverman's (1997) discussion of the emergence of what they call an 'interview society', in which they address the implications of the increasing use of the interview as a method in a range of mass cultural forms, including newspaper articles, sports programmes and chat shows, for its use in social science research.

10 Drawing a similar parallel, Steve Brown notes that 'The situation of a housemate [in the reality TV show *Big Brother*] is then close to that of a participant in a psychological experiment'.

11 In a recognition of the importance of recursivity to method in art, Sanford Kwinter writes, 'Among the most prominent developments that have marked recent art has been the incursion of "method" into the heart of what has long appeared as an array

of miscellaneous, even random art practices. By method, I mean nothing more than an approach in which a certain discipline is sustained over a range of executions, sustained, that is, long enough both to leave a trace of "system" in the deposited production and for that systematic quality to serve as a principal rhetorical feature of the work' (Kwinter, 2009).

References

Adkins, L. and Lury, C. (eds) (2009) 'What is the empirical?', Special Issue, *European Journal of Social Theory*, 12 (1): 5–20.

Agamben, G. (2009) *'What is an Apparatus?' and Other Essays*, Palo Alto, CA: Stanford University Press.

Agee, J. (2001) *Let Us Now Praise Famous Men*, Boston, MA: Houghton Mifflin.

Atkinson, P. and Silverman, D. (1997) 'Kundera's immortality: the interview society and the invention of the self', *Qualitative Inquiry*, 3 (3): 304–25.

Badiou, A. (2008) *Number and Numbers*, Cambridge: Polity Press.

Barad, K. (2003) 'Posthumanist performativity: toward an understanding of how matter comes to matter', *Signs*, 28 (3): 801–31.

Barad, K. (2007) *Meeting the Universe Halfway: Quantum Physics and the Entanglement of Matter and Meaning*, Durham, NC: Duke University Press.

Berlant, L. (2007) 'On the Case', Special Issue, *Critical Inquiry*, 33 (4): 663–72.

Burrows, R. and Savage, M. (2007) 'The coming crisis of empirical sociology', *Sociology*, 41 (5): 885–99.

Buscher, M, Urry, J. and Witchger, K. (eds) (2010) *Mobile Methods*, London: Routledge.

Callon, M., Millo, Y. and Muniesa, F. (2007) *Market Devices*, Oxford: Wiley-Blackwell.

Castañeda, C. (2002) *Figurations: Child, Bodies, Worlds*, Durham, NC and London: Duke University Press.

Cavell, S. (1979) *The World Viewed*, enlarged edition, Cambridge, MA: Harvard University Press.

Connor, S. (2009) 'Wherever: The ecstasies of Michel Serres', available at: www.bbk.ac.uk/english/skc/wherever/ (accessed 3 February 2012).

Clough, P. and J. Halley (2007) *The Affective Turn: Theorizing the Social*, Durham, NC: Duke University Press.

DeLanda, M. (2006) *A New Philosophy of Society: Assemblage Theory and Social Complexity*, London and New York: Continuum.

Deleuze, G. and Guattari, F. (1987) *A Thousand Plateaus*, trans. B. Massumi, Minneapolis, MN: University of Minnesota Press.

Fraser, M. (2009) 'Experiencing sociology', *European Journal of Social Theory*, 12 (1): 63–82.

Fraser, M. (2010) 'Facts, ethics and event', in C. Bruun Jensen and K. Rödje (eds) *Deleuzian Intersections in Science, Technology and Anthropology,* New York and Oxford: Berghahn Books, pp. 52–82.

Foucault, M. (1980) 'The confession of the flesh interview', in C. Gordon (ed.) *Power/Knowledge Selected Interviews and Other Writings*, London: Vintage, pp. 194–228.

Haraway, D. (1985) 'Manifesto for Cyborgs: Science, Technology, and Socialist Feminism in the 1980s', *Socialist Review*, 80: 65–108.

Haraway, D. (1992) 'The promises of monsters: a regenerative politics for inappropriate/d others', in L. Grossberg, C. Nelson and P. Treichler (eds) *Cultural Studies*, New York: Routledge, pp. 295–337.

Harvey, P. (2009) 'Between narrative and number: the case of ARUP's 3D digital city model', *Cultural Sociology*, 3 (2): 257–76.

Highmore, B. (2002) *Everyday Life and Cultural Theory: An Introduction*, London: Routledge.

Holbraad, M. and Pedersen, M. A. (2009) 'Planet M: the intense abstraction of Marilyn Strathern', *Anthropological Theory*, 9 (4): 371–94.

Holmes, G. D. and Marcus, G. (2005) 'Cultures of expertise and the management of globalization: toward the re-functioning of ethnography', in A. Ong and S. J. Collier (eds) *Global Assemblages: Technology, Politics, and Ethics as Anthropological Problems*, Oxford: Blackwell, pp. 235–52.

Karpik, L. (2010) *Valuing the Unique: The Economies of Singularities*, Princeton, NJ: Princeton University Press.

King, K. (2010) '"Knowledge-weaving": befriending transdisciplinarity under the urgencies of global academic restructuring', paper presented at CRESC Annual Conference, 'The Social Life of Methods', Oxford, 30 August–2 September.

Krauss, R. (2010) *Perpetual Inventory*, Boston, MA: MIT Press.

Kwinter, S. (1998) 'The hammer and the song', *OASE*, 48 (21): 31–43.

Kwinter, S. (2009) 'Systems theory: Sanford Kwinter on Matthew Ritchie's the Morning Line', available at: findarticles.com/p/articles/mi_m0268/is_3_48/ai_n 56162855/?tag=content;col1 (accessed 3 February 2012).

Latour, B. (2000) 'On the partial existence of existing and non-existing objects', in L. Dalliston (ed.) *Biographies of Scientific Objects*, Chicago, IL: University of Chicago Press, pp. 247–269.

Law, J. (2004) *After Method: Mess in Social Science Research*, London: Routledge.

Law, J. and Urry, J. (2004) 'Enacting the social', *Economy and Society*, 33 (3): 390–410.

Lury, C. and Moor, L. (2010) 'Brand valuation and topological culture', in M. Aronczyk and D. Powers (eds) *Blowing Up the Brand: Critical Perspectives on Promotional Culture*, New York: Peter Lang, pp. 29–53.

Marcus, G. (2005) 'Multi-sited ethnography: five or six things I know about it now', available at: eprints.ncrm.ac.uk (accessed 3 February 2012).

Marsden, D. (2010) 'Life story interview with Paul Thompson', Pioneers of Qualitative Research. Transcribed by ESDS Qualidata, Colchester: UK Data Archive, University of Essex.

Mills, C. W. (1959) *The Sociological Imagination*, London: Oxford University Press.

Mol, A-M. (2005) *The Body Multiple*, Durham, NC: Duke University Press.

Nowotny, H. (2002) 'Vergangene Zukunft: Ein Blick zurück auf die "Grenzen des Wachstums"', in *Impulse geben – Wissen stiften*, 40 Jahre VolkswagenStiftung, VolkswagenStiftung: Göttingen, pp. 655–94.

Ong, A. and Collier, S. (eds) (2005) *Global Assemblages*, Oxford: Blackwell.

Parker, M. (2012, forthcoming) 'Contraptions: an experimental ethics of scientific collaboration', *Biosocieties*.

Pile, S. and Thrift, N. (eds) (2000) *City A–Z: Urban Fragments*, London: Routledge.

Rabinow, P. (2007) *Marking Time: On the Anthropology of the Contemporary*, Princeton, NJ: Princeton University Press.

Rabinow, P. and Marcus, G., with Faubion, J. D. and Rees, T. (2009) *Designs for an Anthropology of the Contemporary*, Durham, NC: Duke University Press.

Rheinberger, H-J. (1997) *Toward a History of Epistemic Things: Synthesizing Proteins in the Test Tube*, Palo Alto, CA: Stanford University Press.

Riles, A. (2001) *The Network Inside Out*, Ann Arbor, MI: University of Michigan Press.

Serra, R. (1968) *Hand Catching Lead*, video.

Serres, M. (2007) *Parasite*, trans. L. R. Scher, Minneapolis, MN: University of Minnesota Press.

Shaw, J. (1996) 'Surrealism, Mass Observation and Researching Imagination', in E. Stina Lyon and J. Busfield (eds) *Methodological Imaginations*, London: Macmillan: pp. 1–17.

Stark, D. (2009) *The Sense of Dissonance: Accounts of Worth in Economic Life*, Princeton, NJ: Princeton University Press.

Thrift, N. (2004) 'Movement-space: the changing domain of thinking resulting from the development of new kinds of spatial awareness', *Economy and Society*, 33 (4): 582–604.

Thrift, N. (2007) *Non-representational Theory: Space, Politics, Affect*, London: Routledge.

Tsing, A. (2004) *Friction: An Ethnography of Local Connection*, Princeton, NJ: Princeton University Press.

Verran, H. (2001) *Science and an African Logic*, Chicago, IL: University of Chicago Press.

Verran, H. (forthcoming) 'The changing lives of measures and values: from centre stage in the fading "disciplinary" society to pervasive background instrument in the emergent "control" society', in L. Adkins and C. Lury (eds) 'Measure and value', Special Issue, *Sociological Review*.

Wardrip-Fruin, N. (2009) *Expressive Processing*, Cambridge, MA: MIT Press.

2 Anecdote

Mike Michael

Here is a small selection of dictionary definitions of 'anecdote':

> A short narrative of an incident of private life.
> (*Chambers Twentieth Century Dictionary*, Revised Edition, 1982)

> A short amusing or interesting story about a real incident or person.
> (*Oxford Dictionary of English*, 2nd Edition, Revised, 2005)

> A short usually amusing account of an incident, esp. a personal or biographical one.
> (*Collins English Dictionary*, 9th Edition, 2007)

Within these definitions, we have some of the key features of the anecdote on display. It is a story of some sort, though there is an implication that this is about an actual incident, thus it is not simply a fictional narrative, but possibly a report. The narrative is short – once more perhaps connoting reportage – which suggests a focused form of accounting, a pithiness that excludes extraneous detail in order to highlight the importance, or core, of the incident. As such, the incident is something that is worth recounting – it might provide insight, it might yield knowledge. But what about? After all, this is 'an incident of private life' or an account that is 'a personal or biographical one'. Might it tell us something about the participants? Do we gain a better impression of this or that person and so a sounder grasp of their behaviour on a wider or public stage? Moreover, the anecdote is said usually to be amusing. Does that mean that we get a sense of the ironies that assail the particular characters in the anecdote? Or does the anecdote afford a renewed, or even novel, insight into the character of private life itself?

But notice (and this is something these dictionary definitions do not address): an anecdote is, arguably, for the telling. Unlike other narratives that can languish in dusty tomes or loiter in the back of one's mind, anecdotes, perhaps because of the nature of the incident, seem to demand to be told, to be put into circulation. Or rather, such narratives become anecdotes by virtue of their telling, because they are deliberately sent out into the world.

How might all this relate to the doing of social scientific research? At the most superficial level, anecdotes can be a resource or a tool for conducting social scientific research: we study the content and enactment of anecdotes much as we might study the content and enactment of any other textual form that is implicated in interesting social phenomena. We might address such questions as: How do anecdotes feature in the rhetorical structure of a political speech or a lifestyle blog? How do anecdotes contribute to the making of a scientific controversy or the emergence of a moral panic or the mediation of a particular prejudice? However, in the present case, the focus will be less on anecdotes as particular components of social phenomena, and more upon their broader, and hopefully deeper, ramifications for methodology. On this score, anecdotes also become a topic of enquiry. The question becomes: How might we push the anecdote as form and process so that it adds something new (or at least new-ish) to the conduct of research – to the gathering, identifying, marshalling, ordering or making of 'the happening of the social'?

What anecdotes can do

Given that anecdotes entail stories about incidents or events or persons, they can be placed within a lineage of social scientific methods that is broadly ethnographic. The personal dimension of the anecdote suggests that its closest methodological relative is probably auto-ethnography. This is a large and burgeoning mode of research, in which it is the analyst's own experiences that, at base, comprise the data. According to Heewon Chang (2008), auto-ethnography differs from more performance-oriented or descriptive accounts (e.g. autobiography, diaries, memoirs) because the interpretation of self is situated within broader sociocultural dynamics. As such, it enables researchers to examine their relationship to a range of others (e.g. in terms of relations of similarity, difference or opposition). While Chang is clear about the dangers of self-indulgence, over-descriptiveness, and over-dependence on memories, she seems less concerned with the 'processuality' of research: how the auto-ethnographic moment is itself performative of researcher and researched.

Unlike the auto-ethnographic approach, the anecdote is, as we shall see, useful for explicitly incorporating the performativity of research – i.e. the way that research is not a mere reflection of something (e.g. one's experiences in relation to social or cultural process) out there, but is instrumental in, and a feature of, the 'making of out theres'. Thus, the anecdote is, as we shall note below, part of the 'historical record' and as it circulates it shapes the ways in which particular incidents come to be understood. However, there is another level of performativity to take into account. The anecdote relates events that have, in one way or another, affected the storyteller in ways that make those events 'anecdotalizable'. Here, performativity lies in the way prior events come to enact the storyteller as just that – one who 'anecdotalizes' and renders the past in the form of an anecdote. The point is that the anecdote, unlike typical forms of auto-ethnogaphy, can serve as a means for tracing the co-emergence of research, researcher and researched.

One implication of this is that the very categories of doing social science can come to be questioned. Auto-ethnography seems to operate within the confines of standard categories of social and cultural analysis. Thus, self might be narrated in relation to others of difference and similarity: the self is seen to emerge through tacit processes of differentiation from, and/or identification with, groups indexed in terms of class, ethnicity or gender. By comparison, anecdotalization can be thought as a methodological tactic that, in keeping with de Certeau's (1984) version of tactic, at once occupies and overflows, reacts to and momentarily escapes, upholds and undermines, the confines and particular productivities of (the) discipline. Thus, the analytic categories typical for a particular area of social scientific research can come to be interrogated. As we shall see below, in the case of the category of 'lay public' in the field of 'public understanding of science', the anecdote serves in querying not only the category of 'lay public', but also the very parameters of the field of 'public understanding of science'.

We are now in a position to think more systematically about the anecdote. The brief characterization of the anecdote sketched in the introduction can be presented more formally in terms of five key features:

1   According to Fineman (1989; see also Boettger, 1998), the anecdote is at once literary (obviously a constructed story) and exceeds this literary status (manifestly, it is supposed to report or document real events). Thus, it is an openly ambiguous textual form: combining the real and the constructed, holding them in tension. In relation to the patternings of ordering and disordering of broader socio-technical assemblages that I am interested in investigating, the anecdote allows one to start from a specific incident and explore its complex and constitutive range of associations without ever seeing this exploration as uncomplicatedly representational, nor regarding it as exhaustive.

2   Fineman argues that the anecdote as a part of a historical record not only reports events, but also acts upon them. An anecdote reports an episode from social life, but by virtue of being a particular interpretation of that episode, and by virtue of its circulation as a story and reportage, it can go on to influence subsequent events. For some purposes, the anecdote can thus serve as a way of chronically invoking the performativity of both the anecdote and its associated analysis as they 'act upon' the reader and beyond.

3   As noted above, a crucial characteristic of the anecdote is that it documents an 'incident', something out of the ordinary. In the process, there is an enactment of difference and sameness: the unusual event articulated in the anecdote serves to highlight, and is highlighted by, the usual run of events that surround it. Even where anecdotes seemingly convey the ordinary ('nothing happened at work today, it was so boring'), there are tacit claims

to the unusual (it was a working day *particularly* bereft of incident; the quality of the tedium was *particularly* intense). In the context of my own work on technology and everyday life, the anecdote captures moments where things go wrong or are out of sorts in one way or another: the Velcro on a cycle helmet catches a daughter's hair and makes her cry, walking boots are so excruciatingly painful that it is impossible to appreciate a 'wonder of nature', the remote control systematically gets lost and disrupts a particular relation to the television. These are instants and instances of difference that allow us to interrogate the sameness of the taken-for-granted (e.g. Michael, 2000, 2006). In a way, such anecdotes can be seen as reporting on 'naturally' occurring, and heterogeneous (in the sense of involving humans and non-humans), breaching experiments, to borrow from Garfinkel (1967). The extraordinary moment serves in the illumination of the ordinary flow of events. In another way, anecdotes relate to the notable incidents that have been the focus of so much science and technology studies: moments of difference (controversies, fraud, hype) that give insight into the mundane workings of technoscience.

4   The anecdote should enable us to draw broader lessons. We move from the individual to the general: from this particular driver who in this particular car experiences 'road rage', to a view of cars as heterogeneous ordering machines that afford, and enable the warranting of, complex affective performances; from these specific painful boots that preclude this body from experiencing the sublime in this Cretan gorge, to a consideration of the quiet affordances of mundane technology that allow nature to appear 'natural'.

5   As we have already noted, anecdotes concern incidents in 'private life'. This may be understood as a reference to the personal: the anecdote accesses something 'intimate'. As such, anecdotes, insofar as they refer to incidents that have befallen their author, can be a means to writing self into the narrative in order to problematize the authorial voice. This can again evoke the constructedness of the anecdote itself, and indeed the text surrounding it. However, perhaps more crucially, such personal anecdotes can connote how the anecdotal events themselves contribute to the making of their author.[1] That is to say, the author can emerge from the 'incident of private life' that renders the incident 'anectoteable' as it were. Put yet another way, anecdotes can come to mark events of the transition of, and invention in, the research process in which the researcher 'becomes'.

While these features of the anecdote concern 'incidents in private life', they are incidents in a peculiarly un-private private life. They narrate happenings of the social that are, for all their apparent 'intimacy', more or less readily convertible into public (social scientific) goods that can be put into circulation. To be sure, there is something 'private' about feeling road rage, having extremely painful feet, routinely losing the TV remote control, catching a daughter's hair with the Velcro straps of a cycle helmet. But this is private in the sense of a 'happening of the microsocial', as it were: these are everyday, personal, affectively charged incidents that are nonetheless highly recognizable. More importantly, they can be assimilated to ongoing analytic projects – in the above cases, there was an attempt to think of apparently social phenomena (the warranting of road rage, the representation of the couch potato, the social constructedness of the sublime, the enactment of everyday life) in terms of the patternings of ordering and disordering in socio-technical assemblages.

In what follows, I will attempt to push the idea of anecdote a little further in order to explore how it might play a more interesting role in relation to methodology. Rather than seeking anecdotes that can become exemplars of, or analytic fodder in, this or that conceptual framework, I will suggest that anecdotes can operate in ways that disrupt such frameworks and precipitate methodological and theoretical reorientation. Here, there is a move away from anecdotes *about* the 'social-world-as-the-object-of-study' towards the process of anecdotalization – how anecdotes become present in the doing of social research, and so query and refresh that process of research.

From 'anecdotes about' to 'anecdotalization'

In this section I will present two anecdotes about 'incidents in private life', but these are the 'private life' of the social science researcher and their doing of research. Specifically, they are incidents that, respectively, entailed failure to 'gather' data, and signalled an 'inability' to use data within an ongoing programme of research. Each will say something about not only the process of research, but also the role of anecdotalization as an 'irritant' within the process of doing research.

Anecdotalization I: on the uses of 'no data'

Some 20 years ago, I was based at Lancaster University and engaged in fieldwork into the public understanding of science. Specifically, I was conducting interviews with respondents to derive the 'mental models' that underpinned their understanding of ionizing radiation. In one particular piece of fieldwork, I was conducting a second interview with a respondent at her house. After a period of unemployment, the interviewee had recently (indeed, since our last interview session) got a job at Burger King. I was seated on the sofa, the respondent was in an armchair to my right and the tape recorder was placed on the floor between us.

During the preliminary conversation, her pit bull terrier ambled up and sat on my feet. As the respondent said, 'she (the dog) liked to know where people were'. As I tried to open up further discussion of ionizing radiation, it became clear that she would much rather talk about her new job, and the opportunities it offered her: she was evidently delighted with Burger King's career structure and was looking forward to rapid promotion. While this conversation was going on, her cat came into the room, and after a few moments of clawing at the tape recorder began to pull it along the ground by its strap. As the cat played with the recorder, it got further and further away from the interview, which was rapidly turning into a monologue about Burger King, a monologue that I could neither halt nor redirect, being too distracted by the disappearing tape recorder and the pit bull's liking for my feet. Together, the respondent, the dog and the cat had conspired to derail the interview and thus disrupt my connection with my tape recorder, my scholarly project, and my dignity. The interviewee was paid five pounds sterling for the interview. As I could not record anything, and as in any case the topic of ionizing radiation had not been addressed, there was no data.

On one level, this anecdote comprises a story about failure – failure of nerve, failure of professionalism, failure to cooperate. It is the sort of happening that crops up now and again in any research career, and there is a battery of informal epithets that one can mobilize by way of 'explanation': the inexperienced or naive researcher, the recalcitrant participant, the ill-thought-through research design. It can be read as a warning anecdote about the things that can go wrong, and how best to be prepared for the worst. Certainly, that was how I treated it for a long time.

And yet, there was something irritating about this episode: this salutary account was too easy, and had utterly failed to grasp, let alone exhaust, its significance. A long time after this 'disastrous interview', as I shifted from an intellectual commitment to social constructionism to an enthusiasm for the heterogeneous analytics of actor-network theory (e.g. Latour, 1987), it began to dawn on me that this was not an anecdote about failure and 'lessons learnt'. Rather, it could be read in terms of 'differential success'. In brief, I began to see this episode as revealing the ways that social data are made possible by virtue of the disciplining (or silencing) of non-human others (such as the dog and cat). No data were possible, because the cat, dog and their human companion 'misbehaved' in relation to my understanding of the interview. But such 'misbehaviour' was also enabled by the relations between dog, cat and human. Thus the episode entailed a complex set of interactions where humans, animals and technologies were involved in a process of constituting orderings and disorderings by virtue of the various relations into which they had entered. On the one hand, from my perspective, these relations between respondent, animals and corporation generated disorder (or failure), in the sense that data were neither yielded nor gathered: there was, in other words, a thoroughgoing disruption of the relations between interviewer and tape recorder and university. On the other hand, these very relations enabled the successful enactment of (cultural) indifference to, and (financial) independence from, interviewer and their institution. Interestingly, in this dynamic we see the differentiation of institutions (university and corporation) partly enacted through heterogeneous microprocesses involving animals (see Michael, 2004 for a more detailed analysis).

It would be easy enough to see this re-interpretation of the 'disastrous interview episode' as a reworking of the significance of the anecdote in the light of a shift in theoretical commitments. To be attached to a general framework such as actor-network theory is to become sensitized to the role of non-humans in the making of the 'social'. However, that would be to regard the anecdote as simple representation upon which one could do conceptual work, to treat it as analytic fodder. As we have noted above, the anecdote is performative: its irritant qualities work upon the author insofar as it is part of the process through which the material-semiotic events described in the anecdote serve in the 'remaking' of the anecdote's author. Indeed, one could say that that episode, partly through its anecdotalization, affectively haunted 'me'. In the disordering of interviewer, tape recorder and institution, that event, and the subsequent events in which there was a retelling of that event, enacted a different 'me'. This new 'me', now partly composed of and by that episode and its multiple tellings (anecdotalization), some 15 years later, comes to be in a position to reenact that episode as a rather different anecdote. To be sure, that position can be seen to be the product of a series of other episodes – intellectual encounters with Latour and Haraway, Serres and Whitehead. Yet, these (material-semiotic) encounters may have been partially precipitated by that initial episode with a dog and a cat and a recalcitrant participant, and its subsequent anecdotal retellings. The disordering of the 'original' episode comes to yield, down a convoluted line of anecdotalization, a more complex ordering, as Serres (1982) might have it, in which there is a shift in theoretical perspective, a dramatic rethinking of the disastrous interview episode, and a reworking of the significance of anecdotes themselves.

Anecdotalization II: on the uses of the 'wrong sort of data'

Some 20 years ago, I was based at Lancaster University and engaged in fieldwork into the public understanding of science. Specifically, I was conducting interviews with respondents to derive the 'mental models' that underpinned their understanding of ionizing radiation. In one particular piece of fieldwork, I was in Cambridge interviewing people who had undergone whole-body radiation monitoring at Addenbrooke's Hospital. I was attempting to trace public understanding of ionizing radiation on the back of a whole-body monitoring programme that had been set up in the wake of the Chernobyl fallout. I too underwent the monitoring procedure, which involved lying on a hard bed in a tunnel chamber, watching a metal bar – a radiation detector – move up then down the length of my body. In recompense for volunteering, a read-out was made available – a graph with the x-axis showing different types of isotopes, and the y-axis showing level of radiation. The most prominent features of the graph were the two peaks, the larger on the left for Carbon 14, the smaller on the right for Caesium 137.

As part of the interviews with whole-body monitoring volunteers, and informed by a commitment to a mental-models approach to public understanding of science, I asked respondents to describe what they understood by these graphs. One particular interview involved a participant who insisted, in a rather arrogant and dismissive way, that he understood perfectly the meaning of the graph. Nevertheless, I pressed him, arguing that, for the purposes of my research, it would be very helpful if he would still describe the graph. Unfurling the read-out, he said (and I paraphrase from memory): 'Well, it's all very obvious. Except, while I can see why your head is so radioactive, I can't understand why your knees are'. He had misinterpreted the peaks: rather than seeing the peaks as markers of especially prominent isotopes, he read them as indicative of particular parts of the body.

For a long time, I found it hugely difficult to 'accommodate' this bit of data. The respondent seemed to be clearly wrong, though it was an understandable mistake given the nature of the whole-body monitoring procedure. But what particularly struck me was his sheer self-confidence, indeed bravado. Here was someone who was wrong and arrogant and, crucially, a member of the lay public. This was problematic in the context of the political battles being fought at the time, not least against the Royal Society and the deficit model (see Wynne, 1995), in which the public was primarily represented in terms of the deficiencies in its scientific literacy. It was hard to know what to make of this lay arrogance/ignorance: how could it be accounted in a way that did not simply reproduce the deficit model? As before, on one level we have an anecdote about failure: failure of nerve, failure of paradigm, failure of the public to be the public that was politically 'needed' at that time. It is an anecdote about the complex politics of research in which differences in data are situated in relation to ongoing political battles. But this is a politics that seems fixed, with established positions and oppositions (e.g. scientific institutions versus the public).

In retrospect, this anecdote did something rather more interesting. Certainly, it acted as an irritant against what I would later call a 'romantic' view of the 'lay local public' (Michael, 1998). But also, it niggled at a deeper level. Questions that came into focus included: What might be valuable about the participant who does not do what one (politically) expects of them? What does this say about one's politics? How does it disrupt not only one's particular politics around the specific issues associated with the research, but one's very conception of politics more generally?

Let me put it this way. The respondent in this anecdote was an idiot, and the anecdote itself was a medium for reiterating such idiocy, or rather a mediator of such idiocy (see Latour, 2005). In saying this, I draw in part on Isabelle Stengers' technical sense of 'idiot' – an ever-present metaphysical spectre who, by refusing the invitation to the event, and not bothering to explain that refusal (i.e. operating with incommensurable criteria of what is sensible/ meaningful) discomfits us. Here, the anecdote and its idiot serve as a way of enabling us critically to reflect on 'what we are busy doing'. Even if it does not quite suspend 'the habits that make us believe that we know what we know and who we are, that we hold the meaning of what makes us exist' (Stengers, 2005: 1003), it does resource a querying of the 'events' into which respondents are brought, or better still, prehended (Whitehead, 1929) along with the social scientist. This anecdotalization enacts the idiot in terms of the exclusion of the then anomalous figure of the arrogant/ignorant member of the public from a range of interdigitating events (e.g. the 'data gathering' event, the analytic event, the 'relevance' events in which data and analysis circulate to various audiences). But the very the effort exercised in the process of exclusion ironically renders this figure present. This 'excluded presence'[2] can prompt a rethinking of such events. This rethinking goes beyond regarding the event of the difficult interview as a methodological problem in need of a solution; for example, the means with which better to accommodate this analytically and politically bothersome respondent. Rather, it enables, as Fraser (2010) puts it, 'inventive problem-making': how fruitfully to remain sensitive to – i.e. capable of anecdotalizing – those and that which is excluded in the process of research. Indeed, there is a querying of the very field of 'public understanding of science': the excluded idiot resources the questioning of what 'we are busy doing' (Stengers, 2005: 1003) in indexing people's complex relations to science.

Concluding remark: anecdotalizing the anecdotalization

In the foregoing, we have moved from a view of the anecdote as a resource or tool in the analysis of socially interesting phenomena through to a notion of anecdotalization in which the making and enactment of anecdotes is a means of interrogating the research process itself. It will not have escaped notice that this movement from 'anecdotes about' to 'anecdotalization' has itself taken the form of an anecdotalization. As a form of telling that gathers into itself previous tellings and performs critical reflections upon the mutualities of such tellings and retellings and the analytic resources that made such tellings tellable, anecdotalization has both a topological and a nomadic flavour. In terms of the topological, it brings together what might once have seemed distant and disconnected: past episodes that are marginal and trivial illuminate contemporary moments of critical reflection and reorientation, and contemporary concerns render what had long been uninteresting past moments full of relevance. This bringing together of the distant and disconnected is also a marker of the nomadic or the rhizomic, according to Deleuze and Guattari (1988). However, the nomadic serves to emphasize what is processual, iterative, emergent and, crucially, changeable and shifting in anecdotalization. As such, how these anecdotal pasts trigger contemporary reorientations, even as the latter enable the articulation of those anecdotalized pasts and become in their turn anecdotalizations, can be unpredictable, wayward, incomplete and always liable to change.

In any case, insofar as anecdotalization troubles what we are busy doing and is instrumental in inventive problem-making, it suggests that such 'objects' of social scientific study as, say, humans and non-humans and their relations are not simply analytic fodder. Their recalcitrance that is traced in the 'flow' of anecdotalization means that they end up as something akin to, for want of a better term, 'heterogeneous interlocutors' in the inventive doing of research. That is to say, anecdotalization entails a semiotic and material dialogue between past and present through, and with, bodies, memories, stories, objects and texts. If this conversation is any good, uninvited topics, unexpected insights and untoward issues should emerge, and in emerging should go on to feed the very process of anecdotalization.

Notes

1   This version of the personal differs from various feminist treatments that argue for the inclusion of the personal voice in academic work, as well as the valuing of experience as 'data' (e.g. Ribbens and Edwards, 1997), not least by placing emphasis on how the 'I' that emerges within and across anecdotes is marked by distributed-ness, heterogeneity, flows of materials and signs.
2   While there are apparent echoes of Agamben's (1998) 'state of exception' and Serres' (1982) 'excluded third', it is beyond the scope of this chapter to explore these.

References

Agamben, G. (1998) *Homo Sacer: Sovereign Power and Bare Life*, Palo Alto, CA: Stanford University Press.

Boettger, O. (1998) 'From information technology to organising information: an interdisciplinary study', unpublished thesis, Keele University.

Chang, H. (2008) *Autoethnography as Method*, Walnut Creek, CA: Left Coast Press.

De Certeau, M. (1984) *The Practice of Everyday Life*, Berkeley, CA: University of California Press.

Deleuze, G. and Guattari, F. (1988) *A Thousand Plateaus: Capitalism and Schizophrenia*, London: Athlone Press.

Fineman (1989) 'The history of the anecdote: fiction and fiction', in H. A. Veeser (ed.) *The New Historicism*, New York: Routledge, pp. 49–76.

Fraser, M. (2010) 'Facts, ethics and event', in C. Bruun Jensen and K. Rödje (eds) *Deleuzian Intersections in Science, Technology and Anthropology*, New York: Berghahn Press, pp. 57–82.

Garfinkel, H. (1967) *Studies in Ethnomethodology*, Cambridge: Polity Press.

Latour, B. (1987) *Science in Action: How to Follow Engineers in Society*, Milton Keynes: Open University Press.

Latour, B. (2005) *Reassembling the Social*, Oxford: Oxford University Press.

Michael, M. (1998) 'Between citizen and consumer: multiplying the meanings of the public understanding of science', *Public Understanding of Science*, 7 (4): 313–27.

Michael, M. (2000) *Reconnecting Culture, Technology and Nature: From Society to Heterogeneity*, London: Routledge.

Michael, M. (2004) 'On making data social: heterogeneity in sociological practice', *Qualitative Research*, 4 (1): 5–23.

Michael, M. (2006) *Technoscience and Everyday Life,* Maidenhead: Open University Press/McGraw-Hill.

Serres, M. (1982) *The Parasite*, Baltimore, MD: Johns Hopkins University Press.

Stengers, I. (2005) 'The cosmopolitical proposal', in B. Latour and P. Webel (eds) *Making Things Public,* Cambridge, MA: MIT Press, pp. 994–1003.

Ribbens, J.and Edwards, R. (eds) (1997) *Feminist Dilemmas in Qualitative Research: Public Knowledge and Private Lives*, London: Sage.

Whitehead, A. N. (1929) *Process and Reality: An Essay in Cosmology*, New York: The Free Press.

Wynne, B. E. (1995) 'The public understanding of science', in S. Jasanoff, G. E. Markle, J. C. Peterson and T. Pinch (eds) *Handbook of Science and Technology Studies*, Thousand Oaks, CA: Sage, pp. 361–88.

3 Category

Evelyn S. Ruppert

The concern of this chapter is the inventive capacities of the category in the ordering of our lives and that of others. Categories are part of everyday practices through which we sort and classify the material objects we use (tools, furniture, books) and identify ourselves and others (student, British, child). In relation to the latter, some of the identification categories we use in various social settings are the same as those of governmental practices such as population censuses. What, then, is the relationship between the two, between grounded and 'non-authoritative' categories of the everyday and the categories of statistical knowledge-power such as those circulated by censuses? One answer is to think about the category as a device that travels and mediates the relationship between individuals and states, between everyday practices of classification and authoritative state classifications. Rather than a great divide between the two, there are often ruptures when lived experience is ordered against a formal set of state categories.[1] All classification schemes have multiple sets of ruptures arising from such a tension. However, over time there is often a convergence between the two through a 'double process' by which formal classification systems and social worlds come together (Bowker and Star, 1999). On the one hand, a classification system is partially constitutive of a social world; on the other hand, any given social world generates many loosely connected but relatively coherent categories used to classify. In this way, formal categories and social worlds are involved in processes of mutual constitution or 'co-construction' (ibid.). In relation to censuses, identification categories are constituted by and retain an account of the classification work of states but also the work that has been occurring in the social worlds they seek to classify.

As I will argue below, the double process through which formal and everyday categories come together leads to the invention of new people. I will start with an example of census-taking to illustrate this inventive capacity of the category. The example concerns the category 'Canadian', which by the end of the twentieth century became the fastest growing 'ethnic' origin group in Canada. Yet, until 1986, state identification practices such as the census discouraged and advised against 'Canadian' in the classification of racial or ethnic origin (Boyd and Norris, 2001). During the first half of the twentieth century, the census inquired into 'racial or tribal origins' defined on the basis of the father's ancestral lineage: 'as in English, Scotch, Irish, Welsh, French, German, Italian, Danish, Swedish, Norwegian, Bohemian, Ruthenian, Bukovinian, Galician, Bulgarian, Chinese, Japanese, Polish, Jewish, etc.'.[2] With the 1951 census, 'ethnic origin' replaced the racial focus and conflated country of origin, race and religion, which continued to be determined in relation to paternal lineage (until 1981) and the question worded such that the expectation was non-Canadian ancestral designation (until 1986). However, throughout this period of Canadian census-taking, numerous respondents persistently indicated 'Canadian' as their origin and by 1971 Statistics Canada for the first time reported their numbers: over 71,000 respondents insisted on Canadian as their single response (Boyd, 1999). By 1986, when multiple responses to the ethnic origin question were permitted for the first time, one-half per cent of respondents reported Canadian; in 1991, this rose to four per cent and by 1996, when 'Canadian' was added to the list of possible categories, the percentage increased to 31 per cent (ibid.).

Interpreters have variously attributed this phenomenon to state encouragement and promotion of a Canadian identity (Howard-Hassmann, 1999), ethnic intermarriage (Kalbach and Kalbach, 1999), the over 200- to 300-year residency of British and French groups for whom immigration is but a distant memory (Boyd and Norris, 2001), changes in the wording of the question or the influence of media and political campaigns that mobilize dormant responses (Boyd, 1999). The question itself has been criticized for emphasizing identification with ancestral origins (ethnic ancestry) and thus assuming that ethnicity is a biological and primordial identity (Howard-Hassmann, 1999). The alternative interpretations of ethnicity as a social and cultural identity has led to the recognition that there are numerous dimensions and practices of ethnic identification, which census questions cannot possibly capture (Boyd, 1999). Additionally, the meaning of responses has been brought into question since many people conflate ethnic ancestry and ethnic identity (Kalbach and Kalbach, 1999). These debates and issues have led some researchers to conclude that, 'to date little evidence exists as to what is actually captured by the Canadian census question on ethnic origins' (Boyd and Norris, 2001).[3]

Much has been debated, interpreted and theorized about the category of ethnic identity in relation to this specific example. However, the approach I offer here allows us to enter into this debate in a new way. Rather than interpret the meaning or 'reality' of Canadian as a group identity, I pose a different question: What is the role of the category in inventing or making up new people? Ian Hacking, in his various writings, has argued that 'making up people' refers to the ways a new classification can bring into being a new conception and experience of a way to be a person. Censuses are one such method of classification that may inaugurate a new kind of person that had not been self-conscious before through a process he calls 'dynamic nominalism' (Hacking, 1982). Names interact with the named and the classified but the dynamic also involves 'the *experts* who classify, study and help them, the *institutions* within which the experts and their subjects interact, and through which authorities control' (Hacking, 2007: 254; emphasis original). Another way of saying this is that the process of dynamic nominalism involves socio-technical arrangements that include not only human actors such as experts, but also the techniques and material practices of institutions such as census authorities and their paper forms, enumerators and, of course, categories.

The 'Canadian' is different from the kinds of people that Hacking investigates, such as those named in relation to autism, obesity, child abuse, and multiple personality disorder. Rather than medical diagnoses, census identification categories are bound up with practices of political and cultural recognition. Yet a similar process is at work, albeit with a key difference. Census-taking is a process that engages subjects in both the confirmation and creation of identification categories, whereas in Hacking's account of medical diagnoses such engagement occurs when kinds of people resist and try to take back control of the classifications into which they are sorted. However, as I argue below, subjects are always engaged in the categorical work involved in the taking of censuses. So rather than conceiving of the assertion of the category 'Canadian' as resistance, subjects engage with categories that mediate what I call double identification. Through categories circulated by the census, subjects identify as part of the population (subjectification) and the state identifies subjects and assembles all of the categories to make up the population (objectification). It is through such *double identification* – of recognition by both the state and subjects – that census categories come to have an existence, come to be facts that can then in turn not only be measured, analyzed and assembled into population (objectification) but also be identified with (subjectification). But, as the example shows, subjects also claim categories that are transported back to the state on census forms. What both the state and subjects do is put into circulation mediators, 'non-human actors', categories that with centripetal force can mobilize others to identify as well as create new 'others'. The presence of such double identification makes an ostensible division between the real and constructed artificial. That is, the question in this chapter is not whether 'Canadian' as an ethnic category existed prior to being reported by the statistical authority in 1971. Rather, it concerns the role of the category in mediating identification and how it is active in the making up of people. To start, just what kind of an entity is a category?

What is a census category?

It is through census categories that the state identifies the individual. In the hands of a central authority, the category is an objectifying technique of configuring social relations and when all categories are assembled (gender, origins, occupation, income, and so on) the population comes into being. So while the census is often described as the 'counting of noses', or 'taking stock' and knowing 'how many', it is categories that become actionable and governable: the immigrants; the elderly; the 'Indians'. However, it is also with categories that individuals identify themselves in relation to others within a social space. It is through categories or classes of equivalence that the individual passes from their singularity to a generality (Desrosières, 1998). Identification is not in relation to a statistical object, which is what happens when census officials make up a population. Categories are 'conventions of equivalence, encoding, and classification, precede statistical objectification' and are the 'bonds that make the whole of things and people hold together' (ibid.: 236). But then what does identification with a category mean?

A population is an entity divided and differentiated into numerous categories and census-taking involves the subject identifying his or her difference and resemblance in relation to these classifications. The subject is mobilized to participate in the practice of identifying with categories that are circulated and transported by different techniques (the census manuscript form, enumerator instructions). But identification is never with one; rather the census demands that individuals simultaneously identify with numerous classifications: age, gender, marital status, ethnicity, origins, language, and so on. But importantly, individuals are not subjected by categories or the census (connoting disciplinary power) but subjectified through it, that is, made into census subjects. This is the meaning of subjectification that Foucault (1983) articulates. Census-taking is a subjectifying technology through which individuals examine and articulate who they are in relation to others in a population. To do so they must engage in creative acts that involve comprehending and identifying themselves in relation to categories. This requires cognitive tools of generalization, which is also a necessary precondition of statistical reasoning on the part of the state (Desrosières, 1998). It is a capacity that involves 'articulation work' – all of the juggling of meaning that goes along with the task of interpreting categories and then performing in the face of uncertainty (Bowker and Star, 1999: 310). Rather than an objectifying procedure to control bodies, census categories are thus specific ways of encoding and directing the articulation work of the subject.

If the census only involved the state imposing categories, then census-taking would be an easier endeavour. The state could simply do the work of identifying, classifying and categorizing bodies on manuscript forms. However, the state needs to and wants to find subjects who can identify with its census categories, it needs subjects to tell the truth about themselves, and it needs to affirm that they can recognize themselves as part of the population. Consequently, much effort is expended in educating people, training enumerators, creating instructions, and establishing classifications and categorizations through which individuals can identify. This was no more evident than in 1911 with the taking of what was declared to be the first 'scientific' enumeration of 'Indians and 'Eskimos', the aboriginal people inhabiting the Canadian Far North.[4] Aboriginal people could not identify with the categories circulated by the census and did not see themselves as part of the population. The difficulties were not simply a matter of language and translation. Cultural concepts for representing divisions of time and social relations also intervened, shaped and confounded enumerators. Thus, aboriginal people could not be classified or identified, nor could corresponding relations be established between them and others in the Canadian population. In other words, census-taking was not able to bring forth the subjectivities necessary to produce population in the Far North.

Census categories not only require subjects, but are also objects of classification struggles. Bourdieu (1988) makes an important distinction between hypothetical and real groups, that is, between classification struggles and group struggles. The former consists of symbolic and conceptual struggles over the categorization of individuals who occupy similar social positions, and who are thus subject to similar conditions and thus tend to perceive themselves as members of a group. But just because individuals are perceived or classified as a group does not mean they will act as a group, as this requires the practical and political work of organizing and mobilizing. Census categories are thus part of symbolic and conceptual struggles over the classification of people, which in turn can mobilize and reinforce group struggles. The two struggles can overlap in a number of significant ways: through census categories, groups can be 'nominated into existence' (Golderg, 1997), which in turn can reinforce their affiliations and identifications (and of course the reverse is also possible); through numerable mediations between individual actors, categories can be modified, subverted and changed; and through recognized census categories, groups can claim or be denied social and political rights (Kertzer and Arel, 2002; Higgs, 2004; Potvin, 2005).

If authoritative categories arise out of practical ones, then agents must have the capacity to challenge, change, modify, invent and refuse the categories in circulation. To be sure, agents can and do refuse identification with authoritative categories or claim different ones than those circulated by the state. They also can and do obfuscate and misreport their identification and use identification as a tactical resource. As such, census-taking is not only a subjectifying technology, but also a strategy. That is, subjects can and do engage in different strategies of identification (both intentionally and unintentionally). They can absolutely refuse to identify with the census and any of its categories. While legally and ethically compelled to participate (for the good of the collective, they have a responsibility to articulate themselves into the population), they can refuse and remain 'outside' of the population. Alternatively, they can identify and be part of the population through their association or solidarity with its categories. To resist or challenge particular categorizations would thus represent a classification struggle. The understanding I want to develop here is that the census category is not only a subjectifying technology, but also a strategy, and as such always results in categories that are non-authoritative. For while professing completeness and attempting to incorporate all identifications, censuses always produce 'others'.

The processes involved in double identification and classification struggles are well captured in Ian Hacking's definition of 'dynamic nominalism' briefly introduced above. A kind of person comes into being at the same time as the kind itself is invented; the category and the people in it emerge at the same time (Hacking, 1986). The question is not whether categories are real but how they are constituted (Hacking, 1983; Desrosières, 1998). They are constituted as a result of battles over truth, debates, controversies, etc. – or what was described above as classification struggles. Once settled, then, the entity – in this case the category – can be said to exist and can be investigated and acted upon (and I would add, identified with). This is a historically contingent outcome: some categories are 'discovered' and others are not. Hacking says there are many possible descriptions that are true of the world, but the events that establish the truth of one version close off other equally true versions. This contingency does not disqualify the truth status of the versions of the world we arrive at, but does account for why some things become true rather than others, or why some categories become authoritative and others do not. Once authoritative, categories can then be deployed administratively, shape social development, support particular political projects, have practical consequences for the distribution of resources and shape collective identities (Kertzer and Arel, 2002).[5]

Interpreting census categories in this way directs our attention to understanding how particular categories have triumphed over others and have come to be recognized as authoritative. Once they have emerged they survive if it is possible for the state to do things with them (objectification) but only if subjects can also identify with them (subjectification). It is only when the category involves such double identification (state-subject) that it can be said to be 'real'. This understanding marks a departure from those who would argue that census categories are merely state constructed. If the categories of the census are made authoritative by the dual processes of subjectification and objectification and if population is assembled from the categories of the census, then population is not an abstract or theoretical entity. It is a 'real' thing through which the subject can identify him or herself, both his or her resemblance and difference. It is a 'real' thing through which the state can know subjects and their resemblances and differences.

This dynamic is perhaps most visible when we consider the subject's refusal or inability to identify with the categories circulated by the census. While the census imposes a limited repertoire of categories, subjects do not necessarily limit their identifications to it. Can we then consider moments when individuals assert new identification categories as a rupture and indicator of the divergence between the formal and informal categories and when new kinds of people or social beings start to emerge? If so, then authoritative categories could be said to arise out of these moments. This is the point I will develop by returning to the example that opened this chapter, the emergence of the non-authoritative ethnic category of 'Canadian' in the early part of the twentieth century.

The category of Canadian

The process of taking and compiling the 1921 Census of Canada involved a particular dispute and struggle over the classification of origins, a classification that has been included in every Canadian census since its beginnings.[6] But before the controversy in 1921, and as early as the first scientific census of 1871, individuals were claiming their ancestral origins as 'Canadian' despite the fact that this category was discouraged and not recognized by the central authorities (Curtis, 2001). Even though the list of categories circulated by the census did not include 'Canadian', many respondents declared it and enumerators recorded it on the manuscript forms, only to be erased by compilers after the fact when the forms were transported back to the statistical authority, and recategorized often on the basis of surnames.[7] As manuscript forms reveal, the practice did indeed continue throughout all enumerations into the next century.[8] So, while the manuscript forms and enumerator instructions did not encourage or permit the category, respondents stubbornly or habitually claimed it. Regardless of the wording of the question, and no matter how much the state attempted to guide responses through its various relations of communication (formatting of questions and forms, instructions, statements in the media, and so on), the category was asserted. Thus, many governing agents, from the enumerators to the heads of households, engaged actively in the articulation work required to interpret, accept, resist and create categories through which they could identify. Even before self-enumeration (1971) and the contemporary practice of blank boxes for recording 'other' responses, capacities of self-categorization were thus being exercised. Subjects creatively engaged in the practice rather than being simply objectified by it. But this is only one half of the process of identification. Respondents were census subjects in a second way: as subjects of political rule. In the hands of the state, which alone could reveal the truth about the population, the census was a political technology. Through corrections, erasures and reclassification, the state made Canadians disappear from official reports of the population. Subjects were forced into accepted categories, suggesting a much more disciplinary rule than that afforded by the introduction of the 'other' category later in the twentieth century.[9]

However, the category 'Canadian' was still transported and communicated back to the state via the manuscript form, and with each census the state had to contend with 'Canadians' as a disruption to its disciplinary efforts. This is evident in changes to the instructions and the wording of questions in subsequent enumerations, which were in part efforts to subdue insistent citizens. The practice thus involved an interaction between the subject and the state through the census form and mediated by categories and many other devices including instructions, enumerators, and compilers. But in the 1921 enumeration another actor was also involved, the newspaper media, through which we can gain some further insight about how categories mediate classification struggles. A few weeks before the 1921 taking of the census, and in light of just-released enumerator instructions, a media campaign was launched against a change in the wording of the instructions concerning categories of racial origin. The 1911 instructions stated briefly that the 'racial or tribal origin' should be recorded. A list of possible categories was provided

(English, Scotch, Irish, Welsh, and so on). However, in 1921 the list of categories was followed by the direction that 'The words "Canadian" or '"American" must not be used for this purpose, as they express "Nationality" or "Citizenship" but not a "Race of people"'. The explicit direction was perhaps a response to the increasing occurrence of 'Canadian' (and 'American') as an origin in the 1911 census manuscript forms.

One paper reported, 'There is no "Canadian" or "American" race, according to the regulations'.[10] News headlines in the English-speaking press across the country declared 'No Canadian Race, Census Takers Say'.[11] An article reproduced in five Western newspapers asked, 'Who and what are we? Is there such a person as a Canadian? The Government of Canada says there is not'.[12] While many editorialists and letters to the editor used nationality, citizenship and racial origin interchangeably, they nonetheless asserted a challenge to the authoritative categories circulated by the census. Canadian as a bona fide origin category was variously defended on the grounds of patriotism, nationalism, as a means of ethnic integration and assimilation, against watered-down 'hyphenated identities', and with the consternation that 'the only persons who are really entitled to be called Canadians are the hundred thousand Indians whose ancestors held the land when Jacques Cartier sailed up the St. Lawrence almost four centuries ago'.[13] It was thus a category that established the difference of a group – the Canadians – in relation to all others (e.g. immigrants).

What happened as a result? In 1931, an elaborate definition was included in the instructions to enumerators that no longer explicitly singled out 'Canadian' as an incorrect category. However, as manuscript forms reveal, the category 'Canadian' was still not permitted as an origin for when it did appear it was edited. As the foregoing account illustrates, the census subject was not the only actor. While difficult to account for all the possible narratives overflowing census-taking, there are numerous traces that can be identified such as those put into circulation by the newspaper media.[14] Certainly, categorizations and narratives of 'ethnicity' and 'race' were also in circulation. For example, around the time of census-taking there were various discussions and debates about what it meant to define oneself as Canadian, who constituted a 'good' immigrant, and problematizations of foreigners and aliens, which expressed understandings of these different identification categories. It is in this regard that we can conceive of the category as a mediator that circulates between practices, with newspaper narratives providing traces of some of these.

Whatever the political reasons and other factors that might have been at work, census-taking constituted a symbolic and conceptual struggle over the recognition of a particular identification that was mediated by the categories circulated by the census. For it is worth repeating that the census form and its categories mediated the state-subject relationship in the dispute. Census manuscript forms could make individuals do things (identify with its categories) but was also made to do things, that is, transport back to the state alternative and competing categories.

It is also worth remembering that identification with the category 'Canadian' occurred before being recognized on the census form and before the newspaper media took up the issue. I would suggest that the creation of the census subject was a condition that made identification with and the eventual recognition of the new category possible (subjectification). Indeed, after much time and controversy it was finally included among the authoritative categories and reported in the official statistics of the census authority, and could then be investigated and acted upon (objectification) (as well as made an object of social science research). The inclusion of the category also mobilized ever more subjects to so identify, illustrating how categories circulated by the census and the individuals to which they are linked are simultaneously created. That the number of ethnic 'Canadians' increased from 4 per cent to 31 per cent in 5 years attests to the power of the category to mobilize identification and 'make' Canadians. As Hacking reminds, this is a historically contingent outcome, and as I have documented above it was only through political and classification struggles (both represented on the manuscript forms and in the political and media debates) that it came to be included among the authoritative categories. Canadian thus understood is the result of co-construction and convergence: between the authoritative classification system of the census authority and the practical systems of subjects. I am not suggesting that it is only through the census that such practices occur. There are many practices of identification, and census-taking is but one. Rather, I am suggesting that by analyzing census-taking we can gain insights about how categories mobilize identification more generally.

The example brings me back to the concern of this chapter, which is about the role of the category in inventing or making up new people. Census-taking required and brought into being subjects with the capacity to reflect on their similarities and differences in relation to categories circulated by the census, and in turn the capacity to challenge and create new identifications. In the case of being Canadian, it was a process through which subjects claimed a new category and differentiated status. The making up of ethnic Canadians was thus not an event that the census simply recorded. Rather, census-taking helped bring into being a category that travelled across the country, attracted new members, and confounded the state's efforts to exclude. But it was only when the category was recognized by both the state (objectification) and subjects (subjectification) through the practice of double identification (state-subject) that it was possible for someone to be officially recognized as an ethnic Canadian. So, while censuses have been interpreted (and legitimized) as simply the recording of data and the construction of population, census-taking and its attendant practices, including the creation of categories, play an inventive (and constitutive) role in making up people.

Researchers often note that how people respond to a survey or census form is very much influenced by the way questionnaires are formatted to how questions are posed and what categories are included. Rather than technical or operational issues, this chapter suggests that each of these devices is an active mediator involved in making up and inventing people. The category is not a simple recording of who people are, but a device that mediates everyday classifications and those of statistical knowledge-power. The question, then, is not how to improve techniques such as censuses to better 'capture' or describe the social world 'out there', but to examine how these very devices are involved in both making up and legitimizing particular versions of the social world. From this perspective, debates about whether categories of people are 'real' or 'constructed' are redundant, for if we attend to the inventive capacities of categories in the ordering of our lives and that of others we see that categories have a formative and transformative potential. Indeed, it is a potential that has and can be activated by subjects. For example, as part of their political repertoire, social groups have often intervened in census-taking to assert new questions and mobilize new categories (e.g. on ethnicity, religion, sexuality).

What, then, can we say about social science researchers who use methods such as surveys and, in doing so, mobilize categories? No matter what our intentions, we are always in some measure involved in the making of the social world and cannot fall back on claims to neutrality and objectivity. Instead, as Law and Urry (2004) suggest, we need to make transparent how the categories we mobilize also mediate the making of the social world and the 'ontological politics' of these practices. This is not only an invitation to be reflexive about how our interventions contribute to the making of some realities and not others. It is also a call to think about how we can interfere and creatively challenge accepted categories as well as illuminate the choices we make about the social worlds we help make happen.

Notes

1 Bowker and Star (1999) address this question in their discussion of the relationship between formal or scientific classification systems and informal or practical classification systems deployed in the everyday. They cite, in particular, Mary Douglas' work on how practical classifications of the everyday become reified, and Durkheim and Mauss, for whom primitive, practical social classifications are linked to the first scientific classifications.

2 'Instructions to Commissioners and Enumerators', Extract from the Manual of Instructions to Officers Employed in the Taking of the Sixth Census of Canada (1921).

3 Additionally, every census in the twentieth century made changes to the list of possible responses, the wording or presentation of the question, enumerators' instructions and data processing rules (Potvin, 2005).

4 See Ruppert (2009) for a detailed discussion.

5 Similarly, Curtis (2001) argues (as do other researchers) that the census must also 'reflect social relations' (ibid.: 34). He notes, for instance, that 'statistical knowledges are conditioned by the materiality of the social relations they attempt to appropriate; they are historically specific knowledges that are adequate to particular kinds of social objects and, by implication, inadequate to others' (ibid.: 308). The latter, Curtis says, feeds off other ways of configuring and knowing social relations, and in turn comes to shape those very social relations.

6 The inclusion of questions on racial and ethic origins in Canadian censuses is connected to the demographic, economic and political stakes in the relations of power between different minority and majority groups that have constituted Canada – its three 'founding nations' (aboriginal, French and British) and diverse immigrant groups. Census statistics have thus always formed the basis of political and institutional organization, group recognition, constitutional rights, and the implementation of equality and anti-discrimination laws (Potvin, 2005).

7 Curtis (2001) notes how the attribution of origin was based on different criteria in Quebec and other provinces. Census commissioner Taché was concerned with ensuring a high count of French Canadians; in Quebec, children were thus categorized as 'French' if either parent was of French origin. In other provinces, attribution was based solely on the paternal line (ibid.: 284–6).

8 This discussion draws from data compiled by the Canadian Century Research Infrastructure Project (CCRI), a five-year interdisciplinary and multi-institutional initiative that involved building a set of interrelated databases concerning the 1911–51 Canadian censuses of population. As one of eleven Team Leaders from seven universities across Canada, I assisted with the compilation of databases, including digitized data from original census manuscript forms, and documentary data derived from Statistics Canada files, newspaper commentaries and parliamentary and legislative debates. For further information, see Bellavance *et al.* (2007).

9 As far as I know, a genealogy of the 'other' category is yet to be written. In 1951, however, an 'other' box was included for enumerators to write in groups not listed on the census form. Nonetheless, enumerator instructions still discouraged the use of 'Canadian' in this box and the census authority recategorized any such entries based on a set of coding rules. However, in 1971, though still discouraged, the number of people who self-reported 'Canadian' was reported for the first time in the final tabulations.

10 *Sudbury Star*, 7 May 1921: 1.

11 *Victoria Daily Times*, 10 May 1921: 1. Other headlines included: 'Can't say race is Canadian' (*News Chronicle* (Port Arthur), 11 May 1921: 5); 'Census takers now on the job' (*Cobalt Nugget*, 4 June 1921: 6); 'How Census Takers Classify Nationalities' (*Camrose Canadian*, 23 June 1921: 7).

12 *Banff Crag and Canyon*, 2 July 1921: 2; *Strathmore and Bow Valley Standard*, 27 July 1921: 2; *Lloydminster Times*, 21 July 1921: 6; *The Vegreville Observer*, 29, July 1921: 6; *The Gleichen Call*, 10 August 1921: 6.

13 *The Globe*, 15 February 1922: 4.

14 Monica Boyd, for example, concludes that the most influential factor responsible for the upsurge in the number of self-identified ethnic Canadians in 1996 was a high-profile 'Count Me-Canadian' campaign waged by major media outlets (Boyd, 1999). See Bellavance at al. (2007) for an analysis of the influence of the media during 1911 census-taking.

References

Bellavance, C., Normand, F. and Ruppert, E. (2007) 'Census in context: documenting and understanding the making of 20th century Canadian censuses', *Historical Methods*, 40 (2): 92–103.

Bourdieu, P. (1988) 'Social space and symbolic power', *Sociological Theory*, 7 (1): 14–25.

Bowker, G. C., and Star, S. L. (1999) *Sorting Things Out: Classification and its Consequences*, Cambridge, MA: MIT Press.

Boyd, M. (1999) 'Canadian, eh? Ethnic origin shifts in the Canadian census', *Canadian Ethnic Studies Journal*, 31 (3): 1–19.

Boyd, M., and Norris, D. (2001) 'Who are the "Canadians?": changing census responses, 1986–1996', *Canadian Ethnic Studies Journal*, 33 (1): 1–26.

Curtis, B. (2001) *The Politics of Population: State Formation, Statistics, and the Census of Canada, 1840–1875*, Toronto: University of Toronto Press.

Desrosières, A. (1998) *The Politics of Large Numbers: A History of Statistical Reasoning*, trans. C. Naish, Cambridge, MA and London: Harvard University Press.

Foucault, M. (1983) 'The subject and power', in H. L. Dreyfus and P. Rabinow (eds) *Michel Foucault: Beyond Structuralism and Hermeneutics*, Chicago, IL: University of Chicago Press, pp. 208–226.

Goldberg, D. T. (1997) *Racial Subjects: Writing on Race in America*, New York: Routledge.

Hacking, I. (1982) 'Biopower and the avalanche of printed numbers', *Humanities in Society*, 5: 279–95.

Hacking, I. (1983) *Representing and Intervening: Introductory Topics in the Philosophy of Natural Science*, Cambridge: Cambridge University Press.

Hacking, I. (1986) 'Making up people', in T. C. Heller, M. Sosna and D. E. Wellbery (eds) *Reconstructing Individualism: Autonomy, Individuality, and the Self in Western Thought*, Stanford, CA: Stanford University Press, pp. 222–236.

Hacking, I. (2007) 'Kinds of people: moving targets', *Proceedings of the British Academy*, 151: 285–318.

Higgs, E. (2004) *Life, Death and Statistics: Civil Registration, Censuses and the Work of the General Register Office, 1836–1952*, Hatfield: Local Population Studies.

Howard-Hassmann, R. E. (1999) '"Canadian" as an ethnic category: implications for multiculturalism and national unity', *Canadian Public Policy*, 25 (4): 523–37.

Kalbach, M. A., and Kalbach, W. E. (1999) 'Becoming Canadian: problems of an emerging identity', *Canadian Ethnic Studies Journal*, 31 (2): 1–20.

Kertzer, D. I. and Arel, D. (2002) 'Censuses, identity formation, and the struggle for political power', in D. I. Kertzer and D. Arel (eds) *Census and Identity: The Politics of Race, Ethnicity, and Language in National Censuses*, Cambridge: Cambridge University Press, pp. 1–42.

Law, J. and Urry, J. (2004) 'Enacting the social', *Economy and Society*, 33 (3): 390–410.

Potvin, M. (2005) 'The role of statistics on ethnic origin and "race" in Canadian antidiscrimination policy', *International Social Science Journal*, 57 (183): 27–42.

Ruppert, E. (2009) 'Becoming peoples: "counting heads in northern wilds"', *Journal of Cultural Economy*, 2 (1–2): 11–31.

4   Configuration

Lucy Suchman

Methods for studying science and technology, like their research objects, are both already made and always in the making. With respect to technology studies in particular, we have by now a powerful toolkit of conceptual and practical resources to bring to the analysis of objects, ranging from individual artefacts to socio-technical systems, historically and in contemporary formations. To name just two examples among many, Haraway's 'cyborg' alerts us to the history of nationalist and military technoscience as a crucible for contemporary conjoinings of bodies and machines, while also opening up generative resources with which to investigate particular cases in ways that retheorize the nature of human-non-human entanglement (Haraway, 1985/1991). Law's trope of 'heterogeneous engineering' both expands and further specifies how scale is enacted in and through complex socio-technical assemblages, as they draw together and multiply entities through time and across space (Law, 1987). Offered as an addition to this toolkit, the device of *configuration* has two broad uses. First, as an aid to delineating the composition and bounds of an object of analysis, in part through the acknowledgement that doing so is integral not only to the study of technologies, but to their very existence as objects. And second, in drawing our analytic attention to the ways in which technologies materialize cultural imaginaries, just as imaginaries narrate the significance of technical artefacts. Configuration in this sense is a device for studying technologies with particular attention to the imaginaries and materialities that they *join together*, an orientation that resonates as well with the term's common usage to refer to the conjoining of diverse elements in practices of systems design and engineering. In what follows, I attempt to elaborate the sense of configuration as a tool to think with about the work of drawing the boundaries that reflexively delineate technological objects, and as a conceptual frame for recovering the heterogeneous relations that technologies fold together. I offer two case studies of socio-technical projects that, while not done through the trope of configuration, can be read as demonstrations of the sensibilities that it recommends.

Interrogating the trope

How might we reverse engineer the device of configuration, to see what it is made of and what work it can do? We could begin by noting its ambiguity as at once action and effect; as a mode of ordering things in relation to one another (Law, 1994), and the arrangement of elements in a particular combination that results. If we examine the trope as a kind of artefact itself, we see at its pivotal centre the *figure*. To figure is to assign shape, designate what is to be made noticeable and consequential, to be taken as identifying. In Castañeda's words:

> To use figuration as a descriptive tool is to unpack the domains of practice and significance that are built into each figure . . . Understood as figures, furthermore, particular categories of existence can also be considered in terms of their uses – what they 'body forth' in turn. Figuration is thus understood . . . to incorporate a double force: constitutive effect and generative circulation.
>
> (Castañeda, 2002: 3)

Figuration, in other words, is an action that holds the material and the semiotic together in ways that become naturalized over time, and in turn requires 'unpacking' to recover its constituent elements. It is also, however, a mode of production, as the circulation of figures implies their recontextualization, multiplicity and at least potential transformation. So figuration comprises both a method through which things are made, and a resource for their analysis and un/remaking. I develop this method's particular relevance here for the careful tracking of what Haraway names projects of 'materialised refiguration' (Haraway, 1997: 23). More specifically, it was Haraway who most forcefully posed the question of whether it might be possible to formulate new strategies for improving the conditions of humans by reimagining relations of human and machine, rather than premising authentic human existence upon their principled and permanent separation (Haraway, 1985/1991; see also Downey and Dumit, 1997: 7). My own work has been concerned with the question of how humans and machines are figured together – or *con*figured – in contemporary technological discourses and practices, and how they might be *re*configured, or figured together differently (Suchman, 2007).

Reanimating the figure

A first step in our method is to reanimate the figure at the heart of a given configuration, in order to recover the practices through which it comes into being and sustains its effects. Reanimating a figure requires attention to its rhetorical constitution as 'category of existence', and to the forms of embodiment that stand as its instances. As one example, Ahmed (2000) mobilizes figuration as a tool to examine the politics of identification, specifically the discursive practices that constitute the figure of 'the stranger'.

Citing Marx's analysis of commodity fetishism, in which objects appear as autonomous figures endowed with a life of their own, she extends his argument to include fantasy as well as materiality, arguing that the stranger enacts an instance of what she names 'a fetishism of figures' (ibid.: 4; see also Benjamin, 1968; Taussig, 1993; Graeber 2005). Insofar as the stranger is not an ontological being but a relational effect, she argues, the identification of an other as a stranger is an act not of failure to recognize, but of recognition (Ahmed, 2000: 26). Ahmed is interested in understanding how difference is constituted in and through particular 'strange encounters', in a way that resists universalizing the figure that those encounters affect. Her aim, more specifically, is to account for the complex relationship between histories of colonialism and contemporary modes of identification as familial and strange. To recover that complexity, she argues, requires restoring the social relations that are concealed by stranger fetishism, 'to consider how the stranger is an effect of processes of inclusion and exclusion, or incorporation and expulsion, that constitute the boundaries of bodies and communities' (ibid.: 6). Within and between entities, practices of association and differentiation are fundamental.

So how might we bring this process of reanimation to bear on the study of technologies? The answer is already present, of course, in Ahmed's reference to the fetishized object, but she give us further suggestions as well. Ahmed's analysis, and particularly her careful attention to enactments of inside and outside, has relevance for thinking about how other kinds of figurations, including boundaries between the human and non-human, are made. In the centre of her attention are questions of identification and difference, how lines of delineation are drawn around inside(r)s and outside(r)s. Similarly, every artefact enacts its singularity through delineations of that which it incorporates and those things that are beyond its bounds. Following Castañeda (2002), figuration alerts us to the need to recover the domains of practice and significance that are presupposed by and built into particular technological artefacts, as well as the ways in which artefact boundaries are naturalized as antecedent rather than ongoing consequences of specific socio-technical encounters. These are the ontological politics of design and use, and of technology development more broadly.

Configuring socio-material assemblages

Configuration, then, brings things together – at once reiterating the separate existence of the elements assembled, and drawing the boundaries of new artefacts. It alerts us to attend to the histories and encounters through which things are figured into meaningful existence, fixing them through reiteration but also always engaged in 'the perpetuity of coming to be' that characterizes the biographies of objects as well as subjects (see Daston, 2000: 1). Building upon contemporary theorizing, configuration places further emphasis on thinking about the discursive and material together (see Barad, 2007: 91,

171–2). But this device for social theory resonates as well with configuration's currency in the everyday language of information systems engineering. The past several decades have seen an expansion of this latter sense of configuration, redefining systems development from a technical project comprising the arrangement of hardware and software components, to the implementation of extensive organizational infrastructures across myriad and often incommensurate imaginaries and practices. To think through how configuration can work as a methodological device in this respect, I turn to two exemplary cases of ethnographic research into making complex information systems, one based on the West Coast of the US, the other in the state of Andhra Pradesh in southern India.

From 1993 to 1998, Judith Gregory followed a project to design and implement a comprehensive electronic health record software package for the largest health maintenance organization (HMO) in the US (Gregory, 2000, 2009). The software prototype, an attempt to project a future path for the HMO's clinical information systems and broader infrastructure development, was designed by a state-of-the-art clinical informatics software company. Gregory's focus was on communication and coordination among members of the HMO's multi-disciplinary care teams, and between them and the system's developers. A key insight from Gregory's analysis came from her observation that at the heart of the extensive discussions and labours of design that comprised the electronic health record prototyping project were what she termed 'multiple logics', each with a rationality of its own. The HMO's management dreamed of a system for decision-making and control that would finally make it possible to grasp, inventory and standardize the workings of this vast organization in a way that would both cut costs and serve patients more efficiently. The software design company was committed to pushing the technical state of the art in health information systems, including the introduction of forms of automated expertise into diagnosis and treatment, while medical researchers imagined a system that would make it possible to eradicate clinical mistakes, and contribute to the creation of a sound scientific foundation for clinical practice. The health workers, finally – physicians and nursing staff alike (albeit differently) – demanded a system for maintaining patient records that would serve their needs and those of their patients in the practice of clinical care. And all of this took place in the context of a health care regime in the US characterized by deepening tensions between economic and social use values of medicine and related institutions.

The result of this initiative was the dream of a system that would be all things to all users. But the figure of a singular electronic health record, Gregory argues, obscured the multiple logics at play. One way to think about those logics is through the disparate subject/object configurations that animated them, and which actors differently located within the project were aiming to realize through the system's design: the figure of the effective manager made possible through the comprehensive decision support system, the innovative design company with its leading edge prototype, the researcher with a perfect database prescribing error-free clinical practice, and the care provider with an always ready-to-hand patient record. By following the project as it unfolded across locations, Gregory was able to recover the multiplicity of the object in development, the actors' abiding faith in the possibility of its configuration as one, comprehensive system, and the in-built contradictions that such a singularity implied. Gregory's own analytic figuration of this as an 'incomplete utopian project', moreover, names a wider class of initiatives that fail to recognize and acknowledge not only that multiple logics exist within the domains that a system must inhabit, but that they may imply deeply incommensurate directions for system design. Crucial here is the recognition that agencies of subjects and objects are figured together – thus the stakes, the reason that the specificities of configuration matter so much to the actors involved.

So what does this analysis imply for the possibility of configuring effective health information systems? Do we conclude that the design of a workable electronic patient record is impossible? Rather than taking this as the logical conclusion, Gregory explores the possibilities of an alternative approach to information systems development, one that might be able to cope with the multiplicities, and contradictions, that are the reality of complex health care institutions. Among other resources from science and technology studies, she draws inspiration from philosopher of science Helen Verran's experience as a mediator in land rights negotiations between the Yolgnu Aboriginal community and Australian pastoralists during the same period in which Gregory was engaged in her study (Verran, 1998). In reflecting on these negotiations, Verran urges that the recognition of multiplicity and difference, while a crucial first step, is not enough to enable the creation of livable socio-material arrangements. The latter requires what she calls 'working knowledges together'; that is, negotiating the creation of new, *partially shared* imaginaries without – and this is crucial – relying on one homogenizing translation into a dominant party's terms.

The politics of cultural historical imaginaries need to be on the table, in other words, whether the project is negotiations over land or the design of information infrastructures. And identifying those politics may require reanimating the figurations that hold particular relations of persons and things – with land, or with information – in place. Which brings me to the second case, another ethnographic investigation of health information systems development, but very differently located. During 2003 and 2004, C. R. Ranjini, then a PhD student at Lancaster University, undertook the daunting task of tracing out the socio-technical networks involved in a series of initiatives to implement a new health information infrastructure across primary health care centres in rural Andhra Pradesh, one of the poorest regions of southern India (Ranjini and Sahay, 2006; Ranjini, 2007). In 1999, the government of Andhra Pradesh imagined a future for economic and social development in the state through their 'Vision 2020' document. This policy document, developed in consultation with McKinsey and Co., included an IT subsection stating that: 'Andhra

Pradesh will leverage information technology to attain a position of leadership and excellence in the information age and to transform itself into a knowledge society'. With respect to health, 'Vision 2020' included an ambitious programme to stabilize population growth and to improve nutrition, sanitation, personal hygiene, and disease control and prevention, particularly with respect to maternal and infant health. All agreed that these visions could only be realized through a serious commitment to delivering primary health care to the 73 per cent rural population of the state. These initiatives were part of the response, by the technology-savvy Chief Minister of the State at the time, to a series of 'millennium development goals' set out by the United Nations and World Bank. Needless to say, the monetary stakes for the state in meeting these goals were significant.

Through extensive fieldwork, Ranjini traced the rhetorical figurations and practical realities of four information technology initiatives for health care launched during this period. One aim of her analysis was to move beyond any simple evaluation of whether the projects she studied were successful or not. Rather, like Gregory, she worked to identify the multiple actors, relationships, labours and contradictions that shaped the implementation and sustainability of these projects. Her study focused on the practices of women health assistants and other staff at primary health centres. Along with patient care, record keeping is a major preoccupation for primary health care workers. As Ranjini describes it:

> In Andhra Pradesh, an army of health assistants, most of them women, routinely collects enormous amounts of health data. Each health assistant maintains 13 to 15 registers, which have to be updated regularly. By manually calculating aggregates in each of these registers, each health assistant produces about 15 different reports every week. These weekly reports are again aggregated at the end of each month to produce monthly reports. Thus, health assistants devote an enormous amount of time to collecting, manually processing and reporting health information.
>
> (Ranjini, 2007: 97–8)

Ranjini's ethnography includes an account of a day spent traveling, largely by foot, with a health assistant to a village in the latter's jurisdiction in order to update a household survey taken some years earlier – an accurate demographic database being a prerequisite for the ministry's dreams of demonstrating systematic achievement of the millennium goals. Her study creates a picture of the enormous, painstaking and in many practical respects impossible labours of information production in Andhra Pradesh. She looks as well at what becomes of these reports at the district and state level, where reports that do not produce the improvements set by targets mandated by the international funding agencies are met with threats of job loss and humiliating public reprimand. As one of Ranjini's informants at the state level explained,

'Targets are for motivating the workers. The whole thing is about reward and punishment. If they do not achieve targets, they are punished. [Of course], there is no reward. The reward is not being punished' (Ranjini, 2007: 113).

Ranjini's observations of district meetings revealed no opportunity for health workers or supervisors to provide explanations as to why targets could not be met, or to inform the setting of more appropriate ones. These accountability practices had the predictable result; namely, health workers and supervisors worked to produce the numbers required, through practices of manipulation, under- and over-reporting. They did this not through any malice or negligence, but through a combination of self-protection and a desire to continue the work of delivering primary health care, in the face of unrealistic targets and inadequate resources, and in the face of an information 'flow' characterized exclusively by directives from the top that, despite the enormous numbers of reports, systematically discouraged the provision of information regarding realities on the ground. As Ranjini concludes:

> The primary concern of the staff was to present positive accounts of performance on record rather than portraying the actual realities of their work . . . In many respects, the existing accountability regime is part of the problem. That is, targets and grading systems are set up to make people accountable, but targets in turn create 'good reasons' to falsify the data (to avoid punishment). As long as accountability is understood in terms of discipline and punishment rather than learning and co-development, it creates these effects.
>
> (Ranjini, 2007: 132)

So what would it mean to challenge this figuration of a 'knowledge society', and to associate health workers and information in very different configurations? Rather than elements of a data collection machinery aimed at demonstrating the effectiveness of state response to goals set by international institutions, workers would need to be refigured as those most knowledgeable about primary health care delivery and the information needed to support it. During her fieldwork, Ranjini observed two instances where primary health workers effectively reconfigured local information systems for planning health services in their communities. In the first case, this involved drawing out relevant information from records already available; in the second, elaborating those records through further data gathering. In both cases, this was work specific to an immediate health care campaign, which repaid the workers' efforts with resources enabling more effective health care provision. Rather than peripheral components outside of and in service to the health information system, health workers were figured as central to its operation. The health information system, in turn, was figured as an integral part of their practice. These reconfigurations, in turn, enabled new agential possibilities for the provision of primary care.

Configuration as a method assemblage

As a practice of figuring things together, we might consider configuration as one form of what John Law has named a 'method assemblage' (Law, 2004). Methods, Law argues, are enactments that make relations between what is *present* (including knowledges, representations, subjects and objects) and what is *absent* or part of the latter's 'hinterland' (both *manifestly*, for example in the form of things articulated as 'context' for what is present, and *othered*, in the form of an open-ended horizon of the unremarkable and/or repressed). In this sense, the method assemblage of configuration could be understood as a device for articulating the relation between the 'insides' of a socio-technical system and its constitutive 'outsides', including all of those things that disappear in the system's figuration as an object (see also Newman, 1998). In his ethnography of engineering as a discipline, Bucciarelli (1994) formulates the difficulty of reanimating the figure of the engineered object to recover its lost contingencies:

> Standing before the machine, its deterministic functioning so dominates our thought that alternative, more open and complex descriptions of process are rarely forthcoming. The artifact is a rationalization of itself, one that excludes alternative forms and speaks to us thus: 'I am a working, efficient, marketable machine. Knowing how I work, understanding my underlying form as the scientific principles that govern my doings, and reading my documentation (though don't be too distracted by the latter) you can reconstruct the decision-making process that made me (or rather that allowed me to make myself)'.
>
> (ibid.: 14)

The same criteria that Law identifies as defining the Euro-American imaginary of the nature that precedes culture – independence, anteriority, definiteness and singularity – could be said to hold for the technoscientific imaginary of the engineered object. Law's elaboration of an alternative ontology of multiplicity and indefiniteness resonates deeply for a project of reconfiguring relations of humans and the built world. At the same time, unlike the phenomena that are the objects of the natural sciences, socio-technical artefacts are imagined as made, not discovered. Rather than being enacted as antecedent to and independent of the practices of their making, they are figured within design and engineering discourses precisely *not* as already existing and independently agential, but as emerging from and dependent upon the actions of their (human) makers. In this sense, configuration as a critical device calls for a kind of alternate respecification to discovery; a recognition of the historical anteriority of even the most innovative objects, and the material agencies that shape practices of design.

To take configuration as a method assemblage means acknowledging the enacted rather than given nature of delineations of inside and outside, with respect both to object and to subject boundaries. The configuration of an artefact, on Akrich's account, is a 'function of the distribution of competences assumed when an object is conceived and designed', the particular 'geographies of responsibility' implied (Akrich, 1992: 207). Woolgar (1991), in investigating professional practices of computer system development, has famously proposed that 'by setting parameters for the users' actions, the evolving machine attempts to configure the user' (Grint and Woolgar, 1997: 71). The sense of configuring developed by Grint and Woolgar is not of the user as an individual actor, but rather the incorporation of the user into the socio-material assemblage that comprises a functioning machine. It is in this sense that objects make subjects. But just how specific and determining is the user's configuration, in either design imaginaries or specific situations of use? While the tropes of use as 'de-scription' (Akrich, 1992) and of 'configuring the user' have been tremendously generative and are widely cited within the STS literature, they also, on my reading, raise a set of further questions. Both, despite their careful attention to the contingencies of design and use, leave in place an over-rationalized figure of the designer as actor, and an over-estimation of the ways and extent to which definitions of users and use can be inscribed into an artefact. As I believe both Akrich and Woolgar would readily agree, there is no stable designer/user point of view, nor are imaginaries of the user or settings of use inscribed in anything like a complete or coherent form in the object. For tropes of configuration and de-scripting to align with their subjects and objects, I am suggesting, we need to see the designer's view of the user as at once more specific, and less. More, in that it is specifically located within the various sites, imaginaries, exigencies and practices that comprise professional design. Less, in that artefacts are characterized by greater open-endedness and indeterminacy with respect to the question of how they might be incorporated into use. The 'user' is, in other words, more vaguely figured, the object more deeply ambiguous. On this understanding, the fixity of an artefact is an effect of reiterative enactments of a particular subject/object configuration, while fluidity articulates the inherent multiplicity of objects in ways that facilitate their travel (Suchman, 1994, 2002; de Laet and Mol, 2000). Somewhat counter-intuitively, the latter turns out to require a more intimate understanding of the possible circumstances of an artefact's use; not in the sense of a predictive model or comprehensive specification, but of an appreciation for what needs to be made contingent and the kinds of agencies required for the artefact's ongoing (re)configuration.

Taking configuration as a method assemblage means recognizing the contingency and incompleteness of artefacts as irremediable (Garfinkel and Sacks, 1970; Lynch, 1993; Garfinkel and Rawls, 2002), both in terms of a system's description (presupposing as it does 'hinterlands' that it does not, and could not, fully specify) and of its implementation (presupposing always further practices of design-in-use). Even while taking up the call for a more 'user-centred' design, however, many professional designers have continued to locate themselves in ways that reinforce their status as at once primary to the artefact's configuration, but also outside of its boundaries. 'The user' in this method assemblage assumes the position of the manifestly absent, while the labours of configuration in use are othered. The exceptions to this rule, for example within the field of participatory design, work instead from the premise that artefacts – particularly computationally based devices – comprise a medium or starting place elaborated in use (Ehn, 1988; Greenbaum and Kyng, 1991; Schuler and Namioka, 1993; Aanestad, 2003; Simonsen *et al.*, 2008). Rather than holding stable and separate the identities of 'designer' and 'user', the latter work as categories describing persons differently located, at different moments, and/or with different histories and future investments in projects of technology development.

'Agency', Barad observes, 'is not an attribute but the ongoing reconfigurings of the world' (Barad, 2007: 141). The notion of configuration is central as well to Knorr Cetina's analysis of the mutually shaping arrangements of scientists, instruments, objects, and practices aimed at the production of observably stabilized instantiations of 'reality effects' (Knorr Cetina, 1999: 26–33). Considered over time, she argues, configurations comprise what are commonly termed skills or expertise: 'The alignments . . . work through the body of the scientist, but they also involve a drastically rearranged environment, a new life-world in which new agents interact and move' (ibid.: 219; see also Pickering, 1995). Configuration is a practice enacted always from within, in other words, however much its objects may be figured as 'out there' and its concerns focused on how to delineate their relations and boundaries. As Barad reminds us, we are always already inside the worlds that we take as the objects of our actions (see also Ingold, 2008). Like the scientist enfolded within the apparatus, 'we' (whether positioned as designers or users) are internal to the technologies that engage us and with which we engage.

Conclusion

Configuration, I have suggested here, is part of a toolkit for thinking about constitutive and generative, reiterative and (potentially) transformative material-semiotic conjoining. In the case of technology, configuration orients us to the entanglement of imaginaries and artefacts that comprise technological projects. The latter include the 'incomplete utopian projects' identified by Gregory and clearly present in the ICT for development initiatives described by Ranjini, which power the imaginary of a perfect health information system perpetually deferred. They include as well, and as instructive counter-examples, the kinds of modest configurations for care generated out of health workers' own imaginaries and material agencies. The differences between these underscore the question of differential capacities for the articulation and movement of technological imaginaries and enabling resources, as well as the complex relationship between the scale of projects and their effects.

Like any tool, configuration is not a device with inherent boundaries, nor does it carry its own inner logics and instructions for use. While normative methods are designed to define and police boundaries, configuration as a method assemblage aims to articulate method in a way that opens received and/or congealed relations to being reenacted differently (see Law, 2004: 84). And as is the case for the artefacts that the trope of configuration might help us to interrogate, the device generates effects only within a method assemblage comprising an open-ended horizon of socio-material arrangements that it at once presupposes and helps to sustain or transform. Recognizing the simultaneously reflexive and generative character of configuration, as well as the leakages and entanglements that configurational objects obscure, would effect, in Law's terms, a more 'generous' method (ibid.: 40–1). An orientation to configuration reminds us to reanimate the figures that populate our socio-material imaginaries and practices, to examine the relations that they hold in place and the labours that sustain them, and to articulate the material semiotic reconfigurations required for their transformation.

References

Aanestad, M. (2003) 'The camera as an actor: design-in-use of telemedicine infrastructure in surgery', *Computer-supported Cooperative Work*, 12 (1): 1–20.

Ahmed, S. (2000) *Strange Encounters: Embodied Others in Post-coloniality*, London and New York: Routledge.

Akrich, M. (1992) 'The de-scription of technical objects', in W. Bijker and J. Law (eds) *Shaping Technology/Building Society*, Cambridge, MA: MIT Press, pp. 205–24.

Barad, K. (2007) *Meeting the Universe Halfway: Quantum Physics and the Entanglement of Matter and Meaning*, Durham, NC: Duke University Press.

Benjamin, W. (1968) *Illuminations*, New York: Harcourt Brace & World.

Bucciarelli, L. (1994) *Designing Engineers*, Cambridge, MA: MIT Press.

Castañeda, C. (2002) *Figurations: Child, Bodies, Worlds*, Durham, NC and London: Duke University Press.

Daston, L. (2000) 'The coming into being of scientfic objects', in L. Daston (ed.) *Biographies of Scientific Object*, Chicago, IL: University of Chicago Press, pp. 1–14.

de Laet, M. and Mol, A. (2000) 'The Zimbabwe bush pump: mechanics of a fluid technology', *Social Studies of Science*, 30 (2): 225–63.

Downey, G. and Dumit, J. (1997) *Cyborgs and Citadels: Anthropological Interventions in Emerging Sciences and Technologies*, Santa Fe, NM: School of American Research.

Ehn, P. (1988) *Work-oriented Design of Computer Artifacts*, Stockholm: Arbetslivscentrum.

Garfinkel, H. and Rawls, A. (2002) *Ethnomethodology's Program: Working out Durkeim's Aphonism*, Lanham, MD: Rowman & Littlefield.

Garfinkel, H. and Sacks, H. (1970) 'On formal structures of practical actions', in J. McKinney and E. Tiryakian (eds) *Theoretical Sociology: Perspectives and Development*, New York: Appleton-Century-Crofts, pp. 337–66.

Graeber, D. (2005) 'Fetishism as social creativity', *Anthropological Theory*, 5 (4): 407–38.

Greenbaum, J. and Kyng, M. (1991) *Design at Work: Cooperative Design of Computer Systems*, Hillsdale, NJ: L. Erlbaum Associates.

Gregory, J. (2000) 'Sorcerer's apprentice: creating the electronic health record, re-inventing medical records and patient care', unpublished PhD dissertation, University of California, San Diego. Available at: www.love.com.au/PublicationsTLminisite/Publications.htm (accessed 1 February 2012).

Gregory, J. (2009) 'A complex model for international and inter-cultural collaboration in health information systems and higher education', in S. Poggenpohl and K. Sato (eds) *Design Integrations: Research and Collaboration*, Chicago: Intellect, University of Chicago Press.

Grint, K. and Woolgar, S. (1997) *The Machine at Work: Technology, Work, and Organization*, Cambridge: Polity Press.

Haraway, D. (1985/1991) 'Manifesto for cyborgs: science, technology and socialist feminisim in the 1980s,' in *Simians, Cyborgs, and Women: the Reinvention of Nature*, New York: Routledge, pp. 149–82.

Haraway, D. (1997) *Modest_Witness@Second_Millennium.FemaleMan©_Meets_Onco Mouse™: Feminism and Technoscience*, New York: Routledge.

Ingold, T. (2008) 'Introduction', in E. Hallam and T. Ingold (eds) *Creativity and Cultural Improvisation*, Oxford and New York: Berg, pp. 45–54.

Knorr Cetina, K. (1999) *Epistemic Cultures: How the Sciences Make Knowledge*, Cambridge, MA: Harvard University Press.

Law, J. (1987) 'Technology and heterogeneous engineering: the case of Portuguese expansion', in W. Bijker, T. Hughes and T. Pinch (eds) *The Social Construction of Technological Systems*, Cambridge, MA: MIT Press, pp. 111–34.

Law, J. (1994) *Organizing Modernity*, Oxford: Blackwell.

Law, J. (2004) *After Method: Mess in Social Science Research*, London and New York: Routledge.

Lynch, M. (1993) *Scientific Practice and Ordinary Action: Ethnomethodology and Social Studies of Science*, New York: Cambridge University Press.

Newman, S. (1998) 'Here, there, and nowhere at all: distribution, negotiation, and virtuality in postmodern ethnography and engineering', *Knowledge and Society*, 11: 235–67.

Pickering, A. (1995) *The Mangle of Practice: Time, Agency and Science*, Chicago, IL: University of Chicago Press.

Ranjini, C. R. (2007) 'Towards building and implementing public health information infrastructures: An ethnographic study in India', unpublished PhD dissertation, Department of Sociology, Lancaster University.

Ranjini, C. R. and Sahay, S. (2006) 'Computer-based health information systems: projects for computerization or health management? Empirical experiences from India', in M. Gascó-Hernández, F. Equiza-López and M. Acevedo-Ruiz (eds) *Information Communication Technologies and Human Development: Opportunities and Challenges*, London: Idea Group Publishing, pp. 266–92.

Schuler, D. and Namioka, A. (1993) *Participatory Design: Principles and Practices*, Hillsdale, NJ: Lawrence Erlbaum.

Simonsen, J., Robertson, T. and Hakken, D. (eds) (2008) *PDC 2008: Proceedings of the Tenth Anniversary Conference on Participatory Design*, available through the ACM Digital Library or Indiana University Conferences at: www.conferences.indiana.edu (accessed 1 February 2012).

Suchman, L. (1994) 'Working relations of technology production and use', *Computer-supported Cooperative Work*, 2 (1–2): 21–39.

Suchman, L. (2002) 'Practice-based design: notes from the hyper-developed world', *The Information Society*, 18 (2): 1–6.

Suchman, L. (2007) *Human-machine Reconfigurations: Plans and Situated Actions*, revised edition, New York: Cambridge University Press.

Taussig, M. (1993) *Mimesis and Alterity: A Particular History of the Senses*, London: Routledge.

Verran, H. (1998) 'Re-imagining land ownership in Australia', *Postcolonial Studies*, 1 (2): 237–54.

Woolgar, S. (1991) 'Configuring the user: the case of usability trials', in J. Law (ed.) *A Sociology of Monsters: Essays on Power, Technology and Domination*, London: Routledge, pp. 57–102.

5 Experiment

Abstract experimentation

Steven D. Brown

For Rex

Introduction

As I write, the tenth and penultimate UK series of the internationally franchised reality TV show *Big Brother* is coming to the end of its season, accompanied by dwindling audience figures and general disinterest. Despite this ignominious end, in its prime the programme had a profound impact on the way celebrity is created, sustained and managed in early twentieth-century British media. In particular, it demonstrated that it was possible for contestants to achieve a degree of fame and to launch media careers (with varying degrees of success) on the basis of their own 'character' as displayed during the show. That is, on the basis of just being themselves rather than by virtue of any particular talent or other merits.

'Just being oneself' is a complex business. From its very beginning, contestant 'housemates' on *Big Brother* appeared to treat authenticity as an ongoing problem in their minutely recorded interactions. Sanctions would be very quickly applied by the housemates to those among them who were deemed to be 'playing up' too much for the cameras. They were quite right to do so. Being 'just me' is the most valuable and marketable commodity a housemate possesses, and by attempting to expose their fellow housemates as fraudulent traders of inauthentic selves, contestants were in effect adding value to their own stock.

On-screen arguments and heated interaction around authenticity draws attention away from a fundamental paradox in the structure of the programme. Housemates exist in a thoroughly unnatural, inauthentic environment in which their behaviour is recorded, edited and decontextualized in the process of constructing televised 'highlights'. Authenticity is here decoupled from reality. One shows what kind of a person one really is not by going about one's usual business, but rather by displaying how one engages with circumstances that are highly unusual or downright bizarre. The situation of a housemate is then close to that of a participant in a psychological experiment. As Fetveit argues:

Formats like *Big Brother* are . . . referred to as 'reality TV', although a more suitable name would be 'experiment TV'. *Big Brother* is a social (Darwinist) experiment . . . With the right casting and proper impulses and restrictions, this social laboratory will produce 'real life soap characters' that quarrel, insult, bond and seduce each other in front of large television and internet audiences . . . On one level it is dramatizing and normalizing our lives as fully surveilled and incarcerated. On another level it pushes the interrogation of authenticity on from the level of the image and onto the subjects photographed whose 'authenticity' is strongly thematized by the participants themselves as well as marketed by producers.

(Fetveit, 2003: 554)

The similarity between reality TV and formal psychological experiments with human participants has been well noted. Indeed, Big Brother was originally promoted by as a 'social experiment' by its UK broadcaster, Channel 4. Conversely, Philip Zimbardo, the social psychologist responsible for the infamous 'Stanford Prison Experiment' (SPE)[1] is an admirer of the work of Alan Funt, creator of arguably the first 'reality TV' show, Candid Camera. Zimbardo considers Funt to have been:

one of the most creative, intuitive social psychologists on the planet. For 50 years he has been contriving experimental scenarios in which ordinary people face a challenge to their usual perceptions or functioning.

(Zimbardo *et al.*, 2000: 197)

Given this enthusiasm, one might have expected Zimbardo to have appreciated the restaging of the SPE by the British social psychologists Alex Haslam and Steve Reicher in collaboration with the BBC as the reality TV show *The Experiment*. He did not. The replication was, in his view, a 'scientifically irresponsible "made-for-TV-study"' whose findings were riddled with 'inherent inadequacies, exaggerated claims and outright falsehoods' (Zimbardo, 2006: 47). According to Zimbardo, the major difference between the SPE and *The Experiment* is that, while both attempt to simulate the unequal power relations found in prison environments, the former draws upon sound scientific principles (e.g. random assignment of participants, separation of researcher from researched, discreet surveillance) whereas the latter follows the rules and format of a reality TV show, where the interactions of participants are structured, shaped and edited around the goal of providing good entertainment for the audience.

This distinction between science and popular media/culture appears to neatly separate the two versions of the SPE. Both share the common structure of 'ordinary people being challenged' with the goal of thereby displaying something of the machinery of normative social life. But the original SPE does so in the pursuit of a scientific agenda, while *The Experiment* and other forms of 'experiment TV' merely allude to this agenda as a marketing strategy to create good television. This distinction does not, however, stand up to close scrutiny. Throughout the history of psychology, there are innumerable instances of experiments that have blurred the line between media and science. The 'bystander apathy' experiments conducted by Bibi Latané and colleagues (Latané and Darley, 1970), for example, were inspired by newspaper reporting of the violent sexual assault and murder of Catherine Genovese in New York in 1964. As Frances Cherry (1995) argues, it is telling that the experiments which followed focused on a single abstract dimension of the case – the behaviour of bystanders to the assault and murder and why they did not intervene – rather than the concrete particularities of gender, class and race that were so clearly at stake in the way the case was originally reported (see also Manning *et al.*, 2007).

More recently, the cognitive psychologist Elizabeth Loftus has made significant contributions to heated public debate around the apparent 'recovery' of memories of hitherto unknown memories of childhood sexual abuse. Loftus controversially proposes that such memories are technically 'false' and the product of demonstrable social effect akin to suggestion that she terms 'imagination inflation' (Loftus *et al.*, 1996). Her key demonstration is a study known as 'Lost in the mall', where a target participant can be shown to recollect a 'false' childhood memory (of having been temporarily separated from their carers in a shopping mall) through the encouragement and influence of their older sibling, who acts a confederate of the experimenters. The study has a curious genealogy. It was first performed in an ad hoc fashion at a party, then used as a classroom exercise, and only subsequently, after it had been publically discussed in media reports of 'false memory', actually conducted as a formal experiment, using remarkably small sample sizes (see Ashmore *et al.*, 2005).

This use of popular media to report findings (or even to suggest possible findings in advance of having actually done or analyzed the experimental work) is not uncommon. Zimbardo himself chose to report the findings of the SPE through near simultaneous publication of the study in the *New York Times Magazine* and in two well-known mainstream professional journals. His subsequent discussions of the SPE have tended to emphasize the human drama of the experiment in a fashion clearly oriented to popular appeal. In a comparatively recent publication, the decision to end the SPE is described in the following dramatic terms:

> a young woman, recently graduated with a PhD from our department . . . came in from the cold and saw the raw, full-blown madness of this place that we had all gradually accommodated to day by day. She got emotionally upset, angry and confused. But in the end she challenged us to examine the madness she observed – that we had created. If we allowed it to continue further, she reminded us of our ethical responsibility for the consequences and well-being of the young men entrusted to our care as research participants.
>
> (Zimbardo *et al.*, 2000: 203)

There really does not seem to be a sensible distinction to be made here between scientific and media presentation of human drama. Perhaps instead it might be more fruitful to consider the sorts of experiments discussed here, ranging from formal experiments conducted in academic settings to 'experiment TV' and the variety of cases that seem to fall somewhere in-between, as instances of a single *device*, or arrangement of forces.[2] That device has the basic structure of creating a situation of 'ordinary people being challenged' in order to facilitate some form of learning experience. More precisely, we might say the device is a kind of social technology, a practice of identifying and organizing persons in such a way that certain aspects of human experience can be induced in isolation from what are typically thought to be their natural environments. These experiences are usually dramatic – failure to help others, betrayal of loved ones, participation in oppression. The device, however, makes it possible for them to be repeated on demand and in isolation from any concrete particularities. It also renders what then occurs as relatively open for coding, such that what may be learnt from the experience is rarely as straightforward as those who articulate the challenges (i.e. the experimenters) may intend or those who enact the challenges (i.e. the participants) experience at the time. The learning made possible by the device is then often ambiguous and open for contestation.

In this chapter, I want to explore experiments as means of doing a 'second order psychology' (see Brown and Stenner, 2009). That is, to show that learning about human experience is necessarily mediated by cultural awareness of the concepts and techniques of the psy-disciplines (i.e. psychology, psychiatry, psychoanalytic theory and practice). Recent work by Isabelle Stengers (2000), Vinciane Despret (2004a, 2004b) and Brian Massumi (2002) has opened up psychological experimentation as an object of thought and ably demonstrated the tension between the possible forms of learning inherent in their performance. This work takes its cue from Stengers' description of experiments as methods of inventing or creating new forms in which the world is deemed able to 'speak'. To make a new scientific being appear in the laboratory – be it a microbe, a body in motion or a false memory – requires a complex game of construction and mobilization, where a network of interests and stakes are made to pass through the experimental setting (see Stengers, 1997, 2000). But in the case of psychological experimentation, Stengers argues that all too often experiments are, by definition, not creative since they do not bring about anything new. They merely repeat what is already known under the guise of the apparently scientific. In describing the famous obedience studies conducted by Milgram (1962/2005), Stengers writes:

In the name of science' Stanley Milgram has taken on the reponsibility of 'repeating' an experiment already realized by human history, and has shown that torturers could be fabricated 'in the name of science' just as other have done so 'in the name of the state' or 'in the name of the good of the human species' ... 'In the name of science' Milgram submitted them to an apparatus that put himself in the position of Himmler or Eichmann.

(Stengers, 2000: 23)

Here, the device of experimentation is very crudely deployed 'in the name of science' with little understanding of what is at stake in an experiment – allowing the world to speak in a new mode which simultaneously authorises innovative propositions to be made by the experimenter. Milgram, by contrast, says what is already known and, in doing so, takes on the role of the torturer rather than a scientist. Stengers' argument defines 'good' experimentation as that which allows the subject to display intransigence or even resistance to the experimental setting and procedure (see Stengers, 1997, 2010). If there is no possibility of such resistance, then there can be nothing new created in the rapport between experimenter and subject, and hence, she argues, nothing can be learned.

I want to argue that this accusation levelled at Milgram mistakes the very particular way in which the device of experimentation functions in both social/developmental psychological research and in reality/experiment TV. The device may appear to resemble a natural science experiment, not least because it may be described as such by the experimenter, and thus appear to warrant comparison and evaluation against the very demanding normative standards that Stengers proposes for her 'contingent history of science'. But this resemblance is misleading. The arrangement of forces in the experimental device I want to consider here actually places it in relation to two other kinds of practices – theatre and art. Thus there are other kinds of contingent histories in which the experimental device of psychology/TV is inscribed.

Experimentation as theatre

The earliest social/developmental psychology experiments date from the late nineteenth century. From the very beginning such experimentation displayed a high degree of ingenuity and resourcefulness in its attempts to simulate social phenomenon. For example, Triplett's (1898) studies of 'social facilitation' set out to demonstrate that the presence of others increases a tendency towards competitiveness. Triplett, a cycling enthusiast, had formulated his hypothesis by way of a statistical analysis of 'official bicycle records made up to the close of the season of 1897 . . . obtained from the Racing Board of the League of American Wheelmen' (Triplett, 1898: 507), which showed that faster personal times were obtained when cyclists raced competitively as opposed to cycling on their own. The experimental demonstration of this supposed effect was conducted with child participants who conducted a manual task individually with and without the presence of others. The children were, of course, not informed as to the purpose of the task, nor the rationale behind it.

The level of detail that goes into this sort of simulation renders the phenomenon under scrutiny as 'staged' in every sense, being 'performed' by a specially recruited cast under the close direction of a backstage team who monitor and supervise what is enacted. In *The Uses of Illusions*, Thomas Korn (1997) points to a number of common characteristics of social psychological experimentation during the pivotal post-Second World War era that sustain this theatrical appeal. These include:

- The preparation of specially constructed environments, the casting of confederates and the creation of an elaborate 'cover story'. Tremendous attention to detail is usually paid. The entire interaction of research subjects with the various elements of the study is anticipated in advance. For example, the most commonly staged scenario is where an unwitting research subject is told that another subject has failed to turn up as scheduled for the experiment, and would they mind helping the experimenter by completing some additional task?
- The experimentation being entirely conducted by research associates who are required to learn extensive 'scripts' that dictate how they should interact with research subjects. The grant holder or project director is not usually involved in the actual 'production' itself; instead, they usually play an 'executive' role, orchestrating the setting up and monitoring of the experiment itself.
- Research subjects being unaware of the part they are required to play in the unfolding drama. These subjects were and still are typically recruited from large existing subject pools, such as undergraduate students on psychology programmes or military service personnel. Although subjects ostensibly have a choice about whether or not to participate, taking part in studies typically earns required course credits. Hence, there is usually something at stake for subjects in their participation

Taken together, these aspects of psychological experimentation render the practice as thoroughly theatrical. A drama is carefully worked out in advance, scripted minutely and then performed in a dedicated space by the cast using an array of props. Some members of the cast – i.e. the research subjects – may not be fully briefed on their performance, which is therefore to some degree 'improvised'. But this improvisation is already structured in advance by the complex work of setting and enacting the experiment, and repeating it over numerous 'performances' (i.e. trials).

To place experiments within the historical tradition of the theatre might be seen as a direct challenge to the scientificity of the practice. I most certainly do not intend it to be so. Psychological experimentation with human subjects addresses the very difficult task of constructing a controlled artificial situation that can nevertheless be said to resemble some facet of a broader social reality. Yet how could something so thoroughly artificial ever make such a claim? Consider the Triplett study – this involved no ordinary task. It made use of a specially constructed piece of equipment:

The apparatus for this study consisted of two fishing reels whose cranks turned in circles of one and three-fourths inches diameter. These were arranged on a Y shaped frame work clamped to the top of a heavy table . . . The sides of this frame work were spread sufficiently far apart to permit of two persons turning side by side. Bands of twisted silk cord ran over the well lacquered axes of the reels and were supported . . . two meters distant, by two small pulleys . . . The wheel on the side from which the records were taken communicated the movement made to a recorder, the stylus of which traced a curve on the drum of a kymograph. The direction of this curve corresponded to the rate of turning, as the greater the speed the shorter and straighter the resulting line.

(Triplett, 1898: 520)

A significant amount of effort was involved in producing this equipment since it had to serve two major purposes. First of all, it had to be able to communicate with a recording device (the kymograph) automatically in order to register the performance of the operator; and second, it had to create an experience for the participant which could be said to be analogous to competitive cycling, the source of the original hypothesis. The material form this analogy takes is absolutely crucial. There is nothing structurally that links reeling a 'twisted silk cord' to peddling a bicycle, the relationship is instead *morphogenetic* – both the bicycle and the fishing reel apparatus are capable of articulating 'social competition' when they are placed in the right set-up (the track or the laboratory). The point is to create something approaching equivalence rather than direct replication in experiential terms. The laboratory task *feels something like* the bicycle race.

Zimbardo refers to this analogy as 'functional equivalence' (see Zimbardo *et al.*, 2000). That is, the employment of practices or artefacts that are intended to engender reactions that can be taken as reasonable analogues of 'real-world experiences'. For example, the prisoners in the SPE were forced to wear rubber shower caps, which were supposed to generate the sense of having a shaved head – a technique for reducing individuality. Prisoners were also made to wear dress-like smocks without underwear, which led them to restrict their movements under continual fear of exposing themselves physically. The idea of all this is that, despite the lack of realism in the design of the prison itself, the prisoners should be provoked to respond emotionally and practically in ways similar to those which they might engage with respect to the intended real-world equivalent.

Functional equivalence is a delicate operation. It requires that the artificial elicit practical responses that mimetically reproduce supposed 'real' responses. Thus the conduct of participants within a given experiment can be read as authentic by an observer, as a genuine object for reflection and comprehension, while nevertheless recognizing its staged character. The theatrical tradition that is most closely aligned to this operation is the 'epic theatre' of Bertolt Brecht (see Thomson and Sacks, 2006). Brechtian theatre is grounded in a materialist, classical Marxist view of the performing arts. Theatre has a didactic purpose; it should aim to educate the audience to a better understanding of their social and historical conditions. As such, it is critical that the audience is aware at all times that what they are witnessing is not social reality itself, but rather an artifice that enables that reality to become an object of conscious reflection. Brecht rejected entirely a 'psychological' model of the theatre where the audience are lured into emotional involvement (and resolution) with the performance, and are thus able to dispose of what they witness as passive entertainment (Brecht, 1978).

The device deployed in Brechtian theatre to address this problem is known as *verfremdungseffekt* ('distancing effect'). This consists of a set of techniques for reminding the audience of the relative artificiality of the performance. These include performers directly addressing the audience, maintaining the house lights on throughout the performance, minimal stage designs and interruptions to the dramatic action through songs (ibid.). The aim of these techniques is to demonstrate the plausibility, often the necessity, of the actions taken by performers in response to the unfolding dramatic situation, but with the individual-psychological dimension removed. What is performed is not the travails befalling unique personalities, but rather the dilemmas of 'everyperson' in response to particular cultural-historical conditions – these are 'ordinary people being challenged'.

The techniques used in the SPE aim at a similar effect. No one is meant to be convinced that this is a 'real' prison, nor that Milgram's experimental set-up looks anything like the 'real' authoritarian power structures it mimics. The relative shoddiness and ramshackle appearance of the vast majority of psychological experimental settings is not accidental. They must be functionally equivalent but never identical to the social realities that ultimately concern them. This is because psychological experimentation is itself 'non-psychological' in the sense that the particularities of the person – their subjectivity and biography – are remarkably unimportant. Psychological experimentation aims at the same kind of realism-through-abstraction that defines Brechtian epic theatre, and moreover shares with it the ambition of didacticism through dramatics. But in the psychology laboratory the *verfremdungseffekt* is achieved with fake electric shock machines, mock prisons and undergraduate students.

Experimentation as art

It is common to observe that experimentation is reductionist, that it decontextualizes phenomenon from the social relations on which they are dependent, and that ultimately the findings that emerge tell us nothing we did not know already. This seems to be the thrust of Stengers' (2000) comments about the Milgram studies. There is, however, a more interesting aspect of this reductionism. Psychological experimentation aims for a certain kind of purity of expression. It does not seek the complexity of social life as it is lived, but rather the essence of a phenomenon reduced the simplest possible set of coordinates. Or, put slightly differently, it attempts to make visible social phenomenon in a form in which they could never possibly be lived, never otherwise made manifest.

Take the extraordinarily visually striking record of a study by Hamlin *et al.* (2007). In a short video clip, the words 'The hinderer' appear on a screen. This is rapidly followed by a shot of a model sloping landscape. On this slope, a small red ball with eyes appears and starts to ascend until it comes to a faltering halt. From the top of the shot, a pink cube appears, also with eyes, which descends to the ball, and then both move downwards to the bottom of the slope before the cube departs. The words 'the helper' appear. The scene seems to repeat, with the ball moving up the slope again. This time, however, a yellow triangle with eyes appears and moves towards the ball before both ascend and the triangle departs. Finally, the words 'the choice' appear. The scene has moved on to a shot of a baby. From out of shot, a tray appears with the cube and triangle. The baby bangs her hand down near the triangle.

The filmed scenes with the shapes were played to 6- and 10-month-old babies, who acted as unwitting experimental participants. The idea is that babies anthropomorphize the shapes and ascribe social attributes to the cube and the triangle, as respective 'hinderer' and 'helper' of the red ball. Having been primed in this way, they are subsequently shown the two shapes. A movement towards one or the other is taken as evidence of a 'preference'. The findings showed that 26 out of 28 infant participants appeared to prefer the triangle. The team then claimed that such a preference demonstrated that infants must be able to make social judgements. In order to do so, they must already have some formative knowledge of social relations, which, they claim, indicates that sociality is innate.

If we leave aside questions about the conduct of the experiment itself, there are certainly a number of issues we might raise in relation to these conclusions. First of all, it seems peculiar to consider 'helping' as a social act and 'hindering' as anti-social. To make this separation implies a very particular ideological meaning where hindering frustrates individual intentions, thereby corroding social life through restricting fundamental 'freedoms' and 'choices'. Given the cultural and historical specificity of such a view, it would be surprising indeed to learn that this was an innate property of human mentality. It is more likely that such a view would emerge on the basis of the participants' limited life experiences, perhaps even as a consequence of their participation in the experiment, which might then be better viewed as a demonstration of the rapid ideological conditioning of young minds.

An alternative is to follow the Stengers/Despret argument that apparent control over the experimental setting arises because experimenters fail to adequately attend to the range of possible forms of communication or affective engagement that may be possible with participants. For instance, Despret's (2004a) reading of the 'Clever Hans' episode emphasizes the active role played by the subject. The well-known story of the debunking of the supposed ability of a horse – Hans – to count on demand is usually recounted by psychologists as an illustration of behavioural conditioning. Hans learns when to stop 'counting' (i.e. tapping his hoof) by observing minimal movements made by the humans who pose mathematical problems. The horse is, in effect, 'docile'. It simply responds to its environment in ways that are initially puzzling and subsequently predictable. Despret argues instead that Hans renders himself 'available' to the observers in a way that redistributes the locus of action. Hans is teaching the observers how to affectively engage with horses just as much as the humans are teaching Hans:

> Hans was teaching them what made him move. Hans the horse was as much leading them as the humans were leading him. Their human bodies were not only sensitive to their own desire to make the horse succeed, they were also translating the horse's desire to help them to lead him successfully.
>
> (Despret, 2004a: 116)

What happens if we see the infants not as docile participants for Hamlin and co-workers, but as actively 'becoming available' to the experiment? Approached in this way, we might observe that the crucial moment is where the infant moves his or her hand near the triangle. Perhaps they 'choose' the helper because that is what they think the experimenter wishes them to do. In this sense, they themselves are acting as 'helpers'. They are deciphering the present situation and not merely the scene on the film. This might be seen as yet more evidence of innate sociality. However, if we follow the apparent ideology expressed by the researchers' findings, we might have to conclude that the infants do so because they see this as an opportunity to express their own freedom to choose. But surely the best way for them to show this innate capacity would be to not follow the wishes of the experimenter, to reject the apparent attempt at coercion? Would a better demonstration of this individualist version of sociality be for the infants to have chosen the hinderer, or even perhaps to have refused to choose altogether? Perhaps this is indeed closer to what they have actually done: they are not empathizing with the helper by 'choosing' it, but rather are accusing it – 'that one gave too much help, it should have left that useless ball alone'.

Let's turn back to the film itself. What the record of the experiment vividly demonstrates is that the question posed by the experimenters turns on a pivotal moment: what shape will the infant choose? The artifice, the reductionism, the decontextualization of the experiment has as its key aim the desire to make this human drama in miniature turn on a single moment that is apparently under the control of the participant themselves. This is a common feature of experimentation – will the child turn the reel faster? (Triplett); will the 'teacher' push the next button? (Milgram); will the guard stop shouting? (Zimbardo). Now, there is a precedent for this procedure, albeit one that appears in the history of art rather than science. It is the practice of bringing about purity of expression through the stripping away of the majority of the perceptual field, making the phenomenon turn on the vicissitudes of a single event. This was developed by the German expressionist movement of the early twentieth century. As articulated in theoretical terms by Ernst Bloch (1977), expressionism offers 'experiments with disruptive and interpolative techniques', which include 'montage and other devices of discontinuity', all of which in their own fashion 'strive to exploit the *real* fissures in surface interrelations and to discover the new in their crevices' (ibid.: 22, emphasis original). Expressionism seeks to create new worlds through finding and exploiting cracks in the existing world. For example, in John Heartfield's artwork, commonplace images are multiplied and juxtaposed to construct unreal, unworldly images that nevertheless express the essential character of their subjects (e.g. Hitler's guts filled with money; the family about to swallow chains and bicycle handles in *Hurrah, die Butter ist alle!*).

Fortuitously, there is a direct link between the aesthetic practices of expressionism and post-Second World War social/developmental experimentation. As part of the emigration en masse of the German intelligentsia in the 1930s, Kurt Lewin became a founding figure of post-war US experimental social psychology. Lewin, schooled in the Gestalt tradition of experimentalism, emphasized that one might create an artificial situation, but nevertheless one where the actual forces that would be deployed would be equivalent to those that would be present in 'real life'. Since individual experiences are, in effect, produced by the summing up of a variety of environmental forces into a dynamic field, it is possible, Lewin claimed, to construct a mathematically based topological model of experience (Lewin, 1936). The model may then be operationalized in experiments that focus on particular states of the dynamic field. In this way, the ongoing dynamic flow of experience can be captured and isolated in its pure form. Similarly, Fritz Heider, another Gestalt alumni, introduced ideas concerning the perception of social relations into US social psychology. In 1944, Heider, along with Marianne Simmel, used an animated film that depicted geometrical shapes moving around one another as the basis for an experiment. Participants were asked to evaluate the 'character' of each shape and to 'tell the story' of the film. This procedure, to which the Hamlin *et al.* (2007) study is indebted, has become a standard illustration of anthropomorphism.

For both Lewin and Heider, what is important is not reducing the complexities of experience to mechanistically conceived component parts. Rather, they sought to refine particular psychological states of affairs to their most focused and concentrated form. This form would then be abstract, in the sense that it would never appear in this way in the course of normative social experience, but it is nevertheless extracted from something, like a 'real fissure in surface interrelations'. Experimentation of this kind shares with expressionism the desire to uncover the new through a treatment and disruption of the real. A psychological experiment on, say, perception or on group conflict is no less a series of juxtapositions of existing elements into novel combinations that express an essential force than Heartfield's photomontages. Indeed, Heider and Simmel's (1944) animation and Lewin's own experiments with film (see Lück, 1997) have a certain expressionist character. They demonstrate how a recognizably human world can be made available in its 'purest' form, a form in which it could not possibly be otherwise lived.

What can we learn from the experimental device?

There are two alternative contingent histories into which the experimental device common to social/developmental psychology and reality/experiment TV can be inscribed. The first is in relation to techniques of 'theatrical abstract-realism' for which the best exemplar is Brechtian theatre. The second is 'artistic expressionism', particularly of the sort represented by German art and cinema of the inter-war years. I am not claiming that there is a direct historical link between post-war psychology and Brecht or expressionism. Rather that, if we place psychological experimentation within these two alternative contingent histories, then what appears to be a reductionist quasi-scientific practice can be treated instead as one site of activation of a device for dramatizing human conduct that is distributed throughout a variety of cultural and historical settings. There are two aspects of the device. On the one hand, it involves an abstract-realist creation of an artificial version of a matter of concern that can nevertheless be treated as a functional analogue. On the other, it seeks a pure expression of some essence by multiplying, repeating, juxtaposing and reducing everyday elements until they take on an entirely new form. The SPE is one exemplary moment where these two aspects of the device are most vividly at work, as is perhaps the experiment TV of *Big Brother*.

It is often said by art theorists that New York became the art capital of the world from the 1940s onwards when the entire gallery system of Paris relocated there. Abstract expressionism, as a North American movement, became a synthesis of existing forms of modern art and the 'wave of the future' as a consequence. Much the same claim is often made about social psychology, which became a predominantly North American discipline on the basis of the wave of emigration based around people such as Lewin and Heider. If the same device is found configured slightly different ways in both theatre (as Brechtian technique) and art (as abstract expressionism), then I propose to refer to the particular version of the device that became adopted in US social/developmental psychology of the time by the similarly synthetic term *abstract experimentalism*. By this I mean the arrangement of forces that comes from the coupling of the realist tradition in the form of functional equivalence, with the expressionist tradition, in the form of the multiplication of the real to allow for the amplification of what is deemed essential.

Describing the work of Zimbardo or Milgram as abstract experimentalism means that, contrary to Stengers, it will not be necessary to see these studies as poor relations of the creative experimentalism to which science ought to aspire, since what occurs in these experiments does not belong to the same contingent history that might link Galileo with modern physics or Newton with modern chemistry (see Stengers, 2010). However, this still leaves open the question of what can be learned from exposure to the abstract experimentalist device. On this point, it is worth returning to Zimbardo. In a formulation remarkably similar to Stengers' description of the Milgram studies, he argues that:

> From another perspective, the SPE does not tell us anything new about prisons that sociologists and narratives of prisoners have not already revealed about the evils of prison life. What is different is that by virtue of the experimental protocol, we selected good people, randomly assigned to be either guard or prisoner, and observed the ways in which they were changed for the worse by their experiences in the evil place.
>
> (Zimbardo *et al.*, 2000: 208)

What appears to matter here, for Zimbardo and his colleagues, is the transformation that occurred to the participants as a consequence of their exposure to the SPE. According to Zimbardo *et al.* (2000), this included the following: the emergence of the idea for the SPE itself on the basis of a prior brief 'experiential study' conducted by Zimbardo's students, one of whom became a co-experimenter on the subsequent project; participants regularly joining Zimbardo in media discussions about the study, and a number going on to train as clinicians and prison consultants; and Zimbardo himself giving senate evidence in support of prison reform in 1975. The sorts of transformations detailed here approximate to what Stengers calls 'learning'.

But could the same be said of experiment TV? Is there some form of learning that arises from participation here, either on the part of actual contestants, or for us as viewers? It would be an act of supreme aggrandizement to bestow on *Big Brother* the power to have transformed our lives, to have opened up creative becomings. And yet here too a kind of learning is possible. Participants on *Big Brother* appear to very rapidly learn how a certain kind of 'micro-celebrity' is accomplished. They learn that the best response to ever more bizarre and artificial circumstances is to perform increasingly more normative versions of gender, sexuality, ethnicity or class. They learn to hone and refine their performance so it becomes a single exclamation ('Oh. My. *God*'). Or a particular sort of facial expression. Or maybe a certain kind of bodily movement. All of which are then repeated until they become a tic. *Big Brother* accomplishes what psychological experimentation could never even begin to imagine: a form of experience that is so relentlessly non-psychological that it is no longer even human.

Notes

1 The SPE was an experiment conducted to assess the impact of situational factors (such as 'depersonalization' – the loss of individuality caused by anonymity in a situation) on the behaviour of individuals in a setting structured by power and

authority. Student volunteers were randomly assigned the role of either guards or prisoners in a mock prison setting and monitored over several days. The experiment was concluded early due to concerns about the well-being of the 'prisoners'. See Zimbardo *et al.* (2000) for a comparatively recent history of the SPE and its aftermath.

2   In using the phrase 'arrangement of forces', I am making a deliberate allusion to the notions of *dispositif* and *agencement* as developed by Foucault (1976) and Deleuze (1988, 2006; Deleuze and Guattari, 1988). Although there are considerable differences in the elaboration of the terms, both represent analytic attempts to describe the holding together of heterogeneous sets of social, technical and discursive relations in a single – albeit topologically complex – milieu or territory. The forces that I have in mind in the case of abstract experimentalism include practices for performing 'self-authenticity', aesthetic codes, empiricist rationalities, technical arrangements for recording and amplifying behaviour and, not least of all, the embodied engagement of participants.

References

Ashmore, M., Brown, S. D. and MacMillan, K. (2005) 'Lost in the mall with Mesmer and Wundt: demarcation and demonstration in the psychologies', *Science, Technology & Human Values*, 30 (1): 76–110.

Bloch, E. (1977) 'Discussing expressionism', in *Aesthetics and Politics*, London: Verso, pp. 16–27.

Brecht, B. (1978) *On Theatre: The Development of an Aesthetic*, new edition, London: Methuen.

Brown, S. D. and Stenner, P. (2009) *Psychology without Foundations: History, Philosophy and Psychosocial Theory*, London: Sage.

Cherry, F. (1995) *The 'Stubborn Particulars' of Social Psychology: Essays of the Research Process*, London: Routledge.

Deleuze, G. (1988) *Deleuze*, Minneapolis, MN: University of Minnesota Press.

Deleuze, G. (2006) 'Desire and pleasure', in *Two Regimes of Madness: Texts and Interviews 1975–1995*, New York: Semiotext(e), pp. 122–34.

Deleuze, G. and Guattari, F. (1988) *A Thousand Plateaus: Capitalism and Schizophrenia*, trans. B. Masumi, London: The Athlone Press.

Despret, V. (2004a) 'The body we care for: figures of anthropo-zoo-genesis', *Body & Society*, 10 (2/3): 111–34.

Despret, V. (2004b) *Our Emotional Makeup: Ethnopsychology and Selfhood*, New York: Other Press.

Fetveit, A. (2003) 'Reality TV in the digital era: a paradox in visual culture?', in R. C. Allen and A. Hill (eds) *The Television Studies Reader*, London: Routledge, pp. 543–57.

Foucault, M. (1976) *Discipline and Punish: The Birth of the Prison*, Harmondsworth: Penguin.

Heider, F. and Simmel, M. (1944) 'An experimental study of apparent behavior', *American Journal of Psychology*, 57 (2): 243–59.

Hamlin, J. K., Wynn, K. and Bloom, P. (2007) 'Social evaluation by preverbal infants', *Nature*, 450: 557–60.

Korn, J. H. (1997) *Illusions of Reality: A History of Deception in Social Psychology*, New York: State University of New York Press.

Latané, B. and Darley, J. M. (1970) *The Unresponsive Bystander: Why Doesn't He Help?*, New York: Appleton-Century-Croft.

Lewin, K. (1936) *Principles of Topological Psychology*, New York: McGraw Hill.

Loftus, E. F., Coan, J. A. and Pickrell, J. E. (1996) 'Manufacturing false memories using bits of reality', in L. M. Reder (ed.) *Implicit Memory and Metacognition*, Mahwah, NJ: Lawrence Erlbaum Associates.

Lück, H. E. (1997) 'Kurt Lewin: filmmaker', in W. G. Bringmann, H. E. Lück, R. Miller and C. E. Early (eds) *A Pictorial History of Psychology*, Hannover Park, IL: Quintessence, pp. 282–7.

Massumi, B. (2002) *Parables for the Virtual: Movement, Affect, Sensation*, Durham, NC: Duke University Press.

Manning, R., Levine, M. and Collins, A. (2007) 'The Kitty Genovese murder and the social psychology of helping: the parable of the 38 witnesses', *American Psychologist*, 62 (6): 555–62.

Milgram, S. (1962/2005) *Obedience to Authority: An Experimental View*, new edition, New York: Pinter and Martin.

Stengers, I. (1997) *Power and Invention*, Minneapolis, MN: University of Minnesota Press.

Stengers, I. (2000) *The Invention of the Modern Sciences*, Minneapolis, MN: University of Minnesota Press.

Stengers, I. (2010) 'Comparison as a matter of concern', *Common Knowledge*, 17 (1): 48–63.

Thomson, P. and Sacks, G. (eds) (2006) *The Cambridge Companion to Brecht*, 2nd edition, Cambridge: Cambridge University Press.

Triplett, N. (1898) 'The dynamogenic factors in pacemaking and competition', *American Journal of Psychology*, 9: 507–33.

Zimbardo, P. (2006) 'On rethinking the psychology of tyranny: the BBC prison study', *British Journal of Social Psychology*, 45 (1): 47–53.

Zimbardo, P., Maslach, C. and Haney, C. (2000) 'Reflections on the Stanford Prison Experiment: genesis, transformations, consequences', in T. Blass (ed.) *Obedience to Authority: Current Perspectives on the Milgram Paradigm*, London: Lawrence Erlbaum, pp. 193–237.

6 Experiment

The experiment in living[1]

Noortje Marres

'There is nothing that is quite so reminiscent of Garfinkel's demonstrational methodology as the "happening", which, however, usually lacks the unblinking hurtfulness of Garfinkel's technique, and may also have a larger social purpose'.

Alvin Gouldner, 'Sociology as a Happening' (1970)

Introduction

Social researchers and theorists have long taken an interest in experiments as a form of knowledge production and intervention that enjoys particular privileges in societies marked by the invention of the modern sciences (Stengers, 2000). But the 'living experiment' presents a special variation on the theme: unlike scientific experiments, this form of experimentation has been explicitly associated with the moral purpose of the improvement of society since its very inception. Thus, the nineteenth-century philosopher John Stuart Mill, who is widely credited with inventing the term, 'experiment in living', first used it to make the case for the affirmation of social and cultural diversity, as something that is distinctive of liberal societies. These kinds of societies stand out, he proposed, insofar as they 'embrace the variability of human life' and believe that 'the worth of different modes of life should be proved practically' (Mill, 1859/2002).[2]

Today, too, the genre of the 'experiment in living' is put to a variety of moral, political and economic purposes. As such, I would like to argue here that the living experiment presents a notable device of social and cultural research: it provides a format or 'protocol' for exploring and testing forms of life, which is today widely applied across social life. And because of this, these experiments also present a useful site for sociological research in a more narrow sense: they can be used to explore collective practices of researching social and cultural change, as engaged in by actors who do not necessarily identify themselves as 'social researchers'. Finally, these experiments can also be taken as an invitation or challenge to social scientists to come to terms with particular social and technological changes that are currently affecting social research.

In recent years, social scientists have proposed that their disciplines may be undergoing a transformation, as the resources and techniques of social research are being redistributed among a variety of agencies inside and outside the university (Latour, 1998; Savage and Burrows, 2007; Adkins and Lury, 2009; Whatmore, 2009). Thus, social data are today collected by a wide range of agencies, from IT services to product designers and news media organizations, as they are developing new ways of analyzing and using them. Many believe that this situation calls into question the distribution of roles in social research. Some have argued that industry is increasingly claiming the edge of social research, thereby challenging the authority of academic social science (Savage and Burrows, 2007). Others, however, have suggested that this situation is not necessarily exceptional: social research has always relied on the active contributions of actors outside the university, and the division of labour among lay and expert actors in the conduct of social research has always been in flux (Callon *et al.*, 2001). From this perspective, the question is rather how we should come to terms with a recent reconfiguration of research cultures: the active participation of social actors in the conduct of research is today increasingly recognized across social life.

In this chapter, I would like to turn to a particular version of the living experiment, namely experiments in sustainable living, to show how such a normative and conceptual problematic can be explored by empirical means. Sustainable living experiments are today conducted by a variety of actors, from journalists to mothers, engineers and policy-makers, as well as artists. As such, they provide an especially useful site for exploring the changing division of labour of research among agencies inside and outside the university. They invite us to focus not necessarily on what are the distinguishing features of social science that set it apart, or allow it to be demarcated, from research conducted elsewhere in society, but rather to explore how the circulation of social research techniques across social life can be rendered productive for social science. After discussing the phenomenon of the sustainable living experiment, and what it might tell us about the division of labour in/of social research in the current context, I will consider two empirical instances in more detail:

1   Sustainable living blogs, which report on such experiments on the Web.
2   An artistic experiment called Spiral Drawing Sunrise in which I recently participated in Amsterdam.

Neither of these projects was initiated by social researchers, but I think that they both have something to tell us about the redistribution of roles in social research.

The sustainable living experiment as a device of social research

Living experiments that are specifically concerned with our relationship with nature or the environment have a long and intricate history. They can be traced back, for instance, to the 'returns to nature' undertaken by educated men in the second half of the nineteenth century, in their attempts to live a simpler life, which they documented in diaries and philosophical writings (Thoreau, 1854/2000; Heyting, 1994; Rowbotham, 2008).[3] But this type of living experiment can also be characterized in terms of its formal features, and this is especially useful for clarifying its significance for social research today. Thus, experiments in sustainable living can be said to undertake the modification of habits and habitats according to a fixed procedure: they are a way of implementing changes in everyday routines and living spaces according to a protocol. These procedures may take various forms, with some dictating 'one simple change a day', while others set a quantitative target, such as reducing energy use or waste by x per cent. To give an example of the latter, this is how the New York-based 'No Impact Man' defines his project:

> [This] is my experiment with researching, developing and adopting a way of life for me and my little family – one wife, one toddler, one dog – to live in the heart of New York City while causing no net environmental impact. To do this, we will decrease the things we do that hurt the earth – make trash, cause carbon dioxide emissions, for example – and increase the things we do that help the earth – clean up the banks of the Hudson River, give money to charity, rescue sea birds, say.[4]
>
> No Impact Man, 'What you need to know' (22 February 2007)

This description is taken from No Impact Man's blog, and as such it also can be taken to indicate a second feature of sustainable living experiments: they tend to involve the meticulous recording and reporting of everyday practices, the attempt to change them, and the consequences of such attempts, in various media. Arguably, indeed, the living experiment can today be said to constitute a genre of publicity (Marres, 2009): experiments in sustainable living can be encountered 'on all channels', from popular television to the (semi-)professional world of blogs. Many of these projects are undertaken by journalists, though certainly not all: they feature a whole range of professionals and amateurs, from engineers and architects to environmental activists, policy-makers, farmers, students, mothers, and so on. In this respect, the sustainable living experiment is perhaps best understood as a proliferating media form, the circulation of which involves the replication of sustainable living, or versions thereof, across social life. And this proliferation is especially interesting for social science, I would say, insofar as these experiments can be seen to undertake a kind of social research.

Sociologists have long taken an interest in forms of research conducted by non-scientists outside the university, something which Michel Callon and others have called research 'in the wild' (Callon *et al.*, 2001; see also Lynch, 1991). Perhaps most radically, authors working in the sociological tradition of ethnomethodology have argued that the label 'social research' may equally be applied to everyday social practices that are not defined as such by the actors involved: as they put it, everyday actors can be said to deploy social research methods in going about their ordinary activities, insofar as they are engaged in 'render[ing] everyday habits and settings visible-reportable-and accountable for practical purposes' (Filmer, 2003; see also Garfinkel, 1967/1984; Button, 1991). Whether or not one would want to agree with the ethnomethodological argument, it strikes me that this description is very much applicable to the aforementioned sustainable living experiments.

These experiments tend to generate detailed descriptions of everyday activities, such as cleaning, bathing and cooking. To give another example, the living experiment undertaken by the Canadian journalist Vanessa Ferquhson, in which she committed to making one 'green' change a day for the duration of one year, resulted in an endless list of everyday routines and things on her blog, from the hair conditioner that she stopped using to not driving her car on weekends. Initiatives like these can quite literally be said to be concerned with rendering everyday living accountable: by describing the objects and habits that make up everyday living, these experiments aspire to bring into view the environmental and social consequences of everyday living.

Furthermore, sustainable living experiments can be seen to deploy a particular research technique invented by ethnomethodologists: they can be said to perform something akin to 'breaching experiments', the famous exercises performed by Harold Garfinkel and his disciples in the 1960s, which involved the controlled disruption of ordinary scenes (Garfinkel, 1967/1984; Lynch, 1993). In these experiments, sociologists went about deliberately disrupting intimate interactions in their own personal lives, for instance by pretending ignorance of conventional expressions when talking with their husbands and wives. Sustainable living experiments can be said to enact similarly controlled disruptions of everyday ways of doing things: the Welsh blogger Suitably Despairing decided to clean his house with vinegar, and Vanessa Ferquhson, after smaller interventions such as not using hair conditioner, went on to unplug her fridge.[5] In documenting such interventions, these experiments render explicit aspects of social life that are not usually considered noteworthy, such as the ways our hair smells, or the rooms we live in.[6] And, in this respect, sustainable living experiments could be said to apply the social methods of the disruption of everyday routines in order to render visible the objects and settings of everyday life (on this point, see also Michael, 2006).

Importantly, this interpretation of sustainable living experiments, as instances of the deployment of social research techniques in and as everyday life, suggests a particular take on the problematic flagged in the introduction: that of the changing relations between forms of social research conducted inside and outside the university. To begin with, the resonance between contemporary living experiments and older arguments from ethnomethodology can serve as a reminder that the distribution of roles among academic and other agencies of social research has been debated in sociology for many decades already. Accordingly, social researchers should not be surprised to find social actors deploying research techniques similar to those used in academic social research, as in sustainable living experiments. However, this does not of course mean that current processes of the redistribution of roles are not problematic. Thus, we can equally note that, in sustainable living experiments, social research techniques are today put to purposes that social scientists would not recognize as their own. That is, it seems important to acknowledge that sustainable living experiments today serve many different purposes, besides that of social research. Here I would like to argue that, if we are to adequately appreciate living experiments as devices of social research, then we must take into consideration this multiplicity of purpose.

Living experiments as multifarious instruments

Sociologists of science and technology have long characterized scientific experiments as a distinctive form of knowledge production and intervention in society, and some of them have argued that one of their distinguishing features is that they may serve a broad range of objectives all at once. Thus, authors working in the subfield of social studies of science and technology have suggested that scientific and technological demonstrations, especially those that are conducted in public, perform a number of different roles simultaneously. On the one hand, public experiments provide a way of inserting new technoscientific objects into the fabric of society – such as the anti-conception pill or a sub-atomic particle like the neutrino. But, on the other hand, they also provide occasions to actively involve social actors in the process of the societal 'domestication' of these new objects (Latour, 1988; Shapin and Schaffer, 1989).[7]

Experiments, then, have been said to perform at least two functions simultaneously: they perform 'ontological' work, by facilitating the integration of new entities into socio-technical practices; but they also do an amount of social or political work, namely that of enlisting the support of social actors for technological or scientific projects. Recent social studies of public experiments have added to this an important political role of public experiments. According to Andrew Barry (2001), experiments have the capacity to accommodate a very broad range of political and/or ideological agendas – as, for instance, in the case of field trials with genetically modified crops, where experimental demonstrations were used as a vehicle for both pro-science and anti-market, as well as ethical arguments. Which is to say, public experiments also provide important sites for a politics of contestation, and not just for a politics of legitimacy or 'enrolment'.

Sustainable living experiments can equally be ascribed the capacity to serve a multiplicity of purposes. They are performed by a variety of agencies in a range of different settings, and serve to enact a range of different forms of research, and moral and political agendas. Thus, sustainable living experiments are not just undertaken by more-or-less media-genic individuals, but also by a range of governmental, scientific and for-profit organizations. In Britain, an institution such as the Building Research Establishment is involved in administering purpose-built experimental sustainable homes, in which the behaviour of inhabitants and the building itself are monitored by a variety of means, from sensors embedded in walls to smart electricity meters and attitudinal surveys. A whole range of other organizations are engaged in similar initiatives in the UK, such as the Sustainable Cities research programme at University College London, which participates in research on a 'retro-fitted' council home in the London borough of Camden, and equally involves the monitoring of the environmental performance of the building and its inhabitants, by means of sensors, smart electricity meters, and questionnaires. And then there are the community initiatives called Carbon Rationing Action Groups, which keep detailed records of individuals' attempts to use less energy, from wearing more clothes indoors to taking less dirty trains, and so on. As the format of the sustainable living experiment is replicated across social life, it can be seen to take on a variety of forms, serve different objectives and carry multiple normative charges.[8]

In this respect, the sustainable living experiment may usefully be understood as a multifarious instrument. This experimental apparatus, we then say, is being used to serve a variety of objectives, which may not always be clearly distinguished. And this variety, and variability, of its purposes may be what makes this experimental form a potent one. This is not the place to specify these different purposes in great detail, but to give an indication of their scope, they range from technological innovation to marketing to awareness raising. Thus, some versions of the sustainable living experiment can be seen to instantiate a particular regime of technological and social change: the monitoring and reporting of behaviours in and of domestic buildings is here a way of making technology critical to the performance of environmental change. But the 'embedding' of environmental monitoring devices in domestic settings also offers a way to transform utility services: electricity supply becomes a different kind of service when it includes feedback about the customer's environmental behaviour. Third, some sustainable living experiments can be said to generate moral and political sensibilities, and to provide a way of exploring embodied and distributed ways of performing social and environmental change. As Gay Hawkins (2006: 7) notes, what is distinctive about living experiments is that they 'involve the intensities of the body' and as such may enable more intimate ways of 'understanding how new habits and sensibilities emerge' (see also Grosz, 2005; Murphy, 2006). From such a perspective, a media format such as the 'green living blog' can be appreciated as a form of moral inquiry or political experimentation, as it enables personal and embodied attempts to 'try and live green in a world that is not so keen', as the title of one of these blogs puts it.[9]

As the publicity genre of the sustainable living experiment proliferates, it is likely to serve an ever-expanding and varying range of purposes. It is then precisely to the degree that the living experiment takes on the aspect of a multiplying genre that it exhibits the feature of 'multiplicity of purpose' and may be understood as a multifarious instrument. The question now is whether and how social research should be included among its various purposes. If sustainable living experiments can indeed be understood as performing social research, this inevitably goes on in the context of multiple deployments of the living experiment. Indeed, to the extent that some of these other purposes are in tension with those of social research, sustainable living experiments must be defined as a critical site of social research. Social research must then be regarded as a contested objective, and the question is whether and how, under such conditions, an experimental form such as that of sustainable living can be rendered productive for social research; that is, how it can be made to serve this purpose.

Living experiments and the redistribution of research techniques

To address this question, it is important to note that sustainable living experiments do not just deploy social methods in a general sense. They do not just exemplify the abstract sociological idea that social research is performed in and as everyday life, as social actors render it describable and accountable as they go about their lives. Rather, in rendering everyday living accountable, these experiments deploy particular research *techniques and technologies*, which are also part of the methodological repertoire of the social sciences: they make video clips that document mundane interactions, and they use software to do textual analysis. One could say, then, that sustainable living experiments present an especially concrete example of the deployment of social methods in everyday life.

To focus here on the latter example, the use of software tools to analyze textual data has been part of the social science and humanities methods repertoire for a long time, and one instance of this is word frequency analysis – the identification of terms and categories of terms that are most prominent in a given text. Reports on sustainable living experiments on the Web, as on 'green living blogs', also use a version of this technique, as many of these feature tag clouds, visualizations that give an impression of the frequency of terms used by the blogger in question to mark up his or her recent posts (see Figure 6.1). Sustainable living blogs can also be seen to perform network analysis in more-or-less explicit ways, as they maintain blogrolls of other sites and, by linking to them, produce recommendations that search engines and others rely on to rank these sites. By producing such links, bloggers are thus likely to influence the organization of sustainable living networks on the Web (Marres, 2006; Weltevrede, n.d.). And this list of Web technologies that resonate with methods deployed in social research could be extended to include the anthropological method of following objects among distributed sites, as some living experiments use tracking and tracing technologies, such as RFID tags, to follow discarded household items and other waste, on their journey from the home to the processing plant.

TAGS

Age of stupid Algalita Marine Research Foundation animals Bay to Breakers Blog Action Day Blog Carnival Blogher bottled water Brita Climate Action Day climate change Colin Beavan cows dairy farm Earth Day eco-running global warming Green Sangha ice cream JunkRide laundry rack meme Midway Journey milk No Impact Man Ocean plastic Ocean Plastic Pollution Oprah packaging plastic-free plastic-free farmers market plastic bags plastic collection plastic packaging Plastic Pollution Coalition plastic tally plastic trash plastic waste Project Kaisei PVC reusable bottles Strauss Organic Creamery Tapped Thanksgiving yogurt

Figure 6.1 Tag cloud, www.fakeplasticfish.com, Beth Terry's blog (accessed 1 November 2009).

Techniques such as tag clouds and blogrolls have been analyzed as specific to digital culture (Rogers, 2009). But when we consider the use of such techniques in the context of sustainable living experiments, they resonate with the deployments of similar techniques in social research: textual analysis, network analysis and the following of objects are central components of its methodological repertoire.[10] Such a focus on the similarities among research techniques used inside and outside the university opens up a particular perspective on the question of relation between expert and lay practices of social research: it directs attention to the circulation of research technologies, and their adaptation to particular purposes in particular settings, as what partly determines which agencies may take on which research roles. The question of the distribution of roles in social research is, then, not just a question of *who* has access to or can lay claim to *what* resources and methods of social research. Rather, social research has to be appreciated in terms of *how* research techniques are put to use. Arguably, it is not the methods of social research themselves that determine what is distinctive about it. For instance, it was the specific ways in which word frequency analysis was put to work in social research, as in co-word analysis (Callon *et al.*, 1983) that made the decisive difference for social research. And this notion that 'the quality of research methods reside in their use', to use a variation on the Wittgensteinian phrase, may also be extended to research in the wild.

Can the adoption of social research techniques by a variety of social actors, in sustainable living experiments, be made to work for rather than against social research? In posing this question, I am asking whether living experiments, as they are performed across social life, can be approached by social researchers, as 'elaboratories'. This word was historically used to signal that the experimental work conducted in laboratories 'went beyond mere observation', to tempt 'nature to reveal its secrets' (Hankins and Silverman, 1995). But, applying this term loosely, we can also ask whether sustainable living experiments could provide useful elaborations on social research techniques, by deploying them in different ways. In the remainder of this chapter, I will explore this in two empirical studies of sustainable living experiments:

1   A Web analysis of sustainable living blogs.
2   By adopting the role of participant in an artistic experiment in living.

The living experiment as rendering device 1: the multiple ontologies of sustainability

One of the reasons sustainable living experiments can be useful for social research is that they may help to explicate the 'ontologies' of environmental living. As I mentioned above, sociologists have argued that public experiments do 'ontological work': they provide answers to the question of what entities the world is made up. Such an understanding of the public experiment, incidentally, suggests that experiments enable a particular redistribution of research. It namely attributes to the empirical device of the experiment a capacity that is usually attributed to theory: the articulation of the entities making up the world. Such an 'ontological' understanding of experiments also has implications for how we understand the role of social research and theory in relation to it. If ontologies are articulated in experimental practices across social life, what then should be the contribution of social theory to the formulation of ontologies (Law and Urry, 2003)? Should social researchers seek to impartially describe the ontologies that are emerging in practice, or should they actively commit to particular experimental ontologies over others – something that Annemarie Mol and John Law have termed 'ontological politics'?

Web-based analysis of sustainable living experiments provides a way of exploring such questions by empirical means. By analyzing sustainable living blogs, we might give a tentative answer to the question: What is sustainable living made up of?[11] Doing Web analysis of living experiments could then be a way of studying ontologies in the making. And to the extent that the objects deployed in different experiments vary, the resulting ontologies might be rendered as alternatives.[12] With this broader aim in mind, let me turn to a particular information format, which is widely used on sustainable living blogs, that of 'green tips', with list actions individuals can undertake, under various banners: 'ethical things that anyone can do'; 'when simple things you can do really do make a difference'; '10 ways to be more sustainable with your vegetable garden'; and so on.[13] Some of the items on these lists are fairly standard and frequently recur ('don't trash your old electronic equipment'; 'use an indoor drying rack'), while others include more idiosyncratic advice ('Ditch the new year diet. It's not working'). But, as a template circulating among websites, the format of 'what you can do' can also be relied on as a form of generating and organizing data for social analysis.

We can thus decide to treat lists of 'what you can do' as providing inventories of 'environmentalized' everyday objects, and to try to detect variation in the kinds of things composing 'sustainable living' in different sites and settings. To structure the analysis, we can divide websites in two groupings:

1   Green living blogs, on which individuals document their or their household's attempts to lead a sustainable life.

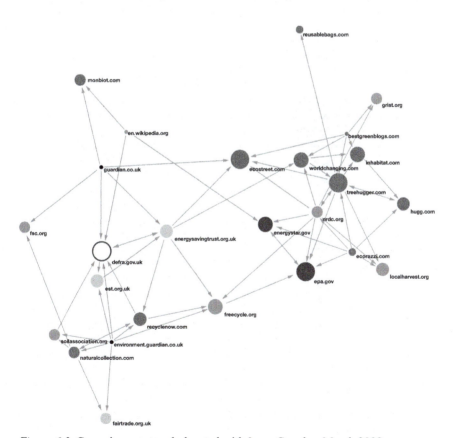

Figure 6.2 Green issue network, located with Issue Crawler, March 2008.

2 A green issue network, consisting of larger organizational websites, maintained by environmental organizations from the governmental, non-governmental and corporate sectors (see Figure 6.2).[14]

We can then select 'what you can do' pages from each of these sites, and extract key terms for each source set, categorizing these terms according to natural and technological kinds (food, technology, chemicals, energy, and so on). In order to bring variations into view, we list only terms that are unique to each of the two source sets, and code these terms according to four different modalities, from 'efficiency measures' to 'materials and natural sources', 'change of use' and 'infrastructural change' (see Figure 6.3 and the appendix for a brief description of the method used).

The resulting diagram shows variations of various sorts in the objects composing sustainable living in the two source sets. Thus, energy and services are big items in the green issue network, whereas food and things – products, appliances, materials – are more prominent on green living blogs. Furthermore, the issue network contains many more objects and activities qualified in terms of efficiency measures (saving, efficient, cost) than green living blogs, and

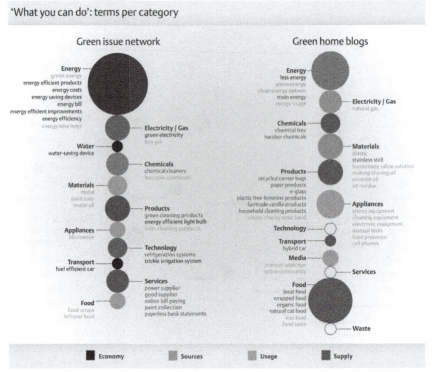

Figure 6.3 'What you can do: green blogs versus the green issue network', designed by Ludic Design.

Figure 6.4 'Spiral Drawing Sunrise: the finished work', Esther Polak (2009), photo: Esther Polak.

this qualification is especially prominent in relation to energy. Green living blogs, by contrast, include many more home-made things, from food to cleaning materials, and they focus on object of use rather than on infrastructural provisions. Such variation can of course be interpreted in various ways, but perhaps we can say that differing ontologies for sustainable living are being put forward by these websites: is it a matter of integrating energy into the service economy, or, rather, of reinventing 'domestic' modes of production such as craft? Web analysis here provides a way of artificially fixing such ontologies, presenting a simple snapshot of what in reality is a dynamic informational space, and rendering comparable what circulates in the absence of clear boundaries.

The living experiment as rendering device 2: the happening of the setting

The rendering of the variable objects composing everyday living is also the accomplishment of a rather different kind of living experiment, an artistic project called Spiral Drawing Sunrise. This experiment, in which I participated in the spring of 2009, was organized by the Amsterdam-based locative media artist, Esther Polak, and had the aim of recording a sunrise, in a public square in Amsterdam, with the aid of a sun-powered robot car, which might be called a 'phototropic' device or mobile hour glass (see Figure 6.4). As Esther explains in the video recording of that morning on the Frederiksplein in Amsterdam:

> The robot car runs on solar energy, it collects a given amount of light each time. When it has gathered enough energy, it will take a step. So you can see, this morning, that was at half past seven, it took much effort to make a lot of small steps, but slowly but surely it has been making bigger and bigger steps and now it's riding and here for instance you have the shade of a tree, so it's going a bit slower, and later on over there it will ride back into the sunlight.
>
> Esther Polak, Spiral Drawing Sunrise (6 April 2009)[15]

The cart was tied to a pole and continuously deposited sand (Esther kept refilling the bottle), which resulted in the spiral pattern, of which we later made prints using spray paint.

Like the living experiments discussed above, this experiment can be said to serve multiple purposes. It was an artistic experiment, which revolved around the idea of producing a record of a site-specific sunrise, and aimed to raise questions about the role of art in inserting technology in public spaces, and more specifically, the question of what happens to its relation with audiences and commissioners of art works in such a context. In this respect, this experiment had little to do with sustainable living in the usual sense of the term, but at the same time it resonated with both sustainable living experiments as well as with experimental social research. Thus, one could say Spiral Drawing Sunrise produced effects very similar to those of a sustainable living experiment: this experiment too involved the modification of everyday habits and habitats, as it introduced an odd technological setup in a square that people pass through every day (as I did myself for many years).

Second, even if the experiment's description that Esther Polak made available on the project's website did not refer to sustainability, the experiment did perform an operation that can be characterized in those terms: it provided a 'distant environment', namely the turning sun, with a tangible presence in the here and now. This fits very well with the technical definition of sustainability, namely to take objects, actors and effects that are distant in time and space into account in the here and now (Meadows *et al.*, 1972). Spiral Drawing Sunrise, then, could be read as a dispositif to render describable and thereby accountable people's relation with the sun. However, importantly it wouldn't be quite right, to say that Esther's experiment had the effect of rendering everyday living or its settings, relations, or objects 'accountable'. Or if it did so, it did so in a particular way. Spiral Drawing Sunrise rendered the setting as a place of activity. And this is also where it resonates with sociological experiments.

Sociologists have recognized in artistic happenings dynamics similar to those of sociological experiments – and more particularly, of Garfinkel's breaching experiments. For example, Alvin Gouldner has noted that there is 'a common impulse' behind the happening and ethnomethodological demonstrations. Describing a famous happening that took place in Amsterdam in the 1970s, involving the release of chickens into a street, he notes that this event involved the disruption of social life in a way similar to a sociological breaching experiment. In both cases, he noted, the aim is 'to bring routines to a halt, to make the world and time stop'. Now it is on precisely this point that Spiral Drawing Sunrise presents an interesting variation or elaboration on the sociological experiment: if this experiment can indeed be said to have disrupted everyday routines and settings in Amsterdam, it did so in a very different way from that described by Gouldner. Rather than bringing routines to a halt, and stopping time, Spiral Drawing Sunrise highlighted movements, of time and of the various entities passing through the square. As I put it on the project's blog:

> So, during this morning we do quite a bit of waiting, of sitting around, and as we sit watching, in a way we adopt the standpoint of this corner of the Frederiksplein. Somehow, the movement of this robot car going its snail-like way amplifies the movements in the square, the changes it is going through: trams passing, traffic picking up, and so on. It turns them into trajectories, and the square a space that unfolds through them. And perhaps these trajectories also 'accentuate' the solar path, becoming so many versions of it. Several of these entities go slow, but none as slow as the sun.
>
> Noortje Marres, Spiral Drawing Sunrise Log (23 May 2009)[16]

In alluding to this possibility, Esther's intervention displayed a rather different experimental dynamic from that described by Gouldner. This experiment did not so much disrupt usual ways of doing in the sense of making them practically impossible, of arresting their movement. Rather, inserting the robot cart into the setting of the public square had the effect of rendering this routine environment as a space of activity. And perhaps we could say that Spiral Drawing Sunrise managed to render the setting as a happening because it performed geometry in/as movement. As Michael Lynch has reminded us, geometry can be translated as 'space tracing' (Lynch, 1993), and Spiral Drawing Sunrise can be seen as performing geometry in this radically circumstantial – and/or perhaps indeed 'environmental' – way. The geometric shape of the spiral here came about through the movement of the sun shedding its light on the car's solar panels, and the car depositing sand.[17] And we might say that, in its spiralling movement, the robot car made room for the sun to exert its capacity to choreograph entities in time and space.

Spiral Drawing Sunrise could then be understood as exploring a different technique, or perhaps indeed method, of enacting sustainability: by rendering things remote in time and space in and as movement, it made them relevant to the here and now, and as such, 'the environment' here lost its more familiar passivity, its status as an 'external' blankness (Whatmore, 1999). Perhaps indeed the topic of sustainability itself was here turned into something rather more happening: not a static way of taking distant environments into account as part of everyday routines, but a technique for rendering 'the environment' as consisting of dynamic entities with trajectories particular to them.

Conclusion

To the extent, then, that versions of the sustainable living experiment multiply across social life, it can be seen to enable various operations of social research. Here I have argued that what is distinctive about the living experiment as a device of social research is that, as it circulates, it can be said to organize actors, practices, data for social research in particular ways. Insofar as it presents a format or template for action and information that proliferates across practices, the living experiment enables the rendering accountable of everyday objects, settings and action – something that ethnomethodologists and others have identified as an important accomplishment of social research. And this has implications for how we may put this device to our own social research purposes. On the one hand, in taking up sustainable living experiments as a research device, to study for instance the 'environmentalization' of everyday life, a researcher aligns himself or herself with an arrangement in which the roles of social research are performed by a variety of agencies. That is, it would be wrong to assume that the sociologist is the sole agent of social research in this situation: the work of the collection, organization and analysis of social data going on here can only be described as distributed labour, performed by a whole range of actors and devices.

However, it would not be quite right either to say that social actors, the journalists, mothers, engineers and policy-makers conducting these experiments, are here doing the work of social research for us: these experiments serve too many other purposes for that to be an adequate description. Indeed, insofar as living experiments are put to a multiplicity of purposes today, social research may have a critical role to play in their analysis. By adding its techniques and modes of research and analysis to those already deployed, social researchers may render or foreground different aspects of it. Thus, we can describe the multiple ontologies articulated in practices of 'living environmentally' and the alternative ways of organizing 'natural political economies' these open up. But we can also show how certain concepts, such as that of accountability, may be transformed in experimental practices across social life: as Spiral Drawing Sunrise made clear, everyday enactments of 'the environment' do not necessarily present it as a static fact to be taken into account, but may render it as a happening. In taking up living experiments as a research device, social research may then produce accounts diverging from those in circulation; but it does so not by opposing, but by aligning itself with researching arrangements that are configuring in/as social practice.

Appendix: 'what you can do', methods used

1 Manually extract pages on 'what you can do' from the sites in the issue network and from green living blogs.
2 Extract terms from these pages with the aid of the textual extraction and analysis application 'Open Calais' (using only industry terms).
3 Manually categorize terms, and count mentionings per category.
4 Use a 'Dorling Visualizer' tool to visualize the relative sizes of categories.
5 Use the 'Analyzer' tool to determine unique terms per category per source set.
6 Manually mark up these unique terms using four values: economy, supply, usage and service.
7 Display unique terms per category per source set.

For tools, see www.digitalmethods.nl.

Notes

1 The author would like to acknowledge the following contributions. The analysis of sustainable living blogs was performed together with Erik Borra, Esther Weltevrede, Michael Stevenson, and Rosa Menkman of the Digital Methods Group at the University of Amsterdam. The figures were designed by Christian Thumer and Matthew Falla, and Marieke van Dijk provided initial ideas. Thanks to Matthew Fuller, Philip Hill, Celia Lury, Esther Polak, Richard Rogers, and Steve Woolgar for suggestions and comments.
2 'As it is useful that while mankind is imperfect there should be different opinions, so is it that there should be different experiments of living; that free scope should be given to varieties of character, short of injury to others; and that the worth of different modes of life should be proved practically, when any one thinks fit to try them'. (Mill, 1859/2002: 58)
3 The term equally resonates with more large-scale attempts to build environmental communities, such as the UK Garden Cities of the early twentieth century where people were to reconnect with nature in buildings open to the skies and built from local materials (Carter, 2007). Perhaps most familiarly, sustainable living was a pivotal genre of American-style post-1960 counter-culture green (Kirk, 2007).
4 No Impact Man, 'What you need to know', 22 February 2007, http://noimpactman. typepad.com/blog/2007/02/what_you_need_t.html (accessed 30 April 2010).
5 Green-as-a-Thistle, 'Hopelessly fridgeless (Day 78)', 17 May 2007 http:// greenasathistle.com/2007/05/17/hopelessly-fridgeless-day-78/ (accessed 30 April 2010). Suitably Despairing, '37 Consequences of Going Green', 26 November 2007, http://suitablydespairing.blogspot.com/2007/11/37-consequences-of-going-green.html (accessed 30 April 2010).
6 There are more similarities. Sustainable living experiments, such as breaching experiments, are not so much concerned with the testing of hypotheses, but rather use experiments as aids to 'the sluggish imagination' (Lynch, 1993). In this respect, one could argue that sustainable living experiments 'ethno-methodologize' ethnomethodology itself. While ethnomethodologists tended to reserve the capacity to 'breach' social life for themselves, in sustainable living experiments all sorts of social actors can be said to make this type of intervention.
7 These arguments about the multiple purposes served by experiments, notably developed in actor-network theory (ANT), also imply a particular understanding of the experiment as a site for the redistribution of research. In actor-network

theory's account of the experiment, it figures as a location for the redistribution of theory formation, namely as a site where ontologies come about. Furthermore, ANT approaches the experiment as a site for building social support for science, suggesting that audiences and social actors play a more active role in the societal embedding of science than conventional theories of knowledge tend to recognize. My account of the experiment as a multifarious instrument draws on these arguments about the redistribution of the roles of research in experimental practice, even if I treat them separately in this chapter.

8   This is how the OED defines multifariousness: 'what inappropriately or confusingly embraces two or more distinct matters'. One could argue that experiments have long been ascribed this feature in the sociology and philosophy of science. Thus, the philosopher of science Pierre Duhem (1906/1982) famously proposed that it is not always possible, in scientific experiments, to distinguish clearly between the empirical content of experimental hypotheses, and their theoretical framework.

9   Suitably Despairing, http://suitablydespairing.blogspot.com/ (accessed 30 April 2010).

10 Debates are ongoing about the implications of the rise of digital technologies such as search engines and blogging for knowledge cultures and the politics of knowledge: Who is allowed access to data? Who can scrutinize which methods are deployed? Who is allowed to modify those methods? However, these debates are mostly not conducted in the vocabulary of social research, but rather in the legal, moral and political languages of intellectual property rights and democracy (Kelty, 2008). The question in this regard is what social research may contribute to such debates. Here I am highlighting that it makes possible an alternative reading of the implications of digitization for research cultures: rather than saying that digitization enables *either* the privatization or the 'democratization' of social research – as in the slogan 'we are all social researchers now' – I am foregrounding the *redistribution* of social research capacities among specific actors.

11 This research was performed as part of the Digital Methods summer workshop in 2009, at the University of Amsterdam.

12 An ontology of multiplicity highlights that things are 'more than one but less than many', to use Mol's (2002) phrase. It is often said that such multiple ontologies precisely do *not* display the neat divisions among separate entities, which comparative analysis seems to require (Strathern, 2004). It is one of the reasons why I characterize social research here as a way of *rendering* ontologies enacted in practice – i.e. to render them comparable involves an 'arteficial' intervention on the part of social research.

13 The endless but rather minimal variations on the theme of green tips on the Web is part of the reason why it can be called an 'information format' – or indeed an 'action template' – and it seems significant the two can be conflated in this instance. One can also think here of the drive to extract information about actors' everyday activities through the collection and analysis of transactional or registrational data (Savage and Burrows, 2007; Rogers, 2009; Ruppert, 2009), with living experiments offering a publicity genre for actors to capture and publicize such data.

14 This network was located with the aid of Issue Crawler, a Web-based tool for network analysis developed by the govcom.org Foundation Amsterdam. We used active, English-language green living blogs as starting points. Issue Crawler crawls hyperlinks going out from these starting points, performs co-link analysis and demarcates a network on this basis (www.issuecrawler.net).

15 Frederiksplein Video, posted 22 May 2009 by Esther Polak, Spiral Drawing Sunrise, http://spiraldrawingsunrise.wordpress.com/ (accessed 30 April 2010).

16 Noortje Marres, 'How long does a sunrise last', posted 23 May 2009, http://spiraldrawingsunrise.wordpress.com/2009/05/23/noortje-marres-log-2-2-during/#more-276 (accessed 30 April 2010).

17 The spiral seems a perfectly suitable form for performing geometry as movement: 'the spiral is not so much a shape, as the evidence of a shape in formation' (Aranda and Lasch, 2009) But in contrast to Aranda and Lash's formal description of the spiral, an ethnomethodologist would emphasize the circumstantiality of method in ths case too. It then becomes noteworthy that Esther would help the winding process by moving the pole slightly, to make sure that the cart's trajectory would pass over the sheets of paper, which we had taped to the ground to record the cart's path. Such circumstantial interventions, we could argue, are here positively constitutive of the performance of method. In this regard, it should also be noted that Spiral Drawing Sunrise runs on an algorithm: one that stipulates the treshhold of stored energy at which the robot cart will start to move (until its battery is empty). Spiral Drawing Sunrise then demonstrates the cirumstantiality of this 'recipe for action' more specifically: it provides a indication of the range of entities that must come into play before the algorithm can 'work', that is, before it can assist in the rendering of a setting as a happening.

References

Adkins, L. and Lury, C. (2009) 'Introduction', in L. Adkins and C. Lury (eds) 'What is the empirical?', Special Issue, *European Journal of Social Theory*, 12 (1): 5–20.

Aranda, B. and Lasch, C. (2006) *Tooling, Pamphlet Architecture 27*, New York: Princeton Architectural Press.

Barry, A. (2001) *Political Machines: Governing a Technological Society*, London: Athlone Press.

Button, G. (1991) 'Introduction', in G. Button (ed.) *Ethnomethodology and the Human Sciences: A Foundational Reconstruction*, Cambridge: Cambridge University Press, pp. 1–9.

Callon, M., Courtial, J-P., Turner, W. and Bauin, S. (1983) 'From translations to problematic networks: an introduction to co-word analysis', *Social Science Information*, 22 (2): 191–235.

Callon, M., Lascoumes, P. and Barthe, Y. (2001) *Agir dans un monde incertain. Essai sur la démocratie technique*, Paris: Seuil.

Carter, S. (2007) *Rise and Shine: Sunlight, Technology and Health*, Oxford: Berg Publishers.

Duhem, P. (1906/1982) 'Physical theory and experiment', in *The Aim and Structure of Physical Theory*, Princeton, NJ: Princeton University Press, pp. 180–218.

Filmer, P. (2003) 'On Harold Garfinkel's ethnomethodology', in M. Lynch and W. Sharrock (eds) *Harold Garfinkel, Sage Masters in Modern Social Thought*, London: Sage.

Garfinkel, H. (1967/1984) *Studies in Ethnomethodology*, Oxford and Cambridge: Polity Press.

Gouldner, A. W. (1970) 'Ethnomethodology: sociology as happening', in *The Coming Crises of Western Sociology*, London and New York: Basic Books, pp. 390–5.

Grosz, E. (2005) *Time Travels: Feminism, Nature, Power*, Durham, NC: Duke University Press.

Hankins, T. and Silverman, R. (1995) *Instruments and the Imagination*, Princeton, NJ: Princeton University Press.

Hawkins, G. (2006) *The Ethics of Waste: How We Relate to Rubbish*, Lanham, MD: Rowman & Littlefield Publishers.

Heyting, L. (1994) *De Wereld in een Dorp: Schilders, schrijvers en wereldverbeteraars in Laren en Blaricum 1880–1920*, Amsterdam: Meulenhoff.

Kelty, C. (2008) *Two Bits: The Cultural Significance of Software*, Durham, NC: Duke University Press.

Kirk, A. (2007) *Counterculture Green: The Whole Earth Catalog and American Environmentalism*, Lawrence, KS: University Press of Kansas.

Latour, B. (1988) *The Pasteurization of France*, trans. A. Sheridan and J. Law, Cambridge, MA: Harvard University Press.

Latour, B. 'Thought experiments in social science: from the social contract to virtual society', 1st Virtual Society? Annual Public Lecture, Brunel University, 1 April 1998.

Law, J. and Urry, J. (2003) 'Enacting the social', *Economy and Society*, 33 (3): 390–410.

Lynch, M. (1991) 'Method: measurement – ordinary and scientific measurement as ethnomethodological phenomena', in G. Button (ed.) *Ethnomethodology and the Human Sciences*, Cambridge: Cambridge University Press, pp. 77–108.

Lynch, M. (1993) *Scientific Practice and Ordinary Action: Ethnomethodology and Social Studies of Science*, New York: Cambridge University Press.

Marres, N. (2006) 'Net-work is format work: issue networks and the sites of civil society politics', in J. Dean, J. Asherson and G. Lovink (eds) *Reformatting Politics: Networked Communications and Global Civil Society*, London: Routledge, pp. 3–18.

Marres, N. (2009) 'Testing powers of engagement: green living experiments, the ontological turn and the undoability of involvement', in L. Adkins and C. Lury (eds) 'What is the empirical?', Special Issue, *European Journal of Social Theory*, 12 (1): 117–133.

Meadows, D., Meadows, D., Randers, J. and Behrens, W. (1972) *Limits to Growth: A Report for the Club of Rome's Project on the Predicament of Mankind*, New York: Universe Books.

Michael, M. (2006) *Techno-Science and Everyday Life: The Complex Simplicities of the Mundane*, Milton Keynes: Open University Press.

Mill, J. S. (1859/2002) 'On individuality, as one of the elements of wellbeing', in *On Liberty: The Basic Writings of John Stuart Mill*, New York: The Modern Library, pp. 57–76.

Mol, A. (2002) *The Body Multiple: Ontology in Medical Practice*, Durham, NC: Duke University Press.

Murphy, M. (2006) *Building Sickness Syndrome and the Problem of Uncertainty: Environmental Politics, Technoscience and Women's Workers*, Durham, NC: Duke University Press.

Rogers, R. (2009) *The End of the Virtual: Digital Methods*, Amsterdam: Amsterdam University Press.

Rowbotham, S. (2008) *Edward Carpenter: A Life of Liberty and Love*, London and New York: Verso Books.

Ruppert, E. (2009) 'Identification technologies and the interpassive citizen', paper presented during CRESC workshop Science and Citizens, Open University, Milton Keynes, 1–2 April 2009.

Savage, M. and Burrows, R. (2007) 'The coming crisis of empirical sociology', *Sociology*, 41 (5): 885–99.

Shapin, S. and Schaffer, S. (1989) *Leviathan and the Air-pump: Hobbes, Boyle, and the Experimental Life*, Princeton, NJ: Princeton University Press.

Stengers, I. (2000) *The Invention of the Modern Sciences*, Minneapolis, MN: University of Minnesota Press.

Strathern, M. (2004) *Partial Connections*, updated version, Walnut Creek, CA: AltaMira.

Thoreau, H. (1854/2000) 'Walden', in *Walden and Other Writings*, New York: Modern Library Classics, pp. 23–231.

Weltevrede, E. (n.d.) 'Studying society, not Google. Repurposing Google for social and cultural research', Department of Media Studies, University of Amsterdam.

Whatmore, S. (1999) *Hybrid Geographies*, London: Sage.

Whatmore, S. (2009) 'Mapping knowledge controversies: science, democracy and the redistribution of expertise', *Progress in Human Geography*, 33 (5): 587–598.

7 List

Andrea Phillips

What is a list? The question is apparently simple and comes with an immediate visual predicate: a list is a set of words organized in a column, sometimes in an order (numerical, alphabetical, temporal, related to value, etc.) and sometimes at random. Lists are general, appearing across strata of organizations from the personal to the institutional: lists of domestic jobs, lists of professional tasks, lists of offers, lists of currency, lists of global statistics, lists of code. As I write, I have a list next to me (as do you as you read, no doubt): finish the article, do the ironing, cancel the meeting, vacuum the house, book the ticket, pay the bill, plan the workshop, write the abstract, collect the children, cook the supper . . . Speaking at once of the technicity of my/your life and the endlessness of our labour, my/your list both absorbs and refracts the stressful intensities of our openings and closings, gaps and double bookings, opportunities and frustrations. They are, of course, blank to us, no help and yet of absolute help. We list at the beginning of the day, at the end of the day, when we are confused, when we need to defer things, when we cannot defer things any longer. In the paradoxically self-annulling character of contemporary immateriality, we no longer need others to impose the list upon us. We do it to ourselves, as Boltanski and Chiapello observe, we do it artistically, as the open spaces of creative freedom demanded by a previous generation of cultural critics are recuperated through forms of advanced capitalism by and in which we utilize our own artistic capacities and skills of autonomous organization to produce more effectively (Boltanski and Chiapello, 2005).

Primarily, lists have a function that can be described as economic in both a cultural and fiscal sense; they provide – or promise to provide – rationalizations of scale, time and space within our lives and those of others, and they do so through contemporary preferences for modes of organization and milieus of practice. Lists are supposed to save time (and money). Lists are distillations of the maps of activity, accumulation, sociability, enterprise, aspiration that motivate action in the widest sense, but they also precede mapping, stand in for mapping, defer the mapping of the organization of the self to some other time and place (the end of the day, the end of the week, the end of the year, the beginning of the future, etc.). While a list might have physical or virtual depth – it might be a series of tiles or links on a web page, for example, or a pile of filing cards – it is usually a spatial device, and one, of course, that has inbuilt (often frustrating) revolution. Closed lists exist on a nominal basis – a list of contents, a list of titles, a list of war dead, an index or codex – but here the function of the list is to always remain partially open in the apprehension of discovery or change (a man is discovered to have survived, an unknown manuscript is revealed, new reference is discovered, etc.). A rolling 'to-do' list haunts contemporary life – from the mundanity of organizing daily practice to the precarious politics of means without ends, offering us opportunities for networked and heterogeneous action (and here the transmogrification of the list into a set of friend-contacts via social networking sites is emblematic). At the same time, 'to-do lists' keep us busy from those 'old fashioned' concerns whereby their contents might reveal a register of power and powerlessness, inclusion and exclusion, access and its lack.

This dynamic capacity of lists to be both open and closed, to suggest both action and the ordering of action, to mark the now ingrained enmeshing of work, play, time on, time off, personal and official orders of behaviour and labour, makes them attractive devices. The attraction is conceptual, affective and aesthetic. But the same attraction to devices that are malleable, that would suggest the enablement of types of paradoxical activity, functions as a sign of the erosive imaginary of contemporary power, and its consistent reinvention of the tools through which it produces its capital.

In advanced capitalist states of labour relations, Weberian definitions of the bureaucratic organization of a clear work/life divide in which official activity takes place within the regime of an office that is segregated from the private sphere have become indistinguished. The dispositif of this indistinction is the list. Whereas in Weber's office (factory, bureau, etc.) work was regulated through abstracted structures of achievement that guaranteed, at least in theory and for Weber with ambivalent results, a distantiated hierarchy of bureaucratic order and authority unsullied by autarchic systems of favour, the shift towards what Richard Sennett identifies as the 'willingness to destabilize one's own institution' through forms of liberal, distributive planning results in a set of contradictions encapsulated by the list (Sennett, 2006: 41). If at one time the list of things to do was imposed, and the worker might well be punished for failing to complete the list, at another (nominally our) time the authority for completion is ours, and failure turns inwards in forms of self-governmentalization that promise to value our resourcefulness and at the same time, as Sennett rightly observes, divorces our displaced and disguised authority from power (ibid.: 62).

In their study of the relation between new forms of immaterial labour organization and developments of neo-liberal capitalism through shifting structures in the organization of work, Luc Boltanski and Eve Chiapello describe a newly emergent subject, 'who is mobile, streamlined, possessed of the art of establishing and maintaining numerous diverse, enriching connections, and of the ability to extend networks'. (Boltanski and Chiapello, 2005: 355). This subject emerges through the absorption of critical attitudes towards the advancement of capitalism (that in order to produce capital, workers and their institutions must be homogenized, hierarchized, subordinated and unequal) into the system of capitalist production itself. In particular, Boltanski and Chiapello label the critique that is absorbed as artistic, pointing to the values championed by artists at the end of the 1960s (and in this they use the term 'artistic' in a very general sense) that prioritized liberation, egalitarianism and freedom of autonomous, creative action. The consumption of this in the 'neo-management mechanisms' and 'especially the self-management movement' of the 1980s and 1990s produces institutional subjects that practice:

> the qualities that are guarantees of success in this new spirit [of capitalism] – autonomy, spontaneity, rhizomorphous capacity, multitasking (in contrast to the narrow specialization of the old division of labour), conviviality, openness to others and novelty, availability, creativity, visionary intuition, sensitivity to differences, listening to lived experience and receptiveness to a whole range of experiences, being attracted to informality and the search for interpersonal contacts.
>
> (ibid.: 97)

For Boltanski and Chiapello, the exemplars, the experts, of this way of working are artists. If they take as their model those radical creative individuals who emerged from May 1968 to develop into the liberal capitalists of the 1980s and 1990s and to invent such novel formations of artistic-capital management for themselves and their employees (the authors cite management gurus such as Peter Drucker and Rosabeth Moss Kanter as examples; the effect of Mitterand's rebranded socialism is also an important example for the authors, locating their argument at times too intractably within a Francophone context), it is easy to see how the ensuing internalization of the conceptualization of capital has emerged not simply through artistic methodologies, but also as art across a similar time period. Much contemporary art, in which relationality and participation are dominant tropes, serves as both an embodiment and illustration of the recuperation of hegemonic organizational structures in the form of ambivalently designed environments and structures (the work of artists such as Liam Gillick, Pierre Huyghe, Elmgreen and Dragset or Iza Genzken are primary examples of this). As Suhail Malik has pointed out, '[contemporary artists'] non-alienated work and informal sociality and exhibition structures are emblematic of the heightened invention of destructured professionalization. Artists are the heroes of the new spirit of capitalism' (Malik, 2006: 41).

Listing, too, is artistic; self-regulated, inventive, adaptable, etc. – it is an activity that joins the stages of this transformation together – from the oppressive and imposed list of Weberian capital analysis to the informal and immaterial processes of labour available to workers in globally advanced capital economies in which it stands as an opportunity (a list of contacts that make a network, a list of potential clients, a list of friends that also constitute a set of economic relations, etc.). The subject of and worker in these environmental conditions (the lister) mimics the shape and form of financial/or all markets in his or her flexibility and mobility. He or she, just as his or her fiscal corollary the market, is able to profit by the manipulation and movement of lists. Movement is essential to continued success. The same open and tolerant socius that produces the potential for heterogeneity also produces the supra-inegalitarianism of new capital. Both proceed via lists.

This double action of the list is mirrored at a structural and linguistic level in Foucault's conception of the dispositif (usually translated as apparatus or device), wherein the paradoxical formats of power involved in its utilization are consistently made manifest:

> With the notion of the apparatus, I find myself in a difficulty which I haven't yet been properly able to get out of. I said that the apparatus is essentially of a strategic nature, which means assuming that it is a matter of a certain manipulation of relations of forces, either developing them in a particular direction, blocking them, stabilizing them, utilizing them, etc. The apparatus is thus always inscribed in a play of power, but it is also always linked to certain coordinates of knowledge which issue from it but, to an equal degree, condition it. This is what the apparatus consists in: strategies of relations of forces supporting, and supported by, types of knowledge.
>
> (Foucault, 1980: 196)

If a dispositif is a mechanism of precarity, it is also one that acts within the power relations of that precarity (this is its 'difficulty'). It is, for Foucault, 'the system of relations that can be established between [. . .] elements' (ibid.:194). As a dispositif, a device, a list is thus a system of relations between elements, those elements being both the contents of any list – the task of ironing, the ordering of the stock market, the alphabetic of the dead – and the structures to which they are linked – the social tensions of private and public labour, the organization of transnational fiscal accumulation and profit, the memorialization of participants in wars of 'national security', etc. Any list performs across registers, its seductive format offering solutions through ordering and naming.[1]

If a list is a dispositif that performs explicitly under the artistic conditions of new capitalism, and if art is generally recognized as a method through which the devices of general cultural and/or social production are held up for (often ambivalently staged) scrutiny, then it is not surprising that artists have produced lists as art. Equally unremarkable is the fact that this experimentation has occurred over the decades that approximate the shift from material to immaterial labour, from the hierarchical divisions of labour to the situated indistinctions performed through informality, flexibility and adaptability that now reconstitute those hierarchies of power. The conceptual turn of art and capital mimic each other, as do the devices with which they invent and maintain themselves. In an attempt to illustrate this compatibility, I propose the figure of Richard Serra, an artist, and here a dispositif, for the performance of the list as art and as the figure of artistic capital. Serra is emblematic not simply because he made a famous work from a written list, but because his career spans the decades through which practices of immaterial labour, arguments over the status of objects and commodities within fiscalized economies and revisions of the value of cultural self-making have developed.

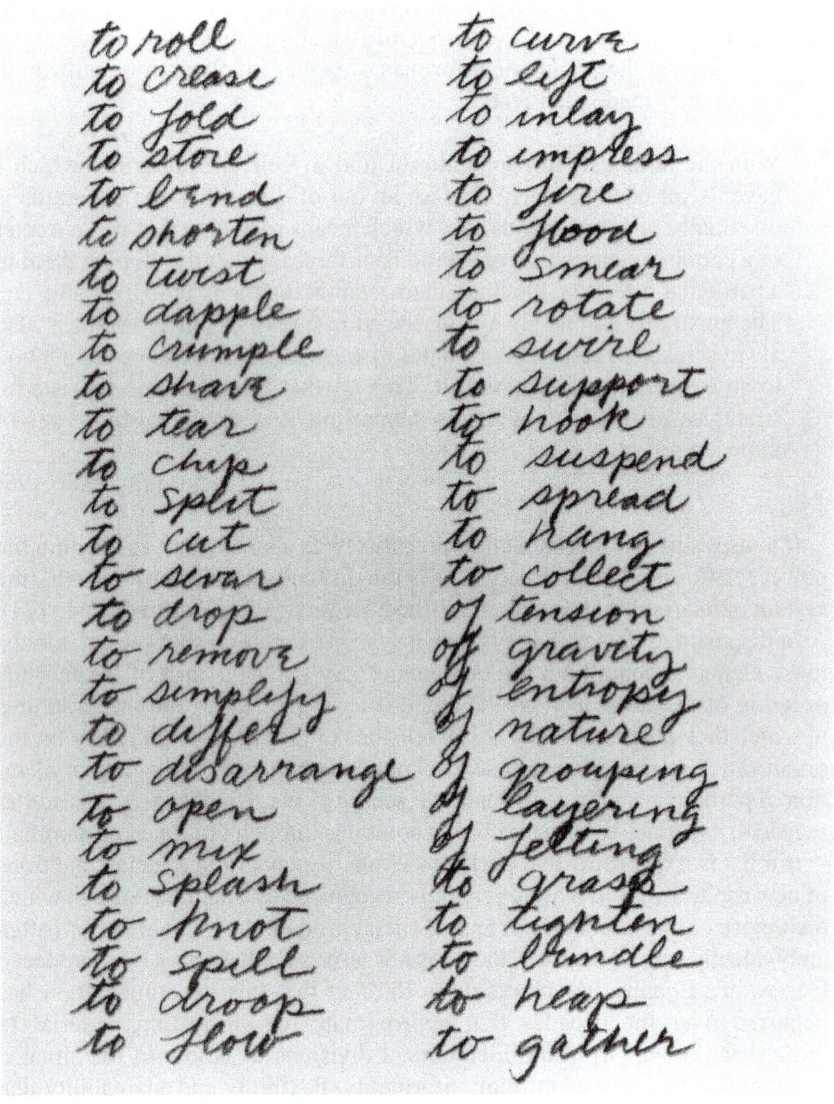

Figure 7.1 Richard Serra, *Verb List Compilation: Actions to Relate to Oneself* (1967–68). (© Richard Serra. Courtesy Gagosian Gallery.)

Serra's *Verb List Compilation: Actions to Relate to Oneself* (1967–68) consists of a column of verbs in prepositional form handwritten on a sheet of paper, reminiscent of the repetitive rote-learning activity that once dominated grammatical education in the classroom. The work was originally presented in published form in a book, but has since been exhibited widely as both a stand-alone artwork and a document that describes the shifting terms of materiality in Serra's – and other artist's – work then and now. The handwritten original is often presented alongside a more legible version in typescript. The actions described are directly related to activities Serra was engaged in his

to scatter
to arrange
to repair
to discard
to pair
to distribute
to surfeit
to complement
to enclose
to surround
to encircle
to hide
to cover
to wrap
to dig
to tie
to bind
to weave
to join
to match
to laminate
to bond
to hinge
to mark
to expand
to dilute
to light

to modulate
to distill
of waves
of electromagnetic
of inertia
of ionization
of polarization
of refraction
of simultaneity
of tides
of reflection
of equilibrium
of symmetry
of friction
to stretch
to bounce
to erase
to spray
to systematize
to refer
to force
of mapping
of location
of context
of time
of carbonization
to continue

studio at the time but they also exemplify an engagement with 'everyday' manual labour indicative of the way in which many artists in the 1950s and 1960s sought to destabilize – and distance themselves from – notions of beaux-arts training.

Verb List appears as both a conceptual artwork, wherein the lack of elite value of its materials underscores its speculative potential, and as a theoretical and descriptive text, published in collections of the artist's writing and catalogues and historical surveys of conceptual art.[2] Its transitive status – part art writing, part instruction manual, part aesthetic object – runs parallel to a set of experiments that Serra was carrying out in his studio at the time.[3]

Peter Osborne describes the tense of *Verb List* as 'the perpetual participal present', a work that is dependent upon its title to establish 'relations to acts of . . . production within the frozen objecthood of . . . results' (Osborne, 2002: 22). Comparing *Verb List* with other works made with lists of instructions as their material by Yoko Ono and Robert Morris, Osborne describes *Verb List* in relation to theatricality:

> Freed from musical or dramatic conventions of performance, and open to interpretation in performance by anyone, instruction pieces are unbounded, in principle, by any particular context. This both draws attention to the indeterminacy or infinity inherent in their linguistic expression and confers a participatory dimension to the work, requiring its audience to 'complete' it, albeit only in this instance and often only imaginatively.
>
> (ibid.: 22–3)

In interviews, Serra has talked of his interest in the 'logic of materials', developing a commitment to the relationship between materiality and the body (his and the viewers') at a time when other critics were involved in the conceptual production and ideologically driven dematerialization of art. The list here stands as a device that allows the artist to move precisely between materialization and dematerialization: if, on the one hand, the work is prag-matically and perceptively insubstantial, proposing a presentness of action over stasis of object, it is also a proposition to get hold of material and make things substantially, in concrete form.

Now best known for *Titled Arc* (1981–89), the monumental rusted steel sculpture sited in, then removed from, Federal Plaza in New York, Serra worked from the age of 16 in steelworks in the Bay Area in order to fund his way through art school. He has consistently described his methodology in direct relation to this experience of large-scale industrial production. He continues to work with steel, and those verbs with which he could be said to have started – roll, fold, bend, twist, etc. – are still clearly present in his work, albeit in highly literal form.

> When I first started, what was very, very important to me was dealing with the nature of process. So what I had done is I'd written a verb list: to roll,

to fold, to cut, to dangle, to twist . . . and I really just worked out pieces in relation to the verb list physically in a space. Now, what happens when you do that is you don't become involved with the psychology of what you're making, nor do you become involved with the after image of what it's going to look like. So, basically it gives you a way of proceeding with material in relation to body movement, in relation to making, that divorces from any notion of metaphor, any notion of easy imagery.

(Serra, n.d.)

Serra's claim has always been that of a relation to unalienated labour, to processes of work of a certain order in which crafting is recognized as the primary tool of artistic endeavour (this fantasy of hard physical labour as both unalienated and true to materiality is a myth that pervaded Northern American minimalism, documented acerbically in Anna Chave's 1990 essay 'Minimalism and the rhetoric of power'[4]). *Verb List* now appears as an anomaly in a career spent building edifices to a bygone industrial age, unless one reads it in purely pragmatic terms: a to-do list of actions to perform upon, say, a large slab of steel. But *Verb List* is never simply a to-do list, however pragmatically the artist might claim his singular relation to the body, to material (and no matter how effectively it apes the form). Rather, its ability to be a to-do list is limited by its ontological status as an art object: a simple but important founding condition.

Figure 7.2 Richard Serra, *The Matter of Time*, Guggenheim Bilbao, 2005.

Verb List, in many ways the most contemporary work Serra has ever produced (far more in sync with contemporary artists' production, say, than the artist's monuments), expresses that which Jacques Rancière describes as 'the absolute singularity of art', which 'at the same time, destroys any pragmatic criterion for isolating this singularity', by which he recognizes contemporary art's ability to appear as both an absolutely irregular artefact within the world at the same time as being constituted by and through regular artefacts and images. Art in what Rancière calls the 'aesthetic regime' (a distinction made on the basis of the need to disassociate the political structure of art's instantiation that interests Rancière from the more didactic or representational work of artists who attempt to illustrate political concerns through their work, as well as in order to describe the performative relationship between art and its discourses) 'destroy[s] the mimetic barrier that distinguished ways of doing and making affiliated with art from other ways of doing and making, a barrier that separated its rules from the order of social occupations' (Rancière, 2004: 23). Serra exemplifies the performance of this indistinction, whereby the acts of writing, working, rolling, folding, spilling, etc. are proposed by the artist and his interpreters as modes of shared knowledge.

The enduring commitment to a relation between materiality and immanence that Serra shares with many artists of a younger generation can here be seen as paradigmatic. Rather than being a device that enables someone to do something, the *Verb List* is, then, a device that performs itself; performs production rather than produces. Here both the limitations of art's ability to produce relations beyond itself and arguments over the political potential of immateriality come together.

The paradox of listing as at once endless ('unbound' in Osborne's terms) and restrictive is the founding interest for artists searching for devices that might develop recognitions of the materiality of practices across social disciplines – Jacques Rancière's 'distribution of the sensible' in literal form is here played out as Serra produces a mimicry of industrial labour that at once alienates artistic forms of production from their relation to everyday life and instantiates the synchronic play of labour across any number of unlimited fields (ibid.: 12). The restrictive aspect of listing is here matched by a repetitive and skilful playfulness; by the act of turning a list into an art. But, as has been established, lists are also homogenizing and powerful devices. This contradiction between boundlessness and stricture, performed by a list, is put into play by my second example, in which art's attempted emancipation from a restrictive and locatable ontology is met by the powerful flexibility of the art's other motivating factor – capital.

The Artfacts ranking to be found at www.artfacts.net/index.php/pageType/ artists/lang/1 changes daily. It is a literal list that uses numerical data to place artists in an order of value. Artists are ranked according to the number and status of their current exhibitions and, since exhibition value is widely regarded as a powerful predicate for market value, the Artfacts list is promoted as a tool

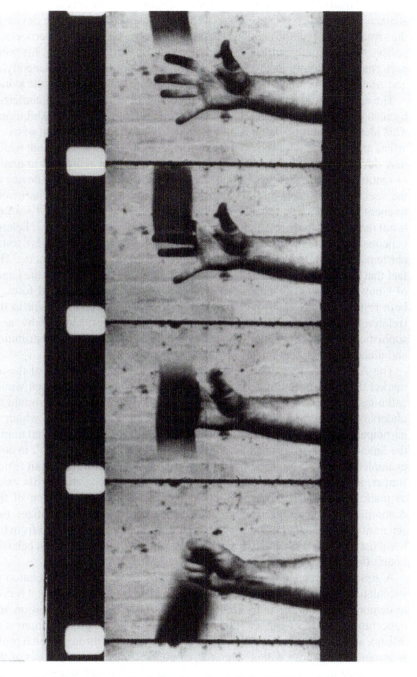

Figure 7.3 Richard Serra, *Hand Catching Lead*, 1968. (© Richard Serra. Courtesy Gagosian Gallery.)

of market analysis and investment choice. Thousands of artists are ranked on Artfacts, and as such it is promoted as an inclusive and democratic device in the same way that public auctions are promoted as mechanisms of meritocratic parity. At the time of writing, Serra's ranking on Artfacts is high; his work performs consistently in this register, with much on display permanently in and around high-profile public museums and private galleries across the world.

The art market is governed by the distinctions of value and taste conferred by such lists with their direct relation to the promotion of artists via exhibitions. This idea of exhibition value is of course vastly contradictory to that of many artists and curators who see exhibitions as spaces in which and through which new devices of the social might emerge and be tested or rehearsed in denial or ignorance of the fact that capital's listing is a dominant framing device of the social that in itself outruns art on a regular basis in terms of its inventiveness and economic reliance on novelty. While a work such as *Verb List* is not recognized in direct relation to the Artfacts ranking (its display is heterogeneous and too regular for the spectacularization the market demands), it still participates in the making of value – capital, conceptual and aesthetic. The fact that *Verb List* is available for anyone to view and download on the pages of Ubuweb and that its materiality is insubstantial, even in original form, is both testament to Serra's ongoing though contradictory commitment to the (relatively free) accessibility of certain of his images and the by now sophisticated understanding of the relation between partially free distribution and niche branding that underpins the art market as a whole.[5]

The Artfacts ranking list is evidence of the invisible mutations of the art market that repurpose old versions of labour into what Saskia Sassen would call a networked assemblage of capital devices; virtually, lists.[6] It should be understood in terms of the economies of transnationalism in which it participates: here the list gains authority from forms of speculation that mimic the finance sector and protect the value of the art sector. The 'art list', in both examples, is thus to be recognized for its paradoxical performance but is not. Rather, art's status as an inventor of cultural value is separated by its value as market value, and the separation defines the ethos and function of the economics that keep art in circulation. The art list, then, dramatizes this separation, as the apparatus through which it is made is disconnected from the fiscal list in which it is valued as a commodity (albeit a commodity that behaves in an often obscure way).

A similar misrecognition – or disconnection – is performed in relation to speculation. The art list has a special relation to the speculative in that it serves to demonstrate both the indeterminate process of guesswork, estimation and opportunism the term implies (this could be said to be the primary interest of artists), and the fact of speculation as an ordering system through which profit is assembled by those with a share (or, of course, shares) on the basis of the labour (both immaterial and alienated) of those that have no share. However, as exemplified by *Verb List*, if this relation were to be recognized – if forms of speculation were to be brought together, a certain devaluation would occur.

If Serra's *Verb List* is an example of an artist attempting to rescue a device from its mundane position in the world in order to reconstitute or capture its aesthetic credibility, the artist's position on the Artfacts list exemplifies, in turn, the conflicted nature of such artistic gestures. This conflict occurs at both a political and ontological level. Artistic gestures as such are consistently striated by the elite mechanisms and economies that sustain their separation from the world. The conditions of production of such devices in art do so at the behest of an economy of alienation that is rarely acknowledged, even when artists turn to dispositifs that enable a relation, broadly, to the realm of the social (for this is what the list does).

Such interdisciplinarity suggests that devices can be turned into the objects of art with ease, and vice versa, but such a premise has political and aesthetic consequences. If the supposition is that art illustrates or exemplifies an equalization between the flexible procedures of artistic invention and the 'plays of power' and 'coordinates of knowledge' that Foucault describes as devices, then the device is rendered problematically as a new political tool the role of which is to act as a mute but quixotic translating implement unencumbered by the problematics of power that it might also serve to instantiate. Artists who ontologize devices in the name of workerist emancipation – Serra and his minimalist contemporaries from the 1960s on one level, a full range of contemporary practices geared towards social engagement on another – do so only to further fantasize the relation between creative freedom and the mundane oppressions of everyday life: by, in other words, suggesting a set of flexibilities that are not available outside the art world and its market, but suggesting them as proper exemplifications of everyday life.

This paradox between use and aestheticization demonstrates the finite potential of art to intercede in an environment and alter social relations, provide services, extend welfare – although these are the aspirations of many contemporary artists on a more or less abstracted level. Thus the concept of a device (a list, an experiment, an archive, a joke, a party, an instruction, a walk, etc.) in contemporary art is double edged. While, on the one hand, artists and their institutions uphold the phenomenological concept of an artefact (an image, an object, a collection) as a productive force in its own right, on the other, the logic of the intra- and transdisciplinary research many artists involve themselves in as part of the process of establishing their work would suggest that an artefact might subscribe to a number of ontological definitions, often concurrently or opportunistically, and this 'ontological precariousness' is the condition of contemporary artistic production – its difference (Bourriaud, 2009: 32). If, as many artists, curators and academics articulate, art is a process of socially situated research influenced by its contact with other disciplines, other geographies, etc., then art is also the production of artefacts whose fiscal and eschatological imperative is towards novel and unique discretion.

Both within the art academy/gallery and at its borders with other disciplines, then, there is both an invitation and a rejection of the acknowledgement of the inclusivity of visual culture and a fear that art objects might be turned from discrete entities into illustrations of something else. This fear emanates from both artistic traditions (rooted in the individualized crafting that Richard Sennett has so easily replanted in his revisionist rejection of immateriality),[7] from the pragmatic root of art's peculiar financing (wherein the art market can only make profit from subscription to the conditions of individual artefactual novelty), and from the belief, as stated above, that art objects do something different from other objects: something that embeds knowing via a unique capacity. This is, of course, the least defensible of claims.

For many artists of Serra's generation, using a device such as a list to produce a work of art instantiated sociality simply by taking place (this predates and mimics much contemporary writing on immersion and affect). To enact that which Osborne calls 'the perpetual participal present' is the desire and goal of much art then as now, a goal upon which production is inevitably – and perpetually – foreclosed. On one level, art proposes the immediate instantiation of new political being in the world (this is its seduction). But on another level, art is only able to propose such aesthetic devices of the social – towards the social – through the specific spaces allotted to it (however ubiquitous art's claim to spaces and processes of the social, its performance within them is limited by its ontology, as has been argued). Artistic production might be any number of processes, but its product can only ever be a mimcry of this process, a simple paradox that serves to both define the limits of any claims for art's politics and pronounces the real coordinates of the devices that order – or facilitate – our lives.

The contemporary list instills in us a form of endless action based on our technical inability to achieve its goal; that is, the utopia of no list, whereby we have checked off all the items and tasks and are free of all forms of labour. But, as art listers exemplify, the excruciating attraction of the list is its endlessness, for within this we are offered the ambivalent imaginary of potential, turned inward in hegemonic forms of self-evaluation. The revolution of the list is not, therefore, an outward sign of change but change turned back upon ourselves – a dubious form of self-participation and pseudo-authorship in which any insurgency comes in the form of gestures of reprioritization: change slips down the list, as necessity reforms labour. Lists roll on, the heavier tasks sinking to the bottom, like so much sediment settling.

Notes

1   Bruno Latour uses a list as an example of an actor-network-theory device: 'If action is limited a priori to what "intentional", "meaningful" humans do, it is hard to see how a hammer, a basket, a door closer, a cat, a rug, a mug, a list, or a tag could act' (Latour, 2007: 71). Critiques of the politics of Latour's conception of ANT, including those by Boltanski and Chiapello, find the politics of ANT wanting in terms of the ability to distinguish between deliberative and assemblaged motivations for action. In terms of my thesis on lists, I would agree with Latour that a list 'acts' – in non-human terms – is exemplary of such types of acting.

2   *Verb List* was initially published in Grégoire Muller, *The New Avant-Garde: Issues for the Art of the Seventies* (1972).

3 For example, *Slow Roll: For Philip Glass* (1968), which consists of three rolls of lead sheeting rolled up and arranged in a triangular stack on the floor, and *Casting* (1969), a series of long hand-cast moldings of the space between the floor and the wall of the artist's studio, repeated and laid side by side. In *Hand Catching Lead* (1968, 16mm film, black and white, 3.5 mins), a film inspired by the work of the choreographer Yvonne Rainer as well as structuralist film and minimalist music, only Serra's hand and forearm is filmed as he repeatedly attempts to catch falling pieces of lead. He says he aimed to explore 'some sort of filmic analogy . . . just by using my hand as a device' (quoted in Michelson, 1979).
4 See Chave (1990).
5 www.ubu.com/concept/serra_verb.html.
6 See Sassen (2006).
7 See Sennett (2008).

References

Boltanski, L. and Chiapello, E. (2005) *The New Spirit of Capitalism*, London: Verso.
Bourriaud, N. (2009) 'Precarious constructions: answers to Jacques Rancière on art and politics', in J. Seijdel (ed.) *A Precarious Existence: Vulnerability within the Public Domain*, Open no. 17, Rotterdam: SKOR/NAi, pp. 20–37.
Chave, A. (1990) 'Minimalism and the rhetoric of power', *Arts Magazine*, 64 (5): 44–63.
Foucault, M. (1980) 'The confession of the flesh', in C. Gordon (ed.) *Power/ Knowledge*, Harlow: Longman, pp. 194–228.
Latour, B. (2007) *Reassembling the Social: An Introduction to Actor-network-theory*, Oxford: Oxford University Press.
Malik, S. (2006) 'Art-critique-capital', in K. Ogg (ed.) *The Showroom Annual 2005/6*, London: The Showroom, pp. 38–43.
Michelson, A., Serra, R. and Weyergraf, C. (1979) 'The films of Richard Serra: an interview', *October*, 10 (Autumn 1979): 68–104.
Muller, G. (1972) *The New Avant-Garde: Issues for the Art of the Seventies*, New York: Praeger.
Osborne, P. (ed.) (2002) *Conceptual Art*, London: Phaidon.
Rancière, J. (2004) *The Politics of Aesthetics*, London: Continuum.
Sassen, S. (2006) *Territory, Authority, Rights: From Medieval to Global Assemblages*, Princeton, NJ: Princeton University Press.
Sennett, R. (2006) *The Culture of New Capitalism*, New Haven, CT: Yale University Press.
Sennett, R. (2008) *The Craftsman*, London: Allen Lane.
Serra, R. (n.d.) 'Ubuweb: Richard Serra', available at: www.ubu.com/concept/serra_ verb.html (accessed 17 September 2011).

8   Number

Helen Verran

The move to market-led environmental policy is obviously not occurring without opposition. Old-guard environmentalists long for the security of command-and-control state policies, while old-guard anti-environmentalists long for the abolishment of environmental bureaucracy and to put it bluntly, the freedom to pillage (Robertson, 2009).

The number at the core of my paper was 'born' in 1997 in the prestigious natural sciences journal *Nature* with the publication of 'The value of the world's ecosystem services and natural capital'. Thirteen authors, representing a wide range of academic institutions and disciplines, presented data that they claimed allowed calculation of a numerical value for the goods and services produced by the world's natural capital stock. As they calculated it, the numerical value of the goods and services provided annually by the environment was somewhere between US$16 and 54 trillion ($10^{12}$), which they averaged as US$33 trillion ($10^{12}$) per year. They compared the value of their newly hatched number to another number: the total of the global gross national product that they estimated at US$18 trillion ($10^{12}$) per year (Costanza *et al.*, 1997).

As contemporary ecological economics tells it, either directly or indirectly, the functioning of ecosystems produces goods (like food, fibres, water, and minerals) and services (like waste assimilation, nutrient cycling and the means to perform culturally significant rituals like bush-walking). These goods and services provide benefit to human societies. Why try to quantify this way of conceiving nature? The authors justified their value generation exercise, criticized by one economist as a 'recklessly heroic attempt to do something that's futile' (Cameron, 1998), by noting that 'because ecosystem [goods and] services are not fully "captured" in commercial markets or adequately quantified in terms comparable with economic services and manufactured capital they are often given too little weight in policy decisions' (Costanza *et al.*, 1997: 253). The calculation of this number (which I will dub Costanza's number after the *Nature* paper's senior author) was then an intervention in the politics around the move to market-led environmental policy. It was not the value of the number that mattered: the authors insisted that the calculation of the number was a political act.

In disputing Costanza and his co-authors' resort to arithmetic, more orthodox economists claim that the number which purports to value the earth's natural capital is nonsense. This is how a small booklet entitled 'How much is an ecosystem worth? Assessing the economic value of conservation', published under the auspices of the IUCN (the World Conservation Union), the Nature Conservancy, and the World Bank in 2004, and expressing more orthodox contemporary economics, deals with what I am calling Costanza's number.

A serious underestimate of infinity

> A landmark paper published in *Nature* in 1997 attempted to calculate the total value of all ecosystems to the earth. By using a range of estimates of the value of individual ecosystems and scaling them up according to the total area covered by each such ecosystem globally, the authors arrived at an estimate of the total value of all ecosystem services . . . This paper has had a significant impact and its results have been widely quoted by scientists and environmentalists. However most economists consider it profoundly flawed both conceptually and methodologically.
>
> (Pagiola *et al.*, 2004: 17)

For more orthodox economists, valuing ecosystem services relates instrumentally to processes of auditing public expenditure on the environment. According to economics orthodoxy, as a representation of total value of the world's natural capital stock, albeit one that does not claim precision, Costanza's number is invalid, a step too far (Bockstael *et al.*, 2000: 1384). Against their more cautious colleagues, Costanza and his co-authors defend the number as leading to good policy: '. . . we do not believe there is one right way to value ecosystem services. But there is a wrong way and that is not to do it at all' (Pearce, 1998). As Costanza and his co-authors see it, their number is 'realpolitik'.

The sentiment that nature can be quantitatively valued is strongly opposed by some natural scientists. They decry the economists' intervention. They assert nature is valuable in and of itself. The effort that is now being devoted to commodifying nature by calculating the economic value of the services it provides should be redirected. These environmentalists argue that the basis for policy should be what they name as the 'intrinsic value' of nature. It is a matter of ethics and aesthetics, they say; nature has its own intrinsic logic that natural science facts represent, and which our policies should reflect. They reject the instrumental anthropocentrism embedded in the processes of quantifying ecosystems services, seeing it as 'selling out on nature'. Nature is not arranged for human purposes, they argue – not marketable. The market has a very short value time span, whereas nature should be conserved in perpetuity. Valuing ecosystems services pits nature against man as competitors providing services, they say. And in fact, they insist, most ecosystems are worth more dead than they are alive (McCauley, 2006).

My critique of Costanza's number is rather different. For me the opportunistic calculation of the purported value of the world's ecosystems services and natural capital in a style designed to appeal to natural scientists exhibits a reckless disregard for number's remarkable capacities. The Costanza paper argues for a particular form of ordering: an order valuing nature as a set of products in a services economy. And so as to 'prove' the reality of that order, it makes an audit of the value of the categories being argued for. As is usual in such exercises, there is a seamless elision of the dual moments of articulating an order so as to create value, and valuing the categories created in the order, to stabilize the order. Costanza's number simultaneously effects a startling ontology – nature as a set of products tradable in an imagined market in environmental services, and warrants that order – makes an epistemic claim, by calculating the values of these products.

Costanza's number reveals itself as a dodgy number. Calculated with the explicit aim of provoking shock and awe, Costanza's number is, or so it claims, mere political spectacle. Perhaps that is why Costanza's number disconcerts and dismays me. In the guise of rationality, numbers speak to a politics of affect (Deleuze, 1988: 48).

Should we be concerned about such a dodgy number getting extensive recognition? Or should we just smile or grimace at the times we live in and pass on to other matters? Perhaps the second is the appropriate response but I want to stay with my dismay for as I see it, the paper and its (in)famous number exemplify a general phenomenon. Modernity itself seems to be afflicted with an ongoing blindness when it comes to the social functioning of number. In my chapter, I use this dodgy number and the controversy around it to begin to develop familiarity with number as a generative device. I aim to sensitize researchers in the social sciences to what is involved in using numbers in informed good faith.

Developing a feel for number

In articulating the social functioning of number, I treat it as a material-semiotic device. This is a quite different way of framing numbers than treating them as either universal abstractions or as culturally relative social constructions. It keeps both numbers and those who use them as present in the here and now. I developed this way of working with numbers when I needed a way to think about how the numbers of science were simultaneously different from and the same as numbers I met in Yoruba classrooms and markets in Nigeria in the 1980s. This way of thinking about numbers takes them as inseparable from the practices in which enumerated material entities come to life, and as semiotically agential (Verran, 2001). It recognizes that the workings of numbers are deeply embedded in and constitutive of the real – they lubricate its happening. Expressing formal relations working simultaneously the distinctions same/different and the idea of ratio, numbers partially configure the ongoing emergence of our worlds.

Numbers participate as order – enumerated entities *are* the real. Yet number-ing is also engaged in *representing* order in a specific way – as value. Numbers sometimes work in ordering and at other times in valuing – it depends. And because it depends, and because often those who love numbers are unaware that numbers have distinct modes of participating in the real, we find dis-sembling in numbering: ends disporting themselves as means; ordering that necessarily distributes benefits differentially, in the guise of merely valuing 'found' orders.

I argue that Costanza's number fails to recognize and respect the difference between numbers working as ordinal number to conserve order and as cardinal number to conserve value. The way the number is presented in the *Nature* paper hides a conflation of number's dual modes of participation in and as the real. The deductive working of number's generalizing, where parts are derived from general, vague wholes in processes effecting ordering, the form of number use familiar in macroeconomics, is conflated with the inductive form of number's generalizing, associated with valuing by engaging a specific one-to-many relation, the way numbers are engaged with by most natural scientists.

Of course Costanza's number is not unique in this, but it is not the conflating that is the problem. If we know what we are doing, flipping between ordering and valuing is generative. The danger lies in the fact that many who love numbers and use them constantly cannot recognize the difference between these two moments of numbering, and hence are unable to discern when conflation is occurring. That we do not know we are conflating number's dual moments of generalizing is a problem. Costanza's number and indeed much of the controversy associated with it, is exemplary in exhibiting this blindness and foregrounding it helps me demonstrate number's duality, a step towards a more realistic recognition of number as a generative device. I use Costanza's number as a means for showing what a feel for number is, or to use Marilyn Strathern's term, I evert it to show what is inside (Strathern, 1992).

I begin with a brief history of the family of numbers to which I see Costanza's number as belonging, explaining why Costanza's number is more controversial than its siblings. Next I consider some of the details of the number's constitution. Using fine-grained textual analysis, I show just where in the paper the elision of order and value occurs. In the next section I introduce another number, the Australian Fire Danger Index, which I claim is unlike Costanza's number in that it explicitly dwells in the mess of the world. It helps me be more explicit about what is left out in Costanza's number. Finally I summarize what, in a material-semiotic way of thinking about number, informed good faith in using number might be.

A family of iconic numbers

In 1997, Costanza's number attempted to join an expanding family of iconic numbers central to aggregate, or macro, economics; however, 15 years later its membership of that family is still contested. The members of this rather exclusive family of numbers have been designed to articulate changes in relationships between various economic flows and 'real-world' processes. They are all temporally dynamic (rates of flow) and for that reason can seem counter-intuitive. All were born in controversy but Costanza's number is probably most controversial.

These iconic numbers name ordering concepts such as 'national income' or 'gross domestic product', or more controversially in the case of Costanza's number, 'natural capital'. Recently, a report 'birthing' a new member of this family of numbers was published by the UK government: Sir Nicholas Stern's number values the costs of reducing the stocks of greenhouse gases (Stern, 2006). With Stern's number, something previously considered as external to economic activity and hence of no interest to economists has been articulated. But like its older siblings, at the time of its birth we are seeing much disagreement over exactly what conceptual and mathematical processes should be used to constitute the number naming the cost of reducing the world's (unwanted) stock of greenhouse gases and coincidently a new economic order (Dyson, 2008; Mendelsohn, 2008).

This family of iconic economists' numbers can be understood as heirs to the project of political arithmetic that came into being along with modernity. In adopting the label of 'political arithmetic' for the process that gives rise to and surrounds the use of Costanza's and related iconic numbers, I am linking the project of macroeconomics to that of William Petty, one of the seventeenth-century founders of the Royal Society of London, whose best known work *Political Arithmetic* was published in 1691:

> Petty promoted his method, which he called political arithmetic, as an explicit antidote both to the excesses of rhetoric and to the theoretical disputes that had provoked the English Civil War. Arguments based on 'number, weight, and measure' he proclaimed, would compel assent as surely as mathematics did – especially if the King was willing to back the knowledge that the supposedly disinterested numbers expert produced.
>
> (Poovey, 1998: xviii)

As Mary Poovey tells the story of this arithmetic, the claim to disinterestedness with which William Petty promoted his numerical cadastral descriptions as 'mathematicals' in the second half of the seventeenth century, was exposed as a fraud by Scottish moral philosophy's 'experimental philosophy' and 'conjectural history' projects. They successfully refuted claims that it is possible for any description, especially numerical description, to be free of embedded theory about the nature of the world. But as she also makes clear, by the end of the eighteenth century the political economy of Adam Smith had reconstituted Petty's cleverly constructed illusion of the disinterestedness and self-sufficiency of numbers (ibid.: 248).

In the twentieth century, a new incarnation of political arithmetic emerged. The still-expanding systems of national accounts now calculate a bevy of numbers that value the various categories of a national economy. But the categories, now routinely valued, first came into existence as contested numbers. The senior member of this family of grand economic numbers is gross national product (GNP). As a number, GNP, or we could call it Kuznet's number, was born at the end of the 1930s in the work of a private research organization under commission from the US Department of Commerce (Kuznets, 1946).

Conceived in the pain and confusion of the Great Depression and seen by all as 'a good thing' at the time of its birth, there was much disagreement over exactly how the number should be algorithmically constituted. The orders engendered in these numbers are controversial among economists who contest them as orders (Mendelsohn, 2008). By the end of the 1930s, this newly hatched number had become the new actuality, the very stuff of the US and other national economies, generating new material, institutional, and textual practices of economic management. In the second half of the twentieth century, the newly articulated entity 'the national economy', named as GNP, intervened decisively in a well-established debate on social development to effect a practical equivalence between society and the monetary economy so that now social development is growth in GNP.

Should we be surprised that, as ordering concepts, these macroeconomic numbers help us focus on troublesome aspects of our world, and that they come to life at particular socio-historical junctures as expressions of social concern about the state of the society or of nature? Just as GNP grew from the view that representing the state of flows of economic activity in society more precisely was unproblematically a good thing, especially as recovering national economies shifted from producing civilian goods to producing war goods, so too there is the sense that at the end of the twentieth century more precise representation of the flows of natural processes as economic flows, is surely a good thing.

That may be so, but Costanza's number differs from these economists' numbers in that it is an order that is argued for as a value using the logic of natural science. Social order conceived as an economy producing goods and services is taken as a template for a natural order similarly imagined: a natural goods and services economy. Rendering flows of natural processes as flows of economic activity, the authors specifically make analogy between the value of 'human production' and the value of 'natural production' in defending their *Nature* paper (Costanza *et al.*, 1998).

One way to understand the critiques of both economists and natural scientists is to see that the paper of Costanza and his co-authors as failing ontologically; a failure that turns on the phrase 'natural capital'. Economists are outraged at this rhetorical flourish because it deprives 'capital' of its conceptual specificity. Economists cannot do without capital meaning something specific such as 'resources, including financial, mobilized in producing goods and services for a market'. The rhetorical use of capital embedded in Costanza's number is a step too far for most economists. Natural scientists, on the other hand, find their conception of nature far too reduced in the notion of natural capital. The narrow specificity it gains in being linked to a rhetorical use of capital means it is not the nature of natural science. Ontologically, 'natural capital' fails in both economics and in natural science – although for different reasons. Why then is the paper and its number so cited? Part of the answer to that question surely relates to the 'numberliness' in which the dubious analogy embedded in 'natural capital' is presented.

While the analogy between an economy and some elements of natural process might make vague intuitive sense, that is as far as it goes. In the end, Costanza's number does a disservice to the market-led environmental policy movement that it sought to promote. But, and this is where Costanza's number understood as an aspect of the endeavour to 'sell' market-led environmental policy, connects up with my attempts to make numbers our familiars so that we might use them knowingly in good faith.

Before I go on to examine the conceptual design of Costanza's number in more detail, I want to consider the sense in which numbers like Kuznet's and Stern's, and the numbers of macroeconomics more generally, are iconic, for I mean that adjective in more than the sense of being emblematic. In a religious sense, an icon is precious because in the actual practices of many religions the image is the god or spirit pictured, and is treated as such. This sense of the term is captured in the Peircian typology of signs where his example of an icon is the lead pencil streak that is simultaneously a mark on a page and a geometrical line (Hoopes, 1991). Just as lead pencil streaks are icons in geometry, numbers such as Kuznet's and Stern's numbers are icons in economics. In generative economic analysis, number and the category numbered are treated as one and the same (MacKenzie *et al.*, 2007).

Such economic categories are, in practice, vague and emergent, and the number actually works as a name. In the case of Stern's number – numbering the cost of greenhouse gases – there are two equally vague parts: the cost of abatement, of curbing emissions, and the cost of damage from climate change. Stern's number is the difference between them – the relative rates of change in the values of these two numbered, that is named, categories. In texts – both spoken and written – Stern's number works in the same way that a pencil streak on a page of a student's geometry book works as a geometrical line.

So is Costanza's number an icon in the way Kuznet's and Stern's numbers are icons? In agreeing with the economists' critique, my answer is no. One can argue that the individual numbers for the values of the many and varied specifically located ecosystem services that economists have invented and named over the past 15 years or so are icons, and that is why it makes no sense to total them. This helps us see that the numbers Costanza and his co-authors recklessly add together are not only invalid extrapolations of values that have very specific referents, but also that adding them together ignores the semiotic character of those numbers as icons. Totalling iconic numbers is to pile icons randomly one on top of the other: Costanza's number can be understood as attempting to convince us that the pile itself adds up to something more than an assortment of icons. As spectacle or stunt, the piling-up seems to work, but as a value of 'natural capital' it does not. To say this more economically, Costanza's number fails both ontologically and epistemologically.

Ecosystem services: many different products in a services economy or plural instantiations of a single measure?

I move on now to considering some details of how Costanza's number is constituted. From my point of view, the nub of the problem is this: in the *Nature* article the total value of the earth's ecosystem services is presented as if it is the total of 17 paddocks of differing areas joined together to make a mega-paddock – total natural capital. It suggests that 'ecosystem service' is self-evidently a unit of natural capital, just as many regard the hectare as self-evidently a unit of area. At the same time, it claims that each ecosystem service is a unique and singular category of product in a (mythical) natural services economy: the table listing ecosystem services articulates an order. Each environmental service product is a category, a whole with emergent parts.

In the *Nature* paper, Costanza's number comes to life in an inductive argument propounded in the style of a naive scientific realism familiar in the natural sciences. The paper by Costanza and his co-authors has the classical structure of a scientific report with introduction, methods, results, interpretations and conclusions. The methods section provides detailed information on the algorithmic methods used, and in addition we learn something about the social process of the two stage methodological procedure of the number's devising. Data initially assembled by one of the authors identifying and extracting appropriate literature sources was intensively workshopped: 'We conducted a thorough literature review and synthesized the information along with a few original calculations during a one-week intensive workshop at the new National Centre for Ecological Analysis and Synthesis (NCEAS) at the University of California Santa Barbara' (Costanza *et al.*, 1997: 258).

In the paper, the number is presented as a one-many generalization based on 17 subtotals of a singular unit 'ecosystem services'. Here is a short description of just 4 of those 17, more or less randomly selected. The first named in Costanza and his co-authors' list is 'Gas regulation', defined as 'regulation of atmospheric chemical composition' and exemplified by the following: 'CO_2/O_2 balance, O_2 for UVB protection, and SO_2 levels'. There are, of course, many more conceivable parts to the category that is the vague whole 'gas regulation'. Passing down the list, fifth is 'Water supply: Regulation of hydrological flows: Provisioning of water by watersheds, reservoirs and aquifers'. Tenth is 'Pollination: movement of floral gametes: Provisioning of pollinators for reproduction of plant populations'. The last named, possibly the most counter-intuitive, is 'Cultural: Providing opportunities for non-commercial uses: Aesthetic, artistic, educational, spiritual, and/or scientific values of ecosystems' (ibid.: 254).

In this process of adding up, there is one issue that the authors are at pains to explain away. Some natural processes – such as flows of the water cycle – are counted twice or three times. The authors claim this does not invalidate their counting:

> for example some of the net primary production in an ecosystem ends up as food, the consumption of which generates respiratory products necessary for primary production [and these are counted as separate ecosystem services]. Even though these functions and services are interdependent, in many cases they can be added [together] because they represent 'joint products' of the ecosystem.
>
> (ibid.: 253)

A conspicuous element in the paper is a tabular matrix with squares for values for 17 proposed ecosystem services across 12 earth biomes (open ocean, coastal, forest, grass/rangelands, and so on). Of the 204 squares so generated a mere 60 have a number. Those biomes that are most complete are, of course, those like forest and rangeland – the parts of the environment most fully integrated into the (social) economy. Should we be surprised? Imagine the institutional effort and money that would be required to fill the empty boxes. In natural science's time-honoured style of managing such 'methodological horrors' (Woolgar, 1988: 30), it is implied that this is an unfortunate circum-stance that will, with effort, be put right in time: 'additional effort in studying and valuing a broader range of ecosystem services' is needed (Costanza *et al.*, 1997: 253).

The numbers that are exhibited in the matrix are working as symbols. They are values representing categories that Costanza and his co-auhors are arguing for in proposing an order. In the Peircian typology of signs, symbols are those types of signs that need a theory (a set of articulated categories) to be made explicit if they are to be meaningful. But the theory that makes them meaningful is exactly what is at stake here. The (few) numbers lined up in rows and columns here are (very slight) evidence for a set of categories precipitated by the 'theory' Costanza and his co-authors are arguing for. In a semiotic sense, the problem here is that these numbers are being presented as simultaneously both icons and symbols. Ordering is being elided with valuing.

How is it done? Like most tricks, it is done with words and misplaced confidence. As I read the *Nature* paper, Costanza and his co-authors make use of the same commonplace illusion that William Petty mobilized some 300 years ago: the comforting idea that numbers carry within themselves everything that is needed to interpret their meaning.

At two crucial places in the paper, words serve to mislead. The first occasion is in the paper's title, 'The value of the world's ecosystem services and natural capital'. I read this as implying 'ecosystem services' is analogous to 'hectare' and 'natural capital' to 'total area', implying: this paper is about (using numbers in) valuing, when it is actually proposing a radically new order of nature. Next, near the top of the second page of their article, the authors begin a section describing the ordering system at the centre of ecological economics. In this section heading, the central terms are reversed: 'Natural capital and ecosystem services'. In beginning to define their analytic categories, Costanza and his co-authors readily admit that it is meaningless to try to value and hence quantify natural capital: zero natural capital is zero humanity, or to put it another way, natural capital is infinite and hence cannot to be valued:

> It is not very meaningful to ask the total value of natural capital to human welfare, nor to ask the total value of massive, particular forms of natural capital. It is trivial to ask what is the value of the atmosphere to humankind, or what is the value of rocks and soil infrastructure as support systems.
>
> (ibid.: 255)

Yet in their paper, they do ask about the quantified value of natural capital and by applying seemingly valid algorithmic processes they do get and give an answer: US$33 trillion. How do they achieve the seemingly impossible task of giving an actual and quite meaningful monetary value for what they themselves announce as a meaningless category – even if they slip from meaninglessness to 'not very meaningful'?

Look at these two consecutive sentences. The first occurs at the end of paragraph five, arguing that the only way to imagine valuing natural capital is to model or represent it as an artificial biosphere: 'Biosphere I (the earth) is a very efficient, least-cost provider of human life-support services' (ibid.: 255). The second sentence begins paragraph six, arguing for the absolute importance of natural capital for humans: 'Thus we can consider the general class of natural capital as essential to human welfare'(ibid.: 255). In the space between these two consecutive sentences 'a many' (human life-support services), a plural set of units of ecosystem services that can be valued, has become a whole: 'a general class'. We have moved seamlessly from value to order. Several 'services' that can be represented and valued become, in the next sentence, the order of the world itself. Something that has been previously named a fiction and necessarily of incalculable value, is, through numbering, confirmed as a specifiable value and real as a specific 'instrumental many' becomes a vague 'metaphysically potent whole'. That is how the ill-designed device that is Costanza's number domesticates 'ecosystem services' as a unit of 'natural capital' and portrays the relation as just a complicated version of the additive process by which (for example) hectares measure area.

Indexical numbers: seeing what is overlooked in iconic numbers and denied in symbolic numbers

There is a sense in which giving a reading of the rhetorical strategies of the 1997 *Nature* paper by Costanza and his co-authors in answer to the question of 'how is it done?', is superfluous. How the authors delude themselves and others about what they accomplish in that paper, and why they think it important, is of secondary importance here. I have used the paper and its (in)famous number as an exemplar to show that numbering accomplishes both ordering and valuing eliding them with seeming ease. I take the moral of the story of Costanza's number to be this. In these seemingly reckless neo-liberal times informed good faith in using numbers is important. But first I want to alert readers to a domain of number use that is almost entirely absent in the paper, although in a paper published in *Nature* this is exactly the domain of number use that we might expect to feature most prominently.

Informed good faith in using numbers is, in part, being familiar with the difference in using them as icons and using them as symbols – recognizing that, in the first, generalizing proceeds as a whole-parts process, and in the second as a one-many procedure. But it is also more than that. When most of us use numbers, we are using them neither as icons nor as symbols. Most of the time, most of us use numbers indexically. Indexical signs are Peirce's third semiotic type. Indexical numbers dwell in the mess of the real and, through them, generalizing can proceed simultaneously as whole-parts and one-many. But, and this is important, in using number indexically, valuing is not used to evidence the truth claims about order as it is in Costanza's number. Rather, we find that the process of valuing can interrupt the ordering prompting a rethink and a redesign. This is how numbering is generative and, for this reason, social as well as natural scientists need to be familiar with possibilities embedded in indexical numbers.

Engaging with numbers indexically involves explicitly working with what using them as icons blithely takes for granted, and using them as symbols insistently denies: the need to wrestle with the always and already overwhelming, blooming, buzzing real. Some numbers are so open about this that they call themselves indexes, not worrying about letting the messy work of rendering them as such show. Such are two numbers that have a high profile where I live – just outside Melbourne, where bushfires raged in the summer of 2009. Like many other things, these numbers were severely challenged by those fires.

What is clear about the McArthur Forest Fire Danger Index (FFDI) and the Grassland Fire Danger Index (GFDI) is that a tremendous amount of work has gone into constituting them as naming an order of danger, and that this elaborate institutional work must continue if they are to continue to work as live numbers. Coming up with values for these clearly highly contrived categories manages to mix up and integrate things that are quite incommensurable. If the elaborate communicating infrastructure embedded in the number fails or is compromised – the number will die. This is how Chapter 5, 'Information', of the 2009 *Victorian Bushfires Royal Commission Interim Report* accounts these sprawling, messy and seemingly uncontrollable numbers:

5.1 These indices are calculated by reference to fuel [wood and grass] characteristics and weather in order to generate a numerical index.

5.2 The FFDI and GFDI indicate expected fire danger and are regularly calculated by the Bureau of Meterology (BoM) for the use of fire agencies.

5.3 The FFDI is calculated with 'inputs' of drought, recent precipitation levels, temperature, relative humidity, and wind speed. The FFDI is calculated on the basis of a normative fuel load.

5.4 The GFDI is calculated using the 'inputs' of curing or fuel moisture, temperature, relative humidity, and wind speed.

5.5 The FFDI and GFDI are together referred to as the fire danger index (FDI). The FDI was originally calculated on a scale 0 to 100. The fire danger rating of extreme corresponds to an FDI of 50 and above. [But, as the Regional Director of the BoM] explained, [while] the FDI was originally designed only to 'go up to' 100 computing models now allow the FDI to exceed this.

The opposite page in the document has a table of 'Fire danger indices forecast for 7 February 2009'. It shows that in the vicinity where I live, the forecast FFDI was 142 and the GFDI was 186. The point of exhibiting these fire danger index numbers is not so much to demonstrate the ways numbers can be mapped on to experience – although that is part of number's indexicality. The significant element I want to bring to the fore in indexicality is the enormous amount of work that is embedded in each value of the FFDI and the GDFI. For these numbers to come to life and to stay alive, there must be an elaborate network of smoothly functioning institutions with trained and willing workers, complex technical procedures and material arrangements and routines, and multiple texts of differing genres must be intercalated. And, as always, there is a slight surprise in the collective action. The order of the fire danger indices exceeds its own definitions in contriving values in showing it has the somewhat surprising capacity to measure up to nearly 200. Working numbers indexically has us taking account of the here and now, and allowing a generative mutual interrogation of ordering and valuing.

Where the stunt that is Costanza's number works to conflate iconic and symbolic forms of number, actively hiding its partiality and promoting the illusion of disinterestedness, the equally arcane, but far less pretentious number the Australian Fire Danger Index recognizes its partiality showing off its generative capacity for unexpected excess, showing how processes of valuing call forth an explicit move to redesign, to reorder. The FDI is exemplary in showing how number intervenes in the happening of the real – and vice versa.

In making the contrast between Costanza's number and the Australian FDI number, I do not want to be seen as claiming that those who work with ecosystems services and accept market-led environmental policy choices are given to using number in ill-informed ways and, motivated by a misplaced enthusiasm, use them in bad faith. Nor do I want to be seen as claiming that, in contrast, those who exercise a logic of environmental care such as those responsible for developing and maintaining the Australian FDI number, exhibit an admirable sensitivity to number's dual moments allowing their number to develop as part of the complex socio-material domain of Australian bush fires, do so out of a sophisticated recognition of number's material-semiotic capacities.

It is clear that on 7 February 2009 the behaviour of the numbers was as surprising as the behaviour of the fires. And it is equally clear that the categorical order of ecosystem services has long since escaped the narrow conceptions of economic ordering, rendering Costanza's number risible. What was originally proposed as a rather strict analogy between nature as a service economy and the capitalist economy has become 10 years later a vague guiding imaginary. As Morgan Robertson, whose opening paragraph I quoted in beginning this paper, puts it:

> It is apparent that nothing approaching 'a market' in the strict economic sense will develop in the foreseeable future . . . [yet] in some cases (but not all), the move towards ecosystem service markets has opened up an entirely new field of action . . . often in spite of, rather than because of, the power of orthodox economic principles . . . finding both progressive political possibilities and positive environmental outcomes in the playing out of market-based policies. It is clear that markets are not going to go away, but neither is their future to be predicted by mere economics. Their potential for surprise is enormous.
>
> (Robertson, 2009)

By delving into the insides of what I experience as a disconcerting and dismaying number, I have shown numbers purporting to objectively value ecosystem services, are an ill-designed device that fails both ontically and epistemically. I emphasized the design flaws of this number by comparing it to a number that the Australian state commits resources to maintaining as an index. Yet I agree with the sentiment of the quotation above. Despite its design flaws, as a device for reporting a purported objective value of ecosystem services, Costanza's number does work in those polities committed to market mechanisms environmental governmentality. It explicitly engages and thus also institutes, a new environmental politics of affect. Recognizing this new sort of politically affective number, we might go on to ask about its agency. But that is not my concern here. My interest here is primarily in learning to recognize number as a device.

What to make of my everting?

In portraying numbers working as a device in the clotting of the real, in everting Costanza's number to show what is inside, and comparing it to the Australian Fire Danger Index, I am seeking to develop a feel for number in a material-semiotic sense. I hope that with a feel for numbers will come an informed familiarity, and a concern among social science researchers to work with numbers in good faith. In separating out the dual moments of numbers' generalizing as working either whole-parts or one-many relations, and relating this to numbers' semiotic capacities, I sought a beginning in sensitizing readers to what is involved in respecting numbers. By explaining my dismay over the bad faith that Costanza's number embeds, and my disconcertment at the excess and spilling over of the Australian Fire Danger Index, my aim was to change the ways social science researchers feel towards and 'do' their own numbers.

My hope is that readers will now be able to characterize the numbers they engender in social science research. Are your numbers symbols representing value mobilizing theory, perhaps in a moment of audit? Or, alternatively, are you working like an economist in using your numbers as icons arguing for a new order of the social? Perhaps your numbers are indexes displaying value in an ongoing project of ordering and reordering effected partly in response to values that become calculable through the ordering moment? In drawing attention to the ways your numbers work as indexes, are you seeking to intervene to promote reordering, perhaps to effect a more just or more discriminating order?

The social sciences are distinguished by a multiplicity of forms of number use. All three forms of numbering – symbolic, indexical, and iconic – are common and are valid usages. My claim is that researchers in the social sciences should know what they are doing with their numbers and how, and most importantly be able to articulate why they want to work with numbers in those ways. That last requirement could be claimed as a distinguishing mark of good social science: using numbers skillfully in articulating problems in terms of how social ordering might be changed to effect distributive justice; asking who benefits from particular orders and how; posing questions about where such orders might be redesigned. Such generative critique can be achieved only by using numbers in informed good faith.

References

Bockstael, N. E., Freeman, A. M., Kopp, R. J., Portney, P. R. and Smith, V.K. (2000) 'On measuring economic values for nature', *Environmental Science and Technology*, 34 (8): 1384–9.

Cameron, T. (1998) 'Audacious bid to value the planet whips up a storm', *Nature*, 395 (1 October): 430.

Costanza, R., D'Arge, R., de Groot, R., Farber, S., Grasso, M., Hannon, B., Limburg, K., Naeem, S. V., O'Neill, R., Paruelo, J., Raskin, R., Sutton, P. and van den Belt, M. (1997) 'The value of the world's ecosystem services and natural capital', *Nature*, 387 (15 May): 253–60.

Costanza, R., D'Arge, R., de Groot, R., Farber, S., Grasso, M., Hannon, B., Limburg, K., Naeem, S. V., O'Neill, R., Paruelo, J., Raskin, R., Sutton, P. and van den Belt, M. (1998) 'The value of ecosystem services: putting the issues in perspective', *Ecological Economics*, 25: 67–72.

Deleuze, G. (1988) *Spinoza: Practical Philosophy*, trans. Robert Hurley, San Francisco, CA: City Lights Books.

Dyson, F. (2008) 'The question of global warming', *New York Review of Books*, 55 (10).

Hoopes, J. (ed.) (1991) *Peirce on Signs: Writings on Semiotics by Charles Sanders Peirce*, Chapel Hill, NC: University of North Carolina Press.

Kuznets, S. (1946) *National Income: A Summary of Findings*, New York: National Bureau of Economic Research.

McCauley, D. (2006) 'Selling out on nature', *Nature*, 443 (7 September): 27–8.

MacKenzie, D., Muniesa, F. and Siu, L. (eds) (2007) *Do Economists Make Markets? On the Performativity of Economics*, Princeton, NJ: Princeton University Press.

Mendelsohn, R. (2008) 'Is the Stern Review an economic analysis?', *Review of Environmental Economics and Policy*, 2 (1): 45–60.

Pagiola, S., von Ritter, K. and Bishop, J. (2004) *How Much is an Ecosystem Worth? Assessing the Economic Value of Conservation*, New York: The World Bank.

Pearce, D. (1998) 'Auditing the earth: the value of the world's ecosystem services and natural capital', *Environment*, 40 (2): 23–8.

Poovey, M. (1998) *The History of the Modern Fact: Problems of Knowledge and the Sciences of Wealth and Society*, Chicago, IL: University of Chicago Press.

Robertson, M. (2009) 'Five hidden challenges to ecosystem markets', The Katoomba Group's Ecosystem Marketplace, 4 January 2009, available at: www.ecosystem marketplace.com (accessed 12 July 2009).

Stern, N. (2006) *The Stern Review on the Economics of Climate Change*, Cambridge: Cambridge University Press.

Strathern, M .(1992) 'The decomposition of an event', *Cultural Anthropology*, 7 (2): 244–54.

Verran, H. (2001) *Science and an African Logic*, Chicago, IL: University of Chicago Press.

Victorian Bushfires Royal Commission Interim Report (2009) Available at: www. royalcommission.vic.gov.au/getdoc/208e8bcb-3927-41ec-8c23-2cdc86a7cec7/ Interim-Report 19/8/2009 (accessed 25 November 2009).

Woolgar, S. (1988) *Science: The Very Idea*, Chichester: Ellis Horwood Ltd.

9   Pattern, patterning

Janis Jefferies

Models of entry

From the simplest spirals cut out of paper, to experimenting with materials to look at mathematical Fibonacci sequences and geometry, to three-dimensional computer programming, pattern excites. Consisting of regularly repeated units, as in a textile quilt, pattern can be a repeat, a motif, a design, a device, a numerical order, or a succession of tones or steps, as in music or dance. There are patterns of behaviour, genealogical patterns, patterned design, grid pattern, fan pattern, patterns of growth, Islamic patterns, pattern books, mosaic pattern, Paisley pattern, weave pattern, coat pattern . . . we live in a universe of patterns, as the American mathematician Ian Stewart puts it in *Nature's Numbers*:

> Whilst human perception is not as perfect as mathematical ideals, people need patterns as a means of creative expression across time and space and as such patterns become devices, methods of investigating personal and social worlds. Pattern is both a noun and a verb but as a verb it is an active way of seeing the world, a process by which to take in and make coherent the random and often chaotic information the world has to offer.
>
> (Stewart, 1998: 11)

Stewart argues that pattern provides a way of seeing the world as if for the first time and can open our eyes to new and unsuspected regularities. For him, pattern denotes a system of thought, or a mode of operation and a means of understanding rules. He presents a pattern method that provides a 'system of thought for recognizing, classifying and exploiting patterns'.[1]

Mathematicians are concerned with pattern as a visible indication of a hidden logic suggesting rules and order. I am taken by the idea of pattern as metaphor that can undo classifying systems and concepts of 'objectivity' to propose a method that is more intuitive, a kind of collaging process that brings other people's voices and writings with my own. Pattern as device encourages us to think in terms of multiple perspectives and mobile subjectivities, of forging collaborations and alliances and juxtaposing different viewpoints.

Pattern

What is it about pattern that I – no mathematician – find so compelling, so endlessly seductive, and so endlessly purposeful for methods of research? Part of pattern's appeal has to do with certainty and predictability. Pattern – generally characterized by rigorously repeated motifs – is the embodiment of order but taken as a metaphor it can change its spots. It can be obsessive, oppressive, unsettling, as is the eponymous 'yellow wallpaper' of the neurasthenic nightmare evoked in Charlotte Perkins Gilman's famous short story. And as the design reformers of the nineteenth century recognized pattern, however logically formulated, can also be deceitful, enabling/fostering disguise and illusion. Such suggestions give us a way of thinking about pattern as a method that is not a system or code, but rather is powerful in its ability to disturb our psychological comfort zones; this can have an impact on how we look, see, write and think. Pattern as a device – as in embroidery or writing – can lead us astray.[2] Araujo (2007: 14) argues that pattern is neither a visible indication of a hidden logic nor a neutralizing backdrop, but rather emerges as play between the two. In this way of thinking, pattern cannot be precisely located, but becomes a device that troubles categories, disturbs the boundaries between fixed meanings and chafes at rational constraint.

In this chapter, a range of spaces will be opened up by an exploration of the material knowledge afforded by pattern: conceptual, emotional, textured; the surfaces of patterning make the invisible, visible. Pattern is physical evidence of abstract knowledge, material evidence of the oscillations of the

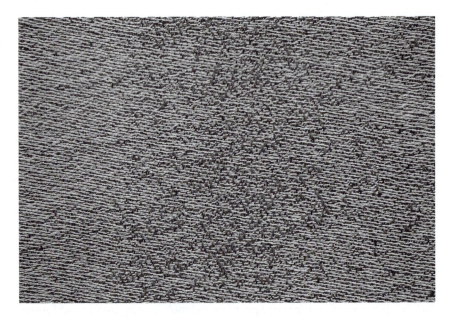

Figure 9.1 Janis Jefferies, Jacquard *Pattern 1*, detail 2004.

world. My approach here, however, is not to focus on what patterns show exactly, but rather how pattern operates as neither quite one thing nor another, refusing to be stabilized into a fixed practice.[3]

Take the example of writing. As Roland Barthes (1990) describes, written text may also be a 'woven fabric' made up of a 'weave of signifiers'. Pattern can exceed itself and act as an open-ended exchange between viewer and audience, text and reader; it can operate within a text, between the text and reader, and then be a method for the reader in becoming a writer. The implication is that all writing – all creative activity – can be located within wider systems of reference: a network of ideas across time and space, launching interdisciplinary procedures and critical discourse. Rather than thinking of the text as something finite, Barthes sees it as open-ended; the reader may join the author as a weaver of texts, a teller of tales, a patterner of practices. This is what leads me to adopt – alongside the practice of criticism – the practice of site-writing, an instance of pattern as device, a way of writing that makes visible the role of the reader.[4]

What I am trying to think about or even perform in this chapter is pattern as a textured medium, a device if you like, for thinking through and reaching out but neither fixing nor restraining the complexities of negotiating the external world we live in: a device for making an active surface through which we may negotiate our place in the world. In writing here, I am temporarily an art critic but I engage with pattern as a device precisely because of its oscillating dynamics, as method and object simultaneously: investigations of surfaces of pattern across the creative arts and material culture can open up and provoke innovative thinking. Thinking by doing, thinking through seeing, probing through writing, pattern opens up a space for practice as a way of knowing and a way of thinking. It is a form of knowledge production.

What drives this writing about acts of looking, feeling and interpretation? On the one hand, my sense of responding and engaging with a text is performative, a live essay, an attempt to create a new form of critical/creative and responsive writing that fosters dialogic engagement with ideas, concepts and a particular artwork by immersing me, the critic and author, in a pattern that confronts how I write and in what method. The format also aims to highlight the conventional downgrading of the senses in Western philosophy and to argue against the sterility of systems of knowledge that are divorced from bodily experience and the ways in which we relate to our surroundings.[5]

As a small child, and as a young teenager, I had an aversion to pattern; most likely it was the garish floral frocks of the 1950s or the large blue blooms of the wallpaper in my bedroom. Either way, pattern for me projected the anxiety of emotional chaos. Reading *The Yellow Wallpaper* (1997) did not help this.[6] The story confirmed my worst fears. Pattern making itself can be playful, repetitive or repressive; pattern can make sense – but not meaning. It can tease, frighten and enlighten. I am not so sure about pleasure. Nonetheless, the patterns that I have admired (and now revere) have been those that were the most restrained and restricted. Small repeats blur the conflicts and emotional tensions between metaphor and abstraction; a delightful sense of play can emerge, a strategy, which saves the viewer who is also a writer (or this viewer at least) from distress.

Interiors

Figure 9.2 Kathleen Mullaniff, *Interiors: Canterbury Bells*, oil on canvas (detail) 2004.

Site-writing part 1

Stand in front or rather move across the surface long enough to give it some play and it starts to play with you. Try to grasp the pattern. It defies you. Try to hold it, finger its details and you are denied. Try to let it 'unfold' itself towards you, perhaps as a musical sequence, then as your eyes flirt and flit around the motifs, listen attentively to its quiet rhythms. There is an eloquent, soft, kind of melody at work here, composed in a funny little speed of brushstrokes that entice a lightness of step in the fingers and the eyes. Observe a field of imprints, traces and gestural marks as you glance from one canvas to another, or perhaps it is a skip. All appears to be remarkably underscored but subtly orchestrated in the coupling of colours that merge as if into a hazy sketch. There's dusty pink here that glides into a blue grey pink and then chases a yellowy pulse. An edge of gold slips over and under a hatched, grey toned slippery grid. Shimmering lines and slivery flicks of black, score and cluster into an optical impression as if it is a Monday or Tuesday.[7] Do not be deceived, something is jostling for attention, but there is no single area of importance to fix your gaze, nor a hierarchy or priority of where you should fix your attention. There is a plaid, corn-like combination (but then it could be Canterbury bells, but aren't they upside down?) that run the length of the horizontal, but it will not be joined up, but then at the bottom of the canvas the motifs congeal. There is no more space. I am falling down. It does not seem safe just now to linger.

Haptic

Pattern holds back from telling you entirely what to do because you are not sure quite where to view it from. The technical crafting of Mullaniff's *Interiors* gives the viewer just enough resistance to make her linger in a flat space and narrow field of memory traces. The whole is restrained, anxiety is held at bay, for just long enough for the imagination to feel at ease (well, almost) until the oscillating dynamics begin once more.

As the surface of *Interiors* is explored in site-writing, ideas of spatial perception are shaped as a fully embodied and emotional experience of the world in which we exist. In their *Thousand Plateaus*, Deleuze and Guattari embody such a pan-sensual collaboration within a single term: haptic. They note that haptic 'may be as much visual or auditory as tactile' (Deleuze and Guattari, 1988: 493), acknowledging within the term a sensory interrelation of the eye, the ear and the limbs. As a concept, 'haptic' speaks to our embodied experience of a space's textural qualities (its weight, mass, density, pressure, humidity, temperature, presences, resonances) as they are simultaneously orchestrated by our vision, hearing and touch.

The term 'haptic' is used by Merleau-Ponty (1964) and Paterson (2007) to also involve emotional connotations and affective response. Translating the words 'haptic', 'sense' and 'emotion' in Greek, there is an obvious interconnection: haptic originates in the Greek word απτό, which means something that can be touched or *grasp*-ed. Sense, translated as aesthesi / αίσθηση, in Greek involves notions of feeling, *grasp*-ing and understanding. Consequently, the concept of 'grasp' is central to both aesthesi (sense) and haptic. Emotion, on the other hand, translated in Greek as αίσθημα / aesthema, shares the same root with aesthesi, as both derive from the word αισθάνομαι / aesthanome, whose ambiguous meaning can be equally translated as 'I sense' or 'I feel'. Among these three words – haptic, sense and emotion – one can find an underlying relation that brings out the very nature of haptic as a term that is ultimately bound up with emotional grasping.

The term 'haptic' is further elaborated in Fisher's 'Relational sense: towards a haptic aesthetics' (1997), where she addresses the haptic as the merging of the bodily senses and affect. Such a concept can be theoretically supported by the work of Berenson (1906), in which he notes that our bodily response to the 'tactile properties' of a space depends on our understanding of that space's ability to affect and 'touch' us. From a haptic point of view, pattern provokes our bodies into a visceral response rather than a purely visual grasping of form alone.

Site-writing part 2

And now, somewhere in the Victoria and Albert Museum, London, Mullaniff comes across a tiny, densely worked eighteenth-century wood block print on stitched cotton. It forms a pleasing textural pattern. The pattern is thought to be made up of Canterbury bells. The dye is madder, the blue is hand painted and the bells appear to bleed one into the other. Recalled and traced from memory, this is where interiors begin their journey, a kernel of an idea that will permit the painter to reflect upon her own interiority. 'I will only like it if it's pretty', she says, when making interiors over an eight-year period.[8] Motion and rest, rhythmic unity combine to indulge perception but the decorative surfaces that I see now both impregnate and transform that which may, at first glance, seem merely pleasing to the eye. A fine line is trodden between excess and modesty. Which is it here? The surface is dispersed, the damp cloth is put down, and the paintings conjure their own disappearance as light floods into the studio. I am left to remember what I might have seen.

Surface space

In pattern-based work within contemporary art practice, repeated forms are presented in merged space. This means that the surface structure is not weighted, balanced or logically coherent, but forms coalesce and converge, they merge in and on the surface of the picture plane. Meaning is derived from the viewer attending to the repeated intervals and arrangements of patterned elements, viewed simultaneously. An overall arrangement is scanned in a never-ending process of engagement within the changeable worlds of appearance, perception and meaning. Robin Leher describes this kind of scanning from the artist's point of view but we can also adopt it as a viewer's perspective as we scan the surfaces of material forms. To repeat and reemphasize, I am using pattern as a verb rather than as a noun. It is a way of seeing the world, a process by which to take in and make coherent the random and often chaotic information the world has to offer. It is the thread of my connections that makes the world intelligible to me. The act of connecting, of 'patterning', provides a structure through which is sieved new information, which in time becomes part of the structure through which new information is sieved.[9]

Detail, the minute and intricate deployment of pattern, has the potential to destabilize an internal ordering of surface structure. Detail participates in a larger semantic field, bounded on the one hand by the ornamental, with its connotations of effeminacy and decadence, and on the other, by the everyday, whose prissiness for masculine critics is rooted in the domestic sphere presided over by women (Schor, 1987).[10] At the beginning of the twentieth century, Adolf Loos accused ornament, and by implication decoration, of the crime of turning back the clock of cultural development. In the essay 'Ornament and crime', Loos (1908/1998) argues that all ornament can be traced to childish graffiti – sexual images smeared with faecal matter.[11] He saw the same impulse manifested in the practice of tattooing, claiming that only savages and criminals bear tattoos. Decoration represents only the lowest of human impulses for Loos, and so it must be stripped from art and design, especially from useful objects.

The taste for the decorative was pathologized as feminine, as embellishment, as style, as frivolous, as excessive and was therefore constantly repressed within the rhetorical devices of modernism. Detail and fabric were viewed as decorative extras and were excluded from the rigid confines of the regularly ordered space of the picture frame. Once released, detail and pattern become excessively magnified and erupted, exceeding the borders that once tried to contain them. In his discussion of ornament, Mick Carter (1997) observes that, with its association with adornment and decoration, it has a tendency to wander from its proper place, threatening and undermining the aesthetic value of an artwork. Drawing on Derrida's suspicions of any rigid distinction between essential and non-essential (supplementary) registers, Carter argues that it is only within the play, the tensions between ornamental errancy and the confines of the picture frame, that meaning may be created.[12] The idea of play, being mischievous, playing off and against the rule that the centre is the focal point of a work, such as in this case a painting, is challenged by pattern as a device – an all-over ornamental pattern or design that goes astray, runs amok, is a supplement that takes centre stage. There is a double sense of the supplement here, the supplementary economy of the feminine as described by Carter above.

Like patterning itself, pattern painting – an art movement situated within the US during the 1970s and 1980s – was viewed as 'two dimensional, non-hierarchical, all over, a-centric, and anionic'.[13] Many of the women artists who participated in this movement, such as Valerie Joudon, Miriam Schapiro and Joyce Kozloff, produced paintings that purposively deployed the decorative: whereas minimalist paintings were often austere, pattern paintings were boldly coloured, and sometimes suggestive of floral patterns.[14] In the 1970s, John Perrault recognized the movement as a challenge to the divisions between fine and decorative arts, referring to weaving and mosaics (Joyce Kozloff made mosaics as wall panel in architectural settings) as having essential qualities that gave pattern its surfaces and details. He went on to claim that the grid was the basis of all patterning and that weaving was its true source by virtue of the way in which the lines of the 'warp and weft make up the primordial square block grid'.[15]

In her essay for the catalogue of the 1996 Jaudon retrospective, art historian Anna C. Chave fully explores the pattern and decoration movement as a context for Jaudon's early work, emphasizing the distinctly feminist inflection of the movement.[16] As Chave observes, quoting the art historian E. H. Gombrich, decorative richness offers 'a feast for the eye without demanding that we should taste every dish' (Chave, 1996: 39) .[17] Interestingly, Gombrich analyzed two functions of perception in respect of decorative richness and pattern. For him, these were associated with the differences between the presentation of form in pictorial and pattern art – looking at order and scanning for order – with the cognitive skills associated with these two functions drawn along gender lines.[18] Pattern art has been historically noted as a sign of the repetitiousness of women's art and was explained away as a reflection of the repetitive nature of women's domestic work.[19] Lucy Lippard's oft-quoted observation in Charlotte Robinson's (1983) *The Artist and the Quilt* that 'the quilt has become the prime visual metaphor for women's lives, women's culture' provided a situated knowledge for a version of feminist art practice that now may be seen as universalizing female experience (Lippard, 1983: 18). In the verbal quilt of (an) other feminist text, Rachel Blau DuPlessis argues that there is an appeal to the voice of the female body 'which speaks of itself as subject as: non-hierarchic . . . breaking hierarchical structures, making an even display of elements over the surface with no climatic movement, having the materials organized into many centres and many patterns of experience' (DuPlessis, 1990: 5) Reflections on self, on writing, on pattern as I write on site are unsettling. When 'I' reflects on 'I', what do I imagine it to be? Perhaps 'I' will only know myself when another is there? Is the 'I' that makes a piece of the work the same 'I' that will write its interpretation? How 'I' move will be in relation to that which coheres the patterning of that which is performed through this text.

Site-writing part 3

I repeat. Which is it here? Where is here now? The surface is dispersed, the damp cloth is put down, and the paintings conjure their own disappearance as light floods into the studio. I am left to remember what I might have seen working with writing and visual devices that probe reflective considerations; between the writer and the reader, the artist and artwork, somewhere between the Victoria and Albert Museum a studio and the yellow wallpaper and an interior on my wall.

Conclusion

Mark Freeman suggests moving towards a 'more poetic way of writing' in research, 'using words in such a way that they can carry the weight, and the depth, of the phenomena in question' (Ruppel, 2008: 32). For me, here, it is about pattern as a device, site-writing and the 'I'. Such writing, Ruppel goes on to say, 'will be less orientated toward arguing, convincing, making a definite case, than toward appealing, suggesting, opening, pointing toward the possible' (ibid.: 33).

Writing in research can produce many sites of interdisciplinary exchange following what can be perceived as a spatial pattern of enquiry. In order to find a place from which to reflect upon new modes of enquiry, new ways of knowing and being, I have to draw on the patterns that emerge out of 'situated knowledges' (Haraway, 1988: 111).[20] The interrelations between where I might be sited and located operate in the slippery exchange between practices of writing and the writing of practices. Sometimes for a nomadic theorist and a theoretical nomad the interstitial relationship between patterns of thinking becomes a compelling device to ask where does autobiography end and theory begin? Where does writing the self blur the boundaries of research as an academic convention and point towards the possible and the experimental? To return to where I think I started, I am taken by the idea of pattern as metaphor, a method that is intuitive, a kind of collaging process that brings other people's voices and writings into 'our' own. This pattern*ing* device opens us to engage in multiple perspectives, mobile subjectivities juxtaposing different viewpoints at the moment of being on site and in view.

Notes

1 Ian Stewart is Professor of Mathematics and Director of the Mathematics Awareness Centre at the University of Warwick.
2 See www.thefreedictionary.com/pattern (accessed 18 January 2010).
3 For an account of the textile origins of pattern and on its prolific qualities, see Kraft (2004).
4 See Rendell (2011), in which she outlines a theoretical framing for the spatialization of art-writing as site-writing, identifying the potential of particular concepts in feminist, art and literary criticism for developing understandings of positionality and subjectivity in critical writing.
5 See Jay (1993).
6 In the short story *The Yellow Wallpaper* by Charlotte Perkins Gilman, it is interesting to note that an otherwise simple plot becomes increasingly complex due to the of the wallpaper. The story describes a woman, her psychological difficulties, and her husband's so called therapeutic treatment of her ailments during the late 1880s. It was first published in *The New England Magazine* in 1892 but the edition I have is the Dover one published in 1997 and called *The Yellow Wallpaper and Other Stories*.
7 This essay is composed as homage of another kind of trace. It attempts to trace Virginia Woolf's (2003) *Monday or Tuesday*, a deliberately fragmentary and experimental sketch in which a woman gazes at a mark on a wall. I am gazing at *Interiors*, three paintings by Kathleen Mullaniff (oil on canvas, 5' × 6', 1995–2003). I return to them in 2009. One is hanging on my bedroom wall in New Cross, South East London. Colour is given an expression in words.
8 Kathleen Mullaniff and Janis Jefferies in conversation, Chisenhale studios, London Friday 21 November 2003 and St. Leonards-on-Sea, East Sussex, 4 July 2009.
9 See Rickey (1990).
10 See Schor (1987).
11 See Loos (1908/1998).
12 See Carter (1997).
13 Perreault, 'Issues in Pattern Painting', 34.
14 See Swartz (2007).

15 Perreault, 'Issues in Pattern Painting', 36.
16 Anna Chave cites Carrie Rickey on this aspect of Jaudon's work. See Chave (1996).
17 Gombrich, E. H. 'The Sense of Order', quoted by Chave (1996: 39).
18 See Kraft (1984).
19 See my essays on the relationship between women's domestic work and textiles, 'Text and textiles: weaving across the borderlines', in *New Feminist Art Criticism* (2001), ed. Katy Deepwell, and 'Textiles: what can she know?' in *Feminist Visual Culture* (2001), eds Fiona Carson and Claire Pajaczkowska. In addition, see *Heresies: A Feminist Publication on Art and Politics* no. 4 on 'Women's traditional arts: the politics of aesthetics', 1978. The special issue also includes essays by Melissa Meyer and Miriam Schapiro, 'Waste not/want not: femmage' and Linda Nochlin, 'Excerpts from women and the decorative arts'.
20 'Situated knowledges' are marked knowledges that produce maps of consciousness reflecting the various categories of gender, class, race, and nationality of who is speaking, who is writing and from where. Donna Haraway (1988) develops these ideas in *Situated Knowledge: The Science Question in Feminism and the Privilege of Partial Perspective*, pp. 575–99.

References

Araujo, A. (2007) 'Introduction: a pattern constellation', Haecceity Papers, 3 (1): *Pattern*, Sydney: University of Sydney Press.

Barthes, R. (1990) *New Critical Essays*, Berkley, CA: New California Press.

Carson, F. and Pajaczkowska, C. (eds) (2001) *Feminism and Visual Culture,* Edinburgh: Edinburgh University Press.

Carter, M. (1997) *Putting a Face on Things: Studies in Imaginary Materials*, Sydney: Power Publications.

Chave, A. C. (1996) 'Disorderly order: the art of Valerie Jaudon' in *Valerie Joudan: A Retrospective*, Jackson, MI: University Press of Mississippi.

Deleuze, G. and Guattari, F. (1988) *A Thousand Plateaus: Capitalism and Schizophrenia*, London: Athlone.

Deepwell, K. (ed.) (2001) *New Feminist Art Criticism*, Manchester: Manchester University Press, pp. 164–73.

DuPlessis, B. R. (1990) *Pink Guitar: Writing as Feminist Practice*, New York: Routledge.

Fisher, J. (1997) 'Relational sense: towards a haptic aesthetics', *Parachute*, 87 (1): 4–11.

Gilman, C. P. (1997) *The Yellow Wallpaper and Other Stories*, New York: Dover Books.

Haraway, D. (1988) 'Situated knowledge: the science question in feminism and the privilege of partial perspective', *Feminist Studies*, 14 (3), University of Maryland.

Jay, M. (1993) *Downcast Eyes: The Denigration of Vision in Twentieth Century Thought*, Berkeley, CA: University of California.

Kraft, K. (2004) 'Textile patterns and their epistemological function', in *Textile: The Journal of Cloth and Culture*, 3 (3), Oxford: Berg Publishers.

Kraft, S. 'Cognitive function and women's art', *Women's Art Journal*, 4 (2), Fall 1983/Winter 1984: 5–9.

Lippard, L. (1983) 'Up, down and across: a new frame for new quilts', in C. Robinson (ed.) *The Artist and the Quilt*, New York: Knopf Press, pp. 32–43.

Loos, A. (1908/1998) *Ornament and Crime: Selected Essays: Adolf Loos*, selected and introduced by Adolf Opel, trans. Michael Mitchell, Riverside, CA: Adriane Press.

Merleau-Ponty, M. (1964) *The Primacy of Perception and other Essays on Phenomeno-logical Psychology, the Philosophy of Art, History and Politics*, Evanston, IL: Northwestern University Press.

Paterson, M. (2007) *The Senses of Touch: Haptics, Affects and Technologies*, Oxford: Berg Publishers.

Rendell, J. (2011) *Site-Writing: The Architecture of Art Criticism*, London: I. B. Taurius.

Rickey, C. (1990) 'Decorating, ornament, pattern and utility: four tendencies in search of a movement', in G. Politi and H. Kontova (eds) *Flash Art: Two Decades of History XXI Years*, Milan: MIT Press, p. 61.

Ruppel, S., Dege, M., Andrews, M. and Squire, C. (2008) 'Tackling problems of qualitative social research: a conversation', *Forum: Qualitative Social Research*, 9 (1): 41, available at: www.qualitative-research.net/fqs-texte/1-08/08-1-41-e.htm (accessed 8 March 2011).

Schor, N. (1987) *Reading in Detail: Aesthetics and the Feminine*, London: Methuen.

Stewart, I. (1998) *Nature's Numbers: Discovering Order and Pattern in the Universe*, London: Phoenix, Orion Books.

Swartz, A. (2007), *Pattern and Decoration: An Ideal Vision in American Art, 1975–1985*, Yonkers, NY: Hudson River Museum.

Woolf, V. (2003) *Monday or Tuesday*, London: Hesperus Press.

10 Pattern

Paul Stenner

Introduction

I am watching in serene amazement. The broken and twisted iron of Brighton and Hove's decadent West Pier sets the stage for the curious air-born dance of thousands of starlings. They swoop in unison towards the sea and then swirl back upwards, dispersing into a multitude of tiny elements, before changing direction once more and clotting into a dense and gently undulating mass. Although I would love to join them, my fate is to remain an observer, and what I observe, it seems to me, is a particularly pure expression of pattern. Not being capable of *defining* pattern adequately, I wish first to use these starlings merely to identify some significant features of the device[1] of pattern before sketching some ways in which it might be relevant to social scientists.

The 'all together' of pattern

At a basic level, pattern concerns the relation between unity and multiplicity. A pattern suggests a multiplicity of elements gathered into the unity of a particular arrangement. As such, it presupposes the concept of distinguishable *modes of togetherness*. Thus the many starlings swarming over Brighton's West Pier form before my eyes as a patterned unity as they swirl into a dense flock, gathering into a dark cloud one moment and dispersing into a looser arrangement the next. One moment the many starlings are unified into a coherent collective, the next they disperse into a more chaotic multiplicity. The many are gathered. The many are dispersed.

In dealing with the device of pattern, then, we encounter something 'synthetic' that is often neglected in science. Science has typically excelled at analysis – at reducing unities to their parts – rather than composing them into patterns, or explaining their mode of togetherness. The recent sciences of complexity that deal with questions of 'emergence' are an exception (Kauffman, 1993; Holland, 1998). Studies of ant colonies or cellular automata demonstrate that a few simple rules applicable at the micro-level to many simple building blocks can generate complex emergent macro-level effects (Holland, 1998). Thus, each of Hoftadter's (1979) ants is conceived as an agent with a modest repertoire of potential (re)actions, and yet, in concert, and without a central 'executive', many ants can generate adaptations that far exceed the capacities of any single agent.

Likewise, given time, the initially rather random clay-gathering activity of termites results in a colossal termitarium, thanks to simple innate inclinations such as the preference to deposit one's ball of clay on larger balls of clay. Each starling need only track the movements of around seven others in the flock in order to generate the fluctuating cohesion of a swarming display.

This relation between gathering and dispersal, however, suggests that if pattern is a unification of multiplicities, then we must be careful not to let this mean that pattern concerns the gathering *and not* the dispersal of multiplicities. Rather, the pattern is precisely the alternation of gathering and dispersal: the gathering of gathering and dispersal into the unity of a pattern. When I observe the pulse of their alternating pattern as it unfolds in time, I observe a higher-order, 'emergent' pattern. I observe the *contrast* between gathering and dispersal, and recognize that contrast as part of a pattern. Gathering, dispersal and their contrast thus take their place among the many that are unified for me into the form of this pattern. The starlings fascinate me because they seem to 'pulse' between order and chaos. By playing the *difference* between gathering and dispersal, pattern can add a little order to chaos and a little chaos to order.

Time is pivotal to the playing of this difference. Just as a termitarium will emerge only through the cumulative iteration of simple activities over time, so it takes time for the starlings to pulse and swarm. The changes in their mode of togetherness are partly explained by the endogenous dynamics of the pattern itself: as they veer too close at time T1, so they will steer apart until they generate a dispersed state at T2, and so on. The pattern is thus not exclusively generated by external efficient causes, but also by self-generated internal dynamics. What applies to a flock of starlings also applies to one. Every cell in a starling's body must continually recreate itself on a moment-by-moment basis according to a distinct biological pattern. A starling is thus a complex pattern of interaction whose 'unity' persists, not despite, but because of an ongoing turnover in 'the many' components of the pattern (Maturana and Varela, 1975). Likewise, each cell is a process of continual regeneration of pattern amidst a flux of energy and matter. As Prigogene's famous work on dissipative structures has illustrated so well, these pattern forming tendencies of self-organization have their origins even in inorganic matter (Prigogine and Stengers, 1984).

Pattern in social science

I deliberately began with examples drawn from the natural sciences, since one value of our device is to invite cross-fertilization between 'natural' and 'social' disciplines. This is important because one clear pattern within sociological discourse is the drawing of an un-crossable line between those disciplines that supposedly deal with 'meaning' and those that deal with meaningless causal forces (Weber, 1903–1917/1949). What possible relevance can a swarm of starlings have to a meaningfully constructed human society?

According to Mark Erickson (personal communication), sociologists rarely write directly about pattern, but spend their whole careers seeking them out. Perhaps the origin of this ambivalence is the highly abstract and temporal nature of social patterns. I have stated that even 'physical' patterns can be understood only as products of process. When it comes to social events such as a conversation or a dance, however, we are dealing with something maximally *temporal* that, like a piece of live music, endures in only a minimally *spatial* manner.

The less spatially evident a pattern is, the harder it is to visualize and understand. It is easier to visualize the built environment of a city than the social processes that sustain it. Sociologists must struggle even to describe their basic subject matter. The classic texts can be read as offering means to grasp abstract patterns in a more concrete and manageable form. Max Weber's 'ideal types', for instance, are patterns in the sense of 'exemplars' that bring out more clearly the contours of otherwise thoroughly abstract matters: charismatic authority is a prototypical pattern to be contrasted with traditional and legal/rational authority (ibid.). Marx saw in the relation to the means of production the key pattern for understanding human history and for predicting and intervening in its future (Marx, 1848/1948). Durkheim sought patterns in suicide rates that could be correlated with different modes of social organization because he recognized that mundane concepts were tacitly patterned by social factors. Parsons hoped to better describe different social systems in terms of the five dichotomies he called the 'pattern variables' (Parsons, 1977). To find a 'social' pattern is to discern a regularity: something predictable that recurs. Micro-sociologists (and also psychotherapists), for instance, have long spoken of repeated interpersonal and intra-psychic patterns, as when certain people appear recurrently to select abusive relationships (Scheff, 1994). A pattern *repeats*. Rather than attempt to survey the sociological application of pattern, I will focus on two exemplars: Kuhnian paradigms and Eliasian figurations.

Paradigms

According to the *Shorter Oxford English Dictionary*, the words 'pattern' and 'patron' became differentiated as late as 1700, and still today the word pattern conveys the sense of a model, exemplar or ideal that deserves imitation. Christ provides a model for Christians to pattern themselves after, for instance. In this usage, the derivation from *pater* – the Latin word for father – is clear, and hence the relation to words such as paternity, patriarchy, patrimony and patronage. Other more familiar meanings of pattern arguably derive from pattern in this sense of exemplar. It easily extends to the notion of pattern as a design or plan for making something (such as a knitting pattern), or to a decorative design (as on a Paisley shirt).

Kuhn (1969) introduced the notion of a scientific *paradigm*. Since the late 1800s, 'paradigm' has meant something like 'thought pattern'. For Kuhn, indeed, paradigms provide exemplary patterns for the activities of 'normal science'. Thanks to the paradigm, these activities become a predictably structured set of values, techniques, educational practices, etc. (a *disciplinary matrix*). In the postscript to the 1969 edition of the *Structure of Scientific Revolutions*, Kuhn attempts to ward off misunderstandings by stating clearly that the primary meaning of paradigm is as *exemplar* rather than as *disciplinary matrix*.

Interestingly, in Kuhn's work we encounter once again our pattern of gathering and dispersal. That is to say, the paradigm/pattern is an exemplary piece of scientific work that has the improbable effect of transforming a state of confused and chaotic dispersal into a gathered unity of scientific practice. The paradigm-as-exemplar (e.g. Aristotle's *Physica*, Ptolemy's *Almagest*, Newton's *Principia* and *Optiks*, Franklin's *Electricity*, Lavoisier's *Chemistry* or Lyell's *Geology*) commands an agreement and a commitment that is unprecedented. It *unifies*. The exemplar organizes the many disparate scientists into one paradigmatic venture, since the paradigm must be 'sufficiently unprecedented to attract an enduring group of adherents away from competing modes of scientific activity' (ibid.: 10). Thus the paradigm, for Kuhn, collects the mulitiplicity into a gathered unity, and puts an end to the scene of rival camps squabbling at cross-purposes in their different theory languages. This discovery was a genuine surprise to Kuhn: 'What is surprising. . . is that such initial divergences should ever largely disappear' (ibid.: 17).

A paradigm thus gathers a previously dispersed multiplicity into an order with clear aims, norms, etc. Not unlike a religion, the paradigm provides a pattern that can be transmitted through time. Not unlike the body of a starling, an established science is a process of continual regeneration of pattern amidst a continual turnover of 'the many' components (scientists) of the pattern. Pattern is thus central to notions of order, structure, stability, and so on. Nevertheless, sciences, like organisms, also *change*, and pattern is also pivotal to an understanding of transformation. We might say that it lends a little stability to change and a little change to stability. Change can thus follow a pattern – e.g. from mechanical to organic solidarity – but such change is also change in pattern.

There are two clear modes of advancement: (1) by gathering more and more details into patterns that are already assigned, and (2) by way of the invention of novel patterns (Whitehead, 1938/1968: 57). In the context of the development of mental patterns ('schemata'), Piaget called (a) 'assimilation' and (b) 'accommodation'. In the context of the history of science, Kuhn wrote of (a) 'normal science' (in which scientists 'mop up' facts in accordance to accepted paradigmatic practice) and (b) 'revolutionary science' (in which a novel pattern of scientific practice accommodates anomalous findings). The history of a given science thus reflects the pattern of our starlings, with periods of (gathered) normal science being interrupted by the dispersal of revolution until the new paradigm establishes itself (cf. Stenner, 2002). When a scientific discipline changes paradigm, or when a child crosses a threshold of development, there is a change in dominant pattern: in form of thought as well as content. We once again begin to see patterns in common between sociology and the natural sciences: 'scientific development is, like biological, a unidirectional and irreversible process' (Kuhn, 1969).

In returning to the pattern of gathering and dispersal, my intention is not to make the absurd claim that there are no relevant differences between swarming starlings and the development of science. Recognizing this pattern demands a feat of abstraction. It is only by dropping practically all of the detail in both situations that their structural equivalence can be grasped. The structural equivalence is the *manner* of the contrast between gathered and dispersed states of a multiplicity. The details about the nature of the multiplicity at play – the differences between birds and scientists (or what we could call the differences in the forms of *matter* involved) – are not necessary for the identification of this *manner*. Indeed, such details of matter are likely to distract us from the pattern. A pattern, as Whitehead (1927/1928: 115) suggests, is the 'manner' of a complex contrast abstracted from the 'matter' of its concrete embodiment. The matter, however, may well be highly relevant for *explaining* the pattern. It is here that differences between the natural and social sciences become distinctly relevant. It makes a considerable difference if the many agents that make up one's pattern are termites, starlings or people. Developments in science involve highly intelligent agency absent among the starlings.

Figurations

Although science has been dominated by *number*, the question of pattern lies beyond all questions of mere *quantity*. One learns little by attending only to the sheer *number* of starlings involved in a swarm. Having said that, number is itself nothing but an extreme (and useful) form of abstraction characterized by pattern. Given three rocks, three rabbits and three Rabbis, their matter is irrelevant to the manner of their 'threeness'. This differential importance of pattern and number is particularly apparent in the social sciences, where number is often used merely as a proxy to help visualize the actual data, as in suicide statistics (Durkheim, 1897/1951). To illustrate the value accorded to pattern in sociology, I will turn briefly to the work of a sociologist who took process seriously: Norbert Elias.

Norbert Elias used the word pattern regularly, but the concept is best expressed in his core construct: *figuration*. As Goudsblom and Mennell (1998) point out, Elias derived figuration from the Gestalt notion of *configuration*. In adapting the notion to sociological matters, Elias emphasized that human beings are interdependent and never to be understood as simply self-contained individuals. More specifically, lives are lived in social figurations that – much like a tango, mazurka or some other dance – require specific men and women to compose them, but exist as a pattern relatively independently of those specific individuals who happen to be 'dancing' here and now. Consistent with our analysis so far, the temporary unity of figuration is a pattern that persists despite the constant turnover of its elements or components, and which accordingly entails dynamics of its own that are engendered by, but not reducible to, the agency of its elements. Like dances and paradigms, figurations change and develop over time, and are nested within larger figurations that also change.

For the most part, Elias concerned himself with changing and historically specific issues, but there is one pattern that he considered universal. This concerns the established-outsider figuration that Elias and Scotson (1965/1994) discuss in a book based on fieldwork with working class communities near Leicester in the late 1950s and early 1960s. An established-outsider figuration, as the name suggests, is a pattern involving the relations between at least two interdependent groups in which the 'established' group reserves good things for itself (such as social positions with a high power potential) and excludes members of the other group(s) from them (and otherwise exploits them). This figuration recurs in numerous forms throughout history, as with feudal lords and their *villeins*; 'whites' and 'blacks'; Gentiles and Jews; men and women; capitalist and proletariat; powerful nation state and relatively powerless; and so on. A key part of the pattern at play is that the more powerful group considers themselves superior as people and as endowed with a unique group *charisma*, which merits their powerful position. The interdependent less powerful group, by contrast, is viewed as deserving its position due to innate inferiority and lack of virtue.

To investigate how these practices, images and beliefs are actually produced and maintained, Elias and Scotson conducted a detailed study of a particular example of the figuration. As Elias puts it:

> one encountered in this small community what appeared to be a universal regularity of any established-outsider figuration: the established group attributed to its members superior human characteristics; it excluded all members of the other group from non-occupational social contact with its own members; the taboo on such contacts was kept alive by means of social control such as praise-gossip about those who observed it and the threat of blame-gossip against suspected offenders.
>
> (ibid.: xvi)

What is particularly instructive about the Elias and Scotson study is that this pattern was played out between two neighbouring communities that seemed identical in practically all respects (class, ethnicity, religion, income, education, standard of housing) except that 'one group was formed by old residents established in the neighbourhood for two or three generations and the other was a group of newcomers' (ibid.: xvii).

The study could thus be thought of as an examination of the *minimal conditions* required to engender the established-outsider pattern (and as such it is a precursor to Henri Tajfel's (1970) Minimal Groups Paradigm in social psychology):

> one could see that 'oldness' of association, with all that it implied, was, on its own, able to create the degree of group cohesion, the collective identification, the commonality of norms, which are apt to induce the gratifying euphoria that goes with the consciousness of belonging to a group of higher value and with the complementary contempt for other groups.
>
> (Elias and Scotson, 1965/1994: xvii)

The phrase 'with all that it implied' is not inconsequential here. Indeed, what 'oldness' of association implied in this case was a significant difference in the cohesion of the two groups. Families that had known each other over generations had evolved a common set of norms and mode of living with an internally complex hierarchy, and this itself constitutes a significant power advantage with respect to a barely integrated set of newcomers. It enabled the established group to reserve influential social positions for its own members, for instance, and this in turn enhances cohesion while denying it to the excluded. In this case, cohesion = power.

In other words, in relation to the pattern that has been the theme throughout this chapter, the 'established' community was relatively *gathered* and the 'outsider' community relatively *dispersed*. Elias suggests that inequalities we typically attribute in other situations to more obviously visible factors, such as race or class, may actually be underpinned by the less visible factor of cohesion. The unexpected parallels with the history of science should be immediately apparent: a paradigm creates an *establishment* in a science, which is to say that it *establishes* it. It is interesting that the discovery of this pattern appears to have been no less a surprise for Elias than it was for Kuhn:

> The sameness of the pattern of stigmatisation used by high power groups in relation to their outsider groups all over the world – the sameness of this pattern in spite of all the cultural differences – may at first be a little unexpected. But the symptoms of human inferiority which a high-powered established group is most likely to perceive in a low-powered outsider group, which serve their members as justification for their own elevated position and as proof of their own superior worth, are usually engendered in members of the inferior group – inferior in terms of their power ratio – by the very conditions of their outsider position and the humiliation and oppression that go with it.
>
> (ibid.: xxvi)

Subject/object

Before concluding, a brief abstract detour is necessary if the device of pattern is to fulfil its potential. Is pattern something in the world or merely something in the eye of the beholder: an illusion that might disappear when properly understood? Carefully conceived, I suggest that the device of pattern can help precisely to avoid this kind of bifurcation of the world into subject and object, observer and observed, in which the subjective mind of the observer projects its imaginary patterns on to a supposedly real material world (patterned or not *as it is,* whether 'experienced' or not). This will require a non-representational (Gibson, 1966; Brown and Stenner, 2009) articulation of the concepts of subjectivity and objectivity in relation to pattern.

First, with respect to subjectivity, it is important not to deny the phenomenon that Bartlett calls *effort after meaning,* whereby people tend to impose meaningful patterns on what may turn out to be random events, or the Gestalt psychological phenomenon of *Prägnanz,* whereby we simplify perceptual data into the most convenient pattern (see Ash, 1998). The swarming starlings clearly do not occupy simply two states, one gathered, one dispersed, but take on innumerable positions, none of which will ever be exactly repeated. In fact, part of the joy of watching them is the experience of 'Bergsonian' duration, whereby one configuration 'melts' into the next as when a musical melody unfolds in real time.[2] There is nevertheless a tendency for my perceptual experience to identify and enhance contrast effects, 'cutting out' or 'parsing' simplified patterns of image from the undivided flux that Bergson called the 'fluid continuity of the real' (Bergson, 1911/1998). As the Gestalt psychologists emphasized, this tendency is nothing less than a search for the relative invariants of regularity, repetition and predictability (i.e. of pattern), without which the complexity and perpetual novelty of the experienced-world would overwhelm us. In principle, this is also why social scientists are interested in patterns: grasping a genuine pattern renders the world more comprehensible, predictable and tractable.

There is no doubt, in short, that 'subjectivity' is characterized by what we might call *patterning*: the more-or-less active and creative tendency to *lend* pattern, rather than to merely receive and transmit what is given. Patterning is characterized by 'subtraction' in that it entails a reduction in complexity with respect to the possibilities offered by the data at issue. Patterning, in short, is a matter of *selectivity*: out of all the possibilities for experience offered by the world, only *this* experience is actualized, and it is actualized in accordance with the present concerns and past experiences of the subject. As Whitehead (1927/1928: 21) insists, an occasion of experience (a *happening*) involves a subject entertaining its objects and selectively patterning them into a unity. Let us call 'subjectivity' nothing but this process of patterning or lending pattern as experienced from the perspective of the emerging event. In a given subjective occasion, the many (data) are grasped as one, and thereby increased by one (the *pattern* enters the world). Once the patterning has happened, we are left with the pattern. Let us therefore call the pattern thus produced an 'object' to distinguish it from the subjective process of patterni*ng*. This pattern/object can then take its place as one of the many patterned objects to be entertained and patterned in the event of the next happening. Since a subject patterns its objects, we might say that subjectivity *objectifies*. The world is objectified in a given pattern. Subjectivity is the becoming of objectivity, and objective reality is the expression of experience. In this resolutely non-representational account, subjectivity is not a stage-play about the real world, but a key ingredient in its concretion, and the device of pattern is pivotal to its articulation.

Elsewhere, following Whitehead and Bergson, I have suggested that a key problem with representational thought based on a bifurcated nature is, first, that subject and object are divorced and, second, that subjectivity, agency, experience and so on are construed as purely a matter of the high-level, conscious experiences of human beings (Stenner, 2008). Instead, subject and object must be seen as intimately related moments of experience and expression (patterning/patterned), and experience, subjectivity and agency must be recognized as being *distributed* throughout nature, albeit with more or less relevance and consequence. It is not by accident, for example, that Hofstadter refers to his ants as *agents,* as it is their (minimal) selectivity, taken in unison, that generates the emergent powers of the colony. Termites, likewise, have comparatively minimal agency, but it is their capacity to differentiate between a large and a small lump of clay and to act differently towards them that provides the generative basis for the termitarium. A common daisy could not produce that effect in the world, but even a common daisy can selectively extract from diverse soils and sunlight the elements it needs to sustain itself. This subtractive operation of selectivity is a germinal form of experience that serves to newly pattern a small portion of the world. As Bergson pointed out, even hydrochloric acid, when it encounters calcium carbonate, acts upon it by picking out the salt from its base, making a 'decision' of sorts (a 'cut', albeit without the trace of consciousness). Each of these is an instance of agency, subjectivity and experience, but what cannot be ignored is that when it comes to human beings, the power and the significance of the subjective is massively amplified and impossible to ignore without gross distortion.

Hence, the experience of watching the starlings and being absorbed in their patterns is *my* experience and not that of the starlings. But that does not make it 'merely subjective'. My experience of the starlings is entirely dependent on the manner in which they are presented to my experience by way of the functionings of my body, especially my brain. What we discern of the world is known through our bodily activity. But my body is at the same time merely one set of functionings within the broader set comprised by the world, including the starlings. The world is implicated in the happenings of my body, and my body is implicated in the happenings of the world. In front of Brighton's West Pier, each occasion of my experience presupposes the antecedent world – including the swarming starlings – as active in its own existence. We are, on one level, part of the same pattern or mode of togetherness. However, although it is true that the alternation of gathering and dispersal is a pattern *for me* (or for those of us with memories allowing us to grasp that the starlings gathered at time T1 were the same as those dispersed at time T2), and not 'for' the starlings, it is nevertheless equally true that the movements I perceive are creditable to the combined (albeit minimal) selective agency of the starlings as they concern themselves with their business of living.

This situation is not adequately understood if we assume that my brain generates a conscious 'representation' of the 'reality' of the starlings, somehow 'adding' pattern to the brute materiality of the latter. On the contrary, one might say instead that, in observing the starlings, my own duration became synchronized with that of the starlings. To watch them, I had to wait for them and their movements. To paraphrase Bergson, my ego had to let itself live in the sense that I had to live through and with the movements of the birds with 'a certain portion of my own duration' (Bergson, 1911/1998: 9–10). It is one thing to imagine or to *think* about such movement (in which case I can protract or contract the temporality at my own whim), it is quite another to *live* it. In the latter case, through my subjectivity, the starlings and their collective activities were objectified. Entering as objects, they became a significant aspect of the environment as active in my own becoming and implicated or 'folded' (Bohm, 1995) into the experience that is me at that moment. The starlings and me were less like a reality versus a representation and more like contemporary isomorphic patterns.

Conclusion

In my opinion, the device of pattern is relevant to social scientists, not primarily because it suggests new methods or techniques which can be shown to improve upon existing methods and techniques, but because it lures us towards an improved general conception of an immanent universe in process of becoming. It suggests and provokes a more adequate cosmology that does not entail the privileging of substance over process and the division of the world into mutually irreconcilable subjects and objects associated in turn with separated social and natural worlds. As a mode of togetherness, it calls for an associated ontology capable of attending to the basic togetherness of things and to the forms of creative synthesis whereby novelty of pattern, and hence qualitative change, enters the world. As such, pattern is a device for a cosmology of immanence wherein the observer is never ultimately separate from the pattern observed, but always part of a broader unity of pattern. Perhaps, after all, I can join them.

Notes

1   The concept of pattern I articulate in this chapter resonates with Foucault's concept of the 'device' or *dispositif*, which he defines as a 'system of relations' established between a 'thoroughly heterogeneous ensemble' of elements (Foucault, 1977: 214). In general terms, a *device* would thus be an arrangement that lends unity to a multiplicity.

2   For Bergson (1913/2001), *duration* involves the extension of the past into the living present such that the past is not separated from the present state but integrated into it as an organic whole, as when the notes of an unfolding melody melt, as it were, into one another. There are obviously parallels here with William James' (1890) notion of a *stream* of consciousness, and both accounts inspired the development of *relational process* thinking (Brown and Stenner, 2009).

References

Ash, M. G. (1998) *Gestalt Psychology in German Culture, 1890–1967: Holism and the Quest for Objectivity*, Cambridge: Cambridge University Press.

Bergson, H. (1913/2001) *Time and Free Will: An Essay on the Immediate Data of Consciousness*, trans. F. L. Pogson, Mineola, NY: Dover.

Bergson, H. (1911/1998) *Creative Evolution*, trans. A. Mitchell, Mineola, NY: Dover.

Bohm, D. (1995) *Wholeness and the Implicate Order*, London: Routledge.

Brown, S. D. and Stenner, P. (2009) *Psychology without Foundations: History, Philosophy and Psychosocial Theory*, London: Sage.

Durkheim, E. (1897/1951) *Suicide,* New York: Free Press.

Elias, N. and Scotson, J. L. (1965/1994) *The Established and the Outsiders*, London: Sage.

Foucault, M. (1977) 'The confessions of the flesh', in *Power/Knowledge: Selected Interviews and Other Writings*, London: Longman, pp. 194–228.

Gibson, J. J. (1966) *The Senses Considered as Perceptual Systems*, Boston, MA: Houghton Mifflin.

Goudsblom, J. and Mennell, S. (1998) *The Norbert Elias Reader*, Oxford: Blackwell.

Hoftadter, D. R. (1979) *Gödel, Escher, Bach: An Eternal Golden Braid*, New York: Basic Books.

Holland, J. H. (1998) *Emergence: From Chaos to Order*, Oxford: Oxford University Press.

James, W. (1890) *The Principles of Psychology*, New York: Holt.

Kauffman, S. A. (1993) *The Origins of Order: Self-organization and Selection in Evolution*, Oxford: Oxford University Press.

Kuhn, T. (1969) *The Structure of Scientific Revolutions*, London: University of Chicago Press.

Marx, K. (1848/1948) *Manifesto of the Communist Party*, New York: International Publishers.

Maturana, H. R. and Varela, F. J. (1975) 'Autopoietic systems', in *Biological Computer Laboratory, Report No. 9.4*, Urbana, IL: University of Illinois.

Parsons, T. (1977) *Social Systems and the Evolution of Action Theory*, New York: Free Press.

Prigogine, I. and Stengers, I. (1984) *Order out of Chaos: Man's New Dialogue with Nature*, London: Flamingo.

Scheff, T. J. (1994) *Microsociology: Discourse, Emotion and Social Structure*, Chicago, IL: University of Chicago Press.

Stenner, P. (2002) 'Social psychology and Babel', *History and Philosophy of Psychology*, 4 (1): 45–57.

Stenner, P. (2008) 'A.N. Whitehead and subjectivity', *Subjectivity*, 22: 90–109.

Tajfel, H. (1970) 'Experiments in intergroup discrimination', *Scientific American*, 223, 96–102.

Weber, M. (1903–17/1949) *The Methodology of the Social Sciences*, New York: Free Press.

Whitehead, A. N. (1927–28/1985) *Process and Reality*, New York: Free Press.

Whitehead, A. N. (1938/1966) *Modes of Thought*, New York: Free Press.

11 Photo-image

Vikki Bell

What is the relationship between sociology and the photo-image? What should it be? Sociology – historically a text-based and text-biased discipline – has yet to decide how to view the photo-image, both what the photograph is and what it should be in relation to the sociological task. Photography, sharing its time frame with sociology, has accompanied modernity, serving as a tool for representing the world. But it is also said to exceed that task. Indeed, the photo-image has been repeatedly held to reveal the world, rendering it visible, working precisely beyond words and better than words in the delivery of truth, not only of how it is but also how it will be. Photography has been understood not merely as record of the past, therefore, but since its beginnings has been admired and deployed insofar as it prompts audiences to imagine a future. So while some sociologists might understand the photo-image as illustrative, enhancing the text with its 'thousand words', as accompaniment to its task of representing the same world that holds the attentions of the sociologist's text, it is never merely in the hands of the researcher, never merely a recording device. As a methodological device, the photo-image is not at our command, such that any 'revelatory' potential it holds cannot be enfolded into sociological analyses without consideration of the peculiarity of that potential, of its distinction, which in turn, I will suggest, quickly raises the question of what sociology imagines its own task to be. Moreover, because photo-images not only represent but capture, they must be understood as intervening in the social world, circulating and partaking in its arrangements, to the extent that there is now a 'photographic contract' (Azoulay, 2008), or several such contracts, to which we are signed up, and are frequently obliged to enter into in order to survive in contemporary times. Thus photography is enmeshed in the processes to which sociology should attend, integrated not only into contemporary techniques of power and processes of subjectification, but also the imaginations of those subjects; the political questions at stake are crucial and integral to the discussion. This chapter discusses one celebrated example in which the photo-image was clearly compared to and preferred over the 'sociological' text; for through consideration of how the image might come to rival the text, we may begin to explore these questions more fully.

When writer James Agee paired up with Walker Evans in 1936 (book appeared in 1941), he did so not as a sociologist, but as a reporter for *Fortune* magazine; they were assigned by the editors to report on the effects of the economic situation on poor white sharecroppers in the South (Alabama). The magazine ultimately decided not to publish Agee's 'experimental' text, moving, as the editors were, away from the radicalism of some of its contributors. Instead, an expanded text was eventually published, without much commercial success, in 1941, as *Now Let Us Praise Famous Men*. Agee's unorthodox writings were prefaced with Evans' selected un-captioned photographs of the environment and the families they met and with whom they spent time. Seven years later, when Dwight MacDonald (the left-wing editor of the publication *Politics*) tried to revive the book's fortunes by distributing unsold copies through his magazine, it prompted a response from sociologist C. Wright Mills. Mills commented that the text's failure was due to Agee, who was too much in his text; Agee had the tendency to 'get in the way of what he would show you', he would 'jump in', 'obscuring the scene and the actors' (Mills, 1948/2008: 35). His gushing text revealed more of himself, in overwhelmed and self-indulgent state, a state made all the more apparent by what Mills judged as the magnificent photographs of Evans into which the cameraman 'never intrudes' (ibid.: 35). To give a flavour of what Mills is undoubtedly referring to, here is an example of Agee's writing: one morning, when left alone in the Gudgers' home after the family has left to work in the cotton fields, Agee shares his every internal sensation as he laments the hardship he is witnessing, before falling into a meandering reminiscence concerning his own adolescence:

> There is a cold beating at my solar plexus. I move in exceeding slowness and silence that I shall not dishonor nor awaken this house: and in every instant of silence, it becomes more entirely perfected upon itself under the sun. I take warmed water from the bucket, without sound, and it brings the sweat out sharply and I wipe it away, remembering the shame his labor, George, at this instant, hard, in the strenuous heat, and upon the tanned surface of this continent, this awful field where cotton is made, infinitesimal, the antlike glistening of the sweated labours of nine million. I remember how in hot puberty, realizing myself alone the whole of a cavernous and gloomed afternoon in my grandfather's large and un-sentineled home, I would be taken at the pit of the stomach with a most bitter, criminal gliding and cold serpent restiveness, and would wander from vacant room to vacant room examining in every secrecy form fungoid underneath to rarehot roof and from the roof would gaze in anguish at the fronded suffocations of the midsummer city; trying to read; trying to play the piano; ravening volumes of soft-painted nudes; staring hungrily and hatefully at mirrors; rifling drawers, closets, boxes, for the mere touch at the lips and odor of fabrics, pelts, jewels, switches of hair . . .: at length I took off all my clothes, lay along the cold counterpanes of every bed, planted my obscenities in the cold hearts of every mirror.
>
> (Agee and Evans, 1941/1988: 120)

For Mills, Agee's self-indulgence becomes romantic to the extent that often 'there is nothing but Agee', whereas, by contrast, Walker's images of 'family groups of share-croppers, individuals among them, children, a house, a bed in a room' are, Mills opines, 'just there, in a completely barefaced manner, in all their dignity of being, and with their very nature shining through' (Mills, 1948/2008: 35) (Figure 11.1).

Clearly, the question as to the distinction and appropriate relationship between text and images that *Now Let Us Praise* raised – not least in its format – concerns, in turn, the perceived purpose of sociology itself. For Mills applauds Agee's objective as 'rare and appropriate', and he calls the result, approvingly, an example of 'sociological poetry'; if it does not 'come off' (ibid.: 35) as a whole, however, it was because Agee fails to become a sociologist in Mills' eyes. Agee's lack of self-discipline, his furious indignation not only at the socio-economic situation of the people of the South, but also at the way he felt complicit in his being sent 'to spy' on them, so clouded his text, Mills suggests, that he removed the possibility that Mills wanted to promote through sociology. Agee was frustrated at not being able to establish a human relationship with the people he met, but by stepping in with his own furies and frustrations, he kept the readers from 'taking it big' (ibid.: 35) in

Figure 11.1 Sharecropper Bud Fields and his family at home, Hale, Alabama, 1935 or 1936, courtesy of the Library of Congress, LC-USF342-008147-A.

Mills' favourite phrase, 'getting in his own way', and consequently failing as critique, that is, failing to facilitate any transformative possibility for readers of the text. By casting too candid and too personal a shadow over things, he left too much Agee on the page. It is not only a question of too much participation and too little observation; it is a question of a text too sated with affect, obscuring or drowning the bald facts that might in themselves – it is implied – have shone like Walker Evans' photographs. And had they shone, Mills suggests, the political reverberations might have had a chance.

I do not mean to simply affirm Mills' charges against Agee by repeating them here. Instead, I mean to show that the questions with which I began concern not only how to think the relationship between texts and photo-images, but also the self-fashioning of the sociologist and the concomitant envisaged purpose of the sociologist's craft. Mills' perspective is possibly as much, if not more, than Agee's in need of revision, but in tandem they set us upon an investigation made contemporary once again by the renewed interest in what is now termed 'visual sociology'.

Walker Evans' photographs are placed before the text of *Now let Us Praise Famous Men* rather than being dispersed through it, as if there were concern that the images would disrupt the text, or vice versa. But it would be wrong to say that there is a strict division between text and image here; as in all ethnographic work, the text seeks precisely to conjure images. Agee worked hard to convey the landscape, the people, the light, the heat – in short, the image of the South – with his words. He clearly struggled to find the right words, his language infused with the terrifying responsibility of his description, his metaphors often convoluted and spiralling out of his control. The pressure he placed upon his own abilities as a writer are made clear when he explains the expectations he had of those who made the effort to open their consciousness to the 'cruel radiance' of what is. In quasi-Heideggerian terminology, he wrote that:

> in the immediate world, everything is to be discerned, for him who can discern it, and centrally and simply, without either dissection into science or digestion into art, but with the whole of consciousness, seeking to perceive it as it stands: so that the aspect of a street in sunlight can roar in the heart of itself as a symphony, perhaps as no symphony can: and all of consciousness is shifted from the imagined, the revisive [sic], to the effort to perceive simply the cruel radiance of what is.
>
> (Agee and Evans, 1941/1988: 9)

For Agee, the writing of another's life is something he felt he had to do without fictionalizing, a task radically opposed to a 'work of the imagination'. The camera, for him, accompanied this task well. He believed the camera, properly employed, was the 'central instrument' of the time, to the extent that he suggests that if he could have, he would have done no writing at all, and had the book consist solely of photographs (ibid.: 10). In the final product, he states baldly that the photographs are 'not illustrative' (ibid.: xix); they are 'mutually independent' but 'collaborative' with the text (ibid.: xix). Perhaps it was because he suspected the image to have greater potential to succeed in the unconcealment of the world's being that Agee struggled so hard with his words. He returned time and again to descriptions of the light – be it the midday sun under which crops slowly failed (ibid.: 30), the image of the black male singers walking into the evening light in their white straw hats (ibid.: 28), or the flickering light cast by the oil lamp on the family table (ibid.: 44–5) – as if he needed to write in the language of photography, as if the text required that language in order to communicate the cruel radiance of poverty in the South. Only by asking us to imagine being under that sun, our eyes squinting, or by that lamp, our eyes straining, would the reader be able to imagine and truly comprehend the scene Agee wanted to paint.

The supposed 'failure' of Agee's attempt aside, what might it mean to attempt to speak of a (sociological) text's ability to convey 'human nature', or any quality; what does it mean to ask our texts to act as vehicles, allowing light to 'shine through' them? And what makes that attempt equal to or different from an image? This seems an important time to pose such questions, when for example, one recent commentator on 'visual sociology' comes close to confessing the inadequacy of sociological texts to express sociological concepts, suggesting that the photo-image might be required to convey aspects – here of Bourdieu's habitus – that 'can't easily be put into words' (Sweetman, 2009); and not only this, but that it is the image that might, in so doing, release that longed-for transformative potential of sociology by allowing subjects to recognize taken-for-granted ways of being (here it is with Bourdieu rather than Mills that such a wish is shared). I am interested in the confessed inarticulacy of the sociologist, in the suggestion that the image achieves better, with more subtlety or clarity and more critical momentum, than the text. How is the photo-image to reveal something of the world, and to prompt the political trans-formations that are so entwined with sociological desires?

What such a perspective acknowledges, with Agee, and rightly I believe, is that images do something other than confirm the text. They accompany but do not merely illustrate; they can exceed the intentions and articulations of the text, and are certainly not simply subordinate to its order(ing)s. As Michel Foucault pointed out some time ago in his eloquent commentary on Magritte's *This is Not a Pipe*, in the movement from image to text (as from text to image), there yawns a crucial panoply of possibilities, of tensions, affirmations and contradictions. So before we give up the sociological text to the image, it might be important to think their relation a little longer.

As Mills' use of the phrase 'shine through' suggests, the photo-image is often spoken of as a passage, but even before one arrives at recent discussions of the photograph's loss of all indexicality, the term underplays the distinction that the image is; for the notion of a passage forgets that the image crucially marks and maintains a division between the viewer's world and that of the subject(s) of the image, such that we are brought into that world only in a

Figure 11.2 Washstand in the dog run and kitchen of Floyd Burroughs' cabin. Hale County, Alabama, 1935 or 1936, courtesy of the Library of Congress, LC-DIG-ppmsc-00242.

manner of speaking. If we are engaged by the image, if something of that world potentially opens up to us, its existence is not re-presented by the image in the way that term is commonly understood. We can no more step into the washroom in the Burroughs' household as we can step back in time (Figure 11.2); and when and if the image allows that step to be imagined, it is an affectively given and most peculiar sensation. For the threshold is not truly within this image, but between us and (the surface of) the image. Jean-Luc Nancy puts it thus:

> We are placed on the threshold, on the very line that divides the outside and the inside, light and shadow, life and art, whose division [partage] is at that moment traced by something that makes us cross it without eliminating it and that this offers itself fully for what it is, a world.
>
> (Nancy, 2005: 5)

So while the image of the sharecropper might be said to convey his humanity, it is not him we perceive, of course, and certainly not a concept such as 'humanity'; it is the sensation of him, preserved, let us say with Deleuze and Guattari, in this technological, chemical and compositional effort and assemblage, that is offered to us as 'a bloc of sensations . . . a compound of percepts and affects' (Deleuze and Guattari, 1994: 164). Simultaneously, however, and crucially, he is withdrawn from us, with that removal marked by the very fact of being before an image. With Nancy, therefore, I would argue that the image always shows and retains, draws and withdraws precisely because it maintains a distinction between the thing and the image, which is another way of saying that the image refers to the materiality of the image itself. Moreover, it is in the withdrawal that any sense of a world or worldliness is possible, but insofar as it withdraws, as it must, that sense is not presented or (re)presentable, not imaged so much as invited. It is not passively shown; it requests an active encounter.

Of course, one might also say that in Agee's text, likewise, for all its blustering and blundering, we are invited 'in'; we are invited, not least, because Agee felt so constrained by the inequities of the South and so unable to articulate them to the people he was among, that he uses his text to express his disgust, as well as his sense of his own inadequacy. He continually invites one to imagine not simply being there, but being him. In one excruciating scene, Agee tries to convey his own humiliation, and those of a young black couple, when he runs after them to ask for their help. He runs precisely because he is chasing a photograph (the light is fading and if Evans is to achieve the image of the little church in the evening light, they need the permission they would prefer to have, quickly). But in chasing the photograph, Agee ends up chasing the couple, who become agitated at this white man running after them, and the young woman begins to break into a terrified run, stumbling on the gravel road 'like a kicked cow scrambling out of a creek' (Agee and Evans, 1941/1988: 38). Agee is mortified by the consequences of his actions and tries to convey that sense in his prose:

The least I could have done was to throw myself flat on my face and embrace and kiss their feet. That impulse took hold of me so powerfully, from my whole body, not by thought, that I caught myself from doing it exactly and as scarcely as you snatch yourself from jumping from a sheer height: here with the realization that it would have frightened them still worse (to say nothing of me) and would have been still less explicable; so that I stood and looked into their eyes and loved them and wished to God I was dead.

(ibid: 38–9)

His text seems to be for him a diary-like compensation for the fact that, in interaction with these people, he was repeatedly unable to articulate what he was thinking. When words fail him or feel inappropriate, Agee often tries to convey things to people he meets through his eyes, as he did with the young couple. So too when paying the black singers who had been asked to sing to entertain the guests at a house he and Walker Evans visited: '[D]uring all this singing' writes Agee, 'I had been sick in the knowledge that they felt they were here at our demand' (ibid.: 28) and he gives the leader 50 cents 'trying at the same time to communicate with my eyes, much more' (ibid.: 28). Or with Emma, the young woman with whom he more or less admits to being in love, who tells him on the day of her departure how much she and her family cared for him and Walker; he holds back his tears and stops himself from taking her in his arms and cradling her. Instead he says: 'the most I did was to stand facing her, and to keep looking into her eyes (doing her the honour at least of knowing that she did not want relief from this)' (ibid.: 58). Between him and these recipients of his gaze, one might say that Agee tries to make himself, momentarily, into a communicative image:

Mrs Ricketts: ... [C]ontinually, I was watching for your eyes, and whenever they turned upon me, trying through my own and through a friendly and tender smiling (which sickens me to disgust to think of) to store into your eyes some knowledge of this, some warmth, some reassurance.

(ibid.: 322–3)

Agee seeks to present himself as caring, attentive, equal, without the barriers that divided humanity at that time and in that place; in an attempt to achieve that effect, he attempts to make himself, or his sentiment, 'stand out' from the scene without speaking but insofar as he is looked upon by those to whom he wishes to communicate. And while of course we cannot know the 'success' of that attempt at non-verbal communication – whatever that would mean – we receive instead Agee's attempt to convey his sentiments in verbal, textual form. In this, therefore already second, attempt to communicate, he requests that we comprehend or even share in his confused exasperation.

Texts, like images, therefore, can catch and even capture us, carrying us with them, moving or appalling us. Indeed, sometimes one feels one has been thrust before Agee's text, shoved in front of his awkward emotions and attractions and made to imagine them, in much the same way that one unwillingly witnesses a horrific image on the evening news. We wince at his desire to compensate 'Emma' (Elizabeth Tengle) for her doomed and hapless marriage by allowing her, 'a rollicking good time in bed with George [her brother-in-law] . . . and with Walker and with me, whom she is curious about and attracted to' (ibid.: 55). We are caught too when reading about Agee's reminiscences of masturbation (ibid.: 335) or his all-too-honest internal struggles with his sexual attractions (to the prostitute in town, or to the young ten-year-old girl, 'Louise').

In *Now Let Us Praise Famous Men*, then, both the images and the text commend themselves to us affectively. The energy of both is drawn from the shared concern and attraction to the presented absence of the workers and their families and the homes and buildings that Agee and Evans encountered. There is an intense absence, which means that the 'absence of the imaged subject is nothing other than an intense presence, receding into itself, gathering itself together in its intensity' (Nancy, 2005: 9). So both text and photo-image, in their necessary materiality, unavoidably present themselves in distinction from the subjects they communicate, which, by the same token, are inevitably drawn and withdrawn there, however we may judge them against each other.

Indeed, the judgement of image over text cannot be uncontroversial; nor can it be a dispute solved in the abstract. All the more intriguing, then, that our contemporary commentator briefly introduced above considers images to express a sociological argument better than the sociological text, or that, elsewhere, the image becomes subordinated to the word insofar as it is used as a part of the sociologist's toolkit to 'elicit' text from respondents in 'photo-elicitation' interviews.

Let us pursue this latter example a while. What is it that happens in the photo-elicitation interview? I show my subject a photograph, and she remembers, as I hoped, something that otherwise she may have neglected to tell me; a barrier is removed that facilitates my 'data-collection'. She is produced anew, performatively, as a new respondent – less shy, maybe, more verbose, more forthcoming, surer. Or perhaps she is overwhelmed by the photograph, unable to speak, tearful because the photograph has brought too much memory, too much affect. Whichever response one provokes – and obviously there are more than these – the photo-elicitation interview rests upon the peculiar 'magic' of the image, long discussed in anthropology (see Taussig, 1993). The human subject here is produced relationally (in relation to the image, and to the situation) and affectively. Through the – on one level – 'dead' artefact of the photograph, the subject is (re)produced as affective, as knowledgeable, as – paradoxically – singular. Simultaneously, the image suggests of itself an intensity and a vitality, with the power to provoke and produce the subject (and, in turn, the desired 'raw' data for a sociological text).

Whatever the employ of such a method is designed to show, and whatever it 'in fact' reveals, it shows the ability of human subjects to be image-literate, to be affected, to 'become' with images. It might prompt us not only to rehearse the much-touted 'power' of images, but also to consider the participation of images in our production of selves. And it is to this emphasis on the production of selves that I wish to turn in the final section of this chapter; for it is also there that the question of critique, of the politics of the image-plus-text, of sociological analysis, in short, of politics, can be raised.

Photo-images – perhaps with most clarity in the portrait – contain a tension between collectivities and singularities (Sekula, 1986); especially in socio-logical hands, with our discipline's tendency to seek to trade on the level of former, this tension is difficult and dangerous. The portrait of the one in the frame also implies his or her exposure to a power-knowledge assemblage, that marks him or her part of a collectivity – a people, a sub-set or a 'way of life' – with a loss of the specificity of the individual. Anthropology has, of course, had much to say about this.[1] And Agee, radical that he was, struggled with this tension. He abhorred the commercial constraints that hung over the project; he thought of himself and Evans as 'spies'. Wanting to expose a structural violence, he was ashamed at his own paid endeavours to make examples of these people and frustrated at the images' inability to capture such violence in its frame.

He understood this even as the first photographs of the families were being set up on the porch of the Ricketts' house, in the evening sun after a day's work picking cotton. He addresses his text to Mrs Ricketts:

> You realised what the poor foolishness of your husband had let you all in for, shouting to you all to come out, children sent skinning barefooted and slaver-mouthed down the road and the path to corral the others, the Woods and the Gudgers, all to stand there on the porch as you were in the average sorrow of your working dirt and get your pictures made; and to you it was as if you and your children and your husband and these others were stood there naked in front of the cold absorption of the camera in all your shame and pitiableness to be pried into and laughed at; and your eyes were wild with fury and shame and fear, and the tendons of your neck were tight, the whole time, and one hand continually twitched and tore in the rotted folds of your skirt like the hand of a little girl who must recite in front of adults, and there was not a thing you could do, nothing, not a word of remonstrance you could make, my dear, my love, my crazy, terrified child; for your husband was running this show, and a wife does as she is told and keeps quiet about it: and so there you stood, in a one-piece dress made of sheeting, that spread straight from the hole where the head stood through to the knee without belting, so that you knew through these alien, town-dressed eyes that you stood as if out of a tent too short to cover your nakedness: and the others coming up: . . . and Walker setting up the terrible structure of the tripod crested by the black square heavy

head, dangerous as that of a hunch back, of the camera: stooping beneath
cloak and cloud of wicked cloth, and twisting buttons . . . and at least you
could . . . you washed the faces of your children swiftly and violently with
rainwater, so that their faces were suddenly luminous stuck out of the holes
of their clothes.

(Agee and Evans, 1941/1988: 321–2)

Clearly Agee was attuned to the immediate politics of image-making, a
politics here of asymmetrical relationships between himself and the share-
croppers, as well as between the men and the women, and between the country
folk and the town folk. One might understand his verbosity, uncharitably, as
a way of talking himself through (and out of) his discomfort in causing
discomfort to Mrs Ricketts (and the others besides). Be that as it may, Agee
understands also that there is a 'photographic contract' being negotiated, as
the subjects agree to partake in the assignment not because but despite the fact
that it is 'them' who is imaged there; the encounter might also involve another
sort of contract, a photographic contract such as that of which Ariella Azoulay
has written, in which the agreement to allow an image to be made is also an
understanding that it may circulate and be witnessed, to provoke the viewer
to confront a situation, enforcing a duty on the recipient of the image to
recognize the subject within the frame as governed, as placed within certain
specific relations of citizenry (or not). Azoulay is discussing an image of a
Palestinian woman who asked to be photographed by a photo-journalist
because she wanted to show the scars that rubber bullets shot by Israel's
Defence Forces had left on her legs; she has her photograph taken so that it
circulates widely and publicly, even though she refuses to allow the male
photographer to see her legs before the female translator takes the image
(Azoulay, 2008: 147–8). Beyond the negotiations that saw Agee and Evans
spend time boarding in the already cramped homes of the workers, Agee is
aware that he is negotiating permission to make a portrait of a people that had
to have political potential to elevate it above pity, to justify itself; he understood
that this was his side of the contract.

Agee was not a sociologist, but he rants because he knows, as Mills seems
to forget, that however much his philosophy wishes it, humanity cannot
simply 'shine through', and if it miraculously did, it does not necessarily light
a political path. He rants because he did not want to present 'sociological
poetry' or any other sort of poetry. Instead, he is chasing a critical analysis,
and like Mills, because he desires political – social and economic – transformation. He knew that Evans' images might have a communicative charge,
one that his text had to enhance and not detract from, but he also worried that
the package they presented would be insufficient to mobilize anyone or
anything.

His text screams that he did not want this document to become merely an
archive, even as he knew that it had all the potential to become just that. Of
course, the archive is full of the political tension between specificity and

collective commitment, between passivity and action (and more, as Derrida (1995) would have us consider) that we are considering here. It can also be revisited and reignited. Thus, looking at Evans' images now, archived as they are in the North, in the Library of Congress, one becomes aware of the fact that the interest of the magazine in the white poor did not mean that Evans neglected to photograph black people. He had already taken many images of poor black homes and of black people for the Farm Security Association, and would take more after this project. Although we get the image of the church rather than a portrait of the young chased couple, therefore, and although only one such image crept into the final selection for the book, in the appendix to the album of photographs he printed and initially chose for the project *Now Let Us Praise*, one finds, for example, an image of two young 'negro children' as he titles it. An appendix is something separated from the main text (but also something that stands out, awkwardly perhaps); it is where we put that information that the reader doesn't need for his or her under-standing, but that would enrich comprehension should he or she choose to refer to it. Here, across a further slim threshold between main part and appendix, Evans suggested that, despite the constraints of their remit, the 'negro houses' and the children's faces, if unnamed, were also a part of this story. Using a literary device unusual for a photograph album, he implies an awareness of the racial politics of his framing.

But even a set of comprehensive photographs is not by its completeness destined to be more politically efficacious. Critique does not magically arise due to the completeness of the archive, and the vitality of the image, its ability to produce selves, cannot predict nor guarantee that a politicization will form around it. The image-and-text combination was, for Agee, an attempt to provoke outrage at the reality of working lives in which these families existed. If he wanted to 'take it big' it was because he wanted the confrontation with the image to become part of a political intervention, not an ethical encounter of which 'shared humanity' was the conclusion; he wanted to describe the working and living conditions of the sharecroppers as part of a system. Agee wanted the reader to see in the photo-images and in the accounts of working lives, a hardship repeated across those who shared such working conditions. In the section entitled 'Work', he describes the 'arduous physical work' that is 'undertaken without choice or the thought of chance of choice, taught forward from father to son and from mother to daughter' in which there is not even the comfort of treating work as a means to an end, for here one is using 'one's strength . . . for another man's benefit' while the ends of this work 'are absorbed all but entirely into the work itself, and in what little remains, nearly all is obliterated; nearly nothing is obtainable; nearly all is cruelly stained, in the tensions of physical need, and in the desperate tensions of the need of work which is not available'(Agee and Evans, 1941/1988: 282). When the cotton is ready for picking, the whole family is out from very early morning, engaged in this 'simple and terrible work' (ibid.: 299):

with their broad hats and great sacks and hickory baskets, they are out, silent, their bodies all slanted, on the hill: and in every field in hundreds of miles, black and white, it is the same: and such as it is, it is a joy which scarcely touches any tenant.

(ibid: 298)

Agee was as clear as he could be, then, that each image was singular, but the eyes into which the reader looked had to be 'multiplied'. He wondered how 'all this' was to be made clear to the reader so that it would 'stay in you as the deepest and most iron anguish and guilt of your existence'; and he hoped that in meeting the 'gentle eyes . . . in the photograph . . . of the young woman with black hair' the reader might be persuaded that these eyes 'are to be multiplied, not losing the knowledge that each is a single, unrepeatable, holy individual' because the 'huge swarm and majority are made and acted upon as she is: and of these individuals, [he asked the reader to] contemplate, try to encompass, the one annihilating chord'(ibid.: 283).

Agee worries that the reader may forget the 'swarm', that the portrait may founder on its specific face, as it were; equally, I would suggest, he implicitly knew that it risks becoming regarded too broadly, as a portrait of 'shared humanity'. Both of these responses allow the withdrawal of the image to settle back across the comfort of the threshold. But between these two poles is the possibility of seeing the specificities of working conditions, the relations of production, of connecting the portraits of the families with other movements and relations such as those suggested by the ubiquitous Coca-Cola signs in Evans' images of the town, Centerboro, the county seat for these tenants (Figure 11.3). It was this possibility that Agee was hoping for. And so although *Now Let Us Praise* is often approached as posing the problem of the relationship between text and image, or of how to represent suffering, these are not the problems that Agee saw himself responding to. If his 'solutions' disappoint, it is because he was not in fact seeking to solve these questions but rather, strategically, to create a problem; he sought to make the viewing and reading uncomfortable to his (Northern) readers in order to force a confrontation that fulfilled his part of the photographic contract, a confrontation that concerned the future of US working conditions and structures of inequality in the context of the growing and changing commercial capitalism of the time. Text and image might work together in this task, but they are dependent upon the responses they generate; Agee's fear is still relevant today, that the viewer's response will be one that contents itself with a sense of singularities, or otherwise of a 'shared humanity', that routinely accompany systematically reproduced inequities rather too easily. The sociologist's task cannot be content to leave it as undifferentiated as that; ours is a more critical, and a more political task.

Figure 11.3 Crossroads store, Sprott, Alabama, 1935 or 1936, courtesy of the
Library of Congress, LC-DIG-ppmsc-00243.

Concluding remarks: for sociology

Photo-images are currently employed and understood rather differently by sociologists; the discipline – that is, the people who make up the discipline – will be the ultimate judges of that diversity. Be that as it may, for my part, I would argue that the photo-image cannot be understood as a device that does the same work as sociological analyses; nor, in my estimation, can it itself replace or become the sociological analysis. But thinking about how the photograph is both indicative of and initiates processes – multifarious processes of creativity, ethics, politics, subjectification – is certainly important and fruitful for sociological endeavours. We need to attend to the processes by which photo-images come to be (how they are produced, how they circulate, how they are obliged or wrought into being, how they are archived, treasured or abandoned); we need also to consider how they do not 'reveal and represent', but provoke or invite responses which they do not control, responses which, indeed, are drawn from them but which cannot be simply read off or assumed from their content and composition, for they rely upon so much else that the image cannot possibly initiate. Nor is this process one-sided, for, as I have argued here, the photo-image draws and itself withdraws, sometimes intensely, profoundly, sometimes even with that sense – which is not a representation – of worldliness of which Nancy writes. In other words, the way in which an image can 'open up' – an emotion, a memory, a new understanding, a new critique, even a new subjectification, a new politics – is a process that cannot be captured as a positivity for social science (as a 'device') not least because it is not something that is in our control. But that may well be an excellent place to reflect upon the sociological task and its ambitions.

Notes

1　A good place to start an exploration of anthropology's ruminations on its deployment of photography would be with the readings gathered in *The Anthropology of Media*, edited by Kelly Askew and Richard Wilk (2002), especially the conversation between Margaret Mead and Gregory Bateson, and essays by John Berger and James Faris. Elsewhere, this history has been explored, inter alia, by Elizabeth Edwards (1992, 2001) and Christopher Pinney (2011).

References

Agee, J. and Evans, W. (1941/1988) *Now Let Us Praise Famous Men*, London: Penguin.

Askew, K. and Wilk, R. (eds) (2002) *The Anthropology of Media: A Reader*, Oxford: Blackwell.

Azoulay, A. (2008) *The Civil Contract of Photography*, New York: Zone Books.

Deleuze, G. and Guattari, F. (1994) *What is Philosophy?*, trans. G. Burchell, London: Verso.

Derrida, J. (1995) *Archive Fever: A Freudian Impression*, Chicago, IL: University of Chicago Press.

Edwards, E. (1992) *Anthropology and Photograph 1860–1920*, New Haven, CT: Yale University Press.

Edwards, E. (2001) *Raw Histories: Photographs, Anthropology, Museums*, London: Berg.

Mills, C. W. (1948/2008) 'Sociological poetry', in *The Politics of Truth: Selected Writings of C. Wright Mills*, Oxford: Oxford University Press, pp. 125–37.

Nancy, J-L. (2005) *The Ground of the Image*, New York: Fordham University Press.

Pinney, C. (2011) *Photography and Anthropology*, London: Reaktion Books.

Sekula, A. (1986) 'The body and the archive', 39 (October): 3–64.

Sweetman, P. (2009) 'Revealing habitus, illuminating practice: Bourdieu, photography and visual methods', *Sociological Review*, 57 (3): 491–511.

Taussig, M. (1993) *Mimesis and Alterity: A Particular History of the Senses*, New York: Routledge.

12 Phrase

Matthew Fuller and Olga Goriunova

1

Different elements of the world make themselves available to different perspectival operations. In the context of computational and networked digital media, one of these has been the device established in hypertext as the link. As realized in the World Wide Web, the link mixes the orders of the semantic or linguistic and the logical. A link asserts a relation between things and also makes one happen. Because of its dual position, the link became a crucial means of understanding and ranking websites and their relative importance. Epitomized in algorithms such as PageRank (Brin and Page, 1998; Langville and Meyer, 2006), HITS[1] or in software that maps the topology of the Web by such links.[2] This understanding of the link allowed a further formalization of this entity of dual character, a formalization that in turn created new volatilities, opportunities and problems.

Our concern in this chapter is with a related entity of multiple character that can be called a phrase. Phrases exist as conceptual, technical and experiential entities in domains that are codified in mark-up languages, choreography, linguistics, but to which they cannot be boiled down. They operate as one of a series of micro-to-macro objects, entities in their own terms at a certain scale, but also as mediations of part-whole relations. We see them as articulating a crucial relation between the formal and the subjective, between the logical and the experiential, between the numerical and the gestural. That is, phrases are means of both understanding and experiencing technosocial relations.

In this text we aim to focus on a particular kind of phrase, those that exist in relation to computational systems and their users. Here, phrases are entities that either individually or together participate in technosocial processes. Just as certain software will view a website as a collection of links, certain perspectival operations may see phrases simply as formally defined objects and couplings between them, but they also provide the means for making connections with objects of other kinds, to more elusively formalizable things and behaviours such as conversational ruses or rhetorical maneuvers, as with dance, they may involve gestures.

Phrases can be largely technical (an algorithm, a comments facility on a website, a filter in a sorting system, a means of gathering votes, an interface element); can be bodily or performative (a gesture, the provision of a mechanism); or they can be both (the offering of a microphone at a public meeting, the movement of a player-object-logic-sound in the use of an electronic instrument such as Michel Waisvisz's 'The Hands'); or they can be largely rhetorical or experienced in language. In terms of scale, although we say that networks are composed of phrases (phrases in software), phrases themselves can be rather large-scale or micro-scaled, but they also act to momentarily suture scales together or make them distinct. The development of phrases allows for the possibility of opening up intersubjective processes and the spaces for the articulation and development of new ones. In such a context, phrases can also act as tools or vehicles for reflexive, performative, enactive, demonstrative and experimental social research.

2

While, in dance, a phrase is often understood as a particular discrete sequence of small movements that flows or stutters together to make a whole nested into or arrayed along with others between pauses: the flowing arch of an arm in relation to the twist of the head; the oscillations of the waist, buttocks, legs, back wineing to a beat coming through a wall of speakers. In sound- and sign-related sciences, a phrase is not a sentence, nor is it simply composed of words. A sentence or collection of words do not necessarily make up a phrase. A phrase can be a single word, consisting of a single phoneme. Strictly speaking, within linguistics, a phrase is the largest phonetic unity; it is a space in-between pauses, a basic component of speech. (Jakobson, 1971; Zinder, 1979; Reformatskii, 2000) The defining characteristic of a phrase is intonation, which is itself melody, rhythm and logic, among other qualities. Phrases are performative and mixed with breathing too much to exist in literature.

All that language-specific music and pulmonological excitation cannot get away from sense. Such sense, though, is related directly to the nonsensical, to beauty. A phrase can be a sticking together of words that do not make the same meaning on their own, i.e. it is undecomposable; in such a case it can be called an idiom. Everyone, and especially everyone different from everyone else, can make idioms and produce a personal phraseology, so that a phrase is not necessarily a basic universal component. At the same time, a phrase communicates expressively, tastily, individually and illogically in the context of a specific language and requires a device of distance in approaching it in translation. Here, phrases are not bricks to build larger constructions with, and they do not surround us in their nicely ordered, gridded and ranked sextillions. A phrase is a lucky device; it can occur, become fashionable or firm, or can dilapidate. It may last only a moment.

In order to expand on this, it is worth noting a related development. In recent theorizations of new media, particularly those coupled with an interest in the articulations of the literary, attention is often paid to the development of an appropriate unit of analysis that mixes the cultural and technical in discussing the operations of computational fictions, games, playable narratives and other such mechanisms. Noah Wardrip-Fruin describes a series of these as 'Terms for Thinking about Processes' and provides a useful overview of the discursive current in proposing his own addition to the series, 'operational logics' (Wardrip-Fruin, 2009). Operational logics happen inside the black box of computers, but are also manifest at the interface and in the behaviours of objects. They form a rich processual vocabulary of behaviours that game designers and writers work with. Examples of operational logics from outside of games would be edge detection in picture editors, find and replace in word processors, or the movement or generation of on-screen objects or interface sounds via a relation between physical controllers and what is handled by them. Operational logics are means by which we learn how a program works, often by analogy to others, without necessarily reading the manual, but they also contribute a lot to the feel of a computational entity or operation. One of the gains to be made by the development of such terms is in being able to abstract a computational logic without always having to drill down to the level of its specific implementation. Thus, one can speak about software without necessarily analyzing code (although this may be essential in some cases) and find a critical vocabulary more adequate to emerging computational cultural forms.

Related to but separate from this current of work, there is also a tendency in new media studies that aims to identify or invent distinct units that can be strapped safely within a taxonomic framework of meaningful units ordered into ranks and sets. While it is not our intention to suggest that such systems are not operative, particularly in computing, such a normative aspiration is one that extends beyond its capacity to describe or work with the ranges of material and aims at producing a skin, rather than the snake that shed it.

3

Mikhail Bakhtin's *Toward a Philosophy of the Act* (1993) is a useful point of triangulation for what we are trying to devise here. Bakhtin's essay establishes a means of understanding the interrelation between the concrete real, or universal, as it is manifest in a particular moment and the individual experience of that moment in historical, subjectival terms. The first of these terms is understood as an abstract scale, that of theory and ideas that move without the necessity of modification from one instantiation to another. The abstract scale of theory, however, is impossible without the other term of experience, the historically actual deed. Each of these scales drives and shapes the other. Theory works by its own autonomous laws, forcing consequences by the momentum of its own inner logic, generating theoretical 'subiectum' or consciousness that must be inhabited. Such a logic might perhaps be found in numbers such as those generated as the Fibonacci series or in reckoning

Champernowne's (1993) number.[3] At the same time, it is impossible to inhabit theory without the contamination and propulsion engendered by the other side of the dualism of cognition and life. Life, which is always too complex for theory, is also what occupies it, drives it.

Bakhtin proposes a quality, answerability, with which to understand the interrelationship of these terms:

> the answerability of the actually performed act is the taking-into-account in it of all the factors – a taking into account of the sense validity as well as of its factual performance in all its concrete historicity and individuality.
>
> (Bakhtin, 1993)

At once ethical and aesthetic, answerability is one of the means by which Bakhtin's work connects to that of those, such as Félix Guattari, who later related it to the machinic volition of functional assemblages of partially incommensurable materials (Guattari, 1995; Lazzarato, n.d.). Early on in the text, Bakhtin relates the scale of the concept, that of the theoretical machine, to that of the 'world of technology' driven by its own 'immanent laws' and which has 'long evaded the cultural task of understanding the cultural purpose of that development' (Bakhtin, 1993: 7). The world of technology is kin to the abstract scale of the concept, uninhabitable, and here it exhibits a tendency to evil. However, it does not permanently lose an ability to live, be lived in and driven with the lived experiences that, in turn, drive it. The scale of abstraction, of scientific reason, has its own distinct modality, its own patterns of accession, diminution or growth, but can also open itself to the unity of life.

The world of cognition in this sense is distinct from the idea of the essences of Plato; it does not need to be discovered, but to be invented. This theoretical world is composed of archipelagos of more or less pure abstraction and reasoning, all of which are alien, provocative, thrilling and incompatible with the historically situated, lively beings who can think through, make real and therefore complexify and make this uninhabitable arid world meet the unity of the real, making it juicy, turning it into something else. Phrases are points at which Bakhtin's world of technology commingles without merging with that of emotional and subjective volition, with historical and fleshy experience to produce identifiable moments of transition between the two, producing new elements which themselves cohere to produce the technosocial and at the same time break up the idea of the 'concept without brains' to capture it in their folds.

4

While mathematically based network analysis has shown that complex, large-scale networks, if that is what one is looking for, can be elucidated across many material and social domains, most researchers working in this area agree that a pressing challenge is to find ways of tracing the articulations of such 'line and dot' networks with more culturally, materially and socially complex forms of understanding (see e.g. the 'Outlooks' chapter in Newman *et al.*, 2006) Phrases make useful objects and methods of study in relation to the larger scale of networks because they often provide a point of indistinction between the technical and the social (and the human). Equally, as phrases, they are in themselves distinct entities. This means that they are, partially, alienable from their context, but not too readily.

Phrases test the degree to which social dynamics in the context of applications and social networking platforms undergo formalizations of relation between people, ideas, objects and processes. They are also a means of entering, triggering and sensing into the grammars and diagrams through which such techno-social dynamics can be built, felt, understood and changed.

Michel Serres asks whether we can 'conceive of an intersubjective origin for simple machines' (Serres, 2007). We wonder how they emerge when one or more of those entities has already gone through such a threshold. Do phrases, as simple machines that cross from the human to non-human and back, emerge as a result of interactions between people, or do they also function as attractors for certain kinds of processes of subjectivation? How do they frame and induce certain kinds of action, imaginary and agency, and how do such things also overflow them? (Cramer, 2009). In an era when relatively crude social networking technologies aim to diagrammatize and interpellate the social, and in turn ask to be gamed and manipulated, this is a crucial question to ask of software development.[4]

Phrases emerge from socio-technical devices, in the contexts of computer-mediated communications and in offline but partly computational events. They participate in building media ecologies, connecting the gestural to the logical, procedural to the bodily, formal to the informal, skills to structures. Phrases are what work well in the performance of the world but they can also be used to understand it. A couple of examples may serve to clarify what we mean.

The IBM Votomatic voting machines that became notorious during the Floridian phase of the 2000 election of President George W. Bush exhibited what might be called a certain expressivity in operation. The punch card-based voting machines gave considerable variation to the way in which a hole was punched in the voting card to indicate the choice of candidate. The 'hanging chads' were scraps of card that should have been punched out by the machines, but which were left attached, rendering the card nominally unreadable. This machinic gesture was carried out each time as a phrase, sloppily, deftly, drawing on the kind of humanization of error supposedly removed by the use of machines. In this case, the phrase is certainly largely technical, but carries a concatenation of relations to other kinds of judgement, action and behaviour.[5] Rather than being a singular unit of action corresponding to an affirmation, the act produced a generalized, perhaps targeted, doubt.

The People Speak is a company of artists, programmers, designers and other people that develop events for 'social decision-making' (The People Speak, n.d.). They mix formats adapted from TV chat and quiz shows with other kinds of structures in order to produce readily understandable and hopefully thus inclusive kinds of public fora. Above, we mentioned that moving a microphone might constitute a certain kind of phrase. One of their projects, Talkaoke, is 'a mobile talkshow' where 'what we're going to talk about is up to you' (Talkaoke, n.d.). The people who come and sit round the portable, neon-lit circular table with a charismatic motormouth host in the middle are those who direct the conversation. The host simply and skillfully picks up the pace, provides a bit of tempo to its fast multiform improvisation. One of the key acts in this is the movement of the mic. The phrase that starts someone's time to speak may include bending the arm at the elbow, proffering the mic, making eye contact, uttering some words. It is a phrase that says, start, say something, seduce, shock, open your mouth, it impels one to think, or to show that one does not, to take part in the game or get out. Its phrasing can be aggressive, quizzical, eager, but it connects the user and interlocutor into a circuit of speech, into video (shown on nearby screens), into the circulation of statements, jokes, questions, thoughts and phrases made by others, and offers amplification.

5

A phrase is both steady and not-already-there, but the genesis and usage of phrases is core to the operation of computational networks as they increasingly entangle the social. Phrases make meaning but escape full description, they are something that happens that makes something happen: just as cards may be shuffled violently, elegantly, with flair or clumsiness, data is sorted with greater or lesser concern for time and resources. Depending on the algorithm chosen, such a sorting process moves one entity about in different ways in relation to others that are not simply equivalent to the fixed execution of instructions, but imply something akin to a dance, where the parts move according to a pattern, but one which is modified according to the characteristics of those elements being sorted as they in turn change the speed and order in which they are sorted. The phrasing of Bubblesort, a slow sorting algorithm (Astrachan, 2003; Martin, n.d.) is tellingly idiosyncratic. The sorting process starts at the beginning of a dataset, swapping neighbouring entities backwards and forwards according to whether they are attributed a smaller or greater value (commonly numeric or alphabetic), returning to the beginning of the dataset once each pass has been made until no swaps are necessary. The permutational movement of such algorithms, the data they come into composition with, the multiple systems they are embedded in is itself expressive, that is, exudes phrases.

A phrase then is not simply a cyborg event, mixing the technical and bodily, formal and fleshy, into one entity of priorly parceled human and non-human which even when fused implies a dualism. In its technosocial manifestation it may encompass such parts, or more, but is also special in its unity, its force, and performance at multiple and tangential scales and is irreducible to any of them. Experimental art practices, such as live-coding,[6] or the durational ensemble performances of Shu Lea Cheang and Martin Howse establish themselves in part as effective collision sites for the generation of unprecedented phrases experienced and endured by all sorts of entity:[7]

> Phrases can be mundane, functional or brilliant, but they are not all units of the same order; in our proposition for the phrase as a device, we think only in as much as we ask questions. How does a phrase assemble itself together to become a real unity of an order and ensemble that is not predetermined? What does it yield to say that the participative drive of its elements mingles together with the technological and conceptual to be experiential? Taking part in the world of mixed matters, a phrase appears as an aesthetic as much as an ethical consideration. Aesthetics implies life and the generation of experiences, the fundamental scale at which phrases are registered and a crucial way to understand what makes a phrase a phrase, a scale that is also, as those of the architectronics of relations established in rationally ordered conditions and of the experiential or participative, induces the need for an ethics.
>
> (Cheang and Howse, n.d.)

The phrase acts, to come back to Bakhtin (1993), in the space where we do not know how to exist, where we are not, and where, nevertheless, we are. Can we study such phrases, technical, computational, emotional, formal, social, at the point of our existence, and not in the abstract aftermath? What capacities would be required to think, interact and act in terms of phrases where we are, and is such a domain somewhere theory can go?

A phrase emerges at a moment of encounter as a force and a formulation that makes a work, an object, real. As a phrase traverses scales, every time along a new vector, making an ensemble come into existence, it becomes key to experiencing and understanding the genesis of the reality in question. The fabric of a phrase however, cannot be limited simply to its multiplicity. Drawing together combinations of codes, forces, statements and energies without the experiential and participative scales that a phrase takes can assist in rather rich interpretative acts, orderings and games but does not necessarily engender an insight.

Equally, it is not necessary that such an approach only has 'intuition' to rely on, leaving the material to speak to us in articulating its own phrases but that such a constitutive suppleness itself implies that in the search for ways to make sense of digital material and in allowing for the technical and networked to appear we do not invent a kind of re-calcified structuralism where all elements are readily searched for and synthesized along the lines of something akin to laws or look-up tables.

Tuning in to the scale, texture and experiential nature of a phrase therefore implies an approach allowing a tenderly close reading, a way of working with things that are materially rich but not cumbersomely materialized, a proximity that requires the taking of a distance sufficient to allow for the phrase to form and give itself over without turning itself in.

Notes

1   The HITS (Hyperlink Induced Topic Search) algorithm is a forerunner of Google's well-known PageRank that sorts pages according to their relative status as 'hubs' (links from) and 'authorities' (linked to). See also Kleinberg (1999).
2   See *I/O/D 4: The Web Stalker*, available at: http://bak.spc.org/iod/ and Martin Dodge's *Cybergeography Research* page, available at: http://personalpages. manchester.ac.uk/staff/m.dodge/cybergeography/ (both accessed 1 March 2010).
3   Champernowne's number was established in 1933 by David G. Champernowne and consists of a decimal fraction in which the decimal integers are concatentated, as one number, in increasing order, one term after another: 0.12345678910111213.
4   The critical analysis of software systems, in software studies and elsewhere, is one place to turn to for the development of such work. How social networking sites are designed to probe, extract, invent and analyze modes of interaction is also a situation in which such sites develop both pre-emptive designs, anticipating use, and post-facto designs, arising out of the non-standard usage of their resources and mechanisms by users. Since we are no longer in the phase of invention of such software but of its infrastructural and strategic normalization an understanding of the networks of phrases meshing the inter-personal and the formalized needs also to recognize the profound degree of serialization and repetition involved, despite, and occasionally because of, the ways in which it may still be lively.
5   The electronic voting machines that largely replaced the card-based ones in some cases were hardly less susceptible to doubt (see Feldman *et al.*, 2006).
6   See, Toplap, the site maintained by a loose alliance of live-coders (Toplap, n.d.).
7   See the documentation for one such event, *Moving Forest*, (Cheang and Howse), available at: www.movingforest.net/ (accessed 1 March 2010).

References

Astrachan, O. (2003) 'Bubble sort: an archaeological algorithmic analysis', *Proceedings of ACM SIGCSE '03*.
Bakhtin, M. M. (1993) *Toward a Philosophy of the Act*, trans. V. Lupianov, and M. Holquist, Austin, TX: University of Texas Press.
Brin, S. and Page, L. (1998) 'The anatomy of a large-scale hypertextual Web search engine', *Computer Networks and ISDN Systems*, 30 (1–7): 107–17.
Champernowne, D. G. (1933) 'The Construction of Decimals Normal in the Scale of Ten', *Journal of the London Mathematical Society*, 8: 254–260.
Cheang, S. L. and Howse, M. (n.d.) 'Moving forest', available at: www.movingforest. net (accessed 1 March 2010).
Cramer, F. (2009) 'Buffer overflows', in W. Sützl and G. Cox (eds) *DATA Browser 4, Creating Insecurity: Art and Culture in the Age of Security*, New York: Autonomedia, pp. 45–51.
Feldman, A. J., Halderman, J. A. and Felten, E. W. (2006) *Security Analysis of the Diebold AccuVote-TS Voting Machine*, Center for Information Technology Policy, Princeton University.

Guattari, F. (1995) *Chaosmosis: An Ethico-aesthetic Paradigm*, trans P. Bains and J. Pefanis, Sydney: Power Institute.

Jakobson, R. (1971) , *Selected Writings Vol. 1: Phonological Studies,* ed. S. Rudy, The Hague: Mouton.

Kleinberg, J. (1999) 'Authoritative sources in a hyperlinked environment', *Journal of the ACM*, 46 (5): 604–32.

Langville, A. N. and Meyer, C. D. (2006) *Google's PageRank and Beyond: The Science of Search Engine Rankings*, Princeton, NJ: Princeton University Press.

Lazzarato, M. (n.d.) 'Bakhtin's theory of the utterance', trans. A. Bove, *Generation Online*, available at: www.generation-online.org/p/fp_lazzarato6.htm/ (accessed 1 March 2010).

Martin, D. R. (n.d.) 'Visualization of the working of common generic sorting algorithms', available at: www.sorting-algorithms.com (accessed 1 March 2010).

Newman, M., Barabasi A. and Watts, D. J. (2006) *The Structure and Dynamics of Networks*, Princeton, NJ: Princeton University Press.

Reformatskii, A. (2000) *Vvedenie v Jazykovedenie [Introduction to Linguistics]*, Moskva: Aspect Press.

Serres, M. (2007) *The Parasite*, trans. L. R. Scher, Minneapolis, MN: University of Minnesota Press.

Talkaoke (n.d.) 'Talkaoke', available at: http://talkaoke.com/ (accessed 1 March 2010).

The People Speak (n.d.) 'The People Speak', available at: www.theps.net/ (accessed 1 March 2010).

Toplap (n.d.) 'Toplap', available at: www.toplap.org/ (accessed 1 March 2010).

Waisvis, M. (n.d.) 'The Hands', available at: www.crackle.org/TheHands.htm (accessed 1 March 2010).

Wardrip-Fruin, N. (2009) *Expressive Processing, Digital Fictions, Computer Games and Software Studies*, Cambridge, MA: MIT Press.

Zinder, L. (1979) *Obschaja Fonetika [General Phonetics]*, Moskva: Vysshaja Shkola.

13 Population

Cori Hayden

In anthropology and social theory, we largely know and do population through Foucault, for whom the term signals a very particular kind of aggregate. Foucault called population 'the biological multiplicity': distinct from a people or a post-marxist multitude (among other terms), population is a collective marked by its vitality and its measurable, optimizable life processes (Foucault, 2003: 252; see also Foucault, 1978). It is, we might say, an aggregate with a pulse. Together with its corresponding biopolitical formula of life itself as politics itself, Foucault's population has been an undeniably fruitful methodological device. One of its key effects, certainly, has been to channel our attention towards the biological sciences as privileged sites for the production of knowledge, power, things, subjects, and value. With population, we have learned very well to think of the biological as the political.

But perhaps we have learned this method too well. What would happen if we were to wrest ourselves loose from population as the bio-aggregate we know, in order to think it otherwise? With an eye on current developments in Latin American pharmaceutical politics, this essay explores the possibility of giving population a chemical turn. While we are accustomed to thinking about pharmaceuticals in the idiom of the biological, insofar as they affect the formation of subjects, the constitution of vital aggregates, and the management thereof,[1] we are not nearly as accustomed as we might be to thinking about pharmaceuticals as chemical objects in their own right (cf. Barry 2005). But most drugs are, of course, chemicals: they are synthesized, stabilized, mass-produced chemical compounds, mixed with and delivered via inactive chemical ingredients. While chemistry has long been seen as profoundly 'uninteresting' – bereft of the kinds of epistemological and theoretical questions that animate and emerge from other sciences, especially physics and biology (Barry, 2005: 51–2; see also Casper, 2003: xvii) – a number of scholars have recently set in motion what we may have to call a chemical turn in science studies more broadly, making compelling cases for chemistry as a site and source of epistemological and methodological interest (see, among many others, Bensaude-Vincent and Stengers, 1996; Casper, 2003; Fraser, 2003; Barry, 2005; Fortun, 2006; Murphy, 2006). Among other things, chemistry is a mode of thinking about and producing taxonomic and material kinds, relationality, and multiplicities. But what kind of multiplicity is a chemical multiplicity? What kind of device might population become when its substance and its operations are thought through the chemical?

This somewhat odd question in fact taps into something fundamentally generative about Foucault's own idiom. As Tiziana Terranova showed brilliantly in the workshop that preceded this volume, Foucault's account of population is strikingly heterogeneous to itself: it shifts continuously, from the regulation of human life to matters of climate, from biological reproductions to statistical repetitions. Its ossification in and through our own analytic habits is thus somewhat ironic. The questions I pose here seek to exploit the concept's own inbuilt heterogeneity. With luck, this move will manage to make population strange again, in part by exploring the consequences of the fact that the 'biological' processes at the heart of biopolitics are also different from themselves (see Murphy, forthcoming).

SimiPolitics: reproduction, replication

My interest in rethinking population's possibilities (bio)chemically has emerged less as a general theoretical quest than as a way in to a specific empirical problem.[2] Working on generic drugs in Latin America has prompted me to think about how familiar biopolitical concerns – such as appeals to the health of the population – are cross-cut with other idioms and mechanisms for making and intervening in collective formations. Given current developments in Mexico, I may have to call these other mechanisms 'SimiPolitical' formations. In the late 1990s and early 2000s, a wildly successful Mexican pharmacy chain, Farmacias Similares (Similar Pharmacies), rose to prominence on the heels of the Mexican government's efforts to promote the consumption of cheaper, generic substitutes for expensive, foreign-made drugs. The chain emerged in 1998 with its savvy proprietor, Victor Gonzalez Torres, profitably reclaiming the rallying cry of 1970s state-led pharmaceutical nationalism: 'defend your domestic economy'! In the first decade of the twenty-first century, Farmacias Similares, their pointed slogan ('the same but cheaper!') and their ubiquitous mascot, Dr. Simi, have made a vivid mark on Mexico's commercial pharmaceutical landscape, and on the kind of political-social arrangements taking form in the name of the copied drug (Hayden, 2007).

Similares' interventions in Mexico (and throughout Latin America, as the chain has expanded rapidly) draw our attention to the many ways in which pharmaceuticals participate in the making of populations – or, to open up Foucault's evocative term again, in the making of multiplicities. Similares thus raises questions about how to characterize these multiplicities, and the mechanisms through which they operate. Certainly, the circulation of cheaper, copied pharmaceuticals implicates bodies, health, and life process at aggregate scales – the population in a biological sense. But, in SimiPolitics,[3] if I may be so bold, something else is afoot. Here, multiplicities are organized at every scale – the industrial-pharmaceutical, the commercial, the political, the social

– around the ever-proliferating copy, and the multiplication of entities (social, political, economic, material) that are simultaneously the same as, yet different from, each other. SimiPolitics, I will suggest, sets in motion some suggestively chemical modes of proliferation, prompting us to think about populations – and 'bio'politics – that are organized nonbiologically, and nongenealogically.

Chemical multiplicities: the same but different

Dr. Simi came to life in 1998, and with his emergence, the kinds of political claims and projects that had been made periodically in the name of the pharmaceutical in Mexico took a particularly vivid turn. Simi's entrée was made possible in large part by economic crisis in Mexico, which in turn had led to significant problems in the provision of pharmaceuticals.[4] While middle- and working-class incomes plummeted following the peso devaluation of 1994, increasingly expensive, foreign-made, brand-name drugs continued to dominate pharmacy shelves, leading to a widespread problem of access and affordability. The state's regulatory solution, beginning in 1998 and 1999, focused largely on creating a 'culture' of, and a market for, generic substitution; that is, paving the way for consumers to buy cheaper generic versions of leading-brand drugs.

Dr. Simi's slogan, *lo mismo pero más barato*! (the same but cheaper!) perfectly captured and popularized this call for enhanced access through substitution. Indeed, many commentators grant Farmacias Similares credit for having made a sceptical public increasingly comfortable with the idea that a brand-name drug could indeed have a cheaper substitute. *But!* The Similares promise of cheaper equivalence (as with the project of generic substitution more broadly, in Mexico, the US and elsewhere) has been marked from the start by some fairly overdetermined interruptions, qualifications, and doubts. Where Simi is concerned, the slight gap that opens up between the name of the chain (*similares*!) and its slogan (*lo mismo*!) taps into the specter of copied drugs that are 'merely' similar and not really 'the same' at all. This potential for slippage has long animated battles over the regulation of equivalence for generic drugs, as patent-holding 'innovator' firms have routinely impugned the quality of generics precisely by casting doubt on their claims to equivalence.[5]

The same but (similar), the same but (cheaper), the same but (different): this syntax, or simi-semiotics, saturates the pharmaceutical field in Mexico. Multiple kinds of generic drugs are approved for sale there, including (regular) generics, interchangeable generics (GI), branded generics, and the 'nonexistent' but very popular 'similars'. These categories correspond in part (but only in part) to different regulatory thresholds of equivalence, such that a generic naproxen, an interchangeable (GI) naproxen, and a branded 'Wal-proxen' could all be 'equivalent' to the brand-name drug Aleve, while also being *different from each other*.[6]

At the same time, in a seeming riot of recursivity, the Similares slogan, 'the same but cheaper', has itself been subject to competitors' perfectly pitched

variations: 'the same substance but cheaper', or 'it's equal but more eco-
nomical!'. Farmacias Similares also finds its retail strategy – specifically, the
practice of setting up low-cost health clinics adjacent to their pharmacies –
mimicked across the nation by bigger chains and smaller, family-run outlets
alike, many of which cheerily tack clinics to the side of their dispensaries
and call themselves 'Farmacias de similares', or 'Simylares'. While Dr. Simi
decries such cheap imitations, these acts of copying are, in a sense, already
anticipated by the ways in which Farmacias Similares has virally replicated itself.
Its remarkably successful franchise model – in the context of Mexican regulation
placing few restrictions on who can open and operate pharmacies – has resulted
in the explosion of the chain's presence across the nation, from an initial 8 outlets
in its first two years to well over 3,000 in the current moment. (Its success in
reproducing itself has earned *Similares* the attention of, among other things,
a Harvard Business School case study (Chu and Garcia-Cuellar, 2007).)

As these myriad repetitions begin to suggest, Simi's semantic operation –
the same but (different) – is very much at home in the commercial sphere.[7]
We could be forgiven in fact for thinking of Simi's formula as 'generic': one
could certainly imagine its deployment in the sale of all kinds of discount
goods, from replacement mufflers for Ford cars, to different brands of facial
tissue (see Schwartz, 1996). But, is it possible that the traction and generativity
of this formula, with which I am taking some nonarbitrary poetic license, is
somehow related to its distinctive pharmaceutical-ness? Its chemical-ness?

I pose the question because the field of chemistry in general, and pharmaceutical chemistry in particular, is peculiarly animated by a rich understanding of the many ways in which molecular entities can be the same as, while
also different from, each other. We might think, for example, of isotopes and
isomeres (such as two water molecules or two fluoxetine molecules) that have
the same chemical elements but are arranged slightly differently, giving them
different geometries, and different molecular weights; or chiral molecules,
which are 'handed', making them the same as each other, and yet not interchangeable, as with your left and right hands; or the importance of molecular
mimickry – the ability of drugs to mimic substances in the body, thus triggering
particular cellular reactions – in drug development. Chiral molecules, isotopes,
isomeres: to invoke the title of chemist Roald Hoffmann's intriguing book
about chemistry's core philosophical concern, chemistry is a field with a rich
repertoire for producing entities that are simultaneously 'the same and not the
same' (Hoffman, 1995).

The density of this potential for chemical entities to be the same as, and also
different from, each other, has drawn science studies scholars' attention to
chemistry as a specific site of interest. Among them are Isabelle Stengers and
Bernadette Bensaude-Vincent's *A History of Chemistry* (1996), and Andrew
Barry's extension of their analysis in a trenchant 2005 article, 'Pharmaceutical
matters'. Bensaude-Vincent, Stengers, and Barry are interested in the dense
layerings of information that molecules can contain or 'embody', and which
allow us to see how the same molecule can exist in countless different material

and informational forms (Barry, 1995: 55). It is this capacity to generate multiple kinds of sameness or identity, always in relation to particular requirements or material-informatic environments, that has prompted Barry, Stengers, and of course A.N. Whitehead before them, to take from chemistry a rich understanding of a materiality that is both 'irreducible' and relational (ibid.: 55–9). This particular mode of proliferative (non)-identity – the multiplication of things that are the same as, and also different from each other – does not just saturate the field of pharmaceutical commerce and regulation in Mexico. It also saturates pharmaceutical politics in a rousingly literal way, prompting my questions about how we might draw chemical substances and modalities into relation with the political.

SimiPolitics: fissiparous reproductions

Dr. Simi (and his competitors) clearly know how to multiply in the commercial sense. But González Torres/Dr. Simi is unique in the degree to which he also makes multiplicities in the political sense. The reverberations – from the chemo-pharmaceutical to the commercial, to the political, and back again – are not subtle, though characterizing their relationship remains the methodological challenge. Dr. Simi has, since the early 2000s, made a name for himself by simultaneously copying drugs and copying 'the state' in order to a pose himself as a viable substitute thereto. Pursuing these combined ends, González Torres (who identifies himself with, or as, Dr. Simi) has, from the outset, tapped into an almost cartoonishly recognizable inventory of popular-political aesthetics, tropes and tactics. This inventory has included a (failed) bid to stand as a presidential candidate in 2006, alongside the adoption of a corporate flag, a corporate hymn, and a mural in corporate headquarters mimicking Diego Rivera's famed depiction of Mexico's glorious past and future in the National Palace.[8] He has engaged in relentless attacks against the state's social security medical system, aired through a well-financed, constant presence on talk radio shows, TV programmes and newspapers. As I have outlined in greater detail elsewhere, González Torres has echoed the populist gestures of both the right and the left in Mexico's constantly re-congealing multi-party democratic field, essentially establishing (the appearance of) an enterprising SimiState, with real effects in the world (Hayden, 2007). His many-tentacled, often lucrative, social-political apparatus works on many fronts. Alongside the franchised, low-cost popular health care infrastructure anchored by Farmacias Similares are González Torres' philanthropic associations, constituent organizations (he has made sure to call into being his own 'civil society'), and a visible presence as a source of social and material aid to the poor, the elderly, and the underfunded organizations that serve *barrios populares* (popular and working-class neighbourhoods).

What kind of a politics is this, and what kind of aggregates are in formation? Political and social theory provide us with a few recognizable points of orientation, which may help us make our chemical turn. On the one hand, similarity and substitutability are not new idioms of politics, or of imagining, intervening in, naming, and even knowing 'a mass of men'. Before Foucault described population as a biological multiplicity, Gabriel Tarde and late nineteenth-century crowd theorists had much to say about how nongenealogical reproductions and multiplications – imitation, repetition and replication – literally constitute sociality (Tarde, 1993).[9] The point has been particularly relevant to theorizations of popular politics in Latin America, especially in the work of Ernesto Laclau (2005).[10] It was Tarde, Laclau reminds us, who freed imitation and repetition from their disreputable association with the unruly crowd, arguing instead that even proper, 'rational' publics are generated by imitative processes across multiple scales. That is, sociality at a collective level is only produced, Tarde argues, through minute acts of repetition and imitation. Taking this argument a turn further, Laclau insists on extracting from Tarde's imitation an account of populism as something that produces – indeed that works through – homogeneity and equivalence.[11] But such a seamless confla-tion of 'imitation' with 'equivalence' deprives us of a way to engage with some of the most generative aspects of populism itself, which, like the chemical, seems to fundamentally trouble unexamined notions of 'the same', the homo-geneous or the equivalent. SimiPolitics, as pharmaceutical politics, demands that we rethink such taken-for-granted terms, attending in fact to how they have 'not the same' at their core.

The chemical-political formula 'the same and not the same' in fact matters very much to how we think about populist politics in Mexico (and elsewhere in Latin America). In conversations about this project, my Latin Americanist colleagues frequently mention the inescapable resonance between the notion of the generic (and the substitute, and interchangeability) with twentieth-century idioms of citizenship and efforts to incorporate the popular masses into 'the state'. This resonance emerges out of the history of twentieth-century Latin American populism, which was largely configured around the political and economic strategy of Import Substitution Industrialization (ISI). ISI provided a state-led language for Latin American nationalist politics of production, consumption and identity well into the 1960s and 1970s. The project of substituting domestic-ally made products for foreign commodities, under the mantle of an explicit protectionism (the very thing to which recent free trade agreements have so deter-minedly put an end), was meant to produce, among other things, employment for the working classes, a sense of identification through the consumption of *lo nuestro* ('ours') and a promise of undifferentiated inclusion for the 'masses' – *la ronda de seres intercambiables*[12] – in state projects of modernization and development (García Canclini, 1995; Lomnitz, 2001; Yúdice, 2001).[13]

Given this history, invocations of 'generic substitution', it seems, cannot help but evoke the making of political multiplicities. And indeed, González Torres/Dr. Simi vividly taps into this storied history of 'the national-popular' configured around the domestic substitute, as in his early quasi-nationalist advertising campaigns ('defend your economy!') and the loud echoes he gen-erates of a corporatist SimiState that will take care of the popular classes.

But! Simi's interruption also draws our attention directly to the other side(s) of this national-popular story: the strong association of the domestic copy and the 'popular masses' with the specter of uncertain authenticity (the same but . . .?), national identities marked by an ambivalently 'imitative' relation to the metropole, and the uncanny powers accruing to the proliferative copy. It also, of course, draws our attention to race, ethnicity, and indigeneity as the modes through which the tensions between sameness and difference within these 'national' projects have long been mediated. It is my contention here that, entangled with the well-documented biopolitical managements of race, sex, gender and reproduction that have defined twentieth-century national-state projects (Leys Stepan, 1996; Nelson, 1999; Appelbaum *et al.*, 2003), Latin American political histories have simultaneously been riven with anxieties about, and the management of, 'fissiparous' reproductions; that is, proliferative, nongenealogical acts of replication or imitation, which have long troubled elites' sense of the sites and sources of political power.[14] (Consider Eva Perón and the multiple copies of her corpse that circulated long after her death (Eloy Martínez, 1996).)

Political and social theory's attention to populism in a broad sense may thus help remind us of the long-standing centrality of the non-genealogical copy to the making of multiplicities. If SimiPolitics brings this legacy into view, it also draws our attention to the possibility that the compound phrase, pharmaceutical politics, might have a very particular traction. To reframe the question baldly, why is SimiPolitics organized around the pharmaceutical at all? Why not organize a SimiPolitics around washing machines, or cars, as in the era of ISI? What does it mean to make the pharmaceutical-ness of this enterprise matter to the operations of a biochemical multiplicity? With Dr. Simi in view, me propose an empirically animated, speculative schema with which to address these questions.

Population, again

Population (biological)

Aggregate organized around vitality, procreative reproduction, regularization of life processes

Proliferation: sexual recombination; statistical repetitions

Populated by people affected by 'the chemical'

Governed by the state

Life = politics (biopolitics)

Population (chemical)

Aggregate organized around nongenealogical replications, generativity of copies

Proliferation: the same, but different; commercial and material replications

Populated by people and chemical substances and modalities

Governed by the SimiState

Chemical relationality = social-political formations (SimiPolitics)

This somewhat tongue-in-cheek exercise does not, of course, hold for very long, especially if it is taken as marking a radical separation between the bio and the chemo, which are in many ways that matter quite difficult to disentangle. More helpfully, we might think of this chemical turn in the same way chemists think about synthesizing the same chemical via a different pathway: shifting our attention from the biological to the chemical is a minor modification, not a wholesale substitution. The columns become, for a minute or two, devices for highlighting different aspects of the substance and operations of pharmaceutical politics. And in particular, they help us think about the kind of aggregate formation a (bio)chemical population could be.

Reproduction as replication; or, the chemical in the biological

Most powerfully, SimiPolitics highlights – because it disrupts and reorients – just how central reproduction has been to the (biological) population we know. I noted above that Foucault's population is marked by its distinctive vitality. More specifically, sexual reproduction organizes and grounds Foucault's biological multiplicity in a strong sense, with sex serving as the fulcrum linking (the regulation of) individual bodies to the larger statistical aggregate, or the population.[15] It is of course precisely this argument that has made reproduction so central to twentieth-century Latin American nation-building exercises organized around race and nation. Population in this biological sense does not simply describe a collection of biological individuals; it is a collective idiom organized in and through the reproduction and management of biological, reproductive life processes.

By extension, a population, organized around the chemical and the copy, might not simply be a collection of 'chemical' individuals (though the possibility raises interesting questions about our units of analysis). Rather, deploying population as a chemical device requires that we open up our notions of reproduction, to consider how nongenealogical reproductions – replications, proliferations – configure aggregates. The chemical and the copy *do something* to the bio-population. In part, they allow us to open it up and redistribute its terms and modalities: to think population 'chemically' means to disaggregate population's constitutive elements and set them in motion in new ways. There is indeed every reason to approach Simi's pharmaceutical politics as a redefined politics of reproduction. There are, among other things, etymological reasons to do so. Before its association with mechanical reproduction, as in the replication of texts and images (Benjamin, 1968; Lury, 1993), the copy's Latin root hewed to notions of abundance and proliferation (see Boon, 2010). The copy (*copier, copieux*, copious) straddles the biological and the 'mechanical', the genealogical and the nongenealogical.[16] The proliferations unfolding in Mexico in the name of copied drugs bring this mixed heritage to the fore.

This move has been engineered in relation to the singular case of SimiPolitics, but the impulse places this rather particular experiment in conversation with other developments in feminist science studies. Michelle Murphy and Kavita Philip, for example, provide a template for posing population's question anew when they consider such things as mid-twentieth-century economic theory and contemporary software piracy as 'distributed ontologies of reproduction'.[17] Their strategy is not to gather pirated software or economic theory back into a conventional notion of biologized reproduction but rather to set our analytic gears in motion in the opposite direction, taking up the challenge to expand reproduction beyond the biological. Opening up and rethinking the reproductive idioms that ground our notions of the political seems an increasingly important tactic. For, as Sarah Franklin's work on Dolly, the cloned sheep, makes clear, even biological reproduction is apt to be different from itself, these days. Franklin makes clear that the biological sciences themselves provide every reason for diversifying our reproductive idioms, as biological reproduction itself is becoming ever more fissiparous. In her account of how Dolly came into being, Franklin tracks how Ian Wilmut and his colleagues experimented to find the optimal mixture of biological reproduction (a mode of recombining cells) with modes of biochemical replication (a much more efficient mode of multiplying cells) (Franklin, 2007: 20). With this mix of reproductive modalities, Franklin notes pointedly, 'Dolly signifies both sameness and difference as a clone, but she also represents a fundamental confusion about how we tell them apart' (ibid.: 28).

As this essay has suggested, this tension between reproduction and replication is itself consequential to how we think the political.

Method and the chemical turn

Finally, it seems apt, given the remit of this volume, that chemistry has proven interesting for such scholars as Barry, Bensaude-Vincent, and Stengers in part for methodological reasons. Barry (drawing on A.N. Whitehead before him) finds chemistry good to think with in large part because its mode of research is *not* guided primarily by theory or general principles. Rather, it is 'attentive to the singularity of the case' (Barry, 2005: 52). As Barry argues, 'chemistry is not so much a positivist science, but a discipline which points to a new form of empiricism' (ibid.: 53). Chemistry's empiricism – a way of *making* (not 'discovering') entities, substances, and the relations between them – may also help us think population's possibilities anew. I argued above that SimiPolitics draws our attention to the many ways in which pharmaceuticals participate in the making of collectives, or multiplicities. It has not been my intention to argue that SimiPolitics 'starts' in pharmaceutical chemistry and emanates out into wider social, political, or economic spheres. Nor is thinking chemically a matter of looking for metaphors of the chemical in the social/political, or vice versa, any more than Foucault's biological operates as a metaphor for the social. Rather, SimiPolitics offers an empirical challenge to which chemistry seems to bind well – both in form, and in content. Science studies scholars have indeed been wrestling with precisely this question, in other ways. For

Isabelle Stengers, chemistry (eighteenth-century chemistry, to be specific) suggests a mode of doing politics that is more auspicious than the idioms provided by either physics or biology. It is one that allows her to think about efficacy, propensity, manipulation, and the ways in which entities act on and influence each other. These relations of efficacy are central to her 'cosmopolitical' project and its delicate matter of theorizing and organizing activist collectives (Stengers, 2005: 1000). With an eye on SimiPolitics, I think there is another case to be made for how chemical relations can configure the collective or the political. Thus when Dr. Simi deftly calls into service resonant idioms of popular politics organized around the copy, he also brings the pharmaceutical into view as an object that can make a series of material demands – irreducible as they are – on our analytic vocabularies. Chemistry's formula – its way of making and thinking substances that are the same as but different from each other, and the way in which these relations of sameness and difference can cross scales, can take form in different environments – offers resources for asking empirically grounded questions about the particularities of form, of syntax, of claims and substance that are configuring politics in relation to and beyond pharmaceuticals. Enacting 'in politics' the operations we might (also) locate in the material production and commercial proliferation of copied drugs, Dr. Simi has made clear the need for an analytic idiom or a methodological device that can account for the relationship between chemical and political modalities. Population, strangely enough, might just do the trick.

Notes

1 The anthropology of pharmaceuticals, one field in which I work, has inarguably delivered a great deal in this idiom, showing how pharmaceuticals reanimate and redefine the boundaries of population by producing new experimental aggregates, eliciting new subjectivities, and stretching population logics themselves beyond the boundaries of the nation-state (Biehl, 2004; Petryna, 2005; Petryna *et al.*, 2006; Sunder Rajan, 2006; Dumit, forthcoming).

2 Insofar as chemistry is a discipline driven by the singularity of the case rather than by general theories (Barry, 2005: 53), this experiment already bears a chemical imprint.

3 Though González Torres has added the prefix 'Simi' to many things, including products such as condoms (the SimiCondón), his 'spokesmodels' (SimiChicas) and his health insurance plan (the SimiSeguro), at this point, I think I have to take the blame for SimiPolitics.

4 In the years following the 1994 peso devaluation, the country's integration into the North American Free Trade Agreement, and the reinstatement of pharmaceutical patents (which had been briefly abolished in a moment of pharmaceutical nationalism in the mid-1970s), medication prices and access had become a significant problem for many people, and hence for the state (see Hayden, 2007).

5 The argument that generic drugs cannot really be 'the same' is an argument that routinely surfaces in efforts to challenge the quality of the generic. As Jeremy Greene's work shows, since the early 1970s, especially in the US, the sites for contesting or asserting sameness have continued to shift, including but not limited to pill size and shape, chemical compound, measures of bioavailability, packaging, etc. (Greene, 2011). In the US, as in Mexico, India, Argentina and elsewhere, the

regulation of standards of equivalence has, not surprisingly, been an intense site of political maneuvering, as leading industries have long exerted pressure to keep the quality of generics under permanent suspicion (ibid.).

6 Among the operative distinctions here is that between chemical equivalence (20 mg of naproxen = 20 mg of naproxen), and bioequivalence, a threshold of sameness established in the US in the 1970s which requires that generic drugs also demonstrated an equivalent (within limits) rate of absorption into the bloodstream. In Mexico, 'interchangeable generics' meet this higher, bioequivalence threshold – they are thus *more* equivalent than their merely chemical equivalent, 'generic' counterparts.

7 I explore these dimensions of the argument in a separate essay, 'New same things'.

8 As we might expect, Dr. Simi (the mascot) does indeed appear in the SimiMural, dispensing pharmaceuticals.

9 Among the prolific commentary on the rise of interest in Tarde, see Latour (2002) and Toews (2003).

10 Laclau insists on assimilating Tarde's argument into his own 'logics of equivalence', wherein different and competing claims are made equivalent through common appeals to 'the people'. But I would suggest that this reading arguably flattens out and misreads some of the most generative aspects of Tarde's idiom (see, in contrast, Deleuze, 1994: 313, n. 3).

11 Thus, for Laclau, populism works through the creation of a relation of equivalence and exchangeability between different and competing claims (so that, for example, in Argentina, both the right and the left can be Peronists, a move that works insofar as both invoke 'the people' as their reference point). In this way, Laclau takes Tarde's idiom of imitation conflates it with the making of equivalences.

12 'The round or series of interchangeable beings'. The phrase belongs to Mexican essayist Carlos Monsivais, discussing how, and to whom, early twentieth-century Mexican novels were addressed (Monsivais, 2000: 21)

13 The production and consumption of an authentic national culture (consider the famously 'folkloric' Mexico) accompanies the consumption of domestically manufactured goods as key mechanisms for incorporation. The fate of the national-popular in the context of the opening of markets and the 'globalization' of popular culture is the subject of much debate among Latin American and Latin Americanist cultural critics and political essayists (García Canclini, 1995; Lomnitz, 2001; Yúdice, 2001).

14 See Daniel Cosío Villegas' critique of his own 'Revolutionary' party, the PRI, which he accused of the sin of reproducing itself fissiparously, 'in the manner of inferior biological organisms' (Cosio Villegas, 1947, quoted in Joseph and Henderson, 2005: 473).

15 Thus Foucault argues, 'Because it . . . has procreative effects, sexuality is also inscribed, takes effect, in broad biological processes that concern not the bodies of individuals but the element, the multiple unity of the population. Sexuality exists at the point where body and population meet' (Foucault, 2003: 251–2).

16 See, for example, the entry for *copier* in the *Dictionnaire de poche de la langue Français, Larousse étymologique, Librairie Larousse* (1971). Many thanks to Hélène Mialet for pointing out this connection.

17 See http://redtechnopolitics.wordpress.com/.

References

Applebaum, N. P., Macpherson, A. S. and Rosemblatt, K. A. (eds) (2003) *Race and Nation in Modern Latin America*, Chapel Hill, NC and London: University of North Carolina Press.

Barry, A. (2005) 'Pharmaceutical matters: the invention of informed materials', *Theory, Culture, and Society*, 22 (1): 51–69.

Benjamin, W. (1968) 'The work of art in the age of mechanical reproduction', in H. Arendt (ed.) *Illuminations: Walter Benjamin, Essays and Reflections*, trans. H. Zohn, New York: Schocken Books, pp. 217–52.

Bensaude-Vincent, B. and Stengers, I. (1996) *A History of Chemistry*, Cambridge MA: Harvard University Press.

Biehl, J. (2004) 'The activist state: global pharmaceuticals, AIDS, and citizenship in Brazil', *Social Text*, 22 (3): 105–32.

Boon, M. (2010) *In Praise of Copying*, Cambridge, MA: Harvard University Press.

Casper, M. (2003) 'Introduction', in *Synthetic Planet: Chemical Politics and the Hazards of Modern Life*, New York and London: Routledge, pp. xv–xxxi.

Cosío Villegas, D. (1947) 'Mexico's crisis', *Cuadernos Americanos*, reprinted in G. Joseph and T. Henderson (eds) *The Mexico Reader*, Durham, NC: Duke University Press, pp. 470–81.

Chu, M. and Garcia-Cuellar, R. (2007) *Farmacias Similares: Private and Public Health Care for the Base of the Pyramid in Mexico*, Cambridge, MA: Harvard Business School, NS-307-092.

Deleuze, G. (1994) *Difference and Repetition*, trans. P. Patton, New York: Columbia University Press.

Dumit, J. (forthcoming) *Drugs for Life*, Durham, NC: Duke University Press.

Eloy Martínez, T. (1996) *Santa Evita*, trans. H. Lane, New York: Alfred A. Knopf.

Fortun, K. (2006) *Advocacy after Bhopal*, Chicago, IL: University of Chicago Press.

Foucault, M. (1978) *The History of Sexuality*, trans. R. Hurley, New York: Pantheon Books.

Foucault, M. (2003) *'Society Must Be Defended': Lectures at the Collège de France 1975–1976*, ed. M. Bertani and A. Fontana, trans. D. Macey, New York: Picador Press.

Franklin, S. (2007) *Dolly Mixtures: The Remaking of Genealogy*, Durham, NC: Duke University Press.

Fraser, M. (2003) 'Material theory: duration and the serotonin hypothesis of depression', *Theory, Culture, and Society*, 20 (5): 1–26.

Garcia Canclini, N. (1995) *Hybrid Cultures: Strategies for Entering and Leaving Modernity*, trans. C. Chiappari and S. López, Minneapolis, MN and London: University of Minnesota Press.

Greene , J. (2011) 'What's in a name? Generics and the persistence of the brand in American medicine', *Journal of the History of Medicine and Allied Sciences*, 66 (4): 468–506.

Hayden, C. (2007) 'A generic solution? Pharmaceuticals and the politics of the similar in Mexico', *Current Anthropology*, 48 (4): 475–95.

Hoffmann, R. (1995) *The Same and Not the Same*, New York: Columbia University Press.

Laclau, E. (2005) *On Populist Reason*, London: Verso Press.

Latour, B. (2002) 'Gabriel Tarde and the end of the social', in P. Joyce (ed.) *The Social in Question: New Bearings in History and the Social Sciences*, London: Routledge, pp. 117–33.

Leys Stepan, N. (1996) *The 'Hour of Eugenics': Race, Gender, and Nation in Latin America*, Ithaca, NY: Cornell University Press.

Lomnitz, C. (2001) *Deep Mexico, Silent Mexico: An Anthropology of Nationalism*, Minneapolis, MN and London: University of Minnesota Press.

Lury, C. (1993) *Cultural Rights: Technology, Legality, Personality*, London and New York: Routledge.

Monsivais, C. (2000) *Aires de Familia: Cultura y Sociedad en América Latina*, Barcelona: Editorial Anagrama.

Murphy, M. (2006) *Sick Building Syndrome and the Problem of Uncertainty*, Durham, NC: Duke University Press.

Murphy, M.(forthcoming) *The Economization of Life*.

Nelson, D. (1999) *A Finger in the Wound: Body Politics in Quincentennial Guatemala*, Berkeley, CA and London: University of California Press.

Petryna, A. (2005) 'Ethical variability: drug development and globalizing clinical trials', *American Ethnologist*, 32 (2): 183–97.

Petryna, A., Lakoff, A. and Kleinman, A. (eds) (2006) *Global Pharmaceuticals: Ethics, Markets, Practices*, Durham, NC and London: Duke University Press.

Schwartz, H. (1996) *The Culture of the Copy: Striking Likenesses, Unreasonable Facsimiles*, Cambridge, MA: Zone Books, distributed by MIT Press.

Stengers, I. (2005) 'The cosmopolitical proposal', in B. Latour and P. Weible (eds) *Making Things Public: Atmospheres of Democracy*, Cambridge MA: MIT Press, pp. 994–1003.

Sunder Rajan, K. (2006) *Biocapital: The Constitution of Postgenomic Life*, Durham, NC and London: Duke University Press.

Tarde, G. (1993) *Les Lois de la Repetition*, Paris: Kimé.

Toews, D. (2003) 'The new Tarde: sociology after the end of the social', *Theory, Culture and Society*, 20 (5): 81–98.

Yúdice, G. (2001) 'From hybridity to policy: for a purposeful cultural studies', in N. Garcia Canclini (ed.) *Consumers and Citizens: Globalization and Multicultural Conflicts*, Minneapolis, MN: University of Minnesota Press, pp. ix–xxxviii.

14 Probes

Kirsten Boehner, William Gaver and Andy Boucher

Introduction

Probes are a method for developing a richly textured but fragmented understanding of a setting or situation. Developed in a design context, their purpose is not to capture what is so much as to inspire what might be. Because their motivations come from design, Probes embody a different set of sensibilities from most other social research methods. Most fundamentally, they make a virtue of uncertainty and risk, acknowledging and celebrating the idiosyncratic interpretations of designers and participants. They aim to open up possibilities, rather than converging towards singular truths, and can be understood as part of a conversation among designers and the people and places for which they design.

Originally conceived of as Cultural Probes, the probe process was developed by designers then at the Royal College of Art (RCA) for Presence, an EU-funded project that aimed to increase the presence of older people in their local communities using new technology (Gaver and Dunne, 1999; Gaver *et al.*, 1999; Gaver *et al.*, 2001; Gaver *et al.*, 2004a). Several educational, governmental, and commercial entities collaborated on Presence and each brought different methods and methodologies to explore the design space from different angles. Example methods included oral histories, concept trials, user forums, user profiles, and relational maps (Hofmeester and de Saint Germain, 2000). These methods were stretched to apply to the unique context of designing technology for older people in local communities, however the techniques and research stance stayed close to the problem solving and optimization approach of traditional usability research methods.

The designers from the RCA, however, set out to take a more experimental approach. They framed the Presence project as facing two fundamental challenges: one conceptual, and one pragmatic. Conceptually, they wanted to subvert stereotypical representations of the elderly as frail and marginalized, as well as assumptions that computation should focus on productivity and efficiency. Instead, the designers intended to tap into people's inherent playfulness and mindfulness in the products they would eventually propose. Pragmatically, they knew this meant getting to know the targets of their design work – groups of volunteers from Norway, the Netherlands and Italy – in ways different than those afforded by traditional research instruments. Rather than focus on problems and needs, they wanted to know about hopes and fears, curiosities and dreams. At the same time, they did not want their research findings to dictate the design, but were anxious to leave ample room for their own interests and imaginations.

In response to these challenges, the designers drew from the theory and techniques of the situationist international (Debord, 1967) and to some extent surrealism (Levy, 1936) in order to articulate a new approach. The surrealist pursuit of the marvellous in the face of apathy spoke to the designers' desire to forge an approach that was playful in intent, delivery, and eventual designs. Surrealist techniques for elevating the unconscious and provoking new dialogue, such as dream writing and games of chance, provided resources of inspiration. Likewise, the situationists' ethos of grounding surrealist ideas more in the everyday and particularly in the fabric of place provided a resonant philosophy for understanding the very different cultures and communities in the Presence project. Techniques such as détournement and dérive were familiar tropes that the designers had played with in previous work and they sought to use their principles in the Presence context as well. More concrete inspiration came from Fluxus boxes, packages of diverse games, cards and suggestions produced as part of the avant-garde movement, which suggested that research materials might also be produced as similarly diverse and loosely organized collections (Kellein, 1995). Hence, the Cultural Probes process emerged as a design led, arts inspired, approach to developing new understanding and perspectives of cultural communities.

In material form, the Cultural Probes consisted of packets of provocative items that set various tasks for the volunteers. These included a customized disposable camera with instructions for taking pictures of 'something beautiful' or 'something you see from your kitchen window', custom-made postcards with questions on the back, kits for annotating maps in various ways, and an album to be filled with personal photos. The designers introduced the Cultural Probe packet to the participants as an experiment – not in the sense of 'you are our subjects' but in the sense of 'try this if you will'. Participants took their probes home, lived with them over a course of a month or so, and returned the individual items separately via post to the designers. The waves of returned responses combined into rich evocative glimpses of the varied participants' lives and communities. These responses themselves became probes or prompts for the designers to respond to in turn, by sketching new ideas and working through possible prototypes with the participants.

This initial experience of the Cultural Probes proved inspiring and engaging for the designers, the participants, and eventually the larger technology and design communities as well. Social scientists as well as designers have taken the Probes into a number of different contexts and in a number of different directions: some more effective than others. In the pages to follow, we will revisit the methodology of probes, examining the way of thinking that underlies the approach and reflecting on how this manifests in the design of particular items.

Case study: Domestic Probes

The tactile and situated nature of probes makes experience the best avenue for understanding them. One needs to receive a probe packet, take the probe items out of the kit, hold them, reflect on them, live with them, and use them. Alternatively, one should be on the design side, creating probes and experiencing their return. In lieu of this possibility, we describe here an example of one probe study in some detail.

The Domestic Probes were designed to provide insight into the context of the home and the possible new roles of technology there. As with the Cultural Probes, the Domestic Probes were employed in order to present rich evocative glimpses into people's home lives as a means of opening new conceptions of what technology for the home should look like and do. The first twenty respondents to a small advertisement placed in citywide newspapers and magazines were recruited for the study (see Figure 14.1). No steps were taken to ensure variety of demographics or to control for participants' motivations, yet the group turned out to be quite diverse in terms of socioeconomic status

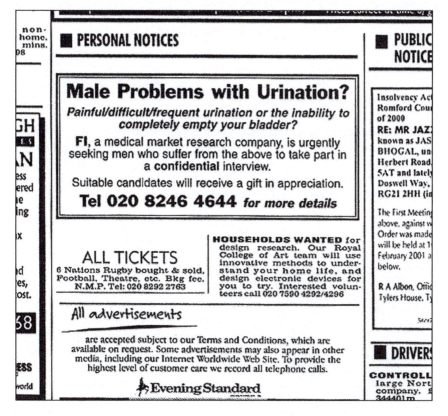

Figure 14.1 Advertisement for Domestic Probe volunteers.

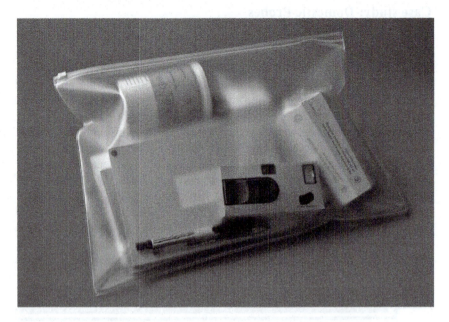

Figure 14.2 The Domestic Probe packet containing 10 individual probes.

and age, and became very engaged with the Probes despite any original preconceptions about the project.

The probes were distributed to volunteers during handoff meetings in which two or three designers met with the volunteers in their homes to give a loose description of the project (e.g. 'It's about designing technology for the home'), an explanation of the probe process (e.g. 'This is a packet for you – fill out the things that seem interesting or useful and send those back. Ignore the rest'), and a brief description of each probe in the packet (see Figures 14.2 and 14.3).

Dream Recorder (14.3.1)

A repackaged digital memo-taker with instructions to use it after waking from a vivid dream. Pulling the attached cord activates the device, turning on the small LED in front. The volunteer has 10 seconds to record an account of their dream, after which the device shuts off. No provision is made for reviewing or editing their recording.

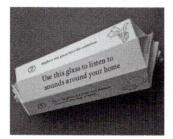

Listening Glass (14.3.2)

An ordinary drinking glass is packaged with a marking pen capable of writing on glass. The instructions suggest that, when interesting sounds are heard around the home, the glass should be held to the ear and placed near the source of sound to amplify it. When the sounds stop or interest dwindles, the volunteer should write what they heard, along with the date and time, on the glass itself. The intention was to sensitize the designers, and volunteers, to sounds around the home.

Bathroom Pad (14.3.3)

A pad with about 20 pages, each printed with a short news feature for comment. Topics range from a description of robotic dinosaurs and jewel-encrusted toilets to a quote from the Queen to the effect that 'one is fortunate to have a garden in central London'. Designed with a built-in hook to facilitate leaving near the toilet, the pad was intended to elicit comments on a variety of topics outside the immediate domestic environment.

Disposable Camera (14.3.4)

A 35 mm disposable camera is repackaged to remove it from its commercial origins and printed with a list of requests for pictures on the back. These ranged from straightforward ('take a picture out your window') to requests requiring interpretation ('the spiritual centre of your home'). Extra pictures are included for participants to photograph whatever they wanted to show us. Overall the intention is to get out-of-the-ordinary photographs, unlike those one might expect if asking for a photographic home tour.

Floor Plan (14.3.5)
An A4 sheet of stiff paper is printed with a dotted grid and instructions to draw a plan of the home. The intention was to receive an overview of the home's layout but experimentation was encouraged. For example, one participant drew the sequence of rooms visited in the course of a morning.

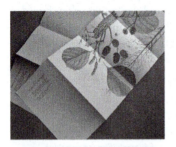

Friends and Family Map (14.3.6)
Participants are requested to draw a diagram showing their friends and family. This common data collection tool from the social sciences is altered by the addition of images, such as the cricket pitch and tidal marine life shown here, intended to suggest unusual metaphors.

Household Routines Camera and Workpad (14.3.7)
An A4 format workpad has 20+ pages for recording domestic routines, labelled with categories such as 'cleaning', 'socializing' and 'cooking'. A repackaged disposable camera allows photographic evidence of the routines to accompany written descriptions.

Household Rules (14.3.8)
A set of various tags is pre-printed with the heading 'house rule'. Participants were instructed to write down domestic rules and leave them in appropriate places. Verbal instructions stressed that rules could range from the mundane ('don't put your feet on the table') to the unspoken ('don't discuss money until I've had my coffee').

Photogram Paper (14.3.9)

A large (A3 format) piece of photograph paper is provided in a cardboard tube. The instructions suggest making a collage of household objects upon it – when exposed to light, unshaded areas turn blue while those under objects remain white. The image can be fixed by immersion in water and returned. The intention was to collect evidence of artefacts in the home through a task that encourages aesthetic play.

Pinhole Camera (14.3.10)

A pinhole camera, constructed from an empty dog food tin, is labelled with instructions suggesting that it be placed in front of an interesting view, the small piece of black tape removed from in front of the hole, and then replaced after about 30 seconds exposure. Volunteers were instructed to write a brief description of what they had photographed (as a back-up in case the photograph failed). The intention was to contrast the casual images taken with the disposable camera with a single image taken in this more ritualistic manner.

Telephone Jotter Pad (14.3.11)

A small (10 cm^2) pad containing a variety of images and occasional writing, including questions. The contents ranged widely over a set of domestic issues, including questions about the home's behaviour, spirituality and aesthetics. The instructions (and name) suggest that people jot down responses, or just doodle, while engaged in other tasks.

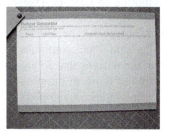

Visitor Pad (14.3.12)

An A4 pad requests comments to be written by every visitor to the household. Based on visitor books found in, for example, cultural attractions, columns are included for recording the visitor's name, the date and time of their visit, and their comments.

After about a month, the designers revisited the participants to collect completed probe packs and have informal discussions about their experiences. Now it was the designers' turn to engage with the probes that trickled back. The returns were displayed in their studio for the designers as individuals and as a group to read through, reflect on, and converse about, ultimately as a context for their design proposals (see Figure 14.4 for examples). Note that the designers did not 'analyze' the returns, at least not in the sense of systematic comparisons or summaries. As with many aspects of the probes, it is difficult to generalize across the returns in terms of proportion returned or nature of responses. As hoped, and indeed designed for, each volunteer chose to complete a slightly different set of the probes. Some volunteers concentrated on items that requested written response, others on taking pictures and drawing images. Some did most of the items, some only a few. Some were terse, others elaborated at length. The varied ways in which participants approached the probes themselves seemed symptomatic of the way they lived their lives. Taken together, the returns created a textural understanding of a home or 'the home', one that was multi-dimensional and shifting depending on the concerns of the time. In addition, some returns – e.g. a house rule requesting that people hang their clothes 'the right way', a photograph of a man lying on the floor gazing into a fish tank, a note of admiration for the Queen – took on the role of landmarks, focusing attention for varying degrees of time.

As the probe returns arrived, the design team started working on sketch proposals. Comprised of little more than an image or two and a short caption, these were the first seeds of what would be developed into fully functional prototypes, some of which made it to the final implementation stage. The History Tablecloth, for example, is a lace pattern tablecloth made with an electroluminescent material that lights up underneath objects left in one place for a period of time. The tablecloth subtly signals the flow of objects in surfaces of the home. Another example, the Drift Table, looks like a modern coffee table, yet includes a video porthole displaying aerial views of the English countryside that shift direction and speed depending on the arrangement of weight on the table's surface. These designs, and the others resulting from the probe process (e.g. Gaver *et al.*, 2004b), subverted familiar notions of what technology in the home could or should do and pushed both the designers and the participants to think about the home and technology's role in the home in different ways.

A natural inclination in reviewing the probe returns and the process in general is to construct a linear narrative. It is tempting to take the History Tablecloth, for example, and try to identify the causal probe and response(s). The process was far more roundabout than this, however. The Domestic Probes had an impact that lasted for years after the study, and continues to influence the design team today. At the same time, the designs that followed were informed by a myriad of influences in addition to those of the probes, including other studies, the availability of technologies developed by project partners, influences from contemporary arts, and the designers' own

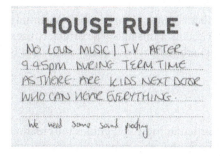

Figure 14.4.1
Sample return of a Household Rule

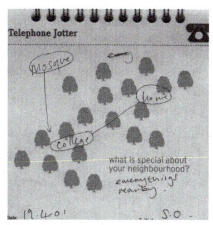

Figure 14.4.2
Sample return from the Telephone Jotter

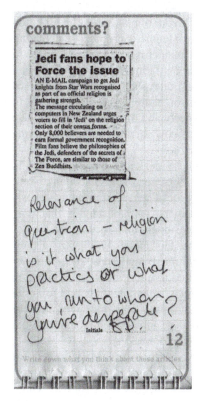

Figure 14.4.3
Sample return from the
Bathroom Pad

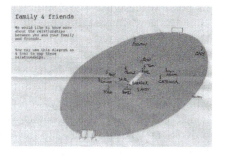

Figure 14.4.4
Sample return of a Friends and Family
Map

inclinations. The designers believe the probes were invaluable in informing the designs, but tracing a path between them is utterly impossible. Assuming an easy link between the probes and designs is a mistake. The artefacts used in the process (the probes, the prototypes) are critical but equally important is the way of thinking that leads to them.

The probe approach

The entire probe process is rooted in a particular logic that guides the creation of the probe artefacts, the framing of the probe engagement, the interpretation of the probe returns, the prototyping of design responses, and the assessment of the design implementations. Fundamental to this approach is its motivation and how this affects the implicit criteria to which the work is held accountable.

In terms of motivation, probes were developed in and for a design process that disregards traditional utilitarian values in favour of playfulness, exploration and enjoyment. They were not intended to support a process of deducing definite truths about target communities in a manner more familiar perhaps to social scientists, nor the problem solving process familiar to many designers. Instead, the designers aspired to find new and unexpected areas in the space of possible designs. The Cultural Probes, for example, were intended to stimulate new ways of thinking about the elderly and their communities. The Domestic Probes were designed to stimulate new thinking about the home. Both aimed to prompt new ideas about technology.

Being motivated by the desire to inspire new ideas rather than understand existing practices has the implication that probes need not be accountable to values such as replicability, representativeness and comprehensiveness, generalizability, or even accuracy. Instead, what is important is that they provoke new design ideas and move both designers and participants out of their comfort zones. For the probe artefacts, this means emphasizing their ability to uncover surprising particularities while giving a sense of familiarity with certain settings. Probe items are designed to elicit individual and often incommensurate responses from people, to resist generalization, and to invite unexpected responses. The assumption is that, in this way, they will uncover previously unexplored possibilities for design that more standard methods, with their emphasis on certainty and generality, would mask.

Allowing surprises to emerge leads to several important design guides for the probe process. In order to avoid surface engagements and support empathetic interpretation, for example, probes such as the Listening Glass encourage participants to take a fresh look or new perspective on familiar surroundings and practices. Others, such as the Camera and the Telephone Jotter Pad, provide prompts for people to produce images and text unlikely to emerge in the context of more expectable research prompts. The richness and diversity of the entire collection invites surprises simply by opening the door to many and varied responses. Finally, the unexpected is courted through deliberately undermining traditional research roles of the researcher versus subject and design roles of problem-solver versus problem-holders. Traditional roles are bound by expectations whereas circumventing these roles holds the potential for new exchanges. The motivation of leaving room for the unexpected drives a probe process that is at once destabilizing and playful, provocative and at the same time inviting.

Courting the unexpected uncovers subjective truths: interpretative, multiple and provisional ways of acting and making meaning in the world. Valuing subjectivity over objectivity shapes the corresponding values embodied in the probe process. Idiosyncratic and felt experiences are valued over majority or statistically significant ones. Evocative glimpses are preferred to complete pictures. Uncertainty is valued as a productive state for exploration rather than a condition to be resolved. Playfulness is valued as an attribute that stimulates creativity and engagement. Intuition is valued as a powerful source of knowing and acting. In short, inspiration for design ideas is valued over information (Gaver *et al.*, 2001).

The uncertainty inherent to the probes prevents the designers from putting too much stock in them. Their interpretation is provisional, and this allows multiple interpretations to coexist. In addition, they are but one resource, but one (incomplete) view into the target community. Designers value their own intuition in constructing interesting interpretations, in the same way that they trust participants to rely on their own intuition in choosing one possible response to complete the probes. Intuition, uncertainty, and subjectivity are taken forward into the designs, so that they are devised to be open to interpretation as well. Just as a single truth is not sought or expected about the communities for design, there is not a singular truth projected on to the eventual designs themselves. Throughout, the intention is to deal with settings and their possibilities in the spirit of literature, with its embrace of nuance, complication and ambiguity, rather than science, with its quest for simplicity and certainty.

Using probes as sources of inspiration and leaving room for the unexpected leads to opening up conversations. The probe process is a back and forth, a gifting (ibid.) between designers and participants. In creating the probes, the designers endeavour to produce something delightful and evocative. The probes are not customized for a particular individual, yet they are customized for a project, and their situated nature is evident in their content and appearance. As highly crafted yet handmade items, the probes carry the designers' fingerprints with them. In other words, the probes are not just aesthetically pleasing questionnaires enticing participants to tell more about themselves. The probes speak about the designers in a way that is designed out of most questionnaires.

As a dialogic exchange, the probe process fosters a two-way relationship. The thought and energy devoted to designing the probes matches the anticipated thought and energy invoked in order to participate with the probes. The designers convey through the probe artefacts and process both a desire to learn about the participants and an acceptance of the designers' own ignorance.

They do not presume that the probes will capture the participants' lives completely or succinctly. Furthermore, the conversation does not end once the probes are returned. The probe returns are a rejoinder in the conversation providing an opening for another response, usually in the form of design proposals and prototypes. Whereas a typical survey or questionnaire asks for input toward a final result, the probe responses start another point of conversation between designers and participants.

From logic to method

Specific probe implementations, such as the Domestic Probes described earlier, flow from the overall logic or mindset behind the probe process. Without this mindset, probes may simply comprise a collection of provocative and aesthetically pleasing prompts without a unifying purpose. In this section, we will outline the movement from approach to methods – considerations and reflections on how the probe logic is articulated through the probes themselves. The popularity of the probe method speaks to its success in terms of its results and its applicability in a number of contexts (Boehner *et al.*, 2007). In reflecting on the actual probe designs, it is worth reflecting on what makes them work.

Prior to suggesting any specific probe items (e.g. a Dream Recorder or Listening Glass), the designers have several guides for keeping their process true to the probe mindset. First, they engage in extensive conversations about the proposed participants and the context for design. For example in the case of the Domestic Probes, what makes a home different from a hospital? How would different people define 'home'? What might they value in the home, and how would they demonstrate this? These questions start priming the designers to think more critically about the broad aspects that characterize settings as well as the fine details that make the setting unique for each individual. Over time, a set of themes of enquiry emerges: routines, spirituality, privacy or community. Potential probe ideas are vetted in terms of whether they would fit these themes and the rhythm of the context, either by working with them or against them.

As the designers begin developing the probe artefacts, they stylize a particular aesthetic. The Domestic Probes are relatively bright, with elements of formality (lists of instructions, grids for filling in responses) undercut by more playful elements and instructions, and a hint of strangeness that overlays the set. Other probes might be quieter and more minimal, or more obviously playful and amateurish. A given probe set both reflects the setting to be explored and the designers' own interests and enjoyments. Unlike standard social science tools, where part of the value is in their generic and therefore generalizable nature, probes thrive on personalization. It is essential that the probes look well finished and sophisticated but also convey that they are not mass produced.

The designers assess the probes holistically in terms of how each probe artefact is situated in the environment as well as how multiple probe artefacts work together. Both the Cultural Probes and the Domestic Probes used a kit of individual artefacts that together provided for a variety of engagement and involvement. Some probes allow for immediate responses; whereas, others will require more thoughtful introspection. Some probes may require a large time investment; whereas, others can be quickly completed. Some probes focus on images, others on text. Silly or fanciful probes are balanced by more searching ones. And so on. The purpose of this variety is two-fold. First, it allows for participant choice. Participants can work with what speaks to or inspires them instead of filling out something they feel required to do. Second, the variety across the probes stymies standardized responses and surface analysis. Comparing responses on the Bathroom Pad with the Dream Recorder, for example, may prove more interesting than trying to draw standard patterns across either alone. As the probe mindset emphasizes, the point is not to whittle down insights but to expand them.

As the name suggests, a probe must be probing. Each probe requires some kind of engagement and gives something for people to react to or do. A probe is a prompt but not a script for engagement. The instructions for the probes are carefully worded so as to allow for a degree of openness and improvisation. At the same time, probes are constrained to address certain topics in certain ways, and often to limit the amount of information that can be returned and to thwart obvious strategies for answering. Filling out the probes is meant to be a fun process and not a chore, a process that rewards the participants as well as the designers. Completing the probes should feel like a process of expression and the artefact one creates should be more beautiful than the empty probe (for instance, an annotated Listening Glass is far more interesting than one that has not been completed). Not everything will be captured in the returned artefact, however, and this is also part of a successful probe – they shouldn't be so authoritative that they prevent imaginative over-interpretation.

Not all probes work. The probe process on a whole is judged in terms of whether it opens up conversation, provides inspiration, and results in innovative ways of thinking about and designing for a particular context. Individual probe artefacts are judged as successful if they do two things: generate some level of engagement and provide interesting responses. No single probe is expected to generate responses from all participants but if a single probe elicits little or no response, or if the responses they elicit are flat, incoherent, or uninspiring, the probe misses the mark. For instance, the Visitors' Comment Book from the domestic probes kit attracted only a few, lacklustre responses. On reflection, the designers realized this probe did not embody several essential attributes, most having to do with how it was situated in its social environment.

The reflections above indicate important aspects of designing probes, however, there are no hard and fast rules for creating successful implementations. The Cultural Probes and the Domestic Probes both used kits of multiple artefacts, for example, but variety of engagement and responses could also be obtained through a single artefact. It is allowing for variety that is important. Likewise, to say that probes should be provocative does not detail how this might be achieved, or even what constitutes a provocative prompt. Probes are situated within the specific contexts in which they are used, so that probes designed for London homes will undoubtedly be quite different from those designed for Tuscan villagers, and probes from one design team are unlikely to resemble those designed by another. In sum, probes themselves are neither a method-ology nor defined by any particular physical artefacts. Instead, probes are a moving target, and risk is one of their essential characteristics.

(Mis)appropriating probes

The design team that developed the original probes anticipated that the approach would inspire the design community. In their playfulness, openness, and embrace of ambiguity and absurdity, probes seemed to mirror aspects of the design process itself. Equally, embodying an appreciation for the limits of knowledge appeared valuable in maintaining room for imagination. Letting go of comprehensiveness, replicability and convergence is liberating in moving design away from the accountability of scientific approaches. The situated and idiosyncratic nature of the resulting process made the originators loath to construct formal probe methods: 'the results might be beautiful but as heartless and superficial as an advertising brochure' (Gaver *et al.*, 2004a). However, the originators also anticipated that the probe process would be taken up in ways that conflicted with the original mindset. We will explore two of the most common approaches to adaptation that veer from the spirit of the probes and examine the drive underpinning this conflict.

The first adaptation uses the probes as a form of discount ethnography – where the probe process is justified as a means for gaining rich insights without the typical time required for an ethnographic immersion in the field. This misunderstanding about the probe process was perhaps sparked by the probes' origin story when the designers acknowledged a gap of time and distance prohibiting extensive field studies (Gaver *et al.*, 2001). Yet, the decision to use probes was not dictated by pragmatic constraints alone, but also by the values the researchers wanted to explore. In the Domestic Probes situation, field studies in a local setting would have been an option but were not selected. In both cases, the probes were chosen not because they could yield rich insights more quickly than field studies but because they would stimulate unexpected responses and provoke new ideas in a playful and open manner.

Furthermore, although there may be discount approaches to the probe process, there is nothing cut-rate about the process itself. Designers may spend less time in the field, but time is shifted, not saved. The possibility of a discount method only materializes by ignoring critical aspects of the process, for instance by recycling an existing probe kit instead of developing a unique one or skipping the essential sketching stage of the process (Boehner *et al.*, 2007). A discount approach to the probe process typically selects a few popular probe artefacts: e.g. a disposable camera with a set of tasks, a journal, and a set of postcards. Results from the probes are used for a brainstorming session that quickly leads to prototype designs. A discount approach to the probes leads to discount designs.

The second adaptation seeks information instead of inspiration for design. In this case, a packet of probes is employed as a data-gathering tool in an effort to reduce possibilities rather than to expand them. The probe results are often combined with interviews or some other data gathering technique, either done in parallel or as a follow up, as the researchers seek clarification about what a participant meant by a particular probe response. Researchers advancing an information approach to probes latch on to the invective to make the process fun, engaging and beautiful. Yet, they ignore the value the probes place on embracing uncertainty, eschewing a formulaic approach and avoiding validation of a single right answer. As a result, this information approach to the probes jazzes up generic surveys or questionnaires, but leaves the survey mindset intact. The information approach proposes a conversation between researcher and researched, but it is a conversation toward a set conclusion.

Both of these common adaptations draw on examples of specific probe artefacts rather than the approach behind them. In other words, the probe kit becomes the methodology as opposed to the methodology influencing the design and implementation of the probes. Although both the Cultural Probes and Domestic Probes used a collection of probe artefacts, this is not the only possible instantiation of the probe methodology. One of the critical elements of probes is that it forces the designers out of familiar patterns of seeing and interpreting – simply relying on a standard tool kit would not meet this requirement.

Both the discount and information approach to the probes spring from a scientific mindset that seeks description, certainty, and a univocal narrative free from the bias of researchers. The probes mindset challenges these values, replacing them with an appreciation for partial access, engagement and inspiration. Using probes embraces intervention, uncertainty and projection in order to balance a grounded account of participants with the kind of openness that inspires design. Those who seek to adapt probes to their own research ends should be aware of what they are taking on and what they might be leaving behind.

... to the social sciences

Probes were developed as a declaration of independence from the implicit requirements of social science methods, in an attempt to construct a design-centred approach to understanding people and settings. Nonetheless, the probes approach has attracted attention within the social sciences as a potential new addition to their repertoire. The discussion above should suggest some of the challenges this may hold. The probes process upends existing roles of researcher and subject. It allows for fabrications, failure and mistakes. It expects different implementations, and different participants, to produce different results. It depends on personal influence and interpretations. It delves into idiosyncratic and singular details as opposed to statistically significant patterns. All these features may make the probe process difficult for the social sciences to digest.

Nonetheless, there are several possibilities for using probes within the social sciences. An obvious approach would be to assimilate them as an information seeking method, as we discuss above. At the simplest level, existing research tools such as questionnaires and tools for self-documentation could be given a more playful, aesthetically crafted appearance to make them appealing to participants. Somewhat more radically, probe tasks could be the basis for more interventionist studies in which participants are urged to think about their orientations and activities more explicitly or from unfamiliar perspectives. In order to ensure that the results provided useful information, the probes could be designed to more readily permit systematic comparison and codification, perhaps in conjunction with some sort of debriefing. Such an approach would maintain some of the active, stimulating qualities of the probes, while relinquishing the ambiguity and openness of results for multiple interpretations.

Another variation of the information-seeking approach would be to maintain the uncertainty and provisional nature of probe interpretation, but restrict their use to the opening stages of research. Probes could be used in early contact with people and settings of interest, to open a conversation and generate a wealth of materials leading to new research topics and hypotheses. After this stage, more definite methods could be used to produce traditionally accountable data.

Beyond adding a new research instrument to a traditional toolkit, however, the probe process could be used to provoke reflection on the core values and practices of the social sciences. Rather than being assimilated to notions of replicability, objectivity and generality, the probes could operationalize a challenge to such assumptions. Joining an emerging movement extending from ethnomethodology to many of the other approaches described in this book, the probes suggest a form of research that abandons 'science' in favour of a more human engagement with the social. This would entail embracing provisional understanding, subjective engagement, particularity and ambiguity not only in the process of research, but in its presentation as well. Rather than presenting authoritative accounts, the aim of such research would be to produce richly textured, situated and idiosyncratic clues for its audience to interpret. In the end, the results of the probe process would themselves be probes, implying respect for the users of research to develop their own multilayered accounts of the evidence.

References

Boehner, K., Vertesi, J., Sengers, P. and Dourish, P. (2007) 'How HCI interprets the probes', *Proceedings of CHI 2007*, 1077–86.

Debord, G. (1967) *The Society of the Spectacle*, Detroit, MI: Black & Red Press.

Gaver, W. and Dunne, A. (1999) 'Projected realities', *Proceedings of CHI 1999*, 600–7.

Gaver, W., Dunne, T. and Pacenti, E. (1999) 'Cultural probes', *Interactions*, 6 (1): 21–9.

Gaver, W., Hooker, B. and Dunne, A. (2001) *The Presence Project*, London: Royal College of Art.

Gaver, W., Boucher, A., Pennington, S. and Walker, B. (2004a) 'Cultural probes and the value of uncertainty', *Interactions*, 11 (5): 53–6.

Gaver, W., Bowers, J., Boucher, A., Gellerson, H., Pennington, S., Schmidt, A., Steed, A., Villars, N. and Walker, B. (2004b) 'The drift table', *Extended Abstracts of CHI 2004*, 885–900.

Hofmeester, K. and de Saint Germain, E. (eds) (2000) *Presence: New Media for Older People*, Amsterdam: Netherlands Design Institute.

Kellein, T. (1995) *Fluxus*, London and New York: Thames and Hudson.

Levy, J. (1936) *Surrealism*, New York: Black Sun Press.

15 Screen

AbdouMaliq Simone

The conundrums of postcolonial cities

What is the work of being in the city today for those whose lives in dense, underserviced, and often dilapidated districts face frequent turbulence, making it difficult to hang on to a sense of stability or predict a reliable future? Continuity is less a matter of anchorage or 'digging in', and more a matter of being prepared to find a way into scenarios for which one is seldom equipped or eligible. Mobility is not so much a practice through which a well-formulated agenda or notion of self seeks information and opportunity, but a series of discontinuous events whereby assumptions, histories, and everyday enactments are dislocated and rearranged. In this essay, I want to say a few things about how various inner city districts in Jakarta, Phnom Penh, Bangkok, Kinshasa, Douala, and Johannesburg act as platforms for the exterior movements of their residents and how these same districts act as both generous and reluctant hosts for the movements of residents from other districts. For in this process of simultaneous accommodation, several critical points about contemporary social research can be highlighted.

Popular understandings of how residents navigate complex urban worlds often centre on sequences of successive states of belonging that mediate relationships to the city. Households belong to neighbourhoods, neighbourhoods to districts, districts to municipalities and so forth. Relationships deliberated at a specific scale thus embody the key logics and practices necessary for residents to map out how to approach a larger field of operations. Yet, the presence of such hierarchical ordering, when it does exist, is only partial, only the result of establishing a specific vantage point from which limited trajectories of extension, transaction, and circulation take place.

While specific geometries are empowered by states and other apparatuses to sediment practices, materials and designs, everything that assumes a discernible location in cities according to specific maps and other locational devices simultaneously occupies multiple positions in other networks that are not readily locatable (Brenner and Elden, 2009). Multiplicity here is not simply the relative and differing weight of components, but a force field that shapes intensity, attentiveness, and resistance – as bodies and materials are enrolled in various projects not simply as counted items, but degrees of participation, affect, and reliability.

Cities are varied distributions of people, infrastructure, services, materials, and information reflecting specific practices of association – i.e. the way places are associated to others; how the experiences of the near or the far are brought into and kept removed from any location's present; how transmissions and circulations are speeded up and slowed down; how engagement and attentiveness is intensified or attenuated. Every place is the manifestation of multiple folds in which various potentialities of action, recognition and assemblage are differentially accessible to those affiliated to that place. The 'management' of a single position, identity, narrative, or trajectory of movement is in large part contingent upon the oscillating activations of other positions that are assumed and 'played with' (Hillier and Vaughn, 2007). People in cities thus step in and out of various 'shells' of operation – i.e. various enfolded identities, ways of moving, networks of circulation and contact, cultural assumptions, and densities of interaction to cite a few.

As Stephen Read (2006) emphasizes, places are always on their way somewhere, always points of relay and transmission, as they are always sites of criss-crossing movements. Given this architecture of urban life, even when specific mediations persist that facilitate the mapping of movement in and out of changing places, circumstances, fields, and times, the switching – i.e. the stepping in and out of different shells or tracks – requires 'research'. It requires a way of experimenting with different ways of seeing and acting. In situations where the re-territorializing forces of government create the effects of hierarchy and stabilized vectors of power, do tangents and disjunctions exist in the networking practices that generate such capacity through which those captured in or captivated by these apparent 'structural effects' can step out of their totalizing circumventions? Likewise, in situations where residents feel that they are unable to consolidate anything, where every provisional actions leads to an endless string of random encounters and diffused impacts, is it possible to mobilize boundaries that make it possible for an assemblage of actors to feel strongly implicated and thus attentive to coming up with mechanisms of coordination and coherence? Here scale and assemblage, flat and vertical ecologies continuously intersect as the multiplex realities of any particular instantiation of urban life posit changing implications and potentials for different actors – and where actors have to continuously 'switch gears' (Legg, 2009). How do residents then perform this research; and if such research is a critical dimension of urban life, how is the research itself 'researched'?

One entry point is the way in which residents in the inner city districts mentioned above undertake hundreds of small efforts to maintain a foothold in one urban district while also becoming involved in places away from home. This may take the form of a collective investment in a trading place in or near a particular market, the construction of a small informal house in an available backyard in a district that is seen as 'up and coming'. It may entail taking over a food-selling operation near the parking lot of a new shopping mall, appropriating abandoned space for storage, inserting small trades in the fringes along busy thoroughfares. Sometimes small social fractures and conflicts or divergences in residential conditions among contiguous micro-territories create underutilized 'no-man's-land' within districts that 'outsiders' take advantage off through using these spaces as platforms from which to offer, for example, repair or protection services, or to set up gambling games.

These movements point to the conundrum of the postcolonial urban situation for many residents. On the one hand, many of the once relied upon forms of mediation that mapped out a range of implications for one's actions and that provided an interpretive framework for deciding how to operate in the city have dissipated. Narratives and institutions that once secured a workable sorting out of bodies, agendas, and practices seem to no longer work, as conflict over entitlements, the use of space, and access to opportunities intensifies. The relationship of residents to the city thus becomes more direct and visceral as if clear categorizations of forces and options are no longer viable and efficacy requires an ability to simply move with diffuse flows no longer held or shaped by intelligible discourses or belief systems. Here, then, the need is for a sense of consolidation, the capacity to be held in place, even momentarily in order to construct a workable vantage point on the city from which one can proceed to make decisions about how to use available resources of all kinds. On the other hand, there is also concern about the ways in which people feel they are stuck in positions from which they are simply the recipients and pawns of the arbitrary games and decisions of others whose power lacks any legitimacy and thus negotiability.

The intensity of concern for many residents of the urban South to circumvent the ways in which their lives can be hemmed in by forces seemingly beyond their control is bleakly depicted in Brilliante Mendoza's film, *Kinatay* – one the most brutal 'postcolonial' films ever made. In this film a freshly married policy-academy student, Peping, helps a drug-gang acquaintance collect outstanding payments from local street hawkers – a banal, low-level job that supplements his meagre income. The film initially captures the vibrancy of Manila as Peping and the mother of his child repeatedly change modes of transportation as they make their way from their home at the periphery to the city hall where they join hundreds of others for a brief marriage ceremony. In the initial part of the film, the importance of extended family ties and friendships are reiterated as critical to the capacity of the young, particularly, to envision normal lives for themselves. Shortly after, as Peping is finishing his rounds, the gang acquaintance requests that he joins in on another quick task from which he could make a little extra money. The quick task turns out to be a seemingly endless ride in a van with high-ranking police officers, moonlighting in their 'real' jobs as a notorious drug gang, on various freeways that seem to be going nowhere but eventually lead to a periphery beyond the periphery. On the floor of the van is a semi-comatose prostitute drug dealer that they had picked up earlier and brutally beaten for supposedly avoiding her debts. The ride to the periphery takes place in almost 'real time' and focuses on Peping's increasing awareness of how the night is going to turn out and his inevitable capture. There is a moment before the film depicts the gruesome details of the way the woman pleads for her life, the affectless and methodical manner in which she is dismembered and the body parts disposed, that Peping has one brief opportunity to escape, but it falls through. Instead, the boss gives him a gun as a sign of his initiation. In the early morning hours as Peping excuses himself from a roadside meal with the gang and is allowed to take a taxi home, he takes out the gun and is startled by the blowout of the cab's tires. Standing on the verge of a downtown freeway in the early morning rush hour traffic, Peping has become the Gregor Samsa of Kafka's *Metamorphosis* – something totally transformed against his will and anticipation, and something completely dislocated.

The prosaic manner in which these events unfold, and the way in which Peping is incorporated into the event in a manner which effectively acts as inescapable coercion but with the discursive flatness of a crew of men performing the most menial of bureaucratic tasks is what indeed frightening about Peping's position. It is frightening to perhaps many others as well caught in the ordinariness of the way that violence is distributed and the complete absence of ethical anxiety in which police, public officials, and local authorities deploy it. The film implicitly points to the exigencies of not being stuck and of having some way out of being implicated in such arbitrary rule.

A range of devices, simultaneously conceptual, cognitive and affective, are important to this aspiration of mobility. For individuals are compelled to simultaneously retain, dispense, and move in and out of their various administrative, familial, and socio-cultural designations – i.e. the way they are 'framed', including both the ways they are interpreted by others and 'set up' to incur certain assumptions about what it is possible for them to do and their concomitant responsibilities. The trajectories of such remembering and forgetting are not volitional or anticipated in advance. So individuals need devices that steer the flows of action towards or away from them as they incessantly change positions, either stealing away from or confronting head-on the projections, anticipations, compulsions and indifference placed on them. Here, I will explore one such device: screen.

The fragile boundaries of urban cognition and space

Research is largely about location – the location of things in cells, curves, correlations, indicators, regressions and context specificities. Even in a world of complexity, it remains a process of locating causes and effects. The possibilities of location assume that any entity can be sufficiently held in a particular place long enough to assign it a location in relation to others or a mechanism, such as global positioning systems, capable of tracking an entity as it moves in real time. In the latter, the larger environment of possible positionalities is largely immaterial as the stability of the entity in movement is a product of algorithmic calculation.

If the proposal here is that research is a critical quotidian process for residents to work out the critical conundrum of how to locate themselves in complex urban environments as a prelude to exerting action, then some overall assessment of where these urban environments are located in the larger scheme of things also is important. Therefore, it is possible to conclude that the dilemmas of intensive territorialization and deterritorialization described earlier are incumbent in all cities and that it is a matter of residents finding out how their 'compatriots' in the most 'advanced' versions of urbanity deal with their historical dilemmas with enough sufficiency to keep the 'wheels turning'.

So, stepping out of the specificities of the urban South for a moment, in a first instance we could understand screens as the construct of cognitive mapping – i.e. a neurasthenic surface of the interplay of various sensations – visual, auditory, olfactory, gestural, and haptic – applicable to all cities. Such mapping then is the intersection of singular sensate experiences projected outward and into the individual's spaces of operation. It is a kind of probe involving various instances and forms of activation of which the individual is either an explicit or implicit target (Liddament, 2000). Here, the screen acts as a membrane, a mediation of interchange that is not important for the arrangements of 'bits' that it displays, but rather as a tissue that relays, switches, speeds up and slows down the 'traffic of semiosis.'

But as many urbanists note, given the profusion of digital production and media saturation, mapping becomes increasingly difficult. Even as a process of regulating intensities, absorption, or attention, mapping may no longer be desirable or possible as discernible anchorage points, trajectories and orientations are incessantly recalibrated in proliferating stochastic modelling systems (Coates, 2000). As Wael Fahmi points out:

> Architecture of cities needs no longer be generated through the static conventions of plan, section and elevation. Instead, buildings can now be fully formed in three-dimensional modelling, profiling, proto-tying and manufacturing software, interfaces and hardware, thus collapsing the stages between conceptualisation and fabrication, production and construction. Iconographic assemblies are absorbed, reworked, and distributed globally in various forms and embodiments. The icons that comprise this new landscape of difference are essentially mediated reflexes of similarity and diversification (constructs that are mirrored endlessly over computer networks, home pages, televised imagery, advertising campaigns).
>
> (Fahmi, 2008: 43)

Whereas scales, hierarchy or habitus could be mobilized as a means of situating the body into a series of discernible and interlocking positions – thus shaping how individuals thought about and represented the urban environment – at the neurasthenic dimension, mapping now verges on the extensionality of the territory itself. Interpretive orders can be displaced or condensed; the interrelationships of built, media and social environments entangle themselves in dream-like webs of affective meaning. Individuals are emplaced in a doubled manoeuvre where, on the one hand, everything remains to be figured out and, on the other hand, there no longer is a need for interpretation. Here, the individual no longer has access to the distance attained by representations but is in one sense always in the 'midst of things' – a direct participant in the flows of events and signs that incessantly recombine to elide distinctions between near and far, here and there, reality and simulation as a criteria for response.

Power is not addressed to a 'social body', but to microphages and synapses, as well as to cognitive phase spaces. In the increasing disjunction of the surface from function and semantic depth, the surface becomes a scene with its own autonomous operations, and thus the promoter of relations among a wider range of actants. In a literal sense, the surface no longer 'screens' anything, but registers the body as immersed in the immediacy of experience (Krupar and Al, 2010). Yet, as Terranova (2004) notes, basins of coalescence and polarization continue to exist, as do the disparate distributions of sense, access, and opportunity. People still find themselves in tightly sealed interest groups, neighbourhoods, markets, or specializations. These fragmented and fractal urban landscapes then require new possibilities and practices of translation and articulation, new ways for people to reach each other as well as to circumvent the 'regime of fear' where the identity of any possible object, what something might be – i.e. how anything, however mundane could become an object of danger or terror – increasingly determines the affective quality of any situation.

So even though all cities may confront the dissipation of mediations in face of more direct confrontations with urban life and the intensifying segregation of access and possibility, does the location of residents within fluid demarcations of north and south, black and white, productive and marginal, centre and periphery say anything about locating what people think, what they assume is possible, or how they engage the world. What is the salience of the 'colonial difference' in terms of the specific characteristics putting together a 'social' and 'economic' life and attaining increasing degrees of autonomous action in face of arbitrary confinement? It is easy to conclude that cities in the Global South are in need of more accountable and transparent governance, economic specialization, and proficient legal and regulatory systems in order to really work. At the same time, it is also possible to conclude that these supposedly unworkable cities do indeed work by virtue of the activation of virtualities at the heart of urbanization – i.e. the unregulated thickening of relationships among things of all kinds. Such virtuality also includes the flexible use of different networks of connections – categorized in different ways – to access resources that are, in turn, distributed in quantities that acquire particular value by again flexibly using categories that point to different kinds of social relationships and responsibilities. Cities of the south are conventionally considered to need to be more formal, transparent, governable, entrepreneurial and rational; whereas they work largely by avoiding all of these things. So where then is the location of efficacy and a viable future, beyond facile claims of hybridity? How do residents do the 'right thing' when that right thing is largely undecidable in advance, but also not meaningful if it is simply something to be discovered at the point of arrival in the sense that the decision and movement 'feels right'? While such feeling indeed is a crucial element of popular research, there must also be a way for residents to generate and uncover evidence that can be shared, translated and converted into an incentive for collective action.

Screens as objects

Here then screens cease to be a seemingly infinite refraction of images otherwise thoroughly indistinguishable if not for long histories of repression, projection, and displacement that enable 'working differentiations' of whites and blacks, citizens and subjects, rulers and the ruled, moderns, pre-moderns and post-moderns. This is not Bhabha's (1994) 'linguistic multivocality' that unsettles the colonial imposition of binaries. Unlike Genet's *The Screens* where politics is a parlour game of cross-dressing that unsettles any possible integrity of the command – the injunction to become developed, modern, in this situation of postcolonial indeterminacy – the screen here is something more visceral and intrusive.

It is commonly assumed that screens do not call attention to themselves. Rather, they subsume their materiality and status as objects to the need to reflect, enchant, engross, or incite. That they are objects of a particular kind is much less important than the images they 'carry', transmit and arrange. But research for residents taking on these postcolonial conundrums is less a process of coming up with an image of things where the constituent elements of the city find their proper place. It is less than a series of best practices and policy prescriptions that hold things in place, in part by specifying their proper 'commitment' to each other. Rather, screens act as material probes churning up events, making things happen in part because they are not supposed to do this, and that these forms of enactment and objectness can be occluded by the predominant role of the screen as either a mechanism of filtering, reflection, absorption, or transmission. Research is then not a matter of identifying locations but explicitly inventing them in a context where residents endeavour to act as if the undecidability of their location in a larger world either does not exist or does not matter.

At the same time, residents may insist that the such indeterminacy – i.e. about whether prevailing notions of doing the 'right' thing have enough persuasiveness to sufficiently turn people's attention away from things that are obviously right for the specificities of a particular place but wrong where the 'real' (big) powers of valuation lie – is crucial to their survival. Screens here intrude upon locations and the ability to locate persons and things within any categories and space definable in advance of an engagement that seems to increasingly hedge its bets. Here, reflection and projection becomes simply an excuse to do something else. The conventional functions of the screen provide a certain amount of cover so that its status as an object can experiment with how connections can be made so as to invent locations that might provisionally resolve the anxiety and inertia possibly associated to the difficulties inherent in solving the riddles of location.

Thus, I want to consider notions of screens, not as devices of mapping but as a switchboard of connections, a mechanism of transplantation and inter-ference, and as such, a vehicle of 'popular research'. Screens are devices that enable residents to try on different ways of being in the city 'on for size' without making definitive commitments to them – a way of acting in conditions of uncertainty but proceeding nevertheless as if the implications were clear.

Reenacting the screen

To set a screen in basketball refers to a teammate inserting their body between the shooter and a defender momentarily creating space and time for the player to get a good shot off. Always as a tactical manoeuvre, screens can be called and anticipated in advance, yet in a fast-paced mobile game, where they take place at any given instance on the floor, they are difficult to plan. With moving bodies always in close proximity, always in 'each other's face', the chances of a getting off a good shot is directly related to having a 'good look' at the basket, and so the screen is in service of such a look.

With their predominantly visual connotations, screens concern practices of looking, and often are deployed to constitute a possible differentiation between 'looking out' and 'looking out for'. Screens, such as those that supplement windows and doors filter out unwanted intrusions, like insects, while maintaining the circulation of sound and air. When constructed of metal mesh, screens also limit the extent to which other aspects of the outside can cross a divide, such as a reaching hand. Constituting a semi-permeable boundary is a minimum condition for the distinctions between these different types of looking. 'Looking out for' steers attention to the identification of targets the viewer already has in mind – a viewer geared towards moments of recognition, be it opportunity or threat, or as part of a sequence of stepping stones in a trajectory of movement – e.g. 'look out for the McDonald's next to the pink house on your right, then turn left.'

To eliminate the 'for' and simply 'look out' opens up potential sight lines, doesn't orient the viewer to specific features or compel particular modes of paying attention. Even if certain features of the environment may be 'screened out' and not paid attention to, this 'editing' of perception can be directed towards vitiating the power of objects otherwise and implicitly demanding preoccupation. With such preoccupation out of the way, different aspects of both familiar and unfamiliar worlds can be considered. By filtering out what potentially irritates, preoccupies or event fascinates, the larger visual field can be seen as an assemblage of impurities – i.e. objects and relations that need not have discernible classifications or uses.

From cinema, we also are familiar with the plurivalent position of the screen as an activity projected on to a surface – i.e. to screen a film; the screen as the very surface on which images are screened, and the 'screening' as the very event that incorporates both action and object. This refractory circuit of references appears, on the one hand, compatible to the virtual world of the filmic process and the play of light, surface, memory and motion that materializes it. Initially, it seems like an insular world, oneiric and apart, yet screening is also a prolific practice, capable of showing up anywhere. Any surface can be transformed into a screen, given the right technique, and not simply of high tech projection but of quotidian shadows, reflections, and even sediment, where seemingly non-reflective or illuminative surfaces still can display a range of histories.

As such, the screen is a mobile device; a device mobilized to facilitate movement, in part by facilitating the process of 'looking out.' Here, screens need not be wire or mesh; they need not be capable of showing projected images or of keeping out certain material impurities. Still, incorporating all of these aspects, more ephemeral screens act as invisible supplements to everyday scenarios. They are acts of non-deliberated collaborations that choreograph specific spacing of bodies, materials, and things; act as unspeakable frontiers, and linguistic and perceptual manoeuvres that momentarily allay vulnerability and threat so as to not foreclose ways of looking that take in many possible routes and opportunities of movement.

Screen test in the flesh

In many cities today, eligibility, preparation, status, and waiting – all elements that have conventionally been associated with the ability to attain certain positions or opportunities are frequently pushed aside. Instead, the willingness to dispense with codes and patience is seen as the criteria to become something, to go somewhere. But this is a claustrophobic game, and no one seems to go anywhere, except to an early death. There appears to be no sense of outside and inside, here and there intruding upon the other.

Yet even in this 'game' other, more ambiguous scenarios come to the fore. For example, the renowned television series *The Wire* centres on the drug trade in Baltimore. It deals with the way the trade has changed – the dissipation of codes and honour, the inevitability of betrayal, and the ease in which violence can be delivered to anyone. A minor character acts as an important 'screen' in this economy of auto-destruction, racial resistance, and neo-liberalized black entrepreneurship. Butchie is a blind bar owner, sometime dealer and banker of stolen money, and a figure resonant with centuries of African and African American 'tricksters'. He always acts blind to what he sees, but he sees anyway. He is not the repository of an archival wisdom; he is not a holdover from another generation; he does not issue cautionary tales or deliver cogent oral histories.

Rather, Butchie sees how the changes in the game, the 'passing' of the old orders are not really that at all. He sees the 'affective ties' of the city – the ways in which self-destruction simply does not mirror a past violence, nor opens up a situation to new developments or formations, but rather moves things 'sideways', where many different implications and possibilities happen all at once (Pandolfo, 2006). Butchie exemplifies inexplicable forgetfulness and memory; it is often not clear to whom he talking or what he is talking about, but he won't bend to the specificity of any request, profit or threat. No one ties him down, yet he is not unavailable to anyone; he knows what is going on. But, it is never clear just how he could possibly know, since it is not clear what he offers except the conviction that there is nothing in the long history of black life that was ever settled or clear, and constantly provides the evidence to back this up.

Butchie lends body and image in a situation where it seems impossible to invest in either the survival of the body or the coherence of any image. He provides a 'crossroads' that exceeds the claustrophobia of the 'game'. This does not tell us that in desperate urban situations there is always hope, or that things will at some point get better, or that there some kind of valiant wisdom embedded in the 'game.' Rather, it makes us responsible to look for more than the body count, more than the impossibility of negotiation, dialogue, or civility. As the game 'takes down' everything that it touches, it cannot survive if it is the only thing left.

The game may be the game, but every time it plays itself out it reminds all of those around it just why the arbitrary use of violence had to be used in the first place – i.e. the possibility that whatever one was or what one did, no matter how much you had in your 'camp', you could always be out-tricked. So in the violent manoeuvring that takes place among residents and which governments also direct toward particular residents within the city, what haunts the situation is this fear of being out-tricked – that somehow there is a way of living in cities that neither those with power nor those without can quite get a handle on, but that each suspects the other really has.

So what happens when a district shows, up front, different ways of being in and using the city? What happens when those actors which constitute the prospective threat to projects of capital accumulation and social control may be precisely those that are turned to in order to demonstrate possibilities for operating outside conventions and laws? Do they leave themselves open to getting slammed, taken apart, manipulated? How do they not leave themselves as an identifiable target?

Setting targets and imagining outcomes

Particularly in contexts where once relied upon mediations grow weak, where clear interpretations of what is taking place are difficult to make with confidence, and where individuals feel they have few opportunities to make recourse to higher authorities or arbitration, individuals 'set screens' all of the time. They insert themselves in the flow of events, transactions and conversations – with what they hope are efficacious words and gestures – to create space, to become that which 'comes to be looked out for' or a means of enabling a changed outlook on the part of others. On various thoroughfares and vehicles of transportation, urban residents repeatedly 'step into' situations where they don't necessarily belong and have no apparent eligibility to participate. But here the setting of the screen is not a territorial claim; it is not an instrument that attempts to secure something that someone else *possesses* nor is it an act of self-aggrandizement. Rather, it is a way of being present in a moment that one is already present in but as something or someone else. It is an act of dislocation and relocation. Seemingly full of risks, setting these screens will at times inevitably raise questions about eligibility – i.e. 'who are you, and with what claims and authority do you insert yourself into this situation?'.

For example, one striking aspects of everyday life in Kinshasa – that vast rambling almost ungovernable megacity of the Congo – is just how often strangers intervene into scenarios on the verge of getting out of hand and come up with the rights sense of things in order to steer them in another direction. In part, efficacy here has much to do with the sheer decision of the individual(s) involved to 'set the screen'. But in contexts where the legitimacy of actions of all kinds can be incessantly contested, where people are always looking out for instances of self-aggrandizement and where veracity has long disappeared as an essential component of believability, the screen must always carry with it the traces of elsewheres – i.e. something inserted that is familiar, desired or reliable. Of course, the person who 'sets the screen' – who 'screens'– cannot be expected to be aware or in control of this. In this way, the screen acts as a kind of 'graft', an image of momentary integrity and completeness that comes from the outside but is capable of acting as if it has been inside of the scenario in question the entire time. An imposition can take place – a different way of keeping things moving, a change in the anticipated story line, where individuals feel variation in the way the experience they are in matters – but with the sense that everything is taking place in the same 'neighbourhood', at the same time, in the same world (Stengers, 2008).

Still, grafts are risks in that what is supplemented in order to maintain the integrity of an image can of course be rejected. So the setting of the screen, as an implicit rejection of the apparent alignment of bodies and things in a particular moment, covers its presence as a voice from elsewhere free to say whatever it wants in the cloak of something the others present are willing to recognize as familiar or desired. If the screen is rejected, then, it is not rejected for what it attempts to do – after all, it is not interested in the integrity of identities, events or scenarios – but rather is rejected as the failure of the ruse under which it operates, so that even the process of rejection does not completely foreclose what the screen attempts to do.

Screen literacy and the littering of screens

Much of urban development has been about cleaning up screens, or only emphasizing a reified aspect of them as the filtering of impurities that enables the reproducible ordering of relations among the various materials, bodies and things which make up the city. But the mobility of urban residents with limited resources depends on such screens; depends upon a built environment littered with them. For the ability of residents to 'go out into the larger world' is largely situated in the messiness of built environments, the seemingly haphazard, incomplete and strewn out arrangements of buildings, infrastructure, and activity that continue to persist in many cities. This environment of multiple screens – temporalities, instruments, designs, insertions – provides a visible yet always contestable rendering of what things are and what people are up against dealing with them. It shows how water and power appear and disappear; it shows that people living, playing, working, eating, sleeping, moving, and interacting together have an effect on places – the land, the buildings, the air. It shows how residents crisscross, incorporate and side-step the markings and physical traces of all these different activities, movements; how everyone implicitly sets screens for each other.

When a place shows all of its wears and tears, its memories, and the impacts of what people have done it, the place then shows that it is always available to deals, small initiatives and renovation. It shows that the relationships among bodies, materials and things need not be the way they are imagined or prescribed by the prevailing policies, norms, or administrative procedures. The city is a messy environment, and people have to step through and around each other, but it is an environment that is available to be 'messed with' – that is, open to engagements of all kinds.

When residents go out into the larger city with their modest projects, they bring these experiences back home, where they face the 'imported experiences' of neighbours, co-workers and other associates, as well as those of outsiders who have come wage their own experiments. All of this propels residents back into the larger world in still different ways, and all constitute wide ranging propositions for how different districts might deal with each other over the long run, how they might put together a different kind of city.

These movements back and forth are screens; they constitute a kind of intrusion. Districts are intruding upon each other, as they in some sense always have been, and in the aftermath of each intrusion, it is difficult to sustain the very notion of intrusion. For what integrity of the district is being intruded upon when so many different realities are being grafted on to the other. Yet what is important is experiencing a game of give and take, now you are something, now you are not. So, these movements to the outside enact a form of recognition that dislodges residents from prior ways of seeing themselves, while not having to discard them completely. For, certain stabilities of self-representation and practice are maintained in order to feel, experience disruption, to trace a line or direction from which an impact arrives, as well as for the person to feel themselves as something instrumental, that makes its way into an external space and has an impact on it.

Taking Nancy's notion of intrusion, ruptures are always coming from two places at once (Nancy, 2002). There is the idea of self-integrity that intrudes upon unprogrammed and plural operations, as in the way conceptions of the good or normal city intrude upon multifarious, fractal urban processes. Then there is the idea of diseases and dysfunctions that intrude upon a coherent sense of self. Here, individuals or collectives discover their dependence on components that do not act on behalf of the whole – when dysfunction takes place from the inside, as when cancer spreads or an organ fails, or traffic grinds to a permanent halt. The critical components of the normal city, its identifiable pieces, built environments, and mobilities, often out of control, intrude on the city's normality. In order to 'treat' this dysfunction, the intrusion is doubled, such as when treatment interventions graft, replace, auto-immunize, or transplant – and in doing so, demonstrate a capacity, as Nancy says, to prolong life that wasn't possible before, 10 or 20 years ago. So when Nancy talks about an organ transplant – 'Life' goes on but is cut off from its 'natural' finitude. Life and death are coupled in an arrangement where life is literally out of its time. In these situations, the self or the collective is that which takes what intrudes from both the inside and outside, that comes from within and elsewhere – the strange that is familiar, and the familiar that is strange, and sutures a workable connection. It does so not with the myth of some overarching integrity or coherence. Rather, the collective is the force that intersects and joins that which otherwise could never fit or go together – makes the link where there could not possibly be one.

So, this movement of residents back and forth, this navigation of intrusions is the occasion through which residents suture together a different kind of connection with each other – one cut off from reliance on a particular way of making reference to each other's lives. This connectivity is not a defence of place, not a protection against the incursion of an outside, for residents themselves are engaged in different elsewheres. Nor it is a connectivity based on being able to take advantage of that which is being brought from the outside – to appropriate initiatives, resources, or labour. For this would then obviate the need for residents to act outside of 'their' districts. Rather, it is a way to configure possibilities for residents of a district to be in a larger world *together* – in ways that do not assume a past solidity of affiliations, a specific destination nor an ultimate collective formation to come. It is way of being together without recourse to being able to see, coordinate, or command each other. If in each individual initiative, back and forth, here and there, is a proposition for how spaces across a city could be articulated, the question is how these propositions are amassed, or rather how they have traction with and imply each other?

Let me take just one critical aspect of this question. Usually, districts rely upon concepts such as 'property', 'neighbour', 'co-religionist', 'co-worker' to help specify and regulate social distance and responsibilities among individuals. But in districts full of people coming and going, the sense of habitation cannot correspond to plots, cadastres, and social demarcations. Rather, residents imagine security and stability as located beyond what they can see and figure out – in dense entanglements of implication, witnessing, and constant acknowledgements of other residents, whether physically present of not. Security is necessarily expansive in that it does not act as if contingency is something measurable or subject to contract in the long term. Rather, it entails efforts to instrumentalize the dissensus and uncertainties that ensue in the interaction of specificities registered as life itself.

Security instrumentalizes through a process of extending the ways in which things are implicated in each other; for example, in expanding circuits of relations that economy – especially in the financial topologies of securitization, derivation, and arbitrage – brings about. Discrepant places, things, experiences are articulated, circulate through each other, not just as matters of speculation, but as a complex architecture of accumulating and dissipating energies and attentions.

Urban security is not a matter of simply excluding unwanted and un-manageable populations, or by drawing walls – even though these processes do take place. Lines, corridors, and conjunctions cross the heterogeneous city, imparting various ways of paying attention, vantage points, blurs, clarities, simultaneities, pasts, access points, and frictions. It is about who can do what with whom under what circumstances and what can ensue from the resultant actions; who can they reach, how can they be made known; how fungible are they, and what kinds of other actions are impeded, compelled, or opened up as a result. Nothing is completely ruled out or disciplined; as not everything is possible.

In this context, then, screens produce an affective density – a thickness of people paying attention to each other, not with wary eyes, but attention to points of mutual entry and implication, where the stability of individual households are enjoined to risk-taking and speculations of other households, practices which, in turn are enjoined to the repetitive domestic rhythms of still others. This does not take place because stable and discrete households are adhering to a common set of rules. Something else in witnessed. Keeping in mind the sense of screens as a simultaneous dislocation and relocation, a concretization of the possibility of 'looking out' as opposed to 'looking out for', this is witnessing which situates that which you see right in front of you as either taking place somewhere else than the space in which it is taking place – to see it as if it is in another place *or* to see what is taking place in front of you as being enacted by someone completely different than the neighbour, kin, or stranger you have before known this person to be.

Here, mutual witnessing acts as a way to muddy the waters, to run interference for households to do different things – with their time, money, and passions. It is also a 'screen' on which to project troubling images, half-formulated questions and concerns from within households to which no one can make a quick conclusion. It is to do things not easily recognizable or classified – and so it is not the witnessing of people checking up on each other, comparing what they've and others don't, or about who is doing what to whom as a matter of prohibitive judgment.

In this way, households do not stand alone as discrete social and economic entities but are tied into various circuitries, positions and ways of being in the city. As these circuits scatter in all kinds of directions, households are not subsumed under a series of successive obligations – in relation to which they must always defend themselves from or be accountable to. This does not mean that districts are free of conflict and manipulation. Claims are made and protected. Individuals have to cultivate relationships with patrons and institutions and are paid to the extent to which they become instruments of their will. But residents with different engagements in the larger city, different paymasters, vested interests, and loyalties continue to pay attention to each other – not as a disciplinary manoeuvre – but with a real interest in what is going. Many times across North Jakarta, Kinshasa and Douala I have seen activists, gangsters, clergy, gamblers, government enforcers, marketers, municipal workers, school kids, women and men engaged in long animated discussions – in mosques, street-corners, cafes and markets – about what they see out there, their theories about what is taking place in the city, and perhaps more importantly, what it is exactly that everyone else is doing – the nuts and bolts of talk and action.

Such observations do not obviate the ways in which such practices sometimes never show up in certain districts or do so only fleetingly. It doesn't mean that conventional mobilizations and organizational politics are not necessary. They do not obviate the fact that in many districts claims to space, resources, and life are made by those who have no right, or where claims to rights simply are based on a game that only involves seizing or being seized.

But the key element again for research is how to think about the simultaneities, the co-presence of such ambiguous differentiations. For the differentiations produced by urbanization are not always clearly differences of advantage, authority and resources. What these differences mean in the intersections of labour, space, tools, time, abilities, and networks does not necessarily directly stem from the apparent visible and hierarchical distribution of capacities and privilege.

Relationships can be simultaneously exploitative and excessively generous, competitive and collaborative. There are unpredictable oscillations of accumulation and loss which potentially introduces a dynamic egalitarianism over a long run that no one individually has the power to define or measure, even if in the present glaring disparities can be documented everywhere. This can be the case in situations where hierarchies appear quite obvious. So given the simultaneities, how do both residents and researchers 'screen' the field – both in terms of screening out those facets that would seem to foreclose collaborative action yet still screen the complexity of these differences and the fact that they carry with them the possibility of contradictory futures.

As implied at the beginning of this essay, a conundrum is how to demonstrate that cities of the Global South will be both viable and worthy cities yet different from the urban logics that subjugated them. The difference that would most clearly embody such a break lies in the relatively invisible piecing together of aspects of city life – people, things, spaces – that are not conventionally thought to be associable. But how can such a difference be demonstrated, and at what cost?

Whether cities completely mirror the purported efficiency of those of Europe or North America, exceed them in the spectacular quality of new built environments, or are full of gang wars, ethnic conflict, parochialism, patronage, and other signs of an impending implosion, none of these aspects serves as evidence that 'different' forms of collective life are being definitively ruled out.

At the same time, for cities to demonstrate 'their own way', 'their own difference' in a highly networked urban world linked through various metrologies, skewed advantages, information systems, investments, controls, and properties, risks choking them off from essential transactions.

For now, what we do have is a constant impetus of experimental research, where residents in Messina, Ikori, Penjaringan, and Klong Toey – to name some of the South's most crowded and heterogeneous districts – use what little they have, not just to put bread on their own tables, but to take small steps with other residents from districts across the city to be in a larger world *together* – in ways that do not assume a past solidity of affiliations, a specific destination nor an ultimate collective formation to come.

References

Bhabha, H. (1994) *The Location of Culture*, London and New York: Routledge

Brenner, N. and Elden, S. (2009) 'Henri Lefebvre on state, space and territory', *International Political Sociology*, 3 (4): 353–77.

Coates, N. (2000) *Ecstacity*, London: RIBA Publication.

Fahmi, W. S. (2008) 'The urban incubator: (de)constructive (re)presentation of heterotopian spatiality and virtual imaginar(ies)', *First Monday*, Special Issue 4: *Urban Screens*: *Discovering the Potential of Outdoor Screens for Urban Society*, available at: http://firstmonday.org/htbin/cgiwrap/bin/ojs/index.php/fm/article/view/1548/1463 (accessed 10 May 2010).

Hillier, B. and Vaughan, L. (2007) 'The city as one thing', *Progress in Planning*, 67 (3): 205–30.

Krupar, S. and Al, S. (2010) 'Notes on the society of the brand,' in G. Crysler, S. Cairns, and H. Heynen (eds) *Handbook of Architectural Theory*, New York: Sage.

Legg, S. (2009) 'Of scales, networks, and assemblages: the League of Nations apparatus and the scalar sovereignty of the Government of India', *Transactions of the Institute of British Geographers*, 34 (2): 234–59.

Liddament, T. (2000) 'The myths of imagery', *Design Studies*, 21 (6): 589–606.

Nancy, J. L. (2002) *L'Intrus*, East Lansing, MI: Michigan State University Press.

Pandolfo, S. (2006) 'Nibtidi mnin il-hikaya [Where are we to start the tale?]': violence, intimacy, and recollection', *Social Science Information*, 45 (3): 349–71.

Read, S. (2006) 'Towards an urban space', in S. Read and C. Pinilla (eds)*Visualizing the Invisible: Towards an Urban Space,* Amsterdam: Techne Press, pp. 7–11.

Stengers, I. (2008) 'Constructivist reading of Process and Reality', *Theory, Culture and Society*, 25 (4): 91–110.

Terranova, T. (2004) *Network Culture: Politics for the Information Age*, London: Pluto Press.

16 Set

Adrian Mackenzie

The 'personal productivity' system, Getting Things Done or GTD stands on the periphery of new economy and network sociality. GTD represents an attempt to organize multiple, overflowing demands of work and life by defining things in terms of sets. Like many personal improvement or development techniques, GTD appeals to North American corporate managers, and business journalists. However, its popularity extends well beyond corporate USA – to research social science and humanities academics, for instance in the UK. The official description runs:

> GTD® is the popular shorthand for 'Getting Things Done®', the groundbreaking work-life management system and book by David Allen that transforms personal overwhelm and overload into an integrated system of stress-free productivity.
>
> (David Allen & Co., 2009)

The popularity of David Allen's GTD could be understood from many perspectives: as a symptom of the chronic dislocation of labour that Barbara Ehrenreich describes in *Bait and Switch* (Ehrenreich, 2005); of what Zgymunt Bauman sees in *Liquid Modernity* as 'free-floating capitalism, marked by the *disengagement* and loosening of ties linking capital and labour' (Bauman, 2000: 149); or what Doug Henwood derides in *After the New Economy* as a 'manic set of variations' on the old American theme of techno-utopia (Henwood, 2003: 1). While there are many practical components of GTD that baldly express the fantasies of weightless, frictionless and clean productivity, rules for making sets are central to its promise of a feeling of efficacy. Set-based determinations guide people in responding to contemporary demands on their attention and time.

Sets are often seen as banal, merely practical, disposable, somewhat ephemeral devices, the very epitome of insignificant social behaviour, not even really a practice. We casually group, encounter, collect or sort things in sets. Set-related inscriptions such as labels, tags or codings are a part of routine knowledge-making across humanities, social sciences, engineering and natural sciences today, and data is itself often seen as a kind of set, the dataset. Many

Figure 16.1 Practical set-making setting (Alldredge, 2005).

methods books in the social sciences advocate quasi-formal set-making habits in researchers (usually in the form of 'coding'). Software to assist in the conduct of qualitative and quantitative analysis of social and economic data (the standard statistics package SPSS – analyzed in (Uprichard, Burrows and Byrne, 2008), or the standard qualitative data packages such as Nvivo and Atlas.ti, etc.) relies on sets and sets of sets as basic ordering devices (coding, grouping, tagging, cases). The *dispositifs* of important contemporary network services and products such as Google search, Facebook pages, Amazon, Wikipedia, YouTube and Flickr; the playlists, libraries, trees, menus, address-books, bookmarks, tags and labels of all manner of mobile devices, software interfaces and databases; or bodies of scientific knowledge such as PubMed or GeneBank: every item in this list can entail set-making. In such settings, informal inscriptive practices of collecting, sorting and grouping are increasingly shadowed by much more formal, intensively organized forms of set-making and set analysis. In the light of the 'coming crisis of empirical sociology' (Savage and Burrows, 2007) occasioned by routine collection and analysis of transactional data, the question of how sets are made, and how forms of relationality materialize from set-specific practices becomes highly significant. Practices of set-making partly established in social sciences now structure the objects of analysis. By implication, social scientists and researchers would benefit from an increased awareness of how people's sense of belonging, group, and inclusion embodies acts of set-making.

Techniques derived from the mathematical expression of set-making, 'set theory', underpin many of the most intense and pervasive instantiations of network media collaboration (for instance, Wikipedia), group discussion

(Facebook), entertainment (Amazon book recommendations; Netflix DVD recommendations, Last.fm scrobbling), blogging, knowledge, profiling and transaction, the profiling of consumers in markets segments, and the predictive analytics used everywhere from Tesco's supermarket shelf-stocking policies to airline flight scheduling. Sets make powerful calls to order, and act as world-making forms of collection and grouping. Here, 'world' means more than community, or social grouping, because it 'because it necessarily includes more people than can be identified, more spaces than can be mapped beyond a few reference points, modes of feeling that can be learned rather than experienced as a birthright' (Berlant and Warner, 1998: 558).

How can we appraise the overflows and excesses of the astonishing proliferation of sets and forms of set-making today? Pierre Bourdieu wrote:

> The structures of the social space . . . shape bodies by inculcating in them, through the conditionings associated with a position in that space, the cognitive structures that these conditionings apply to them.
>
> (Bourdieu, 2000: 183)

GTD can be seen as a process of conditioning that structures space in ways governed by sets. GTD offers a practice of the self that addresses a site of distress where exchanges and communication between habits, values, practices, transactions and institutions intensify:

> We're allowing in huge amounts of information and communication from the outer world and generating an equally large volume of ideas and agreements with ourselves and others from our inner world. And we haven't been well equipped to deal with this huge number of internal and external commitments.
>
> (Allen, 2001: 7)

While the personal productive techniques advocated by Allen are scarcely representative of broader spectrum of set-making, the material specificities of sets and set-making in GTD illustrate in particularly exaggerated form the dynamics of collectively networked and collaborative activities. What social order do sets unroll or inculcate? What kinds of subjectifications do sets engender? How are sets and set-making enrolled in practices of the self? Are they processes through which things happen, or through settings are made? How are sets lived and experienced? Could the dynamics of sets give rise to altered ways of inhabiting the multiple, and different theorizations of the multiple?

Between open and closed sets

GTD promises to handle this dual excess coming from outside and inside, from 'outer world' and 'inner world'. From the outside come demands, deadlines, opportunities and accidents. On the inside arise ideas, worries, hopes, memories, and promises. GTD prescribes the development and maintenance of a system of lists. The construction, organization and handling of these lists is described in great detail in the books, seminars, websites and articles. The lists are well ordered in themselves, and together form parts of a set of lists whose limits are defined and documented, electronically and on paper, in great detail. These lists comprise sets of projects, sets of actions, sets of events and contexts. Many different forms of sub-sets, of inclusion and belonging run across the GTD system. The feeling of being productive in GTD comes from (a) the work of constructing an all-encompassing well-ordered set of lists; and (b) maintaining the currency and completeness of those lists by constant review, resorting and updating. How could sorting out all commitments as projects, and then generating sets of actions, produce an affect of efficacy?

Sets have the property of being closed, open or closed-open. The opposition between open and closed implicitly steers much contemporary social and philosophical thought on events, on difference, on relations and multiplicity (for instance, in much post-representational social theory (Thrift, 2007) and in recent science studies (Law, 2004) (Latour, 2007)). The formal contrast between open and closed in set theory seems relatively straightforward:

> Then the set S is open if every point in S has a neighborhood lying in the set.
>
> (Weisstein, 2009a)

> [A] set U is called **open** if, intuitively speaking, starting from any point x in U one can move by a small amount in any direction and still be in the set U. In other words, the distance between any point x in U and the edge of U is always greater than zero.
>
> (Wikipedia, 2009)

By contrast, a closed set includes its boundary or limits points:

> [A] closed set is a set which contains all of its limit points. Therefore, a closed set C is one for which, whatever point x is picked outside of C, x can always be isolated in some open set which doesn't touch C.
>
> (Weisstein, 2009b)

The difference between open and closed as used in set theory is that an open set always includes some more space to move around. It might not be much room, but there is always space to wriggle in an open set. An open set has an edge that always allows a bit of movement that might touch something else. Put differently, we might regard an open set as always expandable. More room can always be found. A closed set, by contrast, has a boundary and that means

Figure 16.2 Open set.

that things can be isolated from it. For a closed set, inclusion and exclusion have strong effects.

A set is 'closed' when no more entries or elements can be added to it. It is open to the extent that more can be added to it. Of course, in many situations sets are subject to constant reordering, and this allows lists to respond to change. But how does a set respond to something new? It can do that either by being open or closed, by either finding what happens in itself (as an element, as a subset, as a relation between existing elements, etc.) or by adding something new to the set. What is interesting about the predicament of GTD as a set of lists is that it tries to be both open and closed. On the one hand, the feeling of control and productivity comes from the conviction that everything trivial or important has been captured by the system and its workflow. In set language, this means that it is closed. On the other hand, the system must remain constitutively open if only to the bare fact of the presence of others. In that sense, it must be an open set. This dual requirement to engender a sense of openness and closure introduces a certain instability that I find symptomatic of contemporary set-making more generally. One could say that set-making is response to the problem of how to sort things coming from the outside and things generated from the inside. Sets are devices for working on the boundaries and edges of collections. In the case of GTD, the solution to the problem of how to negotiate inner and outer is by controlling time. Timing and calendrical routines ranging from time scales of minutes to years ensure – if they are adhered to – that the sets of lists, projects and events will be regularly updated, resorted and kept current. The constant tension between being open to new things and keeping control of what is already in the system is maintained and regulated by routinized reviews and checks on the list. During these reviews, sets open. Outside the review times, work is devoted to making sure that the set stays closed. This closure is diagrammatically expressed in the GTD workflow diagram (see Figure 16.2) that prompts people on how they should process events.

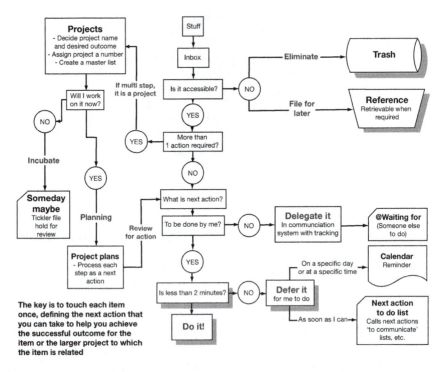

Figure 16.3 GTD workflow (Hsu, 2006).

Outside open and closed: R

Does the opposition, unstable as it is in GTD, between open versus closed sets represent the primary feature of set thinking and set practice? At this point, I think it useful to turn a much larger scale set-making practices: those embodied in the predominating database architecture of the last two decades, the relational database. In a sense – a very broad one admittedly – we could make two connections between GTD and datasets. First, databases are in a sense responses to the same problems of closure and openness. In database design and management, an elaborate panoply of techniques, architectures, query languages, forms of professional expertise, training, product development and intensive research entwine around the problem of keeping datasets sufficiently open so that they can expand and grow, and keeping them closed so that can be manipulated, explored or mined, or in short, controlled. The history of database architectures and database management might be seen as a technological instantiation of the problem that affects all set-making, and all collecting. Second, from a different, more sociological perspective, GTD can be seen as a response to the increasing prevalence of interconnected databases. While I would be hesitant to ascribe the overflow and excess that GTD tries to staunch to databases as such, databases embody in almost exhaustively differentiated form the relational algebra that govern so many contemporary set-making enterprises. If the database, with all its tables, schemas and queries, attempts to construct open-ended processes of set-based relations, it might be that the personal productivity system, with all its lists and folders, attempts to seal out of the productive self the currents and shocks of rapidly transforming patterns of mobility, communication, production and governance generated by database-driven processes.

Database architectures and management run underneath much of the making of knowledge today in various ways. We need only think of the technology of the relational database. Dating from the 1970s, the relational database and its long-lived search syntax called SQL (Structured Query Language), still form the 'engine' of many database-driven activities ranging across commercial, government and academic settings. The technology of relational database has been expanded to gigantic and shrunk to miniature scales. On the one hand, vast enterprise architectures in data centres or increasingly in 'the cloud' (Jaeger, 2009) store trillions of items of data that survey populations, markets, environments and institutions. On the other hand, a variety of more or less embedded personal databases organize and sets preferences, contacts, addresses and references (for instance, in the form of reference and bibliographical management software widely used by academics). Contemporary biopower, in all its guises and facets ranging from clinical drug trials through to patient health records or child protection databases, depends on relational databases or RDBMs (Relational Database Management Systems) such as Oracle's 11g or IBMs DB2 (IBM, 2009; Oracle, 2009).

The mathematics of set theory (dating from the late nineteenth century) quickly becomes unavoidable in making sense of the embedded set-workings of databases and datasets. The relational database relies on set formalisms. Basic technical terms still used today in database design and management such as 'tuple', 'key', and above all 'relation' all date from papers published in 1969 and 1970 (Codd, 1970). The motivation for this turn to a practical instantiation of set theory seems very simple: 'Future users of large data banks must be protected from having to know how the data is organized in the machine (the internal representation)' (ibid.: 377).

This desire to 'protect' users from knowledge still prevails today. The queries, searches, and sorts that organize and animate business processes, certain aspects of scientific work, and the layout of websites bear the traces of the relational database as a prophylactic against knowledge of form. In this setting, what sets provide is a way of bringing data into relation without fixing that relation or making those relations fully visible. Set-making retains forms of flexibility that other figures and devices (network, list, inference, deduction, etc.) find it harder to match. This flexibility, the flexibility that I am suggesting generates the stresses and overheating that GTD tries to quench, pivots on the relation R. What is a relation here? E.F. Codd writes:

> The term *relation* is used here in its accepted mathematical sense. Given sets $S_1, S_2, \ldots, S_n$ (not necessarily distinct), R is a relation on these n sets if it is a set of n-tuples each of which has its first element from S_1, its second element from S_2, and so on.
>
> (ibid.: 379)

A relation R is a set of sets, since a tuple (typically embodied in a 'row' in a database table) itself is a set that possesses some order (for instance, a row of a database table might include a name, an age, gender and address). The relation R allows set-making to become recursive (i.e. as GTDers know to their cost, sets of actions, TODOs, and reminders proliferate across different media, and the relation between these different sets multiplies – this could be seen as a both intrinsic to the relationality of sets, and as a result of the kind of multiples that R gives rise to in contemporary data-driven collectives.)

A whole series of ramifications follow from this. They include techniques of database management. For example, a key technique in relational database design is the process of 'normalization' or 'elimination of non-simple domains' (ibid.: 381). The upshot of the normalization process is constructive – the potential to generate many relations by melding disparate things, by defining relations that observe certain constraints, and by remaining open to production of more relations, always in the simple domain of tuples. The absolute flatness of the normalized form remains indifferent to the difference between sets, to their hierarchical or convoluted intersections and unions.

If we want to see how the set-theoretical processes of normalized database forms impinges on lives not at the level of customer service, surveillance, or loss of privacy (through data-mining, etc.), but as a sensibility, as experiential encounters with the multiple, how do sets and set-making come back into the world? The subjects of set-making, the subjects made by set-making: how do they inhabit worlds? What happens to their senses of open and closed, belonging and inclusion, in the light of the set settings they intimately and impersonally encounter? There are many places we could look for subjects of the set, forms of subjectivities whose practices of self, whose negotiated of the exchanges between self and other, thing and thinking, rest on set-making dispositifs. GTD is one response: make sets against sets, defend yourself against the flow of demands and commitments that carry you through the world by enclosing, grouping and sequencing them. But so many other practices and promises respond to sets.

The relatively austere formalism of the 'relation' as a set of ordered sets underlying the dominant contemporary database architectures does represent the apogee of the set as device. Sometime in July 2007, the Google search engine switched to a different index of the web (Dean 2006; Catanzaro, Sundaram and Keutzer, 2008; Chen and Schlosser, 2008; Ekanayake *et al.*, 2008). A slight reduction in the time taken for search queries might have been the only sign of this change. In the thousands of servers seried in Google's scarcely visible data centre, work on the switch had been going on for several months. A shift in database architecture away from the relational database model to an even more radically simplified set theoretical construct, MapReduce, took place. This change, part of the broader migration of data from single databases to federations of databases – the cloud – also suggests the need to rethink about the experiential dimensions of set-making, to begin to formulate accounts of how the informal processes of grouping and collecting characteristic of so many cultural settings entwine with the ongoing transformations in the technical, economic, scientific and political production of sets.

An animated and motivated engagement with sets can be found in recent European philosophical thought. Here a key point of reference would the work of the French philosopher Alain Baidou. He uses set theory as a 'guide for an ontological thought of the pure multiple' (Badiou, 2000: 47). The intricacies of Badiou's thought are too complicated to follow in any detail here, but his basic notion of 'pure multiple' is 'everything is not one'. It may do to focus on how his re-rendering of the basic opposition between open and closed sets might re-configure the predicament embodied in GTD and in Google's move from a relational database structure to MapReduce.[1] Badiou argues that sets exemplify 'subtraction' from any opposition between open and closed:

> For the set is the exemplary instance of something that is thinkable only if one dispenses entirely with the opposition between the closed and the open . . . We could even say that the set is that neutral-multiple which is originarily subtracted from both openness and closure, but which is also capable of sustaining their opposition.
>
> (Badiou, 2004: 73)

Why does Badiou say that a set is thinkable only if we do without the opposition between open and closed sets? If sets undo the basic opposition between open and closed, then it would be important to track what this means in practice, in the practices of knowledge-making and contemporary world-making. While it would be possible to simply examine the proliferating open and closed sets of the present, the promise of the set as 'neutral-multiple' lies elsewhere, in the potential to understand how new patterns and configurations of open and closed sets materialize today. If this subtraction obtains in practice, a very different perspective on contemporary practices of set-making might open up.

What happens to the open versus closed distinction when Badiou thinks the set as pure multiple? There is no fundamental difference between open and closed at the level of the set as multiple. That means, for Badiou, that any attempt to valourize openness as the locus of vitality, creativity, event or difference is problematic. Despite the many appeals made to openness, the open has no special privilege, and there is nothing intrinsically unethical or negative about being in a closed set. (If Badiou is right, then much contemporary social, political, cultural and organizational thought, in its attempt to locate vitality in openness will run into problems.) Badiou's alternative is try to think how

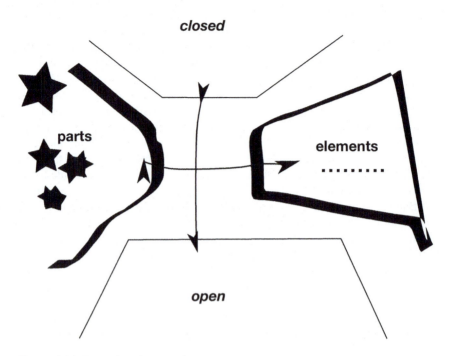

Figure 16.4 Open-closed; parts-elements.

'[e]very multiple is indeed *actually* haunted by an excess of power that nothing can give shape to, except for an always aleatory decision which is only given through its effects' (ibid.: 79). So, while the open versus closed distinction cannot ground any judgment about sets, excess can. What is excess in sets? 'The immanent excess that "animates" a set, and which makes it such that the multiple is internally marked by the undecidable, results directly from the fact that it possesses not only elements, but also parts' (ibid.: 78). This 'fact' sends us back to a different distinction, that between belonging and inclusion. Some things – elements – belong to sets, some things – parts – are included. For instance, a GTDer's lists comprise hundreds of entries or elements (many photographic examples of this can be found on the web, particularly at photo sites such as flickr.com). The notion of the element is recursive – elements or entries can themselves be sets. The GTDer's notebook contains lists of lists (for instance, the GTD central list of projects has elements that themselves must sooner or later, gradually or suddenly, be made into sets of 'next actions'). However, a part can include many elements. What, then, is a 'part'? In set theory, a part is a subset. A set A is a subset of a set B if A is 'contained' or 'included' in B. A part may comprise one or many elements, but it does not belong in the same way to a set. When Badiou writes 'there is an ontological excess of representation over presentation' (ibid.: 78), he refers to a set excess that does not come from the outside, or from life or chaos, but from the internal non-cohesion of the set with itself, from the relation between elements that belong and parts that are included or contained. What he calls the 'actual' or 'immanent' excess of power of the multiple comes from the irreducibly instable relations between elements and parts, between 'the two types of immanence' (ibid.: 78).

If it seems that contemporary databases teem with constant revisions, modifications, additions and almalgamations, it might be because of this ontological excess. If it seems that so many contemporary social-technical processes entail collecting, labelling, tagging, sorting or searching, they might be experiential attempts to determine this excess, to present it, to manage it, to undo it or to politicize it. While differences between open and closed matter greatly in the inhabitation in the topologically connected spaces of databases, they do not exhaust the overflows that animate sets.

Other settings

To what problems in interdisciplinary research does attention to sets respond? I would argue that set-making is already a strong, albeit somewhat latent, impulse in many social science and humanities methods attempts to produce knowledge through narrative, and through explanation. Wherever datasets, practices of coding, grouping or clustering occur, set-making with all its relationality (open, closed, elements, parts, excess) is not far behind. The work of set-making, whose dynamics I have explored in the context of database architectures and in personal productivity systems (a domain not so far removed from the practical exigencies of any academic today), necessarily figures in any of the processes of collecting, sorting, citing and ordering that underpin all research. At the present moment, there is something more specific at stake in sets. Faced with much competition from market research and business analytics that access vast databases of transactions, actions, communication and consumption, sociologists have called for renewed attention to the work of description. Most prominently, Mike Savage argues for a shift away from attempts to provide general or specific causal explanations for particular phenomena to an engagement with the widescale deployment of inscription devices such as websites and loyalty cards (Savage, 2009: 171). These mundane inscription devices constitute a massive capacity to describe what people do, without any reliance on the standard social science research techniques of surveys, statistics, interviews or ethnography. Faced with such abundant descriptive data, Savage suggests that 'a core concern might be how to scrutinize how pattern is derived and produced in social inscription devices, as a means of considering the robustness of such derivations, what may be left out or made invisible from them' (ibid.: 171). Here, alternative theorizations of the intense generativity of set-making may be very useful. Inscription devices, of which GTD would be one example, generate descriptions whose dynamics and potentials stem from the different ways they construct and deconstruct open, closed, closed-open inclusions and belongings. Many of these inscription devices rely directly on mathematical operations on sets. In such settings, many researchers would feel what Donna Haraway described as 'splitting': 'splitting, not being, is the privileged image for feminist epistemologies of scientific knowledge. 'Splitting' in this context should be about heterogeneous multiplicities that are simultaneously necessary and incapable of being squashed into isomorphic slots or cumulative lists' (Haraway, 1999: 179). Splitting, I would suggest, always affects the entangled practices of knowing, not just feminist epistemologies of scientific knowledge. Sets and set-making ontologies are one way of figuring this splitting for researchers who are always in the contradictory position of affirming radical historical contingency and imagining historical change for the better.

Notes

1   The significance of this contrast between open and closed sets can be traced in terms of the theoretical polemic that Badiou conducted with Deleuze around sets over several years in the 1970s. Deleuze, following Bergson, resists set-based thinking as a way to think the multiple. The notion of set, for Deleuze, thwarts thinking multiplicity because a set is an external or analytical multiplicity comprising parts or elements. Nothing happens in sets or lists because the parts are external to each other. A vital multiplicity for him (and for many others who make derive their notion of multiplicity from Bergson) has no parts or elements. It only has intensive differences actualizing as extended things, with boundaries, with orderings. While a set might display boundaries, partitions, forms of inclusion and exclusion, or even hierarchical sites such as the top and bottom we find in lists, the set itself only actualizes something intensive.

References

Alldredge, B. (2005) 'Here's one for David Allen. . .', 8 September, Flickr, available at: www.flickr.com/photos/billypalooza/135447595/ (accessed 26 November 2009).

Allen, D. (2001) *Getting Things Done: The Art of Stress-free Productivity*, New York: Viking.

Badiou, A. (2000) *Deleuze: The Clamor of Being. Theory out of Bounds v. 16*, Minneapolis, MN: University of Minnesota Press.

Badiou, A. (2004) *Theoretical writings*, ed. R. Brassier and A. Toscano, London and New York: Continuum.

Bauman, Z. (2000) *Liquid Modernity*, Cambridge and Malden, MA: Polity Press/Blackwell.

Berlant, L. and Warner, W. (1998) 'Sex in public', *Critical Inquiry*, 24 (2) (Winter): 547–66.

Bourdieu, P. (2000) *Pascalian Meditations*, Stanford, CA: Stanford University Press.

Catanzaro, B., Sundaram, N. and Keutzer, K. (2008) 'A MapReduce framework for programming graphics processors', paper presented at Third Workshop on Software Tools for MultiCore Systems.

Chen, S. and Schlosser, S. W. (2008) *Map-Reduce Meets Wider Varieties of Applications*, IRP-TR-08-05, Technical Report, Intel Research Pittsburgh.

Codd, E. F. (1970) 'A relational model of data for large shared data banks', *Commun. ACM*, 13 (6): 377–87, doi:10.1145/362384.362685.

David Allen & Co. (2009) 'What is GTD®?' available at: www.davidco.com/what_is_gtd.php (accessed 15 September 2009).

Dean, J. (2006) 'Experiences with MapReduce, an abstraction for large-scale computation', *Proceedings of the 15th international conference on Parallel architectures and compilation techniques*, PACT '06, Seattle, WA: ACM Press.

Ehrenreich, B. (2005) *Bait and Switch: The (Futile) Pursuit of the American Dream*, New York: Metropolitan Books.

Ekanayake, J., Pallickara, S. and Fox, G. (2008) 'Mapreduce for data intensive scientific analyses', in *Fourth IEEE International Conference on eScience*, pp. 277–84.

Haraway, D. (1999) 'Situated knowledges: the science question in feminism and the privilege of partial perspective', in M. Biaglio (ed.) *The Science Studies Reader*, New York and London: Routledge, pp. 172–88.

Henwood, D. (2003) *After the New Economy*, New York: New Press.

Hsu, V. (2006) 'GTD workflow', 25 April, Flickr, available at: www.flickr.com/photos/yggg/135181438/ (accessed 15 September 2009).

IBM (2009) 'IBM – DB2 – Data server – database software – database management – open source', CT404, 13 August, available at: www-01.ibm.com/software/data/db2/ (accessed 18 August 2009).

Jaeger, P. T. (2009) 'Where is the cloud? Geography, economics, environment, and jurisdiction in cloud computing', *First Monday*, 14 (5), available at: www.uic.edu/htbin/cgiwrap/bin/ojs/index.php/fm/article/view/2456/2171 (accessed 23 July 2009).

Latour, B. (2007) *Reassembling the Social: An Introduction to Actor-network-theory*, Oxford: Oxford University Press.

Law, J. (2004) *After Method: Mess in Social Science Research*, London and New York: Routledge.

Oracle (2009) 'Oracle 11g, Siebel, PeopleSoft | Oracle, The World's Largest Business Software Company', available at: www.oracle.com/index.html (accessed 18 August 2009).

Savage, M. (2009) 'Contemporary sociology and the challenge of descriptive assemblage', *European Journal of Social Theory*, 12 (1) (1 February): 155–74, doi:10.1177/1368431008099650.

Savage, M. and Burrows, R. (2007) 'The coming crisis of empirical sociology', *Sociology*, 41 (5): 885–899.

Thrift, N. J. (2007) *Non-Representational Theory: Space, Politics, Affect*, London: Routledge.

Uprichard, E., Burrows, R. and Byrne, D. (2008) 'SPSS as an "inscription device": from causality to description?', *Sociological Review*, 56 (4): 606–622.

Weisstein, E. W. (2009a) 'Open set' – from Wolfram MathWorld, Text, available at: http://mathworld.wolfram.com/OpenSet.html (accessed 11 August 2009).

Weisstein, E. W. (2009b) 'Closed set' – from Wolfram MathWorld, Text, available at: http://mathworld.wolfram.com/ClosedSet.html (accessed 11 August 2009).

Wikipedia (2009) 'Open set' – Wikipedia, the free encyclopedia, 5 July, available at: http://en.wikipedia.org/wiki/Open_set (accessed 11 August 2009).

17 Speculation

A method for the unattainable

Luciana Parisi

In his vision of a series of infinite entanglements between methods and objects, cyberneticist Gregory Bateson anticipated the importance of founding a system that would explain the immanence of thought and experience (Bateson, 2000). As opposed to the dominance of deductive and inductive methods that establish a hierarchical relation between the rational and the empirical, Bateson adopted the notion of *abduction*, originally coined by American philosopher Charles Sanders Peirce (Buchler 1940; 2000: 150–6). Abduction points to a quasi-causal process by which patterns of relationship, their symmetry and asymmetry, define complex mental and organic systems. Abduction as a method coincides not with established systems of inference, where for instance *a* is used as an explanation of *b*. For example, 'if it rains the grass is wet'. On the contrary, abduction points at the precondition *a* of '*a* entails *b*' to be inferred from the consequence *b*. In other words, like Peirce, Bateson appealed to the operations of abduction not to establish a derivative use of inferring, but as a method able to create new rules, a quasi-causal process actually inclined to entertain the inference of anything *new* coming from the object. In particular, Peirce suggested that the actual process of generating a new rule should not be 'hampered' by the rules of logic, but rather constituted a probe-head, a speculative device leaning towards the production of the not yet actualized:

> The first starting of a hypothesis and the entertaining of it, whether as a simple interrogation or with any degree of confidence, is an inferential step which I propose to call *abduction* [or *retroduction*]. This will include a preference for any one hypothesis over others which would equally explain the facts, so long as this preference is not based upon any previous knowledge bearing upon the truth of hypothesis, nor on any testing of any of the hypotheses, after having admitted them on probation. I call all such inference by the peculiar name, *abduction*, because its legitimacy depends upon altogether different principles from those of other kinds of inference.
> (Buchler 1940; 2000: 151)

In contrast with the inductive method, which as Peirce explained, implied that 'observations made under certain conditions ought to have certain results', thus extending 'a certain confidence to the hypothesis', abduction was altogether a risky business (ibid.: 154). Abduction, as a method, required the investigator to formulate a hypothesis in no other way than as an 'interrogation' (ibid.: 154). This would eliminate the possibility that a hypothesis could be merely 'a positive falsity'. With this insistence on interrogation, we are fully plunged into a speculative method of approximation and precise modification, which demands a *retroductive* or 'explanatory reasoning' (ibid.: 151). Both Bateson and Peirce therefore were looking for a method that could explain the formation of new knowledge through the re-articulation of both methods of deduction and induction so as to deploy the process (the how) of thought itself.

Abduction therefore provides an all-together different standpoint from both deduction and induction. Deduction for instance can only explain thought as that which relies on a necessary inference according to the causal relation between A and B, whereby only substantial theoretical (pre-established) knowledge can ever offer us the truth. The method of deduction in fact belongs to the tradition of rationalist metaphysics according to which the external world can be known either by intuition or by reason derived from the intuition. An example of this method is thought experiments, which have been used to confirm a hypothetical scenario determined by a theoretical a priori requiring no physical evidence (Galileo, 1632/1953: 186–7). It has been said that thought experiments can be conducted within the laboratory of the mind and never in the materiality of facts (Brown, 1993).

As an instance of deductive methods, thought experiments use deductive truths to sustain a hypothetical scenario, which is able to elicit a common intuitive response needing no further verification. Let's take as an example John Searle's 'Chinese Room': a non-Chinese man in a locked room receives written sentences in Chinese, and returns written sentences in Chinese, following a sophisticated instruction manual (Searle, 1980: 417–57). Searle employed this deductive method to challenge the hypothesis of strong artificial intelligence: if a machine acts intelligently, then it follows that it has a 'mind', 'understanding' and 'conscious experience'. Searle's Chinese Room thought experiment raises doubts about functionalism and the computational theory of the mind (Clark, 2001). In particular, it represents a direct challenge to the Turing test: a human judge engages in a natural language conversation with one human and one machine. All participants are separated from one another. If the judge cannot reliably tell the machine from the human, the machine is said to have passed the test (Turing, 1952). Through the deductive method based on rationalism, Searle insists that the presence of mentality cannot be guaranteed by the physical behaviour of automated machines processing data. For Searle's rationalism, no mental representation can be reducible to algorithmic procedures. Thus, computational systems, such as AI, are to be considered as machines built to *act* intelligently, but not as machines that have a mind or consciousness in the same way as (human) brains do. In this case, the thought experiment deploys an intuitive hypothesis of how mind (qua consciousness) cannot be proven to exist by the physical, mechanical, empirical experiments of AI. The hypothetical scenario of the Chinese Room intuitively points out, and rationally deducts, that only the human mind is capable of cognition.

If, for Peirce and Bateson, the deductive method precluded the construction of any new form of knowledge, the method of induction based on observation is also limited; in this case by its reliance on a predictive hypothesis, where probabilities are pre-set to explain knowledge from past experience. For instance, the extension of inductive methods into sociology has transformed the analysis of society into an evidence-based laboratory derived from empirical facts. The extent to which mobile digital communication has become constitutive of our post-desk society is continuously verified by empirical data provided by users and collected by smart databanks generating profiles and predictions about the experience of being connected. Thus, induction, according to Peirce, implies testing the hypothesis through a prediction, which has already been verified. Abduction, on the contrary, offers us a method for investigating an original suggestion delimited neither by a priori theory or by a posteriori verification. Abduction is rather a method primarily attuned to the unpredictable nature of fact, thought and experience (Buchler 1940; 2000: 153).

In a similar vein, Bateson opposes 'logic as a model of cause and effect' out of which knowledge can be produced. The building of knowledge instead requires the propagation of 'difference or variation' in a complex network (Bateson, 2000: 457–60; 2002: 85ff). The central theme of *Mind and Nature* is that evolution is as much a mental as a natural process.[1] This is because thought and evolution share a 'pattern which connects'. Thought and evolution are processes in which each pattern deploys a link to something new. Both *Steps to An Ecology of Mind* and *Mind and Nature* propose the bio-cybernetic proposition that the mind is not contained in the brain, but is rather given by a complex relationship between the perceiver and the environment. Minds exist in the relationship between things, not in things themselves. Far from relying on an empirical method geared to prove already made predictions applied to objects, Bateson seems to embrace a speculative method strictly aiming at establishing new forms of knowledge defined by the relationships between mind and nature.

However, Bateson's view about the absolute interconnectedness between systems can here be pushed further towards the radical empiricism of William James (1996). Contrary to empiricism, which cannot explain how data relate or form patterns in space-time, James argued that the sole criteria of reality was the experience of pure relations, which are to be conceived as real things and not simply as leaps of imagination (James, 1996: 42). James' notion of experience adds new character to Bateson's insistence on 'patterns of connection'. His conception of radical empiricism points out that any method is to be housed by experience because experience is the sole criterion of reality. Yet to experience is not to bring together what is in reality separated and does not correspond to a way of testing what will happen according to what has already occurred. Experiences occur rather at the interstices, the gaps and the halos that constitute the invisible links or relations between one drop and the next. These relations indeed explain the immanence between thought and experience no matter how abstract, how unthought and unlived these can be (ibid.: 42).[2] According to James, classical empiricism disregarded the reality of relations, imaginations, emotions, contrasts and patterns. Since these could not be reorganized as things or direct impressions of sensation, they had been relegated to a state of mental fiction (such as habits, derivatives, and in general secondary qualities). On the contrary for James, in a world of pure experience relations are to be conceived as being every bit as real as any other thing: 'the relations that connect experience must be experienced relations and any kind of relation experienced must be accounted as real as anything else in the system' (ibid.: 42).

But how does this radical empiricism become a speculative method? How can it embrace the reality of relation and transition, defying any easy correspondence between the physical and the mental as well as between methods and objects? If radical empiricism takes as its point of departure relations, then for knowledge to be new it has to be affected by its prior world, not a rationally determined prior word, but by logically indeterminate sets of large, general, vague thoughts whose feeling or prehension on behalf of actual objects explains how new experience/knowledge can ever occur. From this standpoint, radical empiricism may coincide with a speculative method, whose premises are potential facts releasing an effective power of the new, which can only be *retroductively* explained after an untested hypothesis comes to capture indeterminate conditions, which force new thought and become a new experience.

The retroductive effects of a potential cause are not however experienced retrospectively, but are anticipated as vibrations or tiny excitations intrinsic to the unknown of all hypotheses without which facts would not be worth pursuing. For radical empiricism, the experience of relations involves the transition between given potentials and unknown events. If the method of abduction proceeds by means of interrogation, then these are not simply questions to which sets of probable answers can correspond. In other words, interrogations are not based on already known experiences, but, rather, are inclined towards the feeling-thought of the ingression of the new in habitual patterns. One can define interrogations as the experiencing of *vibes* for something that is not yet there. These vibes constitute the 'whatness' or 'thingness' of any experience, which is ultimately irreducible to an already individuated object. Vibes are more exactly vibrations or excitations intrinsic to and belonging to any unseen object. These vibes may correspond to what Whitehead defines as 'lure for feeling' deriving from an object's capacities of feeling its own spatio-temporal transitions while deploying invisible links between the past and the present, and yet requiring a full immersion in the potential background of the future. Such background however is in no occasion to be conceived as a framework out of which hypotheses can be deduced. A background does not define a general method of application of thoughts to objects. On the contrary, a background must remain fully impersonal, pre-individual, unlived, amodal or virtual. It can only enjoy the company of its own abstract presence. It stays invisible to experience, passing through it as a felt thought in things. It is therefore clear that immanence between thought and experience entails not a direct correspondence between the mind and what is in the world out there. If a radical empiricism admits the superiority of relations, it is because relations are the background that never appears in experience and yet objects incessantly feel these relations as the continuity of thought. In other words, as with abduction, which defines an immanent relation between the thing and its unknown potentials, so for radical empiricism, relations are the lines of a patchwork, where any kind of piece can be sewed in so as to be experienced as yet another thing.

From this standpoint, abduction is neither factual nor logical, neither empirical nor cognitive. It is above all speculative. The method of abduction implies that for each and any theory or observation there is a background of potentialities stemming from within an object. In addition to this, the speculative device specifically admits that a crucial pull of imagination is intrinsic to the workings of rationality. As Whitehead observes:

> The true method of speculation is like the flight of an airplane. It starts from the ground of particular observation; it makes a flight in the thin air of imaginative generalization; and it again lands for renewed observation rendered acute by rational interpretation.
>
> (Whitehead, 1929: 5)

According to Whitehead, in the history of civilization there have been two main views on reason that have dominated its conceptions: either reason is the operation of theoretical realization, whereby the Universe is a mere exemplification of a theoretical system, or reason is only one of many factors within the world (ibid.: 10). Whitehead on the contrary insists that rationality entails the activity of final and not efficient causation. 'The conduct of human affairs is entirely dominated by our recognition of foresight determining purpose, and the purpose issuing in conduct' (ibid.: 13). This final cause characterizes all entities, lower and higher forms of life. The essence of reason in the lower forms entails a *judgement* upon flashes of novelty relevant to appetition (a lure towards, an upward tendency of thought) and not to action (reflexes or sensorimotor responses). However, stabilized forms of life entertain no reason, only repetition. Reason instead is here conceived as an organ of emphasis upon novelty.[3] Reason provides the *judgement* by which novelty passes into realization, in purpose and fact (ibid.: 20). However, Whitehead claims, reason is also, and mainly, speculative: an urge for disinterested curiosity, where reason only serves itself, rather than being a reason for (and of) something else. Reason 'is its own dominant interest, and is not deflected by motives derived from other dominant interests' (ibid.: 36). A tension is here evinced between reason as governed by the purposes of some external dominant interests and those operations of reason, which are instead governed by immediate satisfaction arising from themselves (ibid.: 39). While the history of practical reason is related to the evolution of animal life, speculative reason only belongs to the history of civilization (ibid.: 41).[4] In other words, reason is more than an organ of evolution and does not serve the evolution of biological life. Reason qua thought remains *causa sui,* whose functions are defined by its infinite extensions and not by its biophysical realizations.

The function of speculative reason, for Whitehead, is to pierce into general reasons beyond the limited reason of higher forms of biological life. This is an infinite reason never fully matched by the bounded intelligence of mankind (ibid.: 63). Whitehead's insistence on the generalization of the function of reason is not to be confused with an appeal to a category (as with a deductive method) nor with a proved fact that can be universalized to others (as with an inductive method). Instead, generalization is here the condition describing not cognitive states but rather constituting all order. Generalization here rejects the concept of set as a basic concept and rather points to the 'mapping of the relation between a domain and a codomain' (Bradley, 2008: 3). In other words, to generalize here means to describe the non-separability from particular rules not as a one-to-many relation but as a constructivist endeavour in the nature of finite, actual, terminal entities. But this construction in itself is not infallible. On the contrary, it is in the nature of speculative reason to remain open to unexpected revelations and discoveries forming new epistemologies.

More precisely, however, generalization here alludes to the function of speculative reason: a flight after the unattainable coinciding with the lure for abstract schemes (Whitehead, 1929: 73), where the form, structure and topology of any physical and conceptual system remains composed of related elements. A speculative method therefore will demand of imagination to outrun direct observation, venturing towards the limits of the observable where thought becomes experimental and experiential of the future. In sum, a speculative device is truly a probe-head working in two ways. On the one hand, it depends on the authority of facts – and therefore it cannot overlook the stubborn reality of objects – and yet it cannot cease to transcend the existing analysis of facts to which it returns, after a short journey, mutated. This contrast between fact and thought however entails no bifurcation of nature because, as Whitehead explains, thought is a *factor* in the fact of experience in the same way as a method is a factor in the fact of the object. After all, an immediate fact is what it is, partly by reason of the thought involved in it. The quality of an act of experience is largely determined by the factor of the thinking that it contains. At the same time however, the thought involved in each and any act involves an analytic survey able to go beyond direct experience itself, beyond empiricism and the predictabilities of induction. And yet even the wildest flight of speculative thought has to be relevant to the worldwide experience. This is because even the most speculative device must derive elucidation from experience. From this standpoint, speculations occur all the time, because, as Whitehead claims, we scan the world to find evidence of this elucidatory power not to test or demonstrate a hypothesis, but to find lures for the presence of unknown worlds, adding new drops of experience to existing facts. In other words, a speculative device includes a mutual yet indirect interplay between method and object, a real yet inexact connection of thought and fact, a constructive tension between conditions and occurrences, premises and predictions so that unattainable ideas and experiences can become counter-intuitive kinds of knowledge.

Of propositions

According to Whitehead, besides mental and physical poles, there are prehensions whose objects are propositions (Whitehead, 1978: 259). These involve the union of physical and conceptual feelings, the coexistence of actuality and potentiality. Propositions of this kind can be associated to statements: this stone is grey (but could be red), my body is tired (but could be fit), and my back is stiff (but could be relaxed). Whitehead considers these propositional feelings as constituting a third phase of experience, after the physical and the conceptual phases. Physical feelings are prehensions whose objects are other actualities. Conceptual or mental prehensions demarcate a second phase of an occasion of experience because they are derivative from physical feelings.

For instance, out of a particular set of physical feelings originating from a red object, I may lift out redness as such in abstraction from its particular exemplification. Hence, the feeling of redness itself is a conceptual feeling: it is a mentality. However, while conceptual feelings or mentalities are appetites, a proposition is truly a 'lure for feeling': a propensity towards or away from the conjoining of some indeterminate set of potentialities with some particular facts (ibid.: 184). Propositional feelings are simply feelings in which propositions are entertained.

Propositions therefore are not objects of intellectual judgement but are 'vibes towards' the unattainable, a lure for feeling that can be generalized to non-human occasions of experience. In a propositional feeling, the possibility of this redness, for instance, is a potentiality in abstraction from its presence in the immediate feeling of red. Whitehead distinguishes propositional feelings in this fully-fledged sense from simply physical purposes in which this abstraction from the present feeling is only latent. In a physical purpose, the possibility embodied in the physical feeling is felt with blind appetition either positive or negative. Propositional feelings instead evacuate the present-past axis to occupy the world of futurity without time, by taking the standpoint of an eternal object or a series of eternal objects, existing eternally outside time and space. And yet for Whitehead, propositional feelings are not strictly determined by a special capacity to imagine the future. Organisms as simple as neurons for instance can experience the ingression of the future because of their incipient form of intentionality.

From this standpoint, if a speculative device can be truly constitutive of new thought and experience, it has to exist at all levels and across all scales of the animate and the inanimate. A speculative device is an enterprise determined by the real effectiveness of potential relations occurring in a multiplicity of ways across all kingdoms. These relations are invisible vibrations, minute excitations intrinsic to the irregular patchwork of contrasting colours determined by infinite shades, which acquire togetherness in each and any piece or fragment. Here, each piece is a speculative object made of physical and conceptual relations, immersed between the adjacent patches of colours as a singular assemblage of tonalities, but ultimately deploying a proposition, a lure for a would-be this and not that red. Each and any piece, however, is also and above all a speculative object and method for the next piece as it transports the potentialities of the entire patchwork again and anew at each connection.

From this standpoint, a speculative device does not share the premises of a thought experiment and does not dismiss cognition as yet another instance of functionalism derived from computation. If Searle used a thought experiment to show that cognition and consciousness cannot be explained by computational inductive methods based on the selection of empirical patterns (information processes) extended to generalization, he also maintained that consciousness requires physical properties, the properties of fire or digestion for instance, that can only be *simulated* by computer programs. This thought experiment then relies on the intuition that thought is an organic property. This intuition then constitutes the rational method of deduction through which one has to conclude that thought is not a property of machines. Here the theoretical premises of organic intelligence exclude all speculations not only in relation to what is organic after all, but also in respect of the very object of computation as describing the operations of cognition. A speculative method instead cannot overlook the potential of the object (for example, computation) as pointing to a new level of generalization. No speculative account of an object can be given if the general conditions of the particular are simply pre-set ideas or hypotheses of prediction. What is missing from thought experiments are precisely those indeterminate conditions according to which a particular instance is infected with abstraction and can add new character to general conditions. Far from descending upon the particular, generalizations are not theoretical frameworks but potential thought-objects that admit the actual multiplicities of thought. There is no a priori reason able to explain how these general sets of eternal objects, as Whitehead calls them, should be determined by an organic substrate for thought. Similarly, there is no way of sustaining that these general sets constitute the truth derived by the rational method of deducing knowledge from general intuition. The method of induction would again exclude automatic modes of thought as being unable to ever encompass general sets, indeterminate non-actual states. A speculative method on the contrary embraces the indeterminate conditions of theory, the vagueness of abstraction, the general assemblage of conditions as these are intrinsic to each and any actual mode of thought, which selects the series of eternal objects for itself.

For Whitehead, rationality is above all speculative since it cannot remain isolated from the actual entities in which theory is expressed at once as a logic and an aesthetic, as modes of thought and experience. This does not mean that theory is a practice, a doing, an act or a procedure. On the contrary, as Whitehead insists, only the entertainment of large generality or of incompleteness can explain why we are not concerned with matter of facts but with what is *important*, as generalizations are intrinsically linked to a particular perspective of the universe. Hence, speculation does not lead to vague ideas but starts from them to arrive at particular points of view. The latter always involve the double-sided sword of logic and aesthetic. If logic points at the enjoyment of abstracted details, which together constitute a unity able to increasingly approach the concrete, the aesthetic mode of thought instead defines the feeling of being overwhelmed by an undivided totality disclosing its component parts in any unity. In any case, logic and aesthetic are modes of thought defined by the experience of disclosure: the ingression into the unknown, the unexperienced (Whitehead, 1968: 62). This is why speculative method would admit that automated computation is a mode of thought. Computation is not simply a method of verification based on prediction: probabilities derived from past facts. On the contrary, as Bateson argues, information is a difference that makes a difference. It is not energy but requires energy to become a mental process. However, while the functionalist school is interested in defying a method based on computational procedures of information to hypothesize that cognition and the mind exist outside the biological brain and correspond to algorithmic procedures, a speculative method will disclose algorithms to general assemblages according to which automated thought becomes a specific expression, at once a logical and aesthetic thought never matching the identity of organic form.

This means that a speculative method is not about generalization in the sense that it is based on one flat method that could be applied to any object. On the contrary, the general character of actual objects must describe the unrepeatable articulation of propositions by following the details of logic and the totalities of aesthetic belonging to the object. Hence a speculative method is itself a proposition: neither the result of theories nor of practice, the rational nor the empirical. As a proposition, this method considers the object not as a functional procedure that can be performed everywhere. Similarly, one cannot simply assume that the object always already changes its internal composition according to changing conditions. Instead a propositional method articulates the existence of propositional objects, which can only be defined by 'grades of permanence and compulsive stability' (ibid.: 31). Yet this is not to say that the propositional object remains one and the same. Since an actual object is the assemblage of elements and qualities composing a finite unity, it will not be able to stay the same way at given space-times despite being what it is and nothing else. In other words, a propositional object is defined by 'the interweaving of change and permanence', which constitutes 'a primary fact of experience' (ibid.: 53). The propositional object is therefore a unity and a multiplicity, static and dynamic, irreversible and in variation.

Hence, one must concede that each propositional object is also characterized by enduring effects unleashed by previous conditions. Borrowing from Gilles Deleuze, these could be called 'incorporeal effects' (Deleuze, 1990). Far from determining objects through a linear correspondence with theories or as established by a physical cause, these effects are virtualities establishing an abstract nexus of events (ibid.: 6). In this case, the relation between the object and the method is as incorporeal as it is effective of an unforeseen reality. These relations are virtual causalities or noncausal correspondences between methods and objects, minds and things, or as Deleuze calls it, 'a system of echoes . . . resumptions and resonances, a system of signs – in short an expressive quasi-causality, and not at all a necessitating causality' (ibid.: 170).

These incorporeal effects come before any cause; they are incomplete causes for which physical connections occur. If virtualities are forms determined by relations, these define not simply the place between the ideal and the material but an abstract spatium of singularities determined by an incorporeal series of effects, which are prior to any bifurcation between methods and objects. In other words, Deleuze's virtual causes or incorporeal effects contribute to define speculative devices as being both and at once 'objective and undetermined'. These effects cannot be given or known, and have no form of consciousness or even a subject. A virtual effect possesses a full reality by itself (Deleuze, 1994: 211). This is not the reality of the object and does not prefigure or determine the objects that manifest their virtual effects.

But, how can a speculative proposition become an operative tool for social research? What kind of experience will social research individuate through such retroductive devices? How will propositions incite the formation of new objects and methods, the creation of new knowledge? As with a snowballing effect, a propositional object should not just grow unilaterally, but by its edges, through the additions of routes defining its process as the immanence of the infinite in the finite, the eternal in the actual.

These are only two of the propositions that might be posed here as being attuned to the generalized character of actual objects. These objects include all existing actual entities, whose physical and conceptual prehensions construct infinite spatio-temporal occasions of experience.

1   The immanence between method and object must be a speculative, retroductive construction requiring no testing or demonstrations.
2   A speculative method coincides strictly neither with empiricism nor rationalism, facticity or mentalities, truth or probability.

According to these two propositions, a speculative method:

1   demands of thought to become felt, fact to become potential, imagination to supersede observation, object to affect method, method to become transformative of the object;

2   calls forth the superiority of pure experience: the selection of eternal objects not by perceptive synthesis but by the abduction of the most general and the most particular;

3   exposes how the relations (continuities and discontinuities) between thought and fact become the motor of new social realities;

4   is a lure for feeling or the entertainment of unrealized possibilities characterizing the transition from one experience to the next;

5   may qualify as an event (the nexus of actual occasions), a generalized assemblage of logic and aesthetic thoughts able to supersede, interrupt the seamless continuum of cause and effect, method and object; and

6   may contribute to push social research towards the designing of unknown objects by exposing their particular perspectives about the importance of an event.

For instance, returning to the Chinese Room experiment, and the debates about the validity of deduction versus empirical induction as methods to illustrate or verify the hypothesis of what is mind, rationality, intelligence, thought, it is evident that a speculative device is a thought-experience, which neither demonstrates a method nor explains an object. A speculative method lays out the morphological schemata of thought objects, exposing computing to what is not yet computable or even revealing the incomputable in computation as such. A speculative object is an objectile, bending and twisting the infinite levels of its reality beyond any ultimate point of observation. As a result, a speculative method enters a step-by-step process of permanence and modification to abstract the real potentialities of the object in a new field of relations, a multilayered architecture of conjunctions and disjunctions. This is how a mutual inflection of the method towards the objects and vice versa ultimately works to push their unfamiliar becoming, where a method enters a topological continuity with the object's potential. The method is, as it were, born from within the dissonant facets of the object and yet is not simply there to demonstrate or test the hypothesis of its existence. The method therefore becomes the felt thought of the object, exposing its propensity to extend beyond its own constitution. From this perspective, the Turing Machine as a thought experiment fails to address those incomputable thoughts that neither correspond to symbols nor to facts. The Turing Machine is a method and an object for cognition that explains thought as a functional procedure able to run on any machine: nevertheless, this computational function does not explain the conditions by which algorithms can be executed.

This aspect of the Turing Machine however was only part of Turing's attempt at restoring the axiomatics of formalism and thus indirectly sustaining the identity between computation and cognition. On the other hand, one cannot overlook Turing's discovery of the incompleteness of axiomatics: the fact that although a machine may be able to execute thought (sequential algorithms), it is impossible for any machine to know in advance when the computation will stop and which finite result it will reach. In other words, Turing also insists that infinity is the horizon of computation: starting with a finite set of instructions ends up with indeterminacy. From this standpoint, Turing's thought experiment would point at how from finite rules one can arrive at infinity. But, once again, this is not the conclusion a speculative method would reach. If the Turing Machine forces the empirical method of testing and the rational method of demonstration to confront the incompleteness of logic, it also works to ward off its consequences: the assumption that we know that there are alien modes of thoughts, incomputable realities beyond what can be calculated in advance. A speculative method instead embraces precisely this unmissable consequence: the incompleteness of thought and the reality of uncomputable thought-objects. Only by addressing these consequences will it become possible to conduct research into those societies of ideas that are not directly perceived or cognized. Whereas the Turing Machine is an object defined by the procedure of computing what is computable, for the speculative method this machine is defined by the problem of infinity hanging over the functional operations of algorithmic sets.

This is not, however, to say that Searle's insistence that thought must be limited to a physico-cognitive model that cannot be reproduced by a software system running on mechanical machines is a valid alternative here. On the contrary, Searle's thought experiment is anchored in a deductive method, which always already assumes the completeness of rational thought. From this standpoint, the organicism of his thought experiment fails to admit that thought can be non-physically determined and can be expression of any finite actuality. In contrast, a speculative method will also address the reality of uncomputable thought-objects that infect these actualities and yet are autonomous from them. To conclude, one may suggest that speculation can be a challenging method only if it is allowed to construct abstract schemes able to expose the uncomputable realities of each and any object of thought and experience.

Notes

1   According to Bateson, evolution shares key characteristics with other systemic processes, including thought.
2   James continues: 'Elements may indeed be redistributed, the original placing of things getting connected, but a real place must be found for every kind of thing experienced, whether term or relation, in the final philosophical arrangement' (ibid.).
3   From this standpoint, Whitehead attributes reason to higher forms of biological life, where reason substitutes action. Reason is not a mere organ of response of external stimuli, but rather is an organ of emphasis, able to abstract novelty from repetition.
4   The primary discovery of such reason Whitehead attributes to Greek mathematics and logic, but also to Asiatic, Indian and Chinese civilizations. However, he argues that only the Greeks managed to produce a final instrument for the discipline of speculation (ibid.: 41).

References

Bateson, G. (2000) *Steps to an Ecology of Mind*, Chicago, IL: University of Chicago Press.

Bateson, G. (2002) *Mind and Nature: A Necessary Unity*, New York: Hampton Press.

Bradley, J. (2008) 'The speculative generalization of the function: a key to Whitehead', reprinted in *Inflexions*, 2, available at: www.inflexions.org (accessed 10 February 2011). First published in *Tijdschrift voor Filosofie*, 64: 231–252.

Brown, J. R. (1993) *The Laboratory of the Mind: Thought Experiments in Natural Sciences*, London and New York: Routledge.

Buchler, J. (1940; 2000) *The Philosophy of Peirce: Selected Writings, Volume 2*, London: Routledge.

Clark, A. (2001) *Mindware: An Introduction to the Philosophy of Cognitive Science*, Oxford University Press.

Deleuze, G. (1990) *The Logic of Sense*, trans. M. Lester, New York: Columbia University Press.

Deleuze, G. (1994) *Difference and Repetition*, trans. P. Patton, New York: Columbia University Press.

Galileo Galilei (1632/1953) *Dialogue Concerning the Two Chief World Systems*, trans. S. Drake, Berkeley, CA: University of California Press, pp. 186–7.

James, W. (1996) *Essays in Radical Empiricism*, Lincoln, NE: University of Nebraska Press.

Searle, J. (1980) 'Minds, brains and programs', *Behavioral and Brain Sciences*, 3 (3): 417–57, available at: www.bbsonline.org/Preprints/OldArchive/bbs.searle2.html (accessed 5 September 2011).

Turing, A. (1952) 'Can automatic calculating machines be said to think?', in B. J. Copeland (ed.) *The Essential Turing: The Ideas that Gave Birth to the Computer Age*, Oxford: Oxford University Press.

Whitehead, A. N. (1929) *The Function of Reason*, Boston, MA: Beacon.

Whitehead, A. N. (1968) *Modes of Thought*, New York: Free Press.

Whitehead, A. N. (1978) *Process and Reality*, New York: Free Press.

18 Tape recorder[1]

Les Back

Figure 18.1 A broken device (photograph by Stephanie Back).

My device is broken. After over a decade of faithful service, my Sony Walkman Professional is motionless. One of the quirks of this machine is that it has no speaker: it is a reception device, not a broadcasting one. Its dumb ear caught me out on more than one occasion when I first put it to work. Failing to remember to bring some headphones to an interview to listen to the level and playback, I managed to record two hours of absolutely nothing. Soon I learned I did not need to listen to the playback in order to check that it was working. Rather, keeping a knowing eye on the lights of its VU meter was enough to check the recording level. A few months ago, I loaded it with four AA batteries and pushed the record button but it failed to click into life, no flicker of red light on the meter, the record button pushed back against my thumb. I pushed it again and again – each time more frantically than the last – attempting a mechanical version of CPR in a desperate attempt to revive the beloved device from its state of technological arrest. All to no avail: it was and has remained dead.

I am, of course, making more of this for effect given the neat way my broken device connects with the issues raised in this book. Contained in the nostalgic attachment to a broken machine and the comfortable feel of its weathered case is something telling about the taken-for-granted norms of sociological craft. Over the past 50 years, the habitual nature of our research practice has obscured serious attention to the precise nature of the devices used by social scientists (Platt, 2002; Lee, 2004). For qualitative researchers, the tape recorder became the prime professional instrument intrinsically connected to capturing human voices on tape in the context of interviews. David Silverman argues that the reliance on these techniques has limited the sociological imagination: 'Qualitative researchers' almost Pavlovian tendency to identify research design with interviews has blinkered them to the possible gains of other kinds of data' (Silverman, 2007: 42). The strength of this impulse is widely evident from the methodological design of undergraduate dissertations to multimillion pound research grant applications. The result is a kind of inertia, as Roger Slack argues:

> It would appear that after the invention of the tape recorder, much of sociology took a deep sigh, sank back into the chair and decided to think very little about the potential of technology for the practical work of doing sociology.
>
> (Slack, 1998: 1.10)

In this chapter, I want to assess the advantages and the limitations of the tape recorder as a sociological device. It may be that – like my well-travelled machine – it is a device that has had its day. In keeping with other chapters, I argue that it is timely to rethink the way we work because of the unprecedented opportunities available in a digital age to change the nature of the craft of research. Before discussing these new possibilities, I want to give an account of the emergence of my device.

The rise of the tape recorder

It is hard to imagine today how social research would have been before the tape recorder was invented, such is the nature of its predominance. It became closely connected with the reliance on interviews as a way of knowing or inquiring into social life. As Ray Lee shows, the sociological interview came to prominence before there were sound devices able to record what research respondents said (Lee, 2004). Lee argues that the interview in its modern form had emerged by the early 1920s. However, the documentation of verbatim accounts of what informants said was a far-from-straightforward matter. Through a fascinating discussion of the Chicago school, sociologists such as Clifford Shaw Lee show that interviews were documented by a stenographer – a development that paralleled courtroom stenography – who was often hidden behind a screen (ibid.: 872). This meant that the interviewee would have to travel to the researcher's office, where the stenographer could capture verbatim interview responses.

Thomas Edison invented phonographic recording in 1877 but these early devices were ill suited to pick up individual human voices. Early sound recording equipment was bulky and cumbersome, and it was not until the invention of magnetic recording and transistorization that small-usage tape recorders became widely available to social researchers. Ray Lee points out that citations of the use of tape recorders in sociological journals begin around 1951 (ibid.: 877). Early recorders using open-reel magnetic tape were large, including the deceptively named EMI 'Midget'. They were portable but cumbersome. Robert Perks has shown that oral historians favoured reel-to-reel recording because of its superior sound quality, and the wonderfully named Uher Report Monitor became the standard recorder through the 1970s (Perks, 2010).

Among sociologists, though, there was some initial scepticism about the usefulness of the tape recorder. Michael Young, the driving force behind the Institute of Community Studies and co-author with Peter Willmott of the sociological classic *Family and Kinship in East London* (1957), preferred not to use a tape recorder. In the interviews conducted for their book, Young and Willmott preferred instead to take notes: 'We didn't think that tape recorders added very much' (Young, 2010: 1). Dennis Marsden, co-author of *Education and the Working Class* (Jackson and Marsden, 1966) and an early pioneer of community studies, commented: 'We almost prided ourselves in that method [of interview note taking]' (Marsden, 2010: 14). However, in Marsden's later work, he favoured recording interviews. He told Paul Thompson: 'And you do get something different, you do get something which is heightened and more vivid and less hesitant, and smoothed out, by using those little tape recorders' (ibid.: 14).

The invention of the audio cassette in the 1960s – initially introduced by Phillips – transformed the tape recorder into an essential sociological device. Here, there is a close association between information, technological development and the military. Ray Lee points out that tape recorders were one of the first non-military devices to use transistors and, in a sense, they are the cusp of the adaptation of transistorized military technologies for domestic use (Lee, 2004: 878). Portable, unobtrusive tape recording was now affordable and practical. The invention of the Sony Walkman in 1979 and then the Walkman Professional WM-D6C in 1984 made it possible to make high-quality interview recordings with groups as well as individuals. However, the emergence of the tape recorder, as Lee points out, is part of the development of a particular structure of knowledge production. Rob Perks argues – in the context of oral history – a consensus emerged that favoured one-to-one interviews with a tape recorder being discreetly placed, and 'active listening' without too many interruptions from the interviewer to enable ease of transcription (Perks, 2010).

In 1956, Everett Hughes wrote: 'Sociology has become the science of the interview' (Hughes, 1971: 507). The interview had become the favoured digging tool for mining into people's lives and the tape recorders in the sociologist's bag evidence of a vocational disposition akin to the place of the stethoscope in the professional persona of a medical doctor (Rice, 2008, 2010). The tape recorder provided the means to 'collect voices' then transcribe and re-circulate them. For example, in the aftermath of the Cuban revolution, C Wright Mills wrote *Listen, Yankee* (1960) – a million-selling popular book – that was written in the voice of a young Cuban revolutionary. Dan Wakefield wrote that, in August 1960, Mills went to Cuba 'equipped with his latest beloved gadget, a tape recorder; on his return, working with furious energy, he wrote *Listen, Yankee* in six weeks' time' (Wakefield, 2000: 12–13).

Mills' example is a cautionary tale. The desire to 'give voice' is a lasting impetus for sociologists as they reach for the tape recorder. Mills interviewed Che Guevara and Fidel Castro, and the popularity of the book also brought public pressure – in many respects, Mills' tape recorder was the source of his undoing. *Listen, Yankee* had the kind of public impact so much sought after today in the discussion of public sociology and research relevance (Burawoy, 2005; Grant *et al.*, 2009). In Mills' case, though, that impact was fatal. Mills was scheduled, in December 1960, to debate the Cuban Revolution with a major liberal figure, A. A. Berle Jr, on national television. The night before the debate, Mills suffered a heart attack. In January 1961, a libel lawsuit was filed against Mills and the publisher of *Listen, Yankee* for $25 million damages. The pressure was fatal and a little over a year later Mills died after his second heart attack. His friend Harvey Swados wrote after his death: 'In his last months Mills was torn between defending *Listen, Yankee* as a good and honest book, and acknowledging publicly for the first time in his life that he had been terribly wrong' (Swados, 1967: 207). The danger – a mortal one in Mills' case – is of reproducing the voices of respondents as if they simply correspond to a truth beyond the telling. As Atkinson and Silverman assert: 'We take at face value the image of the self-revealing speaking subject at our peril' (Atkinson and Silverman, 1997: 322).

There is also a sleight of hand in the claim that the authenticity of a person can be rendered through a faithful transcription of his or her voice on tape. It also confers on the person coming to the interview a self that is as much a historical product as it is an authentic biography to be disclosed in the telling. The tape recorder can be interpreted as a surveillance device: 'Caution – be careful what you say!' Loquacious people are silenced by the expectation that they are about to go on record as a single, individuated voice. For Atkinson and Silverman, the speaking self emerges within what they call the 'interview society' - a stylized and particular mode of narrating life. It requires:

> first, the emergence of the self as a proper object of narration. Second, the technology of the confessional – the friend not only of the policeman but of the priest, the teacher, and the 'psy' professional. Third, mass media technologies give a new twist to the perennial polarities of the private and the public, the routine and the sensational.
>
> (Atkinson and Silverman, 1997: 315)

They suggest that the well-intentioned desire to give voice to our subjects and the pervasiveness of the tape recorder and the interview among qualitative researchers draws us into the structure of the 'interview society'. The error is that we mistake the socially shaped account for the authentic voice of truth.

Roland Barthes, in a wonderful collection of his interviews called *The Grain of the Voice*, commented in his introduction on precisely what is at stake in the interview situation:

> We talk, a tape recording is made, diligent secretaries listen to our words to refine, transcribe, and punctuate them, producing a first draft that we can tidy up afresh before it goes on to publication, the book, eternity. Haven't we just gone through the 'toilette of the dead'? We have embalmed our speech like a mummy, to preserve it forever. Because we really must last a bit longer than our voices; we must, through the comedy of writing, inscribe ourselves somewhere.
>
> This inscription, what does it cost us? What do we lose? What do we win?
>
> (Barthes, 1985: 3)

Barthes alerts us here to the issue of what the interview costs. Do we create society in our accounts of it rather than reflect it (Osbourne and Rose, 1999)? If we lose or let go of the idea that we can access the intimate interior of a person through the interview, perhaps we gain other ways of thinking about what might be precious and valuable in what interviews produce or contain (Rapley, 2004). Silverman argues that even 'manufactured' interview data can be useful if understood as an 'activity awaiting analysis and not as a picture awaiting a commentary' (Silverman, 2007: 56). In other words, we should see the interview as a place where social forms are staged rather than a resource to understand the nature of society beyond. For example, in Beverley Skeggs, Helen Wood and Nancy Thumim's study of class and audience understandings of reality TV, interviews provided a 'mode of articulation' infused with classed and racialized moral judgements rather than 'observable realities'. In a sense, reality TV provided the object on and through which modes of class judgement, distinction and taste were rehearsed. They conclude: 'Research practices do not simply "capture" or reveal the world out there; they generate the conditions of possibility that frame the object of analysis' (Skeggs *et al.*, 2008: 20).

One consequence of the critique of the 'interview society' might be to give up on the interview as a tool and consign the tape recorder to the junkyard of outmoded devices. I do not think so. Interviews may well 'manufacture' data but the point that Skeggs and her colleagues point out is that we can identify the social resources, judgments and tools used to 'make society' as they attempt to make sense of their place within it.

As Howard Becker has commented, all representations – including those offered in an interview – are perfect . . . for something (Becker, 2007). The first step in establishing what the account perfectly reveals is to think through the analytical status conferred on the account itself. These questions are settled not in terms of method, but decided theoretically in the analytical framework conferred on what is caught on tape. An interviewer committed to Freudian psychoanalysis will be listening for hidden meanings; a phenomenologist inspired by Merleau-Ponty would be attentive to how the speaker's lifeworld was expressed; while a Foucauldian poststructuralist may not be interested in the specific interviewee as a subject at all, but rather take note of the discourses and forms of power that shape the words articulated. Returning to Barthes' question, perhaps letting go of the idea that interviews capture a deep inner truth about the speaker can alert us to how modes of authority are staged and socially performed for the benefit of the interviewer and his or her tape recorder. This links to the second reason Everett Hughes refers to sociology as the 'science of the interview'.

Sociological sociability and stolen devices

For Hughes, the interview encounter is key because the subject matter of sociology is interaction:

> It is the art of sociological sociability, the game which we play for the pleasure of savouring its subtleties. It is our flirtation with life, our eternal affair, played hard to win, but played with detachment and amusement which gives us, win or lose, the spirit to rise up and interview again and again.
>
> (Hughes, 1971: 508)

There is a lot that might be said about this passage. It contains a certain kind of portrait of sociologists as bemused and yet affected, connected to the social world through the interview encounter and, at the same time, remote and aloof. The tape recorder here issues an invitation, a technological licence to go out in the world and talk to people. Kvale and Brinkmann argue that we can contrast the idea of the interviewer as 'mining' the secret truths of people's lives with the idea of the researcher as a 'traveller' recalling the original Latin definition of conversation as 'wandering together with' (Kvale and Brinkmann, 2009: 48). This conception puts in the foreground the exchange of views captured on tape and the socially produced nature of all data.

Returning to my lapsed tape recorder, I realize that it has been my companion in sociological sociability. Perhaps that is why I was so sad about its demise. It kept me company in encounters with villains and heroines: from the leader of the British National Party to brave opponents to racism, it has provided a physical pretext for conversations with great musicians, athletes, writers, artists, poets and indeed sociologists (Back, 1996; Back *et al.*, 2001; Ware and Back, 2002; Duneier and Back, 2006; Hall and Back, 2009). It has been lots of other things as well. It has produced a record of sociological encounters within a shared time. These encounters are less eternal truths but one-off occasions where life itself is staged. I mentioned at the beginning of this chapter the occasion when my tape recorder recorded two hours of absolutely nothing during an interview. It had been a rich and brilliant telling of a life and my companion had taken me on quite an odyssey. I immediately set up another interview date but the second version was different, more cautious, less free flowing and more inhibited. The lesson here is that, while there may be consistencies in accounts, there are also profound variations in the perform- ances of self that should warn us against making simplistic truth claims. However, I do want to argue that the surface of sonic vitality recorded on our devices has a value that transcription alone cannot capture.

There is something deeply poignant about those cassette boxes full of auditory life. My office is full of hundreds of them. There have been moments when I have been left in possession of recordings of interviewees whose lives have been cut short. I remember a young football fan I interviewed in the 1990s called Carl Prosser. We talked in a local pub for three hours about the triumphs and tribulations of being a devotee of Millwall Football Club. He died in his early 30s. I was holding a full three hours of his emphatic talking, jokes alongside reflections on serious political matters. I had unwittingly become the custodian of his trace in life and the auditory imprint of the person he was. Through a mutual friend, I returned the tape and the copy of his voice to his family and his mother. Here, the value of the interview might be differently conceived as containing an inventory of traces of life passed in living.

I think my tape recorder has also been my protector, a kind of sociological shield in situations when I felt at risk or under attack. There is something about having the tape recorder in the midst of a room full of fascists or people who have histories of violent racism that feels like being in possession of a technological guardian. The device captures the soundscape of the zone of recording. There have been times when I have been threatened with legal action for libel. Having participants admitting or saying incriminating things on tape is protection here in a very direct sense.

While I want to defend the value of the humble tape recorder, I want to argue that we need to break with our dependence on it. Our addiction to the tape recorder has limited our attentiveness to the world. This, in part, is because there lingers the presumption that if it is not on tape it does not exist. In 1967, Ned Polsky, in his classic collection *Hustlers, Beats and Other*, anticipated these limitations:

> Successful field research depends on the investigator's trained abilities to look at people, listen to them, think and feel with them, talk with them rather than at them. It does *not* depend fundamentally on some impersonal apparatus, such as a camera or tape recorder.
>
> (Polsky, 1967/1998: 119)

We do not have to share Polsky's antipathy to gadgets to acknowledge that the reliance on sound recorders has confined our attentiveness to the mere transcription of voices from tape to text.

The tape recorder has been used outside the context of the interview. Anthropologist Jack Goody used recording devices to enhance field accounts of ritual and ceremonial events. During the 1950s, the ethnographer had only pencil and paper available for recording myths in field notes. The result was that the performance of myths had to either be translated *in situ* or recited to the ethnographer at a later point outside of the ceremonial context. The result was that anthropologists generally produced just one version of a myth for the ethnographic record. Goody, in his short essay 'The anthropologist and the audio recorder' (Goody, 2010) noted that taping changed all that. In the 1960s, with the advent of the portable recorder, ethnographers could take them into the ritual context, and myths could be captured in performance and translated at a later point. This made it possible to examine the variations and contradictions and also record the relationship between the audience and the performers. Ethnographers could analyze the significance of variation as well as common repeated patterns. In short, the tape recorder enabled the myth to be brought to life and rendered as a dynamic cultural form and not a fixed text.

If we start to think more imaginatively about the potential of devices to reinvent the nature of recording, it is possible to think beyond the established arrangement where the tape recorder is in the hands of the researcher and is merely directed at people who have to respond. Our devices can be borrowed or stolen. Anthropologist Tobias Hecht took his tape recorder into the field in Brazil, only to have it commandeered by the young people who make the streets their home (Hecht, 1998). Hecht decided to let it go, allowing the young people to become observers of their own lives. The young people conducted 'officinas de radio' or radio workshops, in which they intuitively asked all kind of questions that would have never occurred to the anthropologist.

The days of the tape recorder might be over, however I am not suggesting that we give up on interviews but rather see them as one technique among many. Digital recording has opened a whole new set of possibilities beyond simply doing away with the inconvenience of relying on tapes. Thinking of sociology as more than the 'science of the interview' offers the opportunity to widen the researcher's attentiveness to social life itself.

Sound and the sociological imagination

Mike Savage and Roger Burrows suggest that empirical sociology is facing a crisis (Savage and Burrows, 2007). Academic research is increasingly over-shadowed by the capacity of industry and commerce to know patterns of behaviour and taste in more sophisticated ways than sociologists and social researchers. Implicit in their argument is the charge that sociologists have been complacent. Once methodological innovators, we have been outpaced method-ologically by 'knowing capitalism' (Thrift, 2005) and government agencies and the security services who have developed sophisticated digital measures of human behaviour and social relationships (Savage, 2009). I want to suggest that part of the opportunity we have now is to enliven our methodological creativity but also to extend the scope of the 'sociological imagination' (Mills, 1959) in the twenty-first century.

If we stop listening only to 'voices', then we can reanimate the idea of description and attention. This also links to the appeal to place greater emphasis on 'naturally occurring data' (Potter, 2002; Silverman, 2007) not produced or manufactured by the researcher. The example I want to develop in the final part of this chapter – thinking through sound – offers one such opportunity. This might be summarized as a shift from being concerned only with 'voice' to an attention to soundscape and sound image. A fundamental lesson in Murray Schafer's seminal book *Tuning the World* (1977) is the merit to be found in slowing down modes of analytic attention, to notice that which is looked past and take seriously the soundtrack of the social background. As Howard Becker has commented, this is a matter of noticing what is 'happening when nothing is happening' (Becker, 2007: 267). At the same time, it is also concerned with being attentive to the ways in which the keynote sounds of, say, urban life contribute to the felt environments of cities. These sounds, like the sirens of police cars, have *affordances* and invite imaginative links between the policing of cities, everyday life and the impact of the war on terror (Back, 2007: 117–24; see also Goodman, 2010).

In particular the work connected with CRESSON, Grenoble (Centre de Recherche sur l'Espace Sonore [Research For Sonic Space]), founded by sociologists together with musicologist Jean Francois Augoyard, provides a rich methodological precedent. CRESSON has been active for over 30 years and it has provided a research base for some of the most interesting figures in the field, such as Pascal Amphoux, Olivier Balaÿ, Grégoire Chelkoff, Jean-Paul Thibaud and Henry Torgue. Much of this work is directly relevant to the argument suggested here (Amphoux, 1991a, 1991b; Thibaud and Grosjean, 2001). For example, in 1989, Pascal Amphoux and Martine Leroux published an in-depth study entitled 'Le bruit, la plainte et le voisin' (Noise, complaint and neighbours), which developed innovative measures for the sonic environment. Augoyard and Torgue's *Sonic Experience: A Guide to Everyday Sounds* (2005) outlines a sophisticated glossary of sonic effects that introduce ways of naming otherwise incommunicable aspects of listening experience that is 'halfway between the universal and the singular' (Augoyard and Torgue, 2005: 9). For example, *sharaawadji* is the unexpected perception of beauty or a 'rapture of imagination' with 'no discernible order or arrangement' (ibid.: 117). The term was first encountered by European explorers in China but is transposed to the 'worrisome yet beautiful strangeness' of the city, where multiple and cacophonous sounds – containing rupture and dynamic tension – can produce or create a kind of sublime pleasure. Augoyard and Torgue offer a poetic and rich analytical language to communicate otherwise unnamed sensations and listening experiences.

Thinking with sound in this way invites a sociological sensibility close to George Perec's wonderfully eccentric experiments with cataloguing that which is all around us and yet unnoticed (Perec, 1997). For Perec, the task is 'to describe what's left: what isn't usually noted down, what isn't noticed, what has no importance: what happens when nothing is happening, just the weather, people, cars, clouds' (quoted in Becker, 2007: 266). The police siren, the children laughing in the street, the jet plane's moan overhead along with the crowing birdsong, the sounds of movement of rubber on tarmac, of internal combustion are invitations to develop a different kind of sociological imagination attentive to the rhythm and aesthetics of life.

My 1910 edition of the *Oxford Dictionary* defines 'device' as 'something devised contrived, sometimes with good, usually with evil intent'. Or, as an 'emblem intended to represent a family, person, action, or quality'. These kinds of antecedent meanings are interesting in that they predate the notion of technological devices that are current today. These meanings foreground the notion that devices are representations. They are not simply correspondences to the real. They are facsimiles, they are copies like the tapes loaded in my beloved Sony Walkman Professional. In this sense, I think James Clifford is right to warn that, in order to return to realism, you have to leave it in the first place (Clifford, 1986: 25). The devices create objects that are productive of the social, and an appreciation of this productivity – more than this, I want to suggest an embrace of this productive/creative dimension – might help enable an encounter with 'the real' without a naive realism slipping in through the back door. The recordings made by the sound device provide the illusion of 'being there'. If we leave behind the simple idea that they 'capture' the real but instead produce a realist imaginative object, then they may provide a different kind of possibility for social understanding or revelation.

Working with sound artists Paul Halliday and John Drever, I have been recording the soundscapes that surround the immediate urban landscape where I work at Goldsmiths, University of London. With Paul, I have wandered through the multicultural agora of Deptford Market recording the sounds we found there. It is a strange sight watching Paul with headphones around his neck wandering through the crowded market, waving his wand-like directional microphone at the ebb and flow of Saturday afternoon commerce. People pass him on the market and then turn sharply, rubbernecking to check not only what he is up to but also if their eyes are deceiving them. The recordings often contain a dense proximity that is hard to narrate. In these ground-level sounds, there is laughter and conviviality, as well as the coldness and the frustrations of people treading on each other's toes. I am interested in proximity but I am not interested in creating an illusion of being there, or claiming a simple correspondence between the recordings and a stable unchanging social reality. Rather, I am trying to do something else with these recordings – i.e. to displace, create a kind of amplification or heightened attention to sound images.

With John Drever, I have recorded a very different sound of London. From the top of the 12-storey tower block, a formerly condemned hall of residence called Warmington Tower in which the Department of Sociology is located, we have been recording a kind of sonic panorama, producing a sonic effect close to Augoyard and Torgue's characterization of the experience of *sharaawadji* (Augoyard and Torgue, 2005: 117–23). There is not space here to go into the detail of the projects but what they do highlight is the importance of vantage point – a time and place – in specifying the production of sound data. They are slices of time and not necessarily a sonic portrait that is generalizable or enduring. Tim Ingold has argued that the notion of soundscape is limited precisely because it reduces the appreciation of sound to emplacement or merely reflects a fixed location and its acoustic ecology. Rather, he foregrounds how 'We may, in practice, be anchored to the ground, but it is not sound that provides the anchor . . . the sweep of sound continually endeavours to tear the listener away, causing them to surrender to its movements' (Ingold, 2007: 12).

The recordings we have made from the top of Warmington Tower contain 'sound marks' or 'keynote sounds' that are constantly being repeated but they can equally be very specific compositions of social life in sound. The dull moan of a jet plane passing overhead pulls the listener towards another place or global destination. Here, the listening experience links to the cultivation of a sociological imagination. I love playing the recordings in lecture theatres or events in New Cross close to where they were made. They often produce a sense of dislocation, blurring what is inside the lecture theatre and what is outside. The background is turned up, sometimes as loud as is physically bearable, listeners are unsure whether the sounds they are hearing come out of the speakers or from the world outside. These experiments bring to sociological attention things we are surrounded by but seldom remark upon. As a consequence, what might count as 'data' is extended to the noises and rhythm of life itself and shows the potential of using sound sociologically beyond simply recording human voices that are expected to tell the truth about society.

Conclusions: revitalizing the craft of research

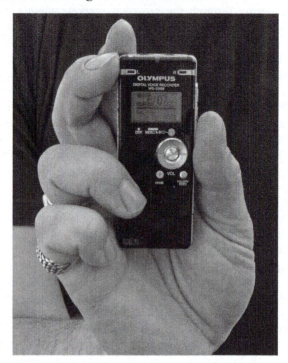

Figure 18.2 Digital voice recorder (photograph by Stephanie Back).

I have a new device. Here it is. The Olympus Digital Voice Recorder WS-320M, with the capacity to record 277 hours of sound data. The emergence in the past 10 years of devices such as this one has made the tape recorder as a collection device a thing of the past. Digital sound recording also makes it possible to think about how we might also transform research texts. I am working on using sound recording accompanied by written accounts. This can easily be done in portable document formats (.pdf), as links to sound files or moving image can be embedded within the documents. As you pass through the document, a sound file is triggered, producing the interplay between word and sound. Silent reading is a modern product and, in the early days of the written word in fifteenth-century Europe, silent reading and writing was prohibited. You had to speak as you wrote or read to show that you had taken in the authority of the religious word. It was called 'the voice of the page' and taken to be more truthful than writing (Morrison, 2000). I have been playing with the interplay between word and sound in order to evoke the unspoken, as well as to enliven sociological text itself as an imaginative object, turning the written page into a screen or speaker.

As Ray Lee has suggested, it is worth imagining what kind of course qualitative sociological research might have taken had the tape recorder not been invented (Lee, 2004: 881). I have argued that the tape recorder as a sociological device has been both enabling and limiting. Enabling in the sense that it allowed for the voices of people to be faithfully transcribed with accuracy. Paradoxically, the fact that the recorder captured the voice and the precise detail of what informants said meant that social researchers have become less attentive as observers. The tacit belief that the researcher needed merely to attend to what was said has limited the forms of empirical documentation. As a result, the technological capacity to record voices accurately meant that researchers became less observant, less involved and this minimized their attentiveness to the social world. As Harvey Sacks warned in a lecture give in the spring of 1965, 'The tape recorder is important, but a lot of this [observational study] can be done without a tape recorder' (Sacks, 1992: 28). In addition, the interview where the tape recorder was deployed normalized a mode of telling the modern self and added to the emergence of the 'interview society' (Atkinson and Silverman, 1997). The mode of telling is a historical product rather than merely a means to document human experience. I am not suggesting that sociologists should turn their backs on the interview, but instead think carefully about the analytic status we give the accounts recorded in these quite specific forms of sociological sociability.

I am arguing for a revitalization of our methodological imagination and to develop new kinds of device to both explore and produce the social. The twenty-first century offers unprecedented opportunities to rethink the nature of sociological craft. For 50 years, sociologists have been dependent on their tape recorders. Now we have to embrace the potential for rethinking the social life of our methods and develop new devices. My own arc of interest has moved towards the possibility that found sounds or sound images have for recording and attending to the rhythm and texture of social life in motion. Here, sound is a repository for what often remains unsaid, a place of surprise, admitting what is often blocked out and offering an opportunity to turn up the background in order to hear what it contains sociologically. Sound flows, as Ingold suggests, and contains pathways and connections across place and time that invite an appreciation of how the 'here and now' connects to a global elsewhere as well as the past.

Unlike the other contributors, I have given up on my device. Abandoning the 'dead tape recorder' has allowed another practice to emerge that displaces the nostalgic attachment to my Sony Walkman Professional, with other gadgets better suited to the task of 'turning up the background'. This is not to say – as I hope I have made clear – that there is no place for 'voice recording' and interviewing in social research. I am arguing that we should not rely on these techniques exclusively or automatically without thinking carefully about the analytical status given to accounts produced in this way. The challenge is not only to find new methodological techniques for attending to life, it also raises the question of how to enliven and transform sociology itself and better communicate the results of our craft.

Notes

1   I would like to thank a number of people for passing on leads, clues and insights concerning my rather eccentric fascination with the academic life of the tape recorder. Sincere thanks to Ray Lee, Tom Rice, Paul Thompson, Rob Perks, Karla Berrens, Shane Blackman, Yasmin Gunaratnam and Nina Wakeford.

References

Amphoux, P. (1991a) *Aux écoutes de la ville: la qualité sonore des espaces publics européennes: méthode d'analyse comparative: enquête sur trois villes suisses*, research report, Lausanne: IREC-EPFL and Grenoble: CRESSON.

Amphoux, P. (1991b) *L'identité sonore des villes européennes: guide méthodologique à l'usage des gestionnaires de la ville, des techniciens du son et des chercheurs en sciences socials*, research report, Lausanne: IREC-EPFL and Grenoble: CRESSON.

Atkinson, P. and Silverman, D. (1997) 'Kundera's immorality: the interview society and the invention of the self,' *Qualitative Inquiry*, 3 (3): 304–25.

Augoyard, J-F. and Torgue, H. (2005) *Sonic Experience: A Guide to Everyday Sounds*, Quebec: McGill-Queen's University Press.

Back, L. (1996) *New Ethnicities and Urban Culture: Racisms and Multiculture in Young Lives*, London: UCL Press.

Back, L. (2007) *The Art of Listening*, Oxford: Berg.

Back, L., Crabbe, T. and Solomos, J. (2001) *The Changing Face of Football: Racism, Identity and Multiculture in the English Game*, Oxford: Berg.

Barthes, R. (1985) *The Grain of the Voice: Interviews 1962–1980*, London: Cape.

Becker, H. (2007) *Telling About Society*, Chicago, IL: University of Chicago Press.

Burawoy, M. (2005) 'For public sociology,' *American Sociological Review*, 70 (1): 4–28.

Clifford, J. (1986) 'Introduction: part truths', in J. Clifford and G. E. Marcus (eds) *Writing Culture: The Poetics and Politics of Ethnography*, Berkeley, Los Angeles and London: University of California Press, pp. 1–26.

Duneier, M. and Back, L. (2006) 'Voices from the sidewalk: ethnography and writing race', *Ethnic and Racial Studies*, 29 (3): 543–65.

Goodman, S. (2010) *Sonic Warfare: Sound, Affect and the Ecology of Fear*, Cambridge, MA and London: MIT Press.

Goody, J. (2010) 'The anthropologist and the audio recorder', in J. Goody (ed.) *Myth, Ritual and the Oral*, Cambridge: University of Cambridge Press, pp. 58–69.

Grant, J., Brutscher, P. B., Kirk, S. Butler, L. and Wooding, S. (2009) *Capturing Research Impacts: A Review of International Practice*, Cambridge: RAND Europe.

Hall, S. and Back, L. (2009) 'At home and not at home', *Cultural Studies*, 23 (4): 660–88.

Hecht, T. (1998) *At Home in the Street: Street Children of Northeast Brazil*, Cambridge and New York: Cambridge University Press.

Hughes, E. E. (1971) 'Of sociology and the interview', in E. E. Hughes (ed.) *The Sociological Eye: Collected Papers*, New Brunswick and London: Transaction Publishers, pp. 507–15.

Ingold, T. (2007) 'Against soundscape', in A. Carlyle (ed.) *Sound and the Environment in Artistic Practice*, Paris: Double-Entendre, pp. 10–13.

Jackson, B. and Marsden, D. (1966) *Education and the Working Class: Some General Themes Raised by a Study of 88 Working-class Children in a Northern Industrial City*, Harmondsworth: Penguin.

Kvale, S. and Brinkmann, S. (2009) *InterViews: Learning the Craft of Qualitative Research Interviewing*, 2nd edition, Los Angeles, London, New Delhi and Singapore: Sage.

Lee, R. M. (2004) 'Recording technologies and the interview in sociology, 1920–2000', *Sociology*, 38 (5): 869–99.

Marsden, D. (2010) *Life Story Interview with Paul Thompson* (extracts), 2002, Pioneers of Qualitative Research, transcribed by ESDS Qualidata, Colchester: UK Data Archive, University of Essex.

Mills, C. W. (1960) *Listen, Yankee: The Revolution in Cuba*, New York: McGraw Hill Book Company.

Mills, C. W. (1959) *The Sociological Imagination*, Oxford: Oxford University Press.

Morrison, B. (2000) *The Justification of Johann Gutenberg*, London: Chatto and Windus.

Osbourne, T. and Rose, N. (1999) 'Do the social sciences create phenomena: the case of public opinion research', *British Journal of Sociology*, 50 (3): 367–96.

Perec, G. (1997) *Species of Spaces and Other Pieces*, London: Penguin Books.

Perks, R. (2010) '"Messiah with the microphone?" Oral historians, technology and sound archives', in D. Richie (ed.) *The Oxford Handbook to Oral History*, Oxford: Oxford University Press, pp. 315–32.

Platt, J. (2002) 'The history of the interview,' in J. F. Gubrium and J. A. Holstein (eds) *Handbook of the Interview Research: Context and Method*, Thousand Oaks, CA: Sage, pp. 35–54.

Polsky, N. (1967/1998) *Hustlers, Beats and Others*, New York: Lyon Press.

Potter, J. (2002) 'Two kinds of natural', *Discourse Studies*, 4 (4): 539–42.

Rapley, T. (2004) 'Interviews', in C. Seale, G. Gobo, J. F. Gubrium and D. Silverman (eds) *Qualitative Research Practice*, London, Thousand Oaks, CA and New Delhi: Sage, pp. 15–33.

Rice, T. (2008) 'Beautiful murmurs: stethoscopic listening and acoustic objectification,' *The Senses and Society*, 3 (3): 293–306.

Rice, T. (2010) 'Learning to listen: auscultation and the transmission of auditory knowledge', *Journal of the Royal Anthropological Institute,* 16, Issue Supplement: 41–61.

Sacks, H. (1992) *Lectures on Conversation: Volume 1*, Cambridge, MA: Blackwell Publishers.

Savage, M. (2009) 'Contemporary sociology and the challenge of descriptive assemblages,' *European Journal of Social Theory*, 12 (1): 155–74.

Savage, M. and Burrows, R. (2007) 'The coming crisis of empirical sociology', *Sociology*, 41 (5): 885–9.

Schafer, R. M. (1977) *Tuning the World*, New York: Alfred K. Knopf.

Silverman, D. (2007) *A Very Short, Fairly Interesting and Reasonably Cheap Book About Qualitative Research* Los Angeles, London, New Delhi and Singapore: Sage.

Skeggs, B., Thumim, N. and Wood, H. (2008) '"Oh goodness, I am watching reality TV": how methods make class in audience research', *European Journal of Cultural Studies*, 11 (1): 5–24.

Slack, R. S. (1998) 'On the potentialities and problems of a www based naturalistic sociology', *Sociological Research Online*, 3 (2), available at: www.socresonline.org.uk/3/2/3.html (accessed 10 September 2010).

Swados, H. (1967) 'C. Wright Mills: a personal memoir', in H. Swados (ed.) *A Radical At Large*, London: Rupert Hart-Davis, pp. 199–208.

Thibaud, J.P. and Grosjean, M. (eds) (2001) *L'espace urbain en methods*, Marseille: Editions parenthèses.

Thrift, N. (2005) *Knowing Capitalism*, London: Sage.

Wakefield, D. (2000) 'Introduction', in K. Mills and P. Mills (eds) *C Wright Mills: Letters and Autobiographical Writings*, Berkeley, Los Angeles and London: University of California Press, pp. 1–18.

Ware, V. and Back, L. (2002) *Out of Whiteness: Color, Politics, and Culture*, Chicago, IL: University of Chicago Press.

Young, M. (2010) *Life Story Interview with Paul Thompson*, 2001, Pioneers of Qualitative Research, transcribed by ESDS Qualidata, Colchester: UK Data Archive, University of Essex.

Young, M. and Willmott, P. (1957) *Family and Kinship in East London*, Harmondsworth: Penguin.

Index